Praise for *Charlott*

This book presents a well-written and scholarly account of Charlotte Mason and her world, placing her firmly in the great tradition of Quaker thinkers, and tracing her development as an educationalist and the influences upon her. The importance of her Quaker background, which has never been explored before, sheds new light on the formation of her educational principles, which are still practised in our schools today.

Heather Eggins,
Visiting Professor of Education,
University of Sussex

'For the children's sake' could surely be the bequest of Charlotte Mason's lifelong work in founding both the Parents' National Educational Union (PNEU) and Home Education in the nineteenth century. Indeed, both organisations, and the magazine, *Parents' Review*, continued well into the twentieth century and still have resonances in twenty-first-century education, with its renewed emphasis on parents. It is to Margaret Coombs' great credit that she has woven an excellent, imaginative and fascinating story of the well-known educator.

Miriam David,
Professor Emerita of Sociology of Education,
UCL Institute of Education

I have long been familiar with Charlotte Mason's Home Education Series and Essex Cholmondeley's *The Story of Charlotte Mason* (1960). I am inspired by Charlotte's passionate opposition to behaviourist, mechanistic and utilitarian approaches to education, which were dominant in her day and remain so in many quarters. But I always felt that the real Charlotte Mason was an enigma. What explains her innovative ideas and her determined, charismatic personality? This scholarly and engaging book provides definitive answers and reveals the origins of Charlotte Mason's passion for universal education. I think everyone who worked or studied at her Scale How 'House of Education' in Ambleside felt her pervading spirit. Now, all readers of this book will have a more complete understanding of this amazing person, her considerable achievements and her continuing importance.

Hilary Cooper,
Emeritus Professor of History and Pedagogy,
University of Cumbria

This much needed book answers longstanding questions about the family background of and influences on Charlotte Mason. Margaret Coombs' meticulous research reveals the hitherto unexplored and unexplained early family life of an often overlooked educator. Charlotte Mason always thought that her work would 'speak for her' but Coombs's detailed scholarship helps the reader to understand the origin of an educational philosophy that spread across the world and across social classes. It is an important addition to the currently available secondary material on an enigmatic woman.

Stephanie Spencer,
Head of Department of Education Studies,
University of Winchester

Margaret Coombs has accomplished impressive archival research in tracking down traces of the illusive Charlotte Mason. Because of this work, it is possible to better understand where Mason came from and how her background influenced her choices later in life.

Rachel Neiwert,
Assistant Professor of History,
Geography and Political Science,
St Catherine University, Minneapolis

Margaret Coombs's diligent research over many years has revealed much that was hitherto unknown about the life of one of the prominent educationists of the late nineteenth and early twentieth centuries. This lively biography reveals how much of Charlotte Mason's beliefs and attitudes were influenced by her family background and, because the book does not finish with Miss Mason's demise in 1923, shows that her theories and method are still in use today. Past students of Charlotte Mason, former pupils of PUS schools and home schools, as well as anyone with an interest in the development of education, will find Margaret Coombs's book an eminently readable insight into the educational and social life of the late Victorian and Edwardian period.

Caroline Heal,
Editor of *L'Umile Pianta*
2002-2014

Margaret Coombs has shown herself a tenacious researcher, tirelessly digging into the life of Charlotte Mason. Her discoveries will surely generate fresh discussions on Mason's life and work, helping us in the twenty-first century to probe further into the life and work of this remarkable educator.

J. Carroll Smith,
Editor of *Essays on the Life and Work of Charlotte Mason* (2014)
and Director of the Charlotte Mason Institute

Margaret Coombs offers the twenty-first educator who is attracted to Mason's design for education an engaging glimpse into the nineteenth century formation of Charlotte Mason that has long been necessary. Coombs writes with a twinkle in her eye and a sparkle in her voice that brings the people and places in Mason's world attractively alive. Curiously, by situating Mason's accomplishments and proposals in the rich detail of her time, Coombs animates Mason's educational ideas in a manner that will make them more appealing than ever to those who care deeply about education in our times.

Deani Van Pelt,
Director of the Barbara Mitchell Centre for Improvement in Education
at the Fraser Institute, Vancouver

Charlotte Mason

Charlotte Mason stands resolutely with her back to the hedge, c. 1894;
Mary Louisa Armitt is probably the seated lady on her left.

Charlotte Mason

Hidden Heritage and Educational Influence

Margaret A. Coombs

Foreword by
John Thorley

The Lutterworth Press

For Martin, Dan, Chantal,
Esme and Anna.

The Lutterworth Press
P.O. Box 60
Cambridge
CB1 2NT
United Kingdom

www.lutterworth.com
publishing@lutterworth.com

ISBN: 978 0 7188 9402 3

British Library Cataloguing in Publication Data
A record is available from the British Library

First Published, 2015

Cover illustration: Charlotte Mason at Ambleside by Fred Yates, 1901,
courtesy of the Armitt Museum, photograph © Dayve Ward, 2014.

Contents

List of Illustrations

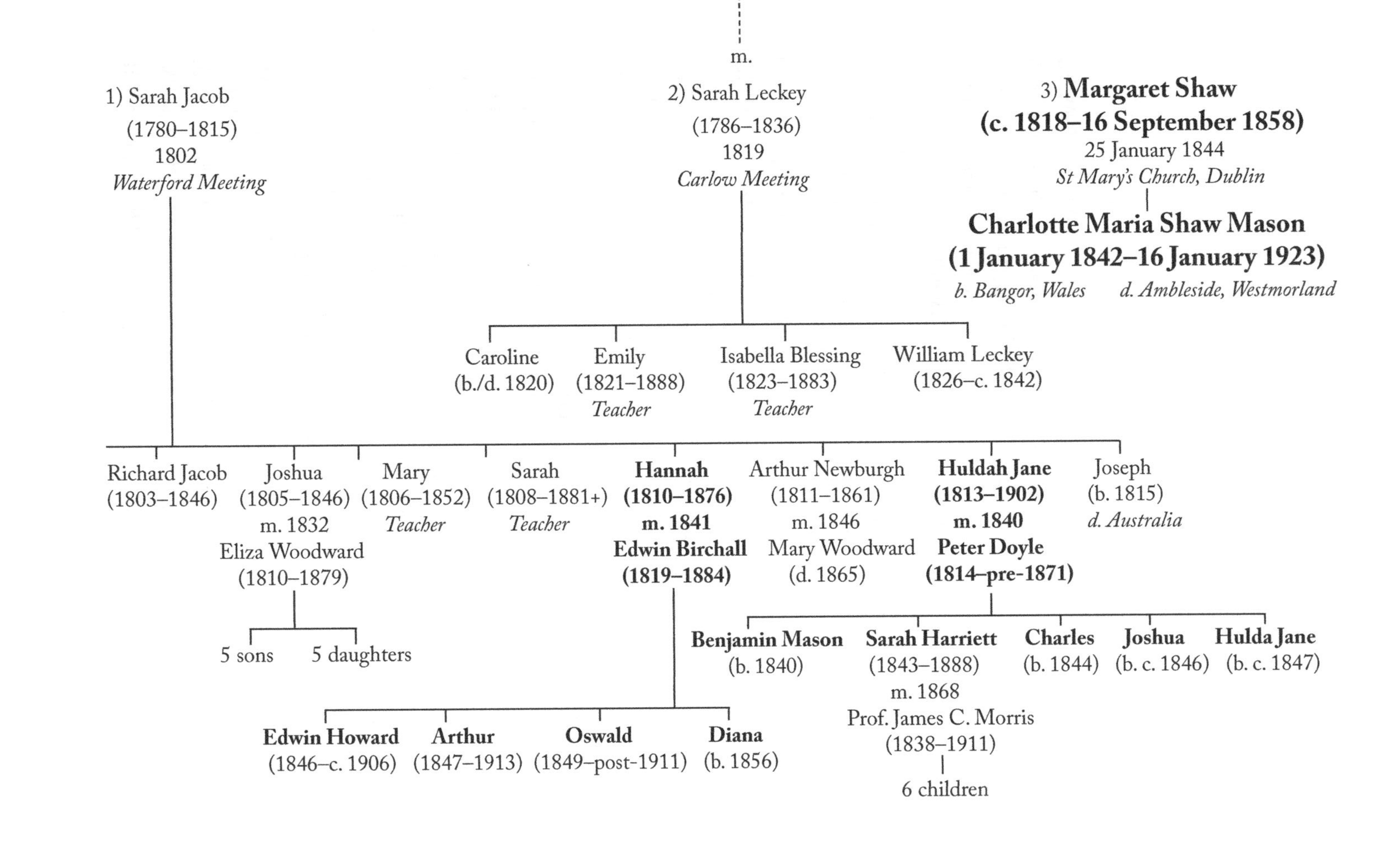

m.
1) Sarah Jacob
(1780–1815)
1802
Waterford Meeting
2) Sarah Leckey
(1786–1836)
1819
Carlow Meeting
3) Margaret Shaw
(c. 1818–16 September 1858)
25 January 1844
St Mary's Church, Dublin
Charlotte Maria Shaw Mason
(1 January 1842–16 January 1923)
b. Bangor, Wales
d. Ambleside, Westmorland
Caroline
(b./d. 1820)
Emily
(1821–1888)
Teacher
Isabella Blessing
(1823–1883)
Teacher
William Leckey
(1826–c. 1842)
Richard Jacob
(1803–1846)
Joshua
(1805–1846)
m. 1832
Eliza Woodward
(1810–1879)
Mary
(1806–1852)
Teacher
Sarah
(1808–1881+)
Teacher
Hannah
(1810–1876)
m. 1841
Edwin Birchall
(1819–1884)
Arthur Newburgh
(1811–1861)
m. 1846
Mary Woodward
(d. 1865)
Huldah Jane
(1813–1902)
m. 1840
Peter Doyle
(1814–pre-1871)
Joseph
(b. 1815)
d. Australia
5 sons
5 daughters
Benjamin Mason
(b. 1840)
Sarah Harriett
(1843–1888)
m. 1868
Prof. James C. Morris
(1838–1911)
6 children
Charles
(b. 1844)
Joshua
(b. c. 1846)
Hulda Jane
(b. c. 1847)
Edwin Howard
(1846–c. 1906)
Arthur
(1847–1913)
Oswald
(1849–post-1911)
Diana
(b. 1856)

The Family Tree of Charlotte Maria Shaw Mason

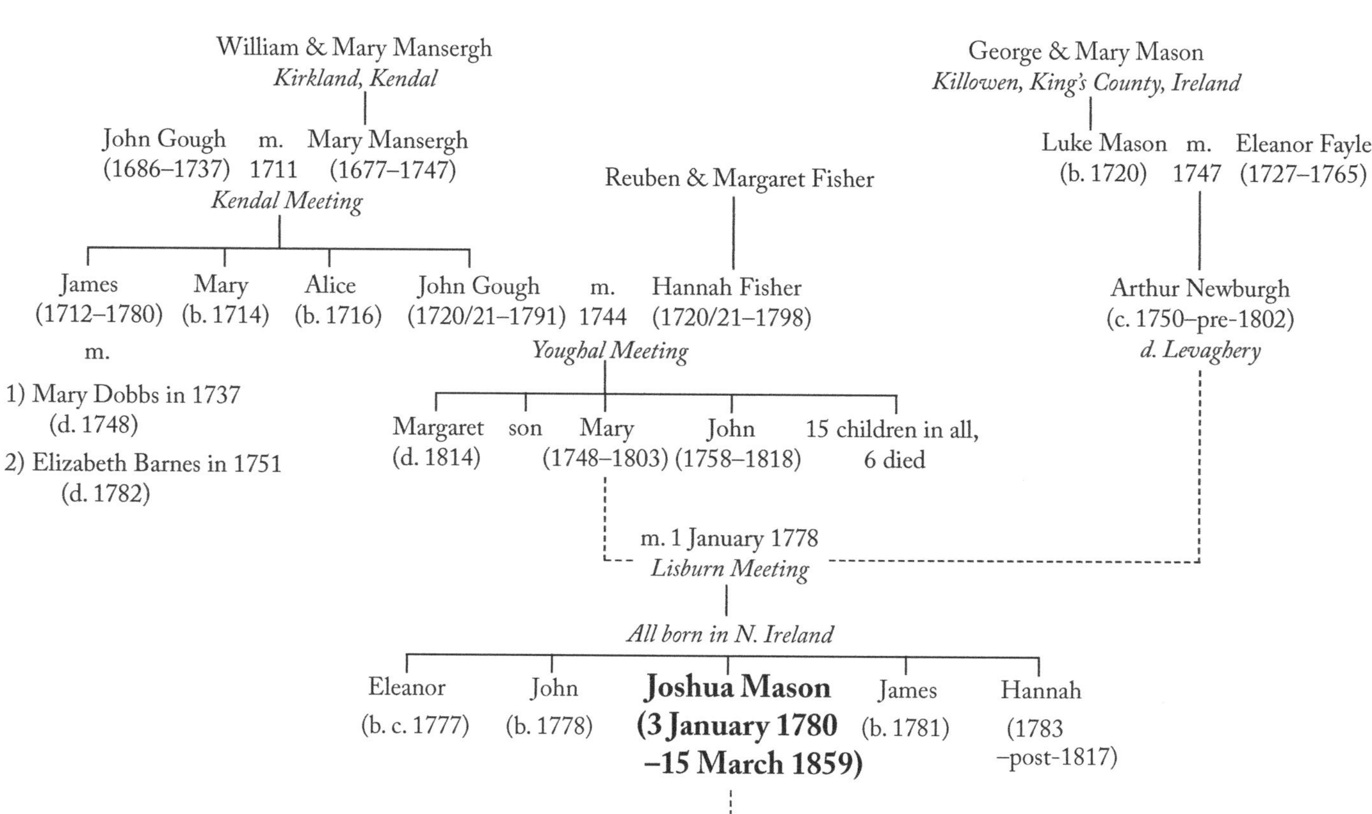

A Timeline for Charlotte Mason (1842–1923)

1720/21	John Gough, Charlotte's Quaker great-grandfather was born in Kendal.
1780	Charlotte's father, Joshua Mason, was born on 3 January at Hall's Mill, Laurencetown, Co. Down, Northern Ireland, to Arthur and Mary Mason, birthright Quakers.
1795	Joshua Mason was apprenticed to Richard Jacob as a tallow-chandler and soap-boiler in Waterford.
1802	Joshua Mason married Sarah Jacob at Waterford Meeting. They had eight children: Richard Jacob, Joshua junior, Mary, Sarah, Hannah, Arthur Newburgh, Huldah Jane and Joseph.
1815	Sarah Jacob Mason died on 15 September, 1815.
1817	Joshua Mason was appointed a freeman of the city of Waterford.
1818	Margaret Shaw was born; the precise date and location of her birth are unknown.
1819	Joshua Mason married Sarah Leckey, a Carlow Friend. They had four children: Caroline, who died in infancy, Emily, Isabella Blessing and William Leckey.
1831	Sarah Leckey Mason's sister, Anna, married Joseph Robinson Pim at Carlow Meeting.
1835	Joshua moved with his second family and Huldah Jane to Staplestown Mill, Co. Carlow; Joshua Mason Esq. was recognised as a gentleman.
1836	Sarah Leckey Mason died on 22 January.
1840	After Huldah Jane Mason married Peter Doyle in church they were disowned by Carlow Friends.

1841	In June, Joshua Mason left Staplestown for Australia with Joseph. It is not known when or where he met Margaret Shaw before embarkation. The Pim family had moved to Birkenhead.
1842	On c. 1 January, Charlotte Maria was born to Margaret Shaw, probably at the home of Huldah Jane and Peter Doyle at 41 Garth Village, Garth Point, Upper Bangor, North Wales.
1843	The Doyle family returned to Ireland; where Margaret Shaw and Charlotte lived is not known.
1844	Joshua Mason returned from Australia and married Margaret Shaw at St Mary's Church, Dublin, on 25 January. Margaret was living in Wellington Street, central Dublin; Joshua was in Kingstown, the port of Dublin.
1844–c. 1852	It is not known where Charlotte and her parents lived. They may have lived in Dublin while remaining in Ireland and probably also stayed at Douglas, Isle of Man, c. 1847.
1849	The Doyle family moved to Oliver Street, Birkenhead.
c. 1851–1852	Joshua, Margaret and Charlotte arrived in Birkenhead. Charlotte must have attended the Holy Trinity National Society elementary school for girls, precise date unknown. The Masons may have lodged near, or with, the Doyles or the Pim family in Holy Trinity parish.
1854	In August, Charlotte began her pupil-teacher apprenticeship at Holy Trinity's girls' and infants' school. The Doyles crossed the Mersey River to Everton.
1855	Joshua Mason, gentleman, was living in Flat 4 at Exmouth Place, 48 Watson Street, with Charles McErithy. Margaret and Charlotte must have been living elsewhere.
1856	Charlotte's half-sister Hannah arrived in Birkenhead with her husband, Edmund Birchall, and their children.
1857–1859	Gore's Directory recorded that Joshua Mason, gentleman, had moved to Victoria Road, Oxton. Margaret Mason was seriously ill.
1858	Margaret Mason died at 15 Whetstone Lane, the home of the Heighisway family, on 16 September. She was buried at St Werburgh's Roman Catholic Church, Grange Road, Birkenhead, on 18 September.
1859	On 15 March, Joshua Mason died in New Road, Tue Brook, West Derby, Liverpool, near the Doyles' house. On 19 March he was interred in the Hunter Street Quaker burial ground. At Christmas, having successfully passed her

	pupil-teaching apprenticeship, Charlotte won a second-class Queen's Scholarship to train at the Home and Colonial Training College (known as the 'Ho and Co') in London.
1860	Charlotte began her first year's training on 25 March (Lady Day). She made friends with Selina Healey, later Mrs Fleming; Elizabeth (Lizzie) Pendlebury, later Mrs Groveham; and Sally, later Mrs Coleman.
1861	Charlotte became ill. She left the Ho and Co a year early, on Lady Day. In April, she was appointed mistress of the William Davison Infantine School in Worthing, Sussex. Lizzie gained her first-class certificate at Christmas.
1862	At Christmas, Charlotte won a first-class certificate for teachers in charge of schools, finally confirmed in 1871.
1863	Probably during this year, Lizzie married John Groveham and moved to Bradford.
1864	An older girls' class was opened within Davison School. Charlotte made her first visit to Ambleside to stay with Selina Healey at her school at Loughrigg View.
1868	Charlotte met Miss Emily Brandreth; this definitive friendship lasted until 1879. Selina Healey married John Fleming, an Ambleside architect.
1874	Charlotte was appointed senior governess at the Bishop Otter Memorial College for gentlewomen in Chichester.
1876	Fanny Williams began the Bishop Otter training.
1877	Charlotte suddenly resigned as senior governess at Christmas, on health grounds.
1878	After working three months notice part-time, Charlotte recuperated with Miss Brandreth. They travelled to Switzerland during the summer.
1878–1879	Charlotte stayed with friends and taught in Selina Fleming's school while writing geographical texts.
1879	Contact with Miss Brandreth apparently ceased. In late summer, Charlotte moved to 2 Apsley Crescent, Manningham, Bradford, where Mrs Groveham had transferred her middle-class ladies' school.
1880–c. 1882	Fanny Williams joined Charlotte at the Groveham household and taught at the Belle Vue Higher Elementary School in Manningham.
1880	Charlotte's first book, *The Forty Shires*, was published by Hatchards.

1880–1884	Stanford published Charlotte's *Geographical Readers for Elementary Schools.*
1882	John Groveham died of appendicitis on 25 October.
1885–1886	Charlotte Mason lectured to ladies on 'Home Education' to raise funds for a new parochial institute for St Mark's Church, Manningham.
1886	Kegan Paul published *Home Education.*
1887	Mrs Emeline Steinthal met Charlotte in the spring. Mrs Steinthal hosted a drawing room meeting at 2 Walmer Place to initiate the Bradford PEU which was established by an autumn meeting at Bradford Grammar School. In November, Charlotte sent a copy of *Home Education* to the Countess of Aberdeen to enlist her support for the new Union.
1888	Lady Aberdeen invited Charlotte to address a meeting at Hamilton House on 5 June.
1889	In November, Miss Clough invited Charlotte Mason to Newnham College, Cambridge, to meet leading educationists and clerics. Lord and Lady Aberdeen hosted a meeting which set up the Central Council. They were chosen as presidents of the Union.
1890	On 18 January the P(N)EU Executive Committee was established.
1890	In February Charlotte Mason launched *Parents' Review*, a monthly journal. On 18 February, the first P(N)EU Council meeting was held. On 3 June, the first AGM at London House constituted the PEU as the Parents' National Educational Union.
1891	In April, Charlotte Mason left Bradford after eleven years in the Groveham household. She stayed at Selina Fleming's school and launched the *Parents' Review* correspondence School (PRS) in June.
1892	In January, with Mrs Parker's support, Charlotte Mason opened the House of Education to train governesses for home schoolrooms at Springfield House, Ambleside and started the Mothers' Education correspondence Course (MEC) in June.
1893	During the summer, Charlotte Mason invited Elsie Kitching to work for her in Ambleside.
1894	Charlotte Mason travelled to Florence with Mrs Firth and was inspired by frescoes at the Church of Santa Maria

	Novella. In late spring, Mrs Henrietta Franklin visited Charlotte Mason at Springfield. In July, Miss Mason defeated the Lady Isabel Margesson who had challenged her authority.
1894	In the autumn, Mrs Franklin opened the first PRS school in London.
1895	In January, Charlotte Mason moved the House of Education to Scale How.
1896	In January, the students launched their journal, *L'Umile Pianta;* Kegan Paul published *Parents and Children.*
1897	Mrs Franklin organised the first PNEU annual conference in London. Miss Mason succumbed to chronic invalidism; up to 1914, she travelled each year to Bad Nauheim, Germany, with Miss Kitching to take the baths treatment. R. Amy Pennethorne started the two-year training.
1898	Fanny Williams was appointed vice principal of the House of Education; the 1898 London PNEU conference was the last one attended by Charlotte Mason.
1900	Ellen Parish started the training; former students established PRS classes and schools.
1901	Agnes Drury began the training
1903	Mrs Steinthal finally relinquished all PNEU commitments for the Anglican Mothers' Union.
1904	On 17 February, Miss Mason's *A Short Synopsis of Educational Theory* was accepted by the Executive Committee who backed publication of her books as the Home Education Series. Mrs. Franklin was finally appointed as *sole* hon. organising secretary of the PNEU. Mrs Franklin introduced PNEU reading courses. *School Education* came out in November
1905	Kegan Paul published *Ourselves* and re-issued *Home Education* and *Parents and Children* for the Home Education Series.
1906	The fifth volume, *Some Studies in the Formation of Character*, was added; Burgess Hill PNEU School was founded.
1907	The *Parents' Review* School was renamed the Parents' Union School (PUS).
1908–1914	Charlotte Mason's life of Christ in verse, *The Saviour of the World*, was published in six volumes.
1911	Government recognition of the Ambleside training was withheld. Miss Mason purchased Scale How with a mortgage.

1912	The Winchester children's gathering was organised by Mrs Franklin. Miss Mason wrote *The Basis of National Strength* in six letters to *The Times*.
1913	These letters were published as a PNEU pamphlet. Mrs Steinthal resigned from the Mothers' Union.
1914	Mrs Steinthal launched the Liberal Education for All Movement pilot at Miss Ambler's elementary school at Drighlington in Yorkshire during the spring. In September, Charlotte Mason and Elsie Kitching were rescued from Germany after war broke out.
1915	Miss Mason took mineral baths in Wales until 1921.
1916	The Liberal Education for All Movement was pronounced a success; teachers' conferences were held. Miss Mason's and Miss Agnes Drury's pamphlets on *The Theory and Practice of a Liberal Education* were widely circulated.
1917	H.W. Household, Director of Education, introduced PUS liberal education methods into Gloucestershire schools until 1936. The movement spread to other LEAs.
1918	Essex Cholmondeley started the Ambleside training.
1919	In April, Miss Mason signed her last will to safeguard the continuation of her work.
1920	The Whitby children's gathering was held in May; Miss Mason's health improved. She attended teachers' meetings in Gloucester and Bradford in September.
1921	In January, Ellen Parish succeeded Fanny Williams as vice principal of the House of Education. Mrs Steinthal died suddenly on 7 August. In October, Miss Mason finished *An Essay Towards a Philosophy of Education*, published posthumously in 1925.
1922	Miss Mason joyously presided over Whitsuntide conferences at Scale How.
1923	Miss Mason died on 16 January. Her funeral was held on 19 January; she was interred in St Mary's churchyard, Ambleside, between W.E. Forster's memorial and the graves of the Arnold family. On 29 March a memorial service was held at St Martin's in the Fields, London, preceded by a memorial conference. Miss Parish succeeded Miss Mason as principal of the House of Education.

Foreword

Charlotte Mason was a prominent and much respected figure on the education scene in the late nineteenth and early twentieth centuries, and in the context of the history of education in the UK, her educational ideas deserve to be more fully understood than they have been in recent years. But Charlotte Mason's educational ideas are not simply of historical interest. Within her educational philosophy, her emphasis on the individuality of each child and on the entitlement of every child to a wide and personally fulfilling curriculum still has a clear relevance to the continuing educational debate today. In the UK, many of Charlotte Mason's ideas did indeed become thoroughly incorporated into primary school practice in the course of the twentieth century. Her distinctive contribution has been largely forgotten, but as an educationist who was a prime mover in the shift from the Victorian classroom, with its almost exclusive emphasis on the three Rs and payment by results, to the child-focussed philosophy of the modern primary classroom, Charlotte Mason deserves greater recognition. In the USA and Canada today, Charlotte Mason is better known, and her ideas are currently the focus of much re-thinking of what education is about, especially among those who have misgivings about what the state system has to offer.

Added to all this, Charlotte Mason's own life story, from the back streets of Birkenhead to the salons of Victorian and Edwardian high society, is a fascinating tale. Margaret Coombs has reconstructed the life of Charlotte Mason here in far greater detail than has ever been achieved before. It was, for instance, previously generally accepted that Charlotte Mason was the only child of her parents. She was probably the only child of her mother, who Margaret has shown was a Roman Catholic, but Margaret has also shown beyond any shadow of a doubt that Charlotte was most certainly not the only child of her elderly father, Joshua Mason, who had a long and colourful history before he fathered Charlotte. Joshua was a Quaker, in his younger days a successful member of the Quaker community of south-eastern Ireland, and descended from Westmorland Friends who set up schools in Ireland. All this was totally unsuspected before Margaret, through her painstaking and detailed research, discovered a whole new dimension in Charlotte's personal history. The implications of this – Charlotte's Quaker connections, the sad death of her father and mother while she was still a teenager, Charlotte's half-brothers and half-sisters in Ireland – have been a major part of Margaret's research. This research has explained much of Charlotte's later beliefs and attitudes.

I first met Margaret about thirty years ago, when I was principal of Charlotte Mason College, and since then we have corresponded about her research, and from time to time have met, usually among the Charlotte Mason archives held in the Armitt Library in Ambleside. Thus I have seen Margaret's investigations develop, often from a mere hint in the records, into a coherent and detailed analysis of Charlotte Mason's history.

It is probably true to say that most biographers find that there are areas of their subjects' lives that are particularly difficult to piece together, either because the subject of the biography has for whatever reason left little trace, or because other sources, relatives, friends or even other biographers have been economical with the truth, or even deliberately misleading. Margaret was faced with all these problems in good measure. Charlotte herself, for reasons that Margaret analyses very thoroughly, had little to say about her early childhood or family. But perhaps even more problematic was the fact that the archive materials available on Charlotte Mason have been through multiple vicissitudes; various parts have been lodged in different locations, brought together only in the 1990s. It is now known for certain that some materials were destroyed. What remains is still a considerable archive, but Margaret's researches have gone far beyond the archive in Ambleside. She has investigated archives in Liverpool, Birkenhead, Lisburn in Northern Ireland, Dublin, Waterford, Kendal and at leading Quaker libraries and the Bodleian, as well as hunting down sources on the internet.

The result is an objective analysis of Charlotte Mason's life, family connections, educational thinking and personal motivations, as she progressed from her childhood on Merseyside to college in London, and then to teaching in Worthing and lecturing at Bishop Otter Memorial College in Chichester, followed by teaching again in her friend's school in Bradford, during which time she established the PNEU as a national organisation to disseminate her educational ideas, and finally to the setting up of her own House of Education in Ambleside to train governesses, many of whom later taught in PNEU schools. In the process, Margaret presents us with a kaleidoscope of the personalities who influenced education and social attitudes, amongst whom Charlotte Mason found her niche.

Margaret Coombs has not only provided a lively account of Charlotte Mason's life, but has also placed it firmly within the social and educational context of the Victorian and early twentieth century periods.

John Thorley,
Former Principal of Charlotte Mason College, Ambleside

Acknowledgements

I first discovered Charlotte Maria Shaw Mason in the journal *Parents' Review* at the former British Library in 1981. After Professor Dennis Smith guided my 1984 thesis to completion, many questions remained unanswered. Twenty-five years later, I returned to the challenge of investigating Charlotte's mysterious past, knowing that the gracious Essex Cholmondeley wanted a new biography to be published. The interest and enthusiasm of myriad friends, relations and colleagues, who cannot all be named, has spurred me on.

Through Hugh Boulter, then Director, WES/PNEU, and Doreen Russo, the guardian of the PNEU movement, I met many Charlotte Mason College Association (CMCA) members who shared their Ambleside memories: Frances Bailey, Esther Card, Essex Cholmondeley, Dorothy Cooke, Beryl French, Lydia Hering, Hedy Joss, Peggy Lane-Roberts (Mrs Steinthal's granddaughter), Sister Sheila Mary SSC and Geraldine Walton, whose husband, Dr Courtenay Walton, delighted in analysing Charlotte's health records. Bill Percival, former Charlotte Mason College (CMC) Principal, introduced me to Joan Fitch and the Revd John Inman, among others. Sadly all have now died. Jane Lane-Roberts kindly gave me permission to quote from the Steinthal papers, lent by her late mother.

Since 1983, it has been a longstanding pleasure to share discoveries with Professor John Thorley, CMC Principal 1983–1994, who painstakingly brought order to scattered PNEU records. At the Armitt Library, Deborah Walsh, Curator, read an early draft and gave permission to use pictures and archive materials. Deborah, Sue Osman and the Armitt volunteers have been unfailingly thoughtful in responding to every request. Caroline Heal (CMCA), former *L'Umile Pianta* editor, cheerfully corrected my grammar, designed the family tree and was on hand with wise counsels. Jeremy Hills skilfully explored census records while Bob Russell, with unstoppable enthusiasm, traced many of Charlotte's numerous paternal connections from the eighteenth century to the 1990s! Victoria Waters unearthed interesting new sources. Professor Heather Eggins read and commented on the text. Canon Brenda Harding, former CMC lecturer, Dr Caroline Ramazanôglu, Dr Carole Satyamurti, Hilary Strudwick and Rae Pearson have been unfailingly supportive. Henrietta Arthur, Josephine Macdermott and Julia Smith recalled their PNEU school education.

The late Robert Drake enjoyed sharing his Mason researches. The late Sir Ian Anstruther elegantly corresponded on the Victorian age, Oscar Browning's sexuality and Patmore's 'The Angel in the House'. In Worthing, Della West, former headteacher, produced the Davison CE High School archives and log book, which the present headteacher, Christopher Keating, has kindly allowed me to cite. Professor Gordon McGregor has enabled me to draw upon his graphic history of Bishop Otter College. Angela Loewi generously gave permission to use all material relating to her grandmother, the Hon. Mrs Franklin, including diaries lent by the late Joe Franklin, grandson.

Archivists at record offices and libraries have been exceptionally generous with their time: Mrs Elen Wyn, Bangor University Library; the Bodleian Law Librarian, Oxford; Janet Carter, Bishop Otter College Archives, Chichester University; Carmel Flahavan and staff at Carlow Local Studies; Kate Greenaway, Cheltenham Ladies' College; John Benson and colleagues, Chester Record Office; The Church of England Record Centre, London; Arabella Woods at the former DES library; Dublin Registry of Deeds; Kate Holliday, Central Archive Collection, Kendal; Lambeth Palace Library; Claire Drinkwater and Nazlin Bhimani, Research Support and Special Collections Officers, Newsam Library, UCL, IOE; Karen B. Morgan, North London Collegiate School; Peter Monteith, King's College Cambridge Library Archives; Mrs Fyfe-Shaw, National Roman Catholic Library, Farnborough; Dr Maureen Watry, Head of Special Collections and Archives, Liverpool University; Dr Raymond Refaussé, Responsible Church Body, Dublin; A. Jones and colleagues, Swyddoc Archifau, for Welsh birth records; Frances Lansley, West Sussex Record Office; Teresa Nixon and staff at West Yorkshire Archive Service; and Francesca Anyon, Wirral Archives.

Liverpool Record Office researcher, Roger Hull, found Joshua Mason's burial note, which led me to Quaker records; Donal Moore, Waterford City Archives, produced Joshua Mason's handwritten freeman application. At Birkenhead Reference Library, I learnt that Margaret Mason was buried in St Werburgh's churchyard. Mrs Margaret O'Brien drove me to Staplestown House, presently owned by Sean Swan.

The Friends have gone the second mile and further. Tabitha Driver and colleagues at Friends' Library London guided my understanding of the early principles of the Religious Society of Friends. Peter Leeming discussed Kendal Friends' history; Joan Johnson, Friends' historian and archivist, showed me Waterford and gave access and permission to draw upon Waterford Friends' and Newtown School Mason archives and pictures, answering numerous questions. At Friends Historical Library Dublin, Christopher Moriarty, Curator, gave unstinting assistance. Kenneth Wigham cheerfully allowed me to quote from his father's Newtown School history.

Eileen Whalley accompanied me to Lisburn, where Muriel Cameron produced key Friends' records. Arthur Chapman, historian and former headmaster of Lisburn Friends' School, cheerfully showed us linen-making, John Gough's grave, Moyallon Meeting House and Hall's Mill. Elizabeth Dickson, present Principal of Lisburn Friends' School, generously gave access to the archives and permission to draw upon Newhouse's history of Lisburn School. With Joan and Roger Johnson, we were welcomed at The Church Restaurant and Bar, set within St Mary's Church in Dublin, where Joshua Mason married Margaret Shaw.

Since we met in Ambleside in 2008, I have enjoyed talking about Charlotte Mason with many Mason enthusiasts associated with the Charlotte Mason Institute, USA, including CMI Director Dr Carroll Smith and Andra Smith, Professor Jack Beckman, Dr Benjamin Bernier, Lisa Cadora, Andrea Eliassen, Nancy Kelly, Tim Payse in Sydney, Gladys Schaefer, Dr Jennifer Spencer, Amy Fiedler and numerous others. Dr Deani Van Pelt also masterminded the digitising of the CM/PNEU archives; Marlene Power, Redeemer University librarian, was on hand to help in difficulty. It is encouraging that twenty-first century British academic historians of women's education are exploring Charlotte Mason's achievements.

I am immensely grateful to Adrian Brink and Emily Reacher at The Lutterworth Press for seeing the point of an inimitable Victorian educationist and to my editor, Lisa Sinclair, for her creative endeavours and friendly encouragement in effectively preparing Charlotte Mason's biography for publication. Steve Calcutt's computer support and Jane Stuart's practical help have been warmly appreciated. Martin, Dan and Anna have cheered me on all the way.

1.
Introduction: Who Was Charlotte Mason?

> Miss Mason was *grande dame, grande âme*. Her thoughts and her tastes had lineage. To be with her, to come under the spell of her courteous and considerate self-possession was to know what it must have been like to meet Madame de Genlis or some other of those great ladies of the *ancien régime* who won fine culture through teaching children and through sharing with them the love of things which are beautiful and true. Miss Mason had a genius for education. She had an inbred good sense and an unfatigued sensibility. Her mind was tempered by great literature. She loved the humanities. She had a very distinguished gift of leadership in co-operation. There was a tenderness, a humility in her self-confidence. . . . And the greatness of the thoughts she lived with made her greater-hearted as her experience deepened and as the circle of her pupils grew nationwide. . . .
>
> Charlotte Mason represented the culture of the home-school at its best. . . . This, I think, was her great contribution to the thought of her time. . . . Through Ruskin and Thomas Arnold of Rugby, she was in direct succession from Wordsworth. . . . The liberal movement through Rousseau found expression in Miss Mason's work as in that of her predecessors. . . . She was steadied by a deep religious conviction, by the reverence for human personality which has in it the quiet awe of faith in divine guidance.[1]

This glowing tribute to Charlotte Maria Shaw Mason (1 January 1842–16 January 1923) was composed for her memorial anthology of eulogy, *In Memoriam: Charlotte M. Mason* (1923), by Sir Michael Sadler CB (1861–1943), distinguished liberal educationist, former government adviser and Master of University College, Oxford, at the time. Sadler greatly admired John Ruskin (1819–1900), a major influence on the Victorian educated classes. For many years, aristocrats and educationists had metaphorically gathered at the feet of Miss Mason, the gracious principal of her House of Education at Ambleside, in the Lake District, the only contemporary training college for governesses. Sir Robert Morant (1863–1920), Permanent Secretary to the Board of Education from 1903 to 1911, and Horace Household (1870–1954), Director of Education for Gloucestershire from 1903 to 1936, admired her liberal educational ideas. Miss Mason's use of *Aids to Scouting* (1899) as a school book inspired Sir Robert Baden-Powell (1857–1941) to found the Boy Scout movement in 1908 after hearing that his brigadier general had been successfully ambushed from a tree-top in 1904 by his son and Katherine Loveday, the House-of-Education-trained governess![2] In Ambleside, Miss Mason made friends with people of standing such as Frances Arnold (1833–1923), the youngest sister of Matthew Arnold (1822–1888); the three gifted Armitt sisters, Sophia, Annie and Mary Louisa; Canon Hardwicke Rawnsley (1851–1920), co-founder of the National Trust; and Gordon Wordsworth (1860–1935), the poet's grandson.

Charlotte Mason's lifestyle, her manners and her morals were quintessentially Victorian. As Victorian social standing was important to our heroine and because she was customarily addressed as Miss Mason by all who knew her at Ambleside, the title 'Miss' will be used throughout this biography as a mark of respect.

In January 1895, Miss Mason settled her House of Education in the stately Georgian mansion, Green Bank, previously owned by Mrs Dorothy Benson Harrison (1801–1890), daughter of Robinson Wordsworth, a cousin of William Wordsworth (1770–1850), the romantic Lakeland poet. This spacious domain gave Miss Mason a gracious setting in which to receive her students and many distinguished visitors. She drew upon Ambleside's rich inheritance of Norse names in renaming the house 'Scale How', meaning 'summer lodge on hill'. Wordsworth used to visit Green Bank regularly as Dorothy, the owner, orphaned at eleven, had lived with his family at Rydal Mount until her marriage to Benson Harrison at the age of eighteen.[3]

As the acknowledged founder and philosopher of the Parents' National Educational Union (PNEU) (1887–1989), Miss Mason was revered as a saintly Madonna figure and leading educational guru, famous for treasured epigrams such as 'Education is an atmosphere, a discipline, a life.' Her credo, 'for the children's sake', founded upon her respect for children as *persons,* lay at the heart of her teaching.[4] From 1914 onwards, her liberal educational programmes, designed for upper- and educated-class home schoolrooms spreading across the British Isles and the colonies, were introduced into state schools, bringing widespread acclaim. As the PNEU movement declined in Britain towards the end of the twentieth century, Charlotte Mason's educational philosophy was transported overseas to America, Australia and other lands, where it is being enthusiastically resurrected, practised and reinterpreted for the new century.

Born in the early years of Victoria's reign, Charlotte Mason grew up during a time of educational ferment and growing recognition of children's rights. Wordsworth's romantic revival and the writings of 'new' Enlightenment educationists such as Jean-Jacques Rousseau (1712–1778), with Johann Heinrich Pestalozzi (1746–1827) and Friedrich Froebel (1782–1852), had engendered a fresh awareness of children as personalities. As the Victorian age progressed, far more children were surviving to adulthood. The sound preparation of succeeding generations for the responsibilities of Empire demanded reverent attention to the education of mothers. For the higher classes, a well-ordered home life was deemed essential for those gentlemen obliged to 'encounter all peril' through toiling at 'rough work in the open world'.[5] Rigid social class divisions, the outcome of a civilising process extended over past generations, were believed by the upper echelons of society to be fixed in accordance with divine laws, although these invisible barriers were already being breached by the emergent new middle classes. By the late Victorian age, the popular image of womanhood as the passively decorative 'Angel in the House' was giving way to matriarchal dominance as upper-class married and independent single women joined committees and engaged in philanthropic works outside the protected domestic sphere, sometimes challenging established patriarchal authority.[6]

The dilemma faced by Victorian female educational pioneers was how to open up academic education and acceptable work opportunities for middle-class women whose families could not support them without prejudicing their health, social standing and chances of marriage. Three educationists who helped Charlotte Mason to establish the PNEU addressed this concern by developing school and university education for women. They were Anne Jemima Clough (1820–1892), the first principal of Newnham College, Cambridge, from 1871; Dorothea Beale (1831–1906), principal of Cheltenham Ladies' College from 1853 and founder of St Hilda's College, Oxford, in 1893; and Frances Mary Buss (1827–1894), headmistress of the North London Collegiate School from 1850 onwards. Miss Buss and Miss Beale were among the first cohort of women attending evening lectures at Queen's College, Harley Street, boldly founded by the Christian socialist Professor the Revd Frederick Denison Maurice (1805–1872) with other King's College London professors in 1848. Linked to the Governesses' Benevolent Institution, established in 1843 to provide training and relief for indigent women, the lectures were intended to raise the standard of governesses' knowledge. Maurice's campaign for higher education and qualifications for women challenged the widespread misconception that intensive academic study not only caused dangerous 'overpressure' and physical prostration, but also wrecked feminine beauty and womanly charm. The pejorative appellation 'the third sex' was crudely applied to campaigning groups

Frances Buss, Principal of the North London Collegiate School.

of strong-minded, intelligent spinsters, as suggested by the well-known ditty attributed by some to J.C. Tarver:

> Miss Buss and Miss Beale
> Cupid's darts do not feel
> How different from us
> Miss Beale and Miss Buss.[7]

Dorothea Beale in her study at Cheltenham Ladies' College.

Apart from marriage, what did the future hold for gently nurtured, less assertively intelligent, single Victorian gentlewomen? After a year or two at a private school, they rejoined the home circle under their parents' protection, their days taken up with acquiring accomplishments, light reading and social calls. For those of slender means, becoming a private governess was usually the only option. Precariously poised between the nursery and the servants' hall, the despised, 'ignorant' governess remained the proverbial butt of unkind humour. As this book will show, addressing this tension while steadily raising her own social and intellectual standing was skilfully achieved by Charlotte Mason in the application of her educational philosophy and methods, first to home and subsequently to school education.[8]

Charlotte Mason was an outstanding personality. She met the challenge of unprotected spinsterhood with a graceful verve that commanded attention and respect. By the 1880s, she was already a published writer. Her lectures to ladies were published as *Home Education* in 1886; they inspired a young mother called Mrs Emeline Steinthal (1856–1921), with whom Miss Mason founded the Parents' Educational Union (PEU) in Bradford in 1887 and launched the cultural journal *Parents' Review* in 1890, the year the PNEU was nationally constituted. In 1891, Charlotte Mason moved to Ambleside and started the *Parents' Review* School (PRS), renamed the Parents' Union School (PUS) in 1907. The PRS offered educational programmes for children under nine learning at home. In January 1892, she boldly opened her House of Education to train governesses for home schoolrooms, followed by the Mothers' Education correspondence Course in June of that year.

A deeply religious woman, Miss Mason was observed to conduct her personal relationships with grace and charm, speaking in a quiet but impelling voice. On the evening of her death, Dr Hough of Clappersgate, who attended select patients, told the House of Education students,

> Wherever she went the charm of her presence brought sunshine and happiness. She made all about her feel at ease and then acted as a magnet for drawing out all that was good in them. Her beautiful face was in her the index of a beautiful soul.[9]

The reverential devotion in which she was held enthralled Miss Mason's far flung followers as much in her absence as in her presence. Nurtured by chosen women disciples at Scale How while quietly reigning from the blue sofa in the drawing room, she was a remote but dynamic presence, missing nothing with her searching blue eyes.

> I can't conceive that there is no Miss Mason lying as usual on her couch, so gentle, so quiet and serene amid the soft greys and blues of her cushions and rugs, that we shall not hear her low, but quite determined voice, or see again that little movement of her hand, that said so much.[10]

Nothing was known of Charlotte's early life. Although her disciples were reluctant to peer behind her veil of secrecy, their tactful reticence did not inhibit eager speculation about what lay hidden.[11] The unspoken question remained: *How* had a previously unknown, frail, spinster school teacher, apparently without patriarchal familial backing or wealth, achieved so much in so short a space of time? Miss Mason's lifestyle at Scale How, fashioned from the best elements of cultured Victorianism, appears to have been deliberately designed to keep spontaneous personal revelation at bay. Her conversation was modelled on the classic Victorian precept, 'Servants talk about people; gentlefolk discuss things.'[12] Everyone knew that Miss Mason suffered from life-long serious heart trouble, restricting all activity. Sometimes breathless, she would claim to be too tired to talk or to meet with more than one person at a time. No one was allowed to drop in without invitation. She was never photographed with the official House of Education groups; snapping by students or visitors was sternly prohibited.[13] Just a few photographs, mostly captured unobserved, have survived; several of these are included in this volume.

> When asked if she would not dictate some notes of her life, her only reply was – 'my dear, my life does not matter. I have no desire that it should ever be written. It is the work that matters and, I say it with all

reverence, it will some day (not in my lifetime) be seen to be one of the greatest things that has happened in the world'.[14]

In this manner Charlotte Mason effectively inhibited her followers from delving into her private past, determined to forestall a biography. Why? This seems inconsistent in one who clearly enjoyed the acclaim she had won towards the end of her life and was not averse to a little 'spin' about past achievements. Reticence was sanctioned by Holy Writ:

> There was another reason why Miss Mason never talked of herself. It was a matter of principle. . . . 'The laws of life and conduct are laid down for us by our Lord and we do well to ponder every hint that the Gospel story gives us'. On this particular point she would, as that part of the Gospel came in its natural sequence, dwell on the words 'If I bear witness of myself, my witness is *not* true' and she would say to the students – 'My dear friends, think of this. Do not dwell upon yourselves, your belongings or even your families unduly, in talking to others. This saying is literally true. If I bear witness of myself my witness is *not* true.'[15]

Fanny Williams (1850–1925) was vice principal of the House of Education from 1898 to 1920. A former student at the Bishop Otter Memorial Training College at Chichester in Sussex, she had known Miss Mason since 1876. Setting a 'daily personal example of utter loyalty' to Miss Mason and her ideals, her reminiscences for *In Memoriam* were said to be 'so typical, so humble and loyal'.[16] After Miss Mason died in 1923, she averred, 'My memory [at seventy-three] fails me sometimes', thus tactfully regretting her inability to recall more than a few fragments.

> Moreover, dear Miss Mason was so much absorbed in her work that she spoke but little of her own life. For many years before her death those who lived with her tried to save her as much as possible from the fatigue of conversation; we always read to her in her few leisure hours.[17]

Daringly disregarding the implicit embargo on investigation, Elsie Kitching (1870–1955), who had lived with Miss Mason for thirty years as her amanuensis, guardian 'dragon', companion and mainstay, could scarcely wait to investigate her leader's mysterious early life. Seeking answers, she confronted the same socially constructed barriers faced by the present writer.

In the spring of 1923, Elsie Kitching wrote to Mrs Elizabeth Groveham (1841–1930), formerly Lizzie Pendlebury, Charlotte's longstanding college friend, also known to Fanny Williams. Elsie must have met Mrs Groveham during her sole recorded visit to Scale How on 8 December 1899.[18] Lizzie's response manifested loving respect for her friend's resolute reticence:

> I fully realise your difficulty and will do my best. . . . I have before me a confused mass of partially faded and undated letters which makes the task of selection difficult. The thought that suggests itself to my mind is this – to go through the letters as they lie, give them an appropriate date and send to you such pages as may be useful for your purpose.[19]

Although Lizzie had received Charlotte's weekly letters from 1861 until 1879, when they lived together in Bradford, because they 'were of so intimate and personal a character' she released only about twenty fragments. Having selected some and copied others, she invited Elsie Kitching to her terraced house in Woodbridge, Suffolk, reluctant to reveal too much.[20]

> The idea of a Memorial Biography is excellent and will be cherished by all who knew and loved her and will be stimulating to those who knew her work. In regard to the letters, there may be much that is helpful to your purpose. . . . At the same time, they are of so intimate and personal a character, that much of their contents would hardly be suitable for publication. I mean in this way. As a girl she was ever spiritually minded, and the letters reveal the earnest striving of the soul for the light, which in after days she found in full measure. . . . I feel that you will quite understand.

Mrs Groveham added a missive from a former pupil at her Bradford Ladies' School, who obliquely hinted at a major transformation, after reading the memorial recollections in the *Parents' Review*:

> In thinking of dear Miss Mason, I always remember her enthusiasm, her true culture and her essential goodness. One can hardly recognise in the printed portraits, the Miss Mason of old days. I think she must have been very happy in her work and evidently found her true sphere.[21]

Mrs Groveham asked Miss Kitching *not* to mention her name and to destroy the few selected excerpts. Both requests were disregarded. Their correspondence lasted intermittently until 1927. Elsie learnt, probably for the first time, that Charlotte had been orphaned as a teenager. She had studied with Mrs Groveham, then known as Lizzie Pendlebury, at the Home and Colonial Training Institution in London before being appointed mistress of the Davison Infantine School in Worthing in 1861. Mrs Groveham inaccurately told Elsie Kitching that the school had nothing to do with the government. She added that Charlotte, affectionately known to her as Lottie, and her parents 'were at times resident in three different places: Dublin – Bangor – Liverpool'. She altered the date given on a postcard from 1841 to 1840, presumably to establish that Charlotte's parents had married in 1840, the year before Charlotte had initially believed she had been born on 1 January 1841. Charlotte's beautiful mother was an invalid. In 1927,

Mrs Groveham unexpectedly added Birkenhead to the list of places where she believed the Masons had lived.[22] Bound to her deceased friend 'by the old kinship spirit', Lizzie did not seriously breach Lottie's sacrosanct confidentiality but sympathised with Miss Kitching's desperate need to learn more.[23] Having obliquely confirmed that Charlotte *had* taught in a government-funded school, Fanny Williams died in 1925 without further revelations.

> She desired to hide behind Miss Mason's greater personality and was unwilling that the least thought should be directed towards herself.[24]

Over the next few years, Miss Kitching collected material for a definitive biography. The archive, now held at the Armitt Museum and Library in Ambleside, abounds with the worn, labelled brown envelopes in which she gathered her findings. *The Times'* obituary had stated that Charlotte Mason's father's name was Joshua; his Liverpool death certificate confirmed he was a merchant. This accorded with Mrs Groveham's recollection that the Mason family had lived in Liverpool.[25] Years passed.

After retiring in 1948, Elsie Kitching, known to Charlotte as 'Kit Kit', undertook further researches and visited Worthing. Information revealed in the statutory Davison School log book, kept by the mistress, and local census records must have perplexed and troubled her. Unable to progress, she spent her remaining years reflecting on her leader's educational philosophy, protesting that, by comparison, the biography was of secondary importance.

> Her devotion, her self-effacing vigilance guarded Miss Mason literally day and night, year in, year out, even through these later years she has lived with the one purpose of guarding and promoting Miss Mason's work.[26]

'The better part of valour is discretion.'[27] Elsie's flat gravestone, adorned with a 'K' at each corner and set at the foot of Miss Mason's Celtic tomb, proclaims that the subservient Kit Kit laid down her life for her leader as, indeed, she gave her all in thirty years of unremitting service. Having purchased the space in Ambleside churchyard on 1 April 1924, Kit Kit's will directed 'that no headstone be erected and the grave space kept flat as a standing place for the visitors to the grave of the late Charlotte Mason'.[28] With this dramatic gesture of extreme docility, Elsie quelled her curiosity and upheld Miss Mason's mythic status in death.

A definitive biography was long awaited. After the Second World War, Charlotte Mason Foundation members believed that the survival of the PNEU critically depended upon making the acknowledged founder's educational ideas more widely known. They asked Essex Cholmondeley (1892–1985) to complete Miss Kitching's unfinished work.[29]

Essex Cholmondeley was a most suitable choice. Distantly connected to Reginald Heber (1783–1826), the well-known hymn writer and Bishop of Calcutta, she was descended from a line of rural clerics.[30] Essex's father, Reginald Cholmondeley (1857–1941), a former army captain, was wealthy. In 1911, he employed twelve indoor servants, from the butler and two footmen to the cook-housekeeper, children's nurse and seven maids. After a home education, Essex stayed with her aunts in London, enjoying the dances and parties of the Edwardian era, and was presented at court. During the 1914 war she taught sick children in hospital. Helen Wix (1882–1982) (CMT 1903) from Sydney, Australia, had gained a first-class House of Education certificate. As governess to Essex's younger sisters, Hester, aged sixteen, and Joan, aged five, in 1911, Helen clearly demonstrated the benefits of an Ambleside education.[31]

A tall, graceful woman, Essex (CMT 1919) took the training under Miss Mason's rule; it was subsequently termed the Charlotte Mason Training. She admired the principal as a frail but impressive elderly matriarch. Aged twenty-six she was appointed senior monitress and drill monitress, gaining a first-class certificate with distinction. Serious and spiritual, Essex probably understood Miss Mason's quest for holiness better than anyone. She protectively concluded that Elsie Kitching's difficulty in finishing the biography lay in the fact that 'Charlotte Mason's story is one of thought rather than incident.'[32]

Did Essex ever tell Miss Mason that her aunt was Mary Cholmondeley (1859–1925), the well-known author of *Red Pottage* (1899), a daring, satirical, best-selling novel? This popular work, which attacked the self-righteous pretensions of the English middle classes and the bigotry of intolerant clergy, was enjoyed by Queen Victoria and preached on at St Paul's by the Bishop of Stepney. Times were changing; *fin-de-siècle* novels of the *new women* genre challenging the probity of cherished institutions from marriage to religion may have delighted the avant-garde but were, assuredly, forbidden at Scale How as 'twaddle'.[33]

After teaching at Hatherop Castle in Gloucestershire, Essex was recalled to Ambleside to assist Miss Kitching with the PUS in 1924. After world travel with her parents and sister Joan in 1929, she was appointed vice principal at the House of Education in 1930. Ellen Parish (1869–1947) (CMT 1902), another first-class student and Miss Mason's chosen successor as principal from 1923 to 1934, was unwell. Essex briefly succeeded her as an innovatory principal from 1934 to 1937, subsequently serving on the Charlotte Mason Foundation and supporting PNEU schools until she was seventy.[34]

After Elsie died, Essex reluctantly agreed to finish the biography. The pressure to publish must have heightened once it was known that Monk Gibbon (1896–1987), a poet and grand old man of Irish letters, was writing about his friend, the Hon. Mrs Henrietta Franklin CBE (1866–1964), who had dominated the PNEU since 1894. Monk Gibbon brought out his lively and endearing account, *Netta*, in June of 1960, the year the official biography, *The Story of Charlotte Mason 1842–1923* by Essex Cholmondeley, was published.[35]

Until now, Cholmondeley's biography has been the main source of information about Charlotte Mason's hidden early life. When the book was re-issued in 2000 for a wider, transatlantic audience, Eve Anderson, a former student, stated unequivocally, 'It is an accurate account.'[36] New evidence, presented here, disproves this assertion.

I first discovered references to Charlotte Mason and the PNEU in the journal *Parents' Review* at the round Reading Room of the old British Library in 1981, where Charlotte Mason studied in 1885.[37] I was researching the history of education for parenthood and sought the PNEU archives.[38] A visit to the offices of the World-wide Education Service of the PNEU in London yielded nothing. Introduced to Mrs Geraldine Walton (CMT 1928), I asked about the archives. This impressively stately lady looked me straight in the eyes and said, '*All the records have been destroyed!*'[39]

Mrs Walton put me in touch with Essex Cholmondeley, whom I visited on 5 April 1982 at Nynehead Court nursing home near Wellington in Somerset, a beautiful mansion, previously owned by Edward Clarke. Coincidentally, in 1684 Dr John Locke (1632–1704) had advised Clarke on his son's education via letter and published these letters as *Some Thoughts Concerning Education* in 1693. A frail but graciously charming lady of ninety-one, Essex was following doctor's orders by staying in bed that day. She explained that it had been necessary to re-write the biography because Miss Kitching had employed a 'rather unreadable, scholarly style'. Within the loving atmosphere enveloping her elegant room, she revealed next to nothing about Charlotte's early life. Fixing her large and beautiful eyes upon me, she whispered dramatically, '*All the papers were destroyed!*'[40] On a sudden impulse, I telephoned the Institute of Historical Research and learnt that Mrs Walton, as Chair of the PNEU Council, had deposited thirty boxes of PNEU records at the University of London Library a few years earlier!

After carefully scrutinising the two supposedly autobiographical extracts entitled 'Memories' and 'Recollections' opening Chapter 1 of *The Story of Charlotte Mason*, I discovered there were *no* original documents. The 'Memories' excerpt was *not* published in Volume 1 of the *Parents' Review* as stated; no manuscript of 'Recollections' has surfaced. Accordingly, I concluded that they were an artificial reconstruction, compiled by the two biographers, perhaps partly from scraps and hints let fall by Charlotte Mason, to present an appropriate background for the founder of the PNEU.[41] Other letters, cited in the early chapters, were either unreferenced or actually altered.

The 'Memories' and 'Recollections' were charmingly composed, painting tender pictures of Charlotte's isolated childhood, apparently spent mainly on the Isle of Man, playing with her mother, whose name was not given. The references to 1840s fashions were authentic. Her mother dressed elegantly; Charlotte wore a Holland overall to play on the beach.[42] Mr Mason, said to have been a Liverpool merchant, was inexplicably given the initials J.H. There is no certain evidence that he was a drysalter. Whoever suggested this must have been unfamiliar with the short story *Angelina or L'Amie Inconnue,* by Maria Edgeworth (1768–1849), in which Lady Diana is appalled at discovering the true background of her companion, Miss Burrage:

> Daughter to a drysalter, niece to a cheesemonger. Only conceive! A person who has been going about with me everywhere. What will the world say?[43]

By way of compensation, Charlotte's father was described as 'a refined and simple man, very fond of books'. The mention of seaside holidays at Douglas on the Isle of Man suggested that Miss Kitching had discovered Charlotte Mason's 1861 Worthing census return. In 1982, the late Robert Drake was the first to show that Charlotte gave Douglas, Isle of Man, as her birthplace for the 1861 census and recorded her age as twenty. Ten years later, she was twenty-nine and had been born in Bangor, Caernarvon.[44] A copied letter, allegedly sent by Mrs Groveham, underpinned *The Story*'s claim that Charlotte was an only child of only children.

> As regards family ties Miss Mason's position was unique. From herself I understood that both her parents were only children, of whom she was the only child. If corroboration were needed, it would lie in the fact, that during her period of training, her holidays were spent in College as she had no relations. . . . With my much love, yours affectionately, E. Groveham. 7th May 1924.[45]

Significantly, this note labelled 'COPY' is the only *typed* letter to be found among Mrs Groveham's boldly handwritten screeds in the archives. No hand-written original has appeared. Did Miss Kitching, who typed up many copies of later correspondence, file a fabricated letter with the handwritten others? The phrase 'If corroboration were needed' is telling. What Lizzie really knew about Lottie's family remains obscure.

'Recollections' plausibly traced Charlotte's teaching career, her love of books and some of her educational ideas back to her early childhood. Mr Mason was said to have lost all his money in 1848 and 1849. These years may have been carefully chosen to explain why Charlotte trained as a teacher. Less disgrace was attached to severely reduced circumstances during the 'hungry forties', at the peak of Chartist political unrest, economic downturns and the far-reaching effects of the Irish potato famine. Anne Jemima Clough, one of Charlotte's leading advisers, opened her Ambleside school in 1852 because her father, a respectable cotton merchant, had lost

Four torchbearers, Agnes Drury, Essex Cholmondeley, Ellen Parish and Elsie Kitching, with the students.

money through trading with America, where the expanding cotton industry was in direct competition with Great Britain. Mrs Groveham also challenged Miss Williams's incorrect assertion that Charlotte's father had been ruined by the American Civil War (1861–1865), which further curtailed cotton imports to Lancashire factories, causing mass unemployment.[46]

'Memories' and 'Recollections' offer a confusing mixture of stereotype and realism in the lightly sketched picture of an impoverished, lonely childhood, spent with erudite parents who read all the time but probably educated her at home. Both pieces echo aspects of the literary home education recommended by John Ruskin (1819–1900), Charlotte's later Lakeland neighbour, but curiously none of the hallmarks of the Victorian upbringing of home-bred girls familiar to Miss Cholmondeley, such as languages, embroidery, watercolour sketching, singing pretty melodies or playing the pianoforte, are described. Instead, the strange pictures in Austen Henry Layard's *Nineveh* (1848/9), allegedly opened up a 'sort of Milky Way of Knowledge' for little Charlotte.[47] The explanation for these anomalies must surely lie in the difficulty faced by such partial, yet essentially honest, disciples in reconciling the little they knew of her background with traditional veneration for her cultured social standing.

Respectability and gentility were integral to the domestically oriented civilising process during the Victorian age. These concepts helped to pinpoint the different levels of status within a hierarchical social order undergoing rapid change. Respectability was held by the aristocracy, the upper class and the new middle class to represent the summit of male and female working-class ambition. It was associated with docile industry, orderly family life, cleanliness and godliness. Respectability marked off the deserving from the undeserving poor. In contrast, gentility incorporated subtle nuances, which popular advice manuals were endeavouring to expound to the upwardly mobile. It suggested more gracious social standing than that conferred by industrious respectability. By late Victorian times, when education was everywhere discussed, the 'educated classes' emerged. Differentiated from the bulk of the rising new middle classes by their preference for culture over ostentatious displays of wealth, the educated classes advocated 'plain living and high thinking', usually because they could not afford conspicuous consumption. Some argued that while a lady could be made, the status of 'gentlewoman' was conferred only by birth. Reduced circumstances did not necessarily destroy gentility, which was thought, by those who laid claim to it, to have slowly evolved after centuries of civilisation. Charlotte Mason was destined to prove, if only to her secret satisfaction, that it was possible to absorb centuries of civilisation within one lifetime and to rise within the rigid society that was opening up by the late Victorian age.[48]

Essex Cholmondeley told me the biography was not very good without explaining why. Her subsequent letters expressed an overpowering desire to learn of any new discoveries: 'I am so glad the work progresses; indeed I can hardly wait for it.' After her death in 1985, Mrs Walton kindly commented, 'Little did her readers realise the long and devoted labour that lay behind this not entirely satisfactory book.'[49] Sadly she died at the age of ninety-three before the more complete story she had quietly expected could be told. Having done her best with her troubling commission, she was not prepared to compromise Miss Mason's reputation by revealing the few secrets that, assuredly, Miss Kitching had discovered. Instead she concluded that any attempt to tell the story of Charlotte Mason must lay stress on that 'life hid with Christ in God' upon which she based her teaching.[50]

The time has come to cast aside the earlier anxieties and subterfuge that have obscured Charlotte Mason's secret past and early education. Since the 1980s, her educational ideas have been embraced with enthusiasm across the Atlantic, in America, Canada and in Australia and other lands. Led astray by the Cholmondeley biography, which misrepresented her early life out of misplaced loyalty, Charlotte Mason has been lifted out of her Victorian historical context and family background. Painstaking research, described elsewhere, has thrown fresh light on her secret early life before the PNEU, revealing her remarkable spirit and determination to overcome all obstacles.[51]

Who *was* Charlotte Mason? Thanks to gaining access to meticulous records kept by the Religious Society of Friends, I learnt that she was *not* the only child of only children. Charlotte was the thirteenth child of her ageing

Irish Quaker father, Joshua Mason, and her young Roman Catholic mother, Margaret Shaw, about whom little has been discovered. On her father's side, Charlotte was descended from a multifarious family, solidly rooted in the egalitarian, puritan ethos of the Religious Society of Friends, reaching back to the seventeenth century in Westmorland and the eighteenth century in Ireland. By uncovering the hidden backdrop to Charlotte Mason's life and the emergent picture of her father's life and times, subtly transformed in the Cholmondeley biography, we surely gain a better understanding of the roots of her personality. These were expressed by her earnest searching for the Light, her capacity for immensely hard work and her bold business acumen, which powered her educational aspirations and dreams of validation as a writer and philosopher. Respected for their honest business dealings, Quakers valued education and endeavour in all walks of life, as shown by Charlotte's family history. Joshua Mason's own rise from a mundane apprenticeship to the status of gentleman miller foreshadowed Charlotte's arduous journey to high standing. Accordingly, the unfolding of Charlotte's interesting paternal Quaker background and her parents' problematic relationship and religious differences sets the scene for her remarkable rise and unexplained break with all family ties.

2.
A Westmorland Quaker Heritage

Charlotte Mason's Irish father, Joshua Mason (3 January 1780–15 March 1859), a birthright member of the Religious Society of Friends, was sixty-two when she was born. Their Quaker heritage has been traced back to the seventeenth century in Westmorland and to the eighteenth century in Ireland. Charlotte's later absorption with the writings of seventeenth-century divines and philosophers from John Bunyan (1628–1688) and Benjamin Whichcote (1609–1683) to John Locke (1632–1704) suggests her father's influence. Did stories of her Westmorland ancestors engender a longing to settle in Ambleside?

Charlotte's paternal great-grandfather was John Gough (1721–1791); her great-great-uncle was his older brother, James (1712–1780). They were born in Kendal, Westmorland, where the Religious Society of Friends was powerfully established from 1652 onwards.[1] James's remarkable memoirs give a graphic account of their lives and the spiritual challenges they faced.[2]

The Religious Society of Friends, known as 'The Children of the Light' or 'Friends of the Truth', was founded by George Fox (1624–1691) in northern England. A weaver's son, he started out as a shoemaker and shepherd. From 1647 he travelled to encourage seekers after truth to join with him as Friends. His original conception of an *inward* or *divine* principle, which he defined as 'that of God in every man', resonates with Charlotte's later emphasis on 'true inwardness'. As a distinctive, reforming, puritan movement, the Religious Society of Friends emerged during a century of religious dissent, beleaguered by the troubled years of the Cromwellian English Civil War (1642–1651). The appellation 'Quaker' may have been first used after Fox's trial before Justice Bennett in Derby in 1650, when he reputedly called upon the judge to *tremble* before the Lord.[3] During the seventeenth century, the Friends faced decades of fierce opposition and persecution. George Fox was a victim of such persecution; in 1651 he was imprisoned for preaching, for blasphemy and for refusing to fight in the Civil War. As the power of the established Church was reinvigorated with the Restoration of Charles II to the throne in 1660, other dissenters, notably Baptists and Presbyterians, shared the Friends' dissatisfaction with the Church's dominant clericalism. Quaker worship and objections to paying tithes to maintain the Church were deemed illegal, leading to harassment and prosecutions. Suffering Friends drew up their historic Peace Testimony in 1660 to tell the whole world that 'All bloody principles and practices we do utterly deny.'[4]

William Edmondson (1627–1712), also from Westmorland, took the movement to Northern Ireland, where the first Friends' meeting was established at Lurgan in 1654. George Fox gave Edmondson an inspiring epistle to read to Lurgan Friends and visited Ireland in 1669 to set up an agreed structure for the discipline of members.[5]

Inspired by the revelation of the inner light of Christ in everyone regardless of gender, race or class, Fox's preaching was rooted in Scripture. Clear understanding of the Bible was achieved through the working of the Holy Spirit in each believer, a view that Charlotte would hold dear. Quakers were set apart from other Protestant groups and Roman Catholics by their profound understanding of the Scriptures. Their direct approach, which bypassed the established Church's doctrine, was condemned as blasphemy.[6] Undeterred and guided by Fox, the Friends rejected the need for priests and the sacraments of baptism or marriage. As local groups of Friends formed, they met together for worship in reverential and companionable silence. There was no leader; men or women might speak in the silence, guided by the inner light of the Holy Spirit.[7]

This enlightened movement spread across England, Ireland and the New World, proclaiming a humane philosophy of social justice, equality and philanthropy, which later found expression in anti-slavery campaigns. Notwithstanding theological controversies, there was remarkable uniformity in matters of practice. Both James and John Gough were raised in the tradition of plain dress, without frills, wigs or ribbons. They adopted plain speech, using 'thee' and 'thou' in treating everyone without undue deference. Except when praying to God, Friends did not doff their hats before any person, superior or otherwise. Simplicity in behaviour was integral to their passion for Truth. Quakers did not swear oaths as there was no need for a truthful person's testimony to be ratified.[8]

Led by Fox, Quakers valued a broad, practical education for boys and girls to enable them to study the natural world and to prepare for life.[9] Fox advocated apprenticeships for boys in suitable trades. Honesty and fairness were key elements. Well-schooled in mercantile arithmetic, Quakers earned a justified reputation for trustworthiness in trade, banking and other business dealings, as well as for quality of workmanship. Quaker families prospered, consolidating the membership in close networks within a relatively small but effective body of Friends.

A clear framework of local monthly meetings, regional quarterly meetings and national yearly meetings, organised by clerks of both genders, was established to foster communication between Friends. Business-oriented meetings and meetings for discipline or the conduct of local affairs were conducted quietly. Quakers paused to discuss the issues patiently without scoring debating points, until general agreement was reached by consensus to achieve clear resolution.[10]

Before Charlotte's Quaker great-great-grandparents, John Gough (1686–1737) and Mary Mansergh (1677–1747), were born, George Fox arrived in Kendal at Whitsuntide in 1652. Perhaps Mary Mansergh's parents, William and Mary Mansergh, were taken to hear Fox preach as young children. The Mansergh family came from Kirkland, later attached to Kendal Meeting. Fox met large numbers of 'seekers' and preached at several meetings. On Pendle Hill at Firbank, by a ruined chapel of ease, about 1,000 people stood on the hillside in the afternoon to hear Fox preach. Now marked with a plaque, the rock where he stood is called Fox's Pulpit. This Westmorland fortnight was described as 'the creative moment in the history of Quakerism' that launched the movement.[11]

On 18 January 1711, John Gough, possibly a tobacconist and Quaker travelling minister, married Mary Mansergh at Kendal Meeting House, thus setting the couple on the path to becoming Charlotte's great-great-grandparents.[12] Growing up towards the end of the seventeenth century, they benefited from greater freedom to worship conferred by the 1689 Toleration Act and from a religious movement that was settling into the organised framework put in place by George Fox. Although Kendal Friends established a strong presence in Westmorland, their first meeting house was not built until 1687. The third elegant meeting house built in 1816 still stands on the former site. Charlotte's Quaker ancestors lie at rest in one of the older burial grounds for Kendal Friends.[13]

Mary and John Gough had four children. Their firstborn, James, arrived two days after Christmas in 1712. Their daughters, Mary and Alice, were born in 1714 and 1716 respectively, but may not have survived to adulthood. Charlotte Mason's great-grandfather, John Gough, was the last born on 30 October in 1720 or 1721.[14]

Aged twelve, John Gough senior had been one of the first day pupils at the Friends' school opened at Stramongate in Kendal town centre in 1698, which remained active until 1932. Thomas Redbank (1694–post-1764), who gave his name to the school, started as the teaching assistant to the first headmaster, John Jopson. Rising to become a forceful headmaster himself, Redbank conducted the school for forty years from 1715 until his retirement in 1764.[15] The Friends sought 'to provide their children with a sound and thorough education, as they regarded education in the same light as George Fox, as a power which might be of great use in supporting their sect'.[16]

John Gough junior was devoted to his older brother and always ready to be at his beck and call. James was intellectually brilliant and a significant role model. Many Quakers, notably George Fox, wrote memoirs. Much may be learnt from James's fascinating *Memoirs,* which he recorded at the age of sixty-six. They were edited by John and published after James's death in 1781.

> I was born at Kendal in Westmoreland on 27.12.1712 and from my parents, John and Mary Gough, professing the Truth as held by the People called Quakers, I received my education in the same profession.

James recalled that their mother,

> who was an industrious, careful, well-minded woman, taught me to read and when I was a little turned of five years I commenced at School in a Friends' School . . . until my fifteenth year.[17]

James worked hard; 'having a good genius and a propensity to learning', he mastered Latin and Greek and was famed locally as a fine scholar.[18] John followed James to Redbank's school from about 1726 until 1736 and did well, if not as noticeably.

James and John were greatly influenced by their mother. Their father may have often been absent, travelling in ministry. As a thoughtful Quaker mother, Mary Gough took responsibility for her children's home education, a duty that would re-emerge in her future great-great-granddaughter's critique of late Victorian parenthood. Writing in a gentler, more child-centred age, Charlotte would have challenged her ancestor's belief in the puritan method of suppressing rather than fostering the development of the child's 'will'.[19]

> My mother made it her maxim in her plan of education to accustom her children to useful employment, frugal fare and to have their wills crossed, in order hereby to render us better fitted to undergo any future hardships in life that might be allotted to befal us.[20]

Alas, James, who was said to have a certain 'gaiety and sweetness of temper', felt that his mother's strictness was as 'bread cast upon the waters, Eccl. 11'. He wriggled out of doing the useful occupations she set for him out of school hours by asserting he had school exercises or talks.[21] Like most boys, he loved to be at liberty; he would grow into seriousness.

> But if my mother seemed to err on the side of severity, indulgence and connivance would have been more pernicious in its effects. . . . I was sensible of my mother's anxious care for my preservation from evil.[22]

In contrast, 'John Gough was seriously disposed from his youth and of exemplary conduct.'[23] No doubt John strove diligently to live up to his brother's lively personality and exceptional academic record, as well as to his mother's firm but loving discipline. If not as well-versed in Latin and Greek as James, John, who had a gift for arithmetic, would go on to advocate thorough study of English.[24] James reflected in old age,

> The great duty of education, to discharge it rightly, needs divine instruction and assistance as much as any duty in life, and therefore parents have need fervently to pray for it and faithfully to follow it when received.[25]

Over a century later, Charlotte would preach the same doctrine and also emphasise the value of English studies.[26]

Both brothers were destined for teaching. As most universities refused admission to dissenters, the brothers, true to their Quaker upbringing, developed their intellectual powers through practical teaching as ushers, comparable to Charlotte's future pupil-teacher apprenticeship. Aged fifteen in 1727, James was sent to Skipton in Yorkshire until 1732 as usher in a school run by David Hall, known to his father and 'for whom my mother had an honourable esteem'.[27] Although James's *Memoirs* were enlivened by graphic descriptions of his various scrapes and experiences when taking a three-month mathematics course in Liverpool, he felt that his mother's tough upbringing had equipped him to accept the plain fare, long hours and plain dress expected at Skipton Friends' School.

While John was still at Redbank's school, James, aged twenty, went to Bristol to teach at Alexander Arnscott's Friends' school, first visiting his mother in Kendal. James noticed that many Bristol Quakers had given up plain dress and plain living but resolved to stick to the way of life he had learnt from his mother's loving care and 'to act faithfully in all the duties of his place and station in life'.[28] In 1735, at the age of fourteen, John was appointed usher at Thomas Bennett's Friends' school at Pickwick in Wiltshire for five years, 'his talents, education and example, having fitted him for the tuition of youth'.[29]

In 1737, James led the way to Ireland; Alexander Arnscott had died of diabetes. He visited John at Thomas Bennett's school before travelling to Kendal. He found his father seriously ill with a fever and stayed on until his death. After the funeral, sorrowfully leaving his widowed mother, James departed for Cork to teach in a new Friends' school. The Friends were well-established in Cork. Here the Quaker preacher Thomas Loe (d. 1668) had twice inspired William Penn (1644–1718). James would have read Penn's famous treatise, *No Cross, No Crown* (1682), written during his imprisonment in the Tower of London. He may have sought comfort from the well-known words 'No pain, no palm; no thorns, no throne; no gall, no glory; no cross, no crown' during his depressingly tedious sea passage to Cork.[30]

After his five years' apprenticeship in Wiltshire, John Gough returned to Kendal in 1740 to bring his mother on a five-week visit to James in Cork, having felt a strong desire 'to fix his residence in the same nation as his brother'.[31] By this time, James had already met and married Mary Dobbs (d. 1748), a birthright Quaker from Youghal, Co. Cork, on 29 August 1738.

In 1739, having doffed his hat and with much trembling, James had found the courage to testify at meeting for the first time. This deep spiritual experience inspired him to begin his travelling ministry, the most treasured part of his life. John's timely arrival enabled his persuasive brother to leave the Cork Friends' school in his inexperienced hands. James travelled to the north of England, via Kendal, to see his widowed mother, who had found 'peace and quiet'.

At around the age of 19, John was placed in charge of the school; 121 years later his future great-granddaughter would be mistress of the Davison School at about the same age. After James returned in 1742, John left to tutor Benjamin Wilson's children in Edenderry, before returning to the Cork school from 1744 to 1748. At Youghal Meeting, Co. Cork, on 18 September 1744, John Gough married Hannah Fisher (1720/21–1798), a birthright Quaker related to James's wife, Charlotte's great-grandmother.

In 1745, James left Cork to run Thomas Boake's school in Mountmellick, King's County (now Co. Offaly). In 1747, the year his mother died, James and Mary lost their first son, Nathaniel, on 30 November, the day he was born. Mary, of whom it was said that 'she had been convinced of the Truth before their marriage', died after giving birth to their second son, John (1748–1769).[32]

Alone with his infant son John, James summoned his brother John and sister-in-law Hannah to run the Mountmellick school. John responded unhesitatingly, releasing James for travelling ministry. They stayed until after James's second marriage to Elizabeth Barnes (d. 1782) in April 1751 at Mountrath, Queen's County (now Co. Laois). Money was very tight during these years. Elizabeth, whom James insensitively described in his journal as having a 'weakly constitution', bore him seven children between 1753 and 1760![33]

Encouraged by Dublin Friends, John was appointed superintendent of the Dame Street school in 1851. James recorded, 'He seemed inclined there, and as the prospect seemed promising, I freely assented to his removal.'[34] John and Hannah had fifteen children between 1844 and 1864; six died in infancy. Born in Mountmellick, their second daughter, Mary (1748–c. 1803), was destined to be Charlotte's grandmother.

To run the struggling school, John was initially offered £40 per annum plus £20 for defined duties for Dublin Friends: the clerkship of Dublin Yearly Meeting and preparing topics from the minutes to send to provincial meetings. By 1854, his headmaster's salary was raised to £60; every year brought more responsibilities for the conscientious superintendent.

James returned to Bristol in 1760 to run the day school there. At last, John felt released from his dominating, charismatic presence. Achieving distinction among the Friends in his own right, John was said to have the ability to reconcile differences of opinion; he was modest in urging his own views but 'clear and concise in expressing them'.[35] Similar traits would characterise Charlotte's calm approach to tricky situations. In addition to assiduously conducting the Friends' day to day business, carrying out duties related to Dublin civil society and running the school, John also wrote many reports, epistles and minutes. A distinguished elder, he attended the London Yearly Meeting on behalf of Irish Friends. His tracts included *Some Brief and Serious Reasons why the People called Quakers do not pay Tythes* (1777).

During their twenty-three years in Dublin, the Gough family struggled to make ends meet. Hannah sold linens sent up from the country, probably from Gilford or Moyallon. The extra money John earned by writing also helped. By 1764, John was feeling 'fettered in Dublin', both in the 'inward and outward'. He longed to travel in ministry.[36]

In 1767, John Gough produced his highly successful *Treatise of Arithmetic in Theory and Practice* in four books: *Whole Numbers, Weights and Measures; Fractions Vulgar and Decimal; Mercantile Arithmetic* and *Extractions, Progressions, Logarithms*, hoping to raise subscriptions. His cheaper, abbreviated text for schools, replacing the sheets of manuscript on which teachers usually wrote out arithmetical rules, was so widely used in Irish schools that it was known as 'The Gough.' His invaluable compendium of arithmetical rules and sums to be worked was introduced in a typically modest style:

> But I only mean just to hint my apprehension of the use to be made of such a book, without pretending to prescribe to teachers, many of whom, without doubt, are men of much more experience than myself and of greater attributes, likewise.[37]

The Gough is a practical textbook consisting of 340 pages of problems with their corresponding answers. Randomly selected questions give a quaint picture of eighteenth-century Irish life:

> A person dying left his wife with child and by his will ordered that if she went with a son, two thirds of the Estate should belong to him and the remainder to his mother, and if she had a daughter, he appointed the Mother two thirds and the daughter one third; but it happened she was delivered of both a son and a daughter, by which she lost in equity 2000l more than if it had only been a girl. What would have been her dowry if she had only a son? Answ: 1750 [l=£].

> It is rule in some Parishes to assess the inhabitants in proportion to three tenths of their Rents. What is the yearly Rent of that House which pays £81.10s to the King under this limitation? Answ: 1421.10s.

> How many dozen of gloves at 8d the pair will pay for 36 dozen and 8 pair of stockings at 3s 6d per pair? Answ: 192½ dozen.
>
> Suppose Cork, Clonmell and Dublin lie in a straight line, and the distance between Cork and Dublin is 121 miles and from Cork to Clonmell is 41 miles. I demand the difference between Clonmell and Dublin. Answ: 80 miles.[38]

John edited and published James's original tome, *A Practical Grammar of the English Tongue containing the Most Material Rules and Observations for Understanding the English Well and Writing It with Propriety* (1764). His apologetic Preface put his own stamp upon the work with an impassioned plea for the greater use and development of the English language, rather than Latin and foreign languages. He offered a 'rational method of education purely in English' for the service of young women as well as children. As Charlotte would also discover, he said children should start with reading and spelling before they learnt the application of grammar from 'some proper English Book', such as *Aesop's Fables* or books of travel and voyages. Quaker education excluded frivolous literature such as plays or novels. John explained that after instructing the pupil, the teacher should ask him to give an account of everything remarkable he had learnt from his lesson, such as examples of where any of the rules he had learnt were to be found.[39] This method was broadly comparable to narration, the flagship method of securing the pupils' attention by expecting them to tell back what they have learnt subsequently devised by his future great-grand daughter.

> And continually as they advance to have their memories refreshed by constant exercise in regard to every branch in which they have already been taught.[40]

While these methods would have been too constrained for a liberal educationist, Charlotte would have welcomed John's inclusion of geography; she thought that every school should have a set of good maps. Using John Gregory's popular *Manual of Modern Geography* (1739), the pupils were expected to follow the author's words and use of grammar in their own descriptions of every place, its location and any other remarkable things they had learnt. History should include the account of history given in the Old Testament, ancient classical history and Persian history, using chronology to give the pupils a sense of the passage of time as the teacher leads up to the history of England, later making use of newspapers, pointing out the situation of every place that occurs in their reading.

Writing followed: '[As] it is so useful and ornamental, two hours a day should be devoted to this art.' Arithmetic followed grammar and geography after the pupils had tolerably mastered those subjects. Given more time for further progress in the English language and arithmetic, the pupils were encouraged to study practical subjects: book-keeping for future merchants and traders or practical geometry and advanced mathematics for those to be employed in surveying or navigation. Each individual's education would be extended or limited according to his capacity to understand what had been taught. Lastly, John explained that he had said little about the Holy Scriptures because few Christian schoolmasters needed reminding of the importance of daily study of the sacred truths.[41]

James stayed at the Friends' Day School in Bristol for the next fourteen years. He travelled in ministry and composed several evocative poems as well as *A Practical Grammar of the English Language Tongue,* an *Epistle to Friends,* several edited *Lives* and his *Memoirs.* In 1774, 'Dear James Gough' was recalled to Dublin by the Friends to run the Dame Street school in order to enable John to open the new school in Lisburn, Co. Antrim, Northern Ireland. But by 1777, James was again fatigued by school mastering. 'His heart overflowing with love', he took up full-time ministry. During the last three years of his life, he travelled throughout Ireland, attending meetings in Lurgan and Lisburn with John. Apart from his second son, John, who died in London in 1769, James was glad that he had lived to see his children well-settled in life. Previously in good health, he died suddenly from neglected dysentery in Cork on 16 September 1780.[42]

> His conversation was entertaining and instructive; his manners were social, cheerful and kind, which added to innocence, simplicity and humility, endeared him to his friends.[43]

James was 'known as a conservative Friend who sought to maintain the standards of Friends during a time of great laxity and lukewarmness of belief'. John followed his example by 'establishing the simple, stern discipline practised by Friends'.[44] He kept James's memory alive by editing his *Memoirs* and other literary works.

During the eighteenth century, Lisburn was an important centre for the linen trade. Johnny Gough junior (1758–1818), Charlotte's great-uncle, would observe in *A Tour of Ireland 1813–14* (1817) that the elegant market square made Lisburn 'the handsomest country inland town' he had seen in Ireland.[45] Low overheads and developing large-scale manufacture of linen brought prosperity to Lisburn drapers and owners of bleach greens. It was still a countryside cottage industry; farmers grew the flax while the whole household prepared the yarn for spinning. Woven webs of unbleached cloth were sold to Lisburn traders and returned for summer bleaching on greens beside the swift flowing River Bann.

The Friends had flourished in Lisburn since 1655. The first thatched Friends' meeting house in Schoolhouse Lane (now Railway Street), erected in 1674, was rebuilt in 1709 and replaced in 1795, beside the graveyard where John Gough lies buried. The modern meeting house on Prospect Hill, built in 1995, stands in the grounds of the Friends' school.[46]

In 1764, John Handcock (d. 1766), a prosperous Lisburn linen merchant, left £1,000 in trust to Thomas Greer II (1724–1803) from Dungannon, grandfather of Joshua Mason's future first wife, and to John Christy, Robert Bradshaw and John Hill to purchase twenty acres of land on Prospect Hill to establish a school within the present bounds of Lisburn Men's Meeting for the 'Education of the Youth of the people called Quakers'. Ten free places were to be kept for poor Quaker children. John Handcock told Thomas Greer that Lisburn seemed 'the properest place' and 'a soil and situation a school will thrive best in'. Two years of tough negotiations with the Earl of Hertford, the land owner, culminated in a six-year lease on 9 June 1766; the school opened eight years later.[47]

As clerk to the Dublin Friends Special Schools' Committee, usually attended by Thomas Greer, from 1764 to 1769, John Gough doubtless heard of the Lisburn school plans while feeling 'fettered in Dublin' during the 1760s. To forestall his departure, Dublin Friends, who clearly valued his abilities, raised his school income to £150 per annum and paid half his house rent, funded by two guineas annually contributed by each pupil, in addition to his earnings as clerk. Thomas Greer calculated that if the Lisburn school accepted fifteen boys and fifteen girls, their fees would give John Gough £150 per annum. His strategy depended upon persuading James to take on the Dame Street school.

Aged fifty-four, John Gough accepted the Lisburn school challenge; as noted, James ran his Dublin school for the next three years. Moving to Lisburn in 1774 was a significant step for John Gough as the first headmaster of the new Friends' school. His older daughters, Margaret (1746–1814), aged about twenty-seven, and Mary (1748–1803), aged twenty-six, were doubtless expected to help their mother with the housekeeping and teaching the girls. Jonathan Hill also left Dublin to be John Gough's assistant master and release him for travelling ministry.[48]

Richard Shackleton (1728–1792), second headmaster of Ballitore Friends' School, open from 1726 to 1837, observed to Thomas Greer that since moving north, John had grown more boldly confident in public and was no longer mild and self-effacing. John followed the usual Quaker practice, said to have persisted in Ulster until 1900, of intoning while ministering to large crowds of Friends. Some felt that what he said was 'too highly set' to music and far too 'harmonious and sweet'.[49]

The new headmaster worked immensely hard. At times he also felt 'fettered' in Lisburn. As Quakers regarded every day as holy and did not keep Christian festivals with pagan origins, such as Christmas, John never relaxed. A 'driven person', dependent upon his wife and daughters for all domestic arrangements, he lacked the easy charm and gaiety of his charismatic older brother but shared his strict puritan discipline. Like many Quakers, John refused to pay tithes to support the established Church of Ireland. The school was regularly deprived of pewter plates, which were distrained in lieu of tithes. While his epistle on tithes argued that there was no precedent in the New Testament, John's views were peaceably prefaced:

> To the Church by law I bear no degree of malignity; but have ever esteemed the civil government in the hands of her members of moderate principles best suited to the nature of the constitution and to the peace and public welfare of the State. To the power by this excellent constitution vested in the legislature, to the sovereignty in the present reigning family, we bear allegiance without dissimulation from duty, gratitude and interest because under them we have enjoyed an ease and protection in our civil and religious rights unknown to our ancestors, who suffered long, unjust and cruel persecutions with Christian meekness, patience and fortitude under most or all successive governments previous to the Revolution.

In his Preface to James's *Memoirs,* John explained that plays, novels and romances were inherently harmful, alongside playhouses, horse races, cock fighting and ale houses. In another epistle, he regretted the ostentation pursued by many Friends. Through the gaiety of their clothes and by living in grand houses with rich furniture, they were seeking to 'gratify the vain and ambitious cravings of the unmortified part of them'.[50] No doubt his words were ignored by the wealthy Quaker linen merchants comfortably residing in large country mansions. John's definitive early home training and tight financial circumstances prevented him from succumbing to these temptations.

It surely suited John Gough to run the school independently on traditionally strict puritan lines with *no* oversight by the Ulster Provincial Quarterly Meeting. There were no pictures at the school, as pictures were considered mere representations of the Truth. 'Heathenish authors' were replaced by works of piety. Did the children study any of the 3,000 copies of *The Dying Sayings of Hannah Hill* printed by the Ireland Yearly Meeting in 1718 or the seven gloomy volumes of *Fruits of Early Piety*, incorporating the sayings of those who had died young?

Although the Lisburn curriculum has not survived, in Friends' schools the boys were kept busy from 6:00am in the morning until 7:00pm at night while the girls, whose timetable included housework and domestic crafts, such as spinning, knitting and sewing, spent less time on academic study. The mistress corrected any unseemly gestures during the girls' daily walk. The food was simple, with Sunday meals consisting of bread and broth in the winter or bread and potatoes with milk or butter and cheese in the summer. Three days a week, meat and vegetables alternated with pudding or suet dumplings, while potatoes with milk or butter were served on two days, leaving the leftovers for Saturdays; beer was drunk at dinner. Assuredly 'the grave and stolid' John Gough followed the broad curriculum set out in his 1771 Preface to James's *English Grammar*, which included history and geography as well as the three Rs (reading, writing and arithmetic), the Catechism and Bible readings.[51]

From 1762 onwards, John Gough worked on the first four volumes of his extensive and earnest *History of the People called Quakers from their First Rise to the Present Time*, unfinished when he died. He sought to rebut the various charges made against Quakers he had heard in Lisburn. Like James, travelling in ministry was central to his life. For example, from 17 March to 14 August 1785 he visited several English counties and attended London Yearly Meetings. In 1790, he journeyed south to meetings in Munster and Leinster.[52]

Always restless and anxious, he fretted constantly about the finances, lacking funds to pay the workmen or meet the cost of materials for the school buildings. Suffering from 'bonds and afflictions', his health was poor. A feverish cold, possibly hay-fever, dogged him for years. Throughout 1790, John Gough worked hard as usual, though it was evident that his strength was failing. Warmly regarded as a good neighbour and Friend, he ministered at the grave of a Friend a few days before his own death. Mary Leadbeater (1758–1826) recalled how he had ministered at his own meeting in 1791:

> He was led by a remarkable transition to supplicate for himself as if sensible of his own dissolution.[53]

On 25 October 1791, five days before his seventieth birthday, John was 'seized with a fit of apoplexy' (a fatal stroke) and died within a few hours.

> He was of a sober, circumspect life, as becometh the Gospel of Christ, plain and humble in his appearance, and grave in deportment, showing himself a pattern of good works and, in doctrine, showing . . . gravity and sincerity.[54]

Lisburn Men's Meeting's warm testimony to John Gough was read at the Ulster Quarterly Meeting, held at Moyallon on 18 February 1792, and at the Dublin Half-Yearly Meeting in May. While thought to have been not especially original as a schoolmaster, he was the first headmaster of a school that is still flourishing over 200 years later.[55]

3.

Charlotte Mason's Grandparents: Arthur Mason and Mary Gough, 1744–1795

Charlotte Mason's Irish paternal grandparents were Arthur Newburgh Mason (c. 1750–pre-1802), a flax grower, and Mary Gough, the second daughter of John Gough and a teacher. Both were birthright Quakers who would bring their children up in the Truth after a youthful dalliance of which their unborn granddaughter would certainly have disapproved. In 1774, Mary was twenty-six; whatever she may have felt about leaving Dublin for Lisburn, she sought change. William Nevill had told Thomas Greer II that 'if Jonathan Hill should go as his [John Gough's] assistant and there fall *again* in love with the second daughter and marry her we might have the prospect of a good schoolmaster and the succession in the right line continued.'[1] Mary was obviously regarded as a good teacher, having doubtless inherited the Gough intelligence. Whatever may, or may not, have occurred in Dublin is unknown, but, as mentioned, Jonathan Hill did accompany the Gough family to the Lisburn school. Instead of marrying him, Mary escaped to the countryside.

Arthur was the son of the late Luke Mason of the city of Dublin and the grandson of George and Mary Mason of Killowen, a Quaker centre in King's County (now Co. Offaly), Leinster. As a member of Dublin Meeting, Luke may have been well known to John Gough. He had married Eleanor Fayle (1727–1765), a birthright Quaker from Kilcomin, King's County, in 1747. Eleanor died in Dublin on 28 December 1765. About that time, Luke Mason may have arranged his son's apprenticeship with a flax grower through Friends' networks in Northern Ireland. Arthur may have felt bereft of his mother's care if he was despatched to an apprenticeship a long way from Dublin soon after her death.[2]

Arthur Mason was a loyal Quaker who might have known Mary in Dublin, at meeting or as a pupil at her father's Dame Street school.[3] By 1777 and probably much earlier, Arthur had settled in Gilford, Co. Armagh, a rural centre for the linen trade, in beautiful countryside, about a mile from Moyallon townland. By 1685 the Friends had begun to establish a community near the meandering River Bann flowing down from the mountains of Mourne to Lough Neagh, where flax growing abounded. Moyallon Meeting began informally in a Friend's house in 1692. The first meeting house was built on land given by John Christy and enlarged in 1780.[4] John Christy and Thomas Greer II, leading Lisburn School trustees, were prosperous linen merchants.

Bleaching linen by the River Bann began in 1710. There was a continuous line of water-powered mills and bleaching greens from Moyallon to Banbridge by 1794, as the cottage industry gave way to mechanisation. After the flax seeds were sown by the men in spring, Arthur must also have been engaged throughout the year in the complex preparations required for transforming raw flax into linen. To meet the Friends' expectations, Arthur must have been an established flax grower before his marriage in 1778.

In Dublin, Hannah Gough had augmented the family finances by selling linens. She probably continued trading through the Friends' school contacts, as she would leave Prospect Hill free of all debt in 1794. If Margaret stayed behind at the Lisburn school to work with her mother, Mary gained permission to move to Gilford during the 1770s, perhaps not only to avoid Jonathan Hill's attentions but also to escape her father's puritan discipline. Hannah Gough may have asked her to deal with the local linen markets on her behalf. Mary may also have taught local children, as Moyallon Friends' School did not open until 1788.

Mary then encountered Arthur Mason, perhaps either at a linen market or at Moyallon Meeting. They fell deeply in love. The proverbial Mason charm, with which Charlotte would be graciously endowed, may have sprung from Arthur's genes. Mary's determination to break the rules suggests an independent spirit that may also have been handed down to her unborn granddaughter. Having already courted trouble in Dublin, rebellious Mary's overly strict upbringing by her strait-laced father did not protect her from Arthur's affectionate advances. Possibly conceived early in 1777, Eleanor, surely named for Arthur's late mother, was born while Mary was living in Gilford. The Friends tactfully recorded little Eleanor's undated birth at Gilford. Sadly, she probably died in infancy before the year's end.

Lisburn Friends were aware that Arthur and Mary had got together by 1777. In deference to the Friends' marriage rules, Arthur and Mary obediently attended Lisburn Monthly Meeting on 23 November 1777 to declare their intention to marry. At this meeting,

> A Paper of Acknowledgement by Arthur Newburgh Mason condemning his fault for seeking to draw out the affections of Mary Gough without the consent of her parents . . . was read.

Notwithstanding this revealing admission, they were advised to publish their intention of marrying at both Lisburn and Moyallon Meetings. Although Mary's father may have pleaded their case, doubts were expressed by conscientious Friends. They directed that the matter should be laid before the Provincial Meeting. Arthur and Mary were asked to return to Lisburn Monthly Meeting for a second time on Christmas Day 1777 to discuss their proposed marriage. Happily the men and women Friends appointed to make the necessary enquiries explained that they had found *nothing* to hinder the marriage because their 'said clear intentions' had been duly published at Lisburn and Moyallon Meetings. Thanks to Arthur's profound apologies, his satisfactory work record, the pair's shared Quaker birthright and manifest affection for each other, the bride's father's spotless reputation and the consent of both Mary's parents, they were permitted to take each other in marriage. Arthur and Mary escaped the disgrace of disownment by the Religious Society that had nurtured them from childhood.

Thus approved by Lisburn Friends, on New Year's Day 1778 Arthur and Mary took each other by the hand and promised to be loving and faithful to each other until death separated them. A company of sixty-four local Friends, including ten members of the Gough family, but no Masons, witnessed their marriage. Duly celebrated, it was no hole and corner affair.[5]

The Masons stayed on in Lisburn, which suggests that Arthur was warmly accepted by the Gough family. Mary's health and second pregnancy may have been the main reason, although Arthur might have been needed for the spring flax sowing. Their removal certificate from Lisburn Monthly Meeting, dated 30 August 1778, confirmed the joint transfer of Arthur and Mary to Lurgan Meeting, of which Moyallon was a constituent member. Arthur and Mary moved to Hall's Mill by the River Bann, between Gilford and Laurencetown, before their second child, John, named for Mary's father, arrived on 5 October 1778.[6] A 1910 photograph shows the Hall's Mill Inn, hemmed in by a row of little cottages. The Masons may have initially inhabited one such thatched cottage with mud walls encased in lime. Charlotte's father, Joshua, was born at Hall's Mill on 3 January 1780. Today Hall's Mill is a large modern hotel and conference centre on Banbridge Road, near a modern close named Hall's Mill Green in Laurencetown.[7]

By the time James was born on 5 July 1781, the family had moved to the Course, possibly a misnomer for Coose or Coove, a small townland near Hall's Mill. Hannah, named for Mary's mother, was born there on 11 March 1783. In later life, Joshua may have recalled walking as a young child with his family to Sunday meeting for worship at the historic ochre-coloured Moyallon Meeting House. Beautifully kept, it still stands proudly in spacious grounds beside the graveyard today.[8]

Like her grandmother and as a former teacher, Mary must have given her children a good educational start at home, grounding them in sound

Moyallon Meeting House, where Joshua Mason worshipped as a child.

Quaker principles – though perhaps with a less strictly puritan slant. Joshua and his siblings could have attended Moyallon School after 1788; more probably, the boys boarded at Lisburn School from the age of eight until it closed down after 1791. Joshua's grandfather, who died when he was eleven, may have developed his business acumen by teaching him from The Gough alongside lessons on Quaker history. While Joshua followed his hard-working father into taking on equally heavy, insalubrious work, did his mother, Mary, instil in him a love of books? If Joshua upheld the Friends' belief in the importance of sound, practical education for life, passing it on to his unborn thirteenth child, he would have been untroubled by the harsh domestic chores imposed on female pupil-teachers such as his daughter.[9]

Clearly, Arthur did not earn enough to share the good fortune of the wealthier Quakers who owned profitable bleaching greens or drapers' shops and settled in large country mansions. The fact that the Irish Linen Board listed Arthur Mason as eligible to receive spinning wheels and looms under the Flax Growers' Bounty in 1796 suggests that he must have been working co-operatively in a cottage industry with nearby Friends and his family, when the children could be spared from school.[10]

Although mechanisation was developing apace, much linen production was still carried out by hand. The women weeded the rows to prevent the flax stems from warping. The plants, adorned with blue flowers, were harvested in August when the metre-high stalks were brown. Bunched into sheaves, the flax stalks were dried in the fields before the seeds were 'rippled' into a trough for oil or next year's crop by pulling the plants through iron teeth set in a wooden block. The flax stems were again dried after rotting in 'still ponds' for several days. Before the days of 'scutch' mills, the men 'broke' the flax on grooved rollers and 'scutched' the stems by banging them between two flat wooden boards to remove the outer skin. A 'hackler' combed out the tangled fibres before they were carded and combed again into sleek 'slivers' ready for spinning by the women. Swirls of dust raised by hand 'hackling' and 'scutching' caused serious disorders of the chest and lungs.

After spinning on a low wheel with a foot treadle, the yarn was wound on to bobbins, often by the children, before being boiled in soapy water and dried. In households with looms, the women wove the yarn into a brown-coloured cloth, called Holland, a material that would seemingly come to mean much to Charlotte in 1894. Before the use of chemicals such as vitriol, which halved the bleaching time, the woven cloth was bleached by boiling in lye, a solution of water and ashes, before being spread out to dry for the first airing. The web was then repeatedly steeped in buttermilk during the 6 to 8 months of summer bleaching on the greens. The final pounding of the cloth closed up the weave to give the linen an attractive sheen. By 1783 there were 20 bleach greens between Gilford and Banbridge, bleaching 90,000 pieces of linen annually.[11]

For Arthur Mason, this poorly paid, unremitting work doubtless took its toll on his health. If Joshua left Lisburn School after his grandfather's death in 1791, helping his father with flax preparation by making lye and potash for the bleaching process would have acclimatised him to the noxious smells of tallow-chandling and soap-boiling that would pervade his future apprenticeship. The Masons lived near Gilford at least until 1794, as Arthur was an active member of Moyallon Men's Meeting.[12]

In 1791, Hannah Gough, aged about seventy-one, was left in a precarious situation as the Goughs' 'good house', built with subscriptions from Lisburn Quakers, was attached to the school. John Gough had not named his successor. Their son, Johnny junior (1758–1818), had married Sarah Manliff (1764–1840) from Roosk, King's County, at Edenderry Meeting House (erected in 1707) on 27 April 1791. Ostensibly returning to Lisburn to support his widowed mother, Johnny planned to take over the school like other Quaker headmasters' sons. However, the Ulster Friends, already deeply critical of the way John Gough senior had run the school without external oversight since 1774, refused his request. One trustee, Robert Bradshaw, commented that Johnny was

> deficient in the following particulars viz. a natural good temper, common sense, want of competent knowledge in literature, arithmetical, mathematical and classical for which reasons I conclude that he is not a suitable person to commit the care of the school to.[13]

Johnny left Lisburn in September 1792 but was appointed to a Limerick school, later becoming a well-known Dublin publisher. The trustees expressed greater sympathy for the headmaster's widow. Hannah and Margaret stayed on, presumably to look after the empty school as all the pupils had left by 1792. On 13 February 1794, Lisburn Women's Meeting approved their removal to the compass of Lurgan Meeting. The clerk, John Handcock junior, commended their orderly conduct and sober conversation. They had regularly attended meetings for worship and discipline at home and left Lisburn

> When ability of body permitted when with ease to their own minds they could withdraw from the cares of the boarding school in which they were then engaged. They left us clear of debt and in solvent circumstance.

With regular oversight from Ulster Quarterly Meeting, the school re-opened in the autumn of 1794 and is flourishing successfully at the present day.[14]

Hannah and Margaret Gough settled near Moyallon. In that year, John Mason was sixteen, and may have left for an apprenticeship. Joshua was fourteen, James was thirteen and Hannah was eleven. Their grandmother died at Gilford in January 1798; Margaret stayed on, attached to Moyallon Meeting, until her death in 1814.[15]

On 18 July 1795, Joshua Mason left his family for his apprenticeship with Richard Jacob, whose Waterford soap-making and tallow-chandling business was well established by 1788. No doubt Richard's father-in-law, Thomas Greer II, had recommended Joshua as an industrious fifteen-year-old.[16] By 1796, the Mason family had moved to Levaghery in the parish of Seagoe, close to Portadown, and were still involved with flax growing. Setting an example for Joshua, Charlotte's grandparents clearly remained true to their Quaker upbringing after their youthful fling. They had worked hard to bring up their family. Sadly, Arthur died in his late forties before Joshua's marriage in 1802.

Did Mary Mason remain at Levaghery as her sister Margaret was nearby? Nothing is known of John's life story; Hannah junior probably moved to Dublin. James went to Dublin but returned to Lurgan before settling in Ross, Co. Wexford, by 1802. Did Joshua later share treasured memories with Charlotte about his formative early childhood spent in beautiful countryside, enfolded within the close-knit compass of Moyallon Friends and his family, as together they sought the Light in darker days?

4.

Joshua Mason's Forty Years in Waterford, 1795–1835

Discovering Joshua Mason's previously unknown life story offers further understanding of the person Charlotte Mason became as we sense his sterling influence from behind the scenes. It is sad to reflect that his thirteenth child would only know him as an old man in his sixties and seventies, living far from the city in which he had spent forty eventful years. In this chapter, Joshua Mason will be shown to have been true to his puritan Quaker upbringing as he rose in the world through unremittingly hard labour while securing his children's education and future work as he saw fit. New evidence suggests that he would exercise similar responsibility in launching Charlotte's future teaching career.

Aged fifteen-and-a-half, Joshua Mason travelled from Ulster to Waterford City 'to serve a regular apprenticeship to Richard Jacob, Merchant' in tallow-chandling and soap-boiling. The Waterford Friends welcomed him warmly. Strong and resourceful, Joshua mastered the unrelenting, odorous work. Developing sound business acumen, he would achieve status as a freeman of the city, marry twice and father twelve children during his forty years in Waterford. Joshua's interest in education would grow with the founding of the new Friends' school at Newtown in 1798. Here he would send his sons. His first marriage to Sarah Jacob (1780–1815), granddaughter of Thomas Greer II, would link him to the forceful founder of his grandfather's Lisburn School. Decades later he would pass on the torchlight to Charlotte.[1]

Sarah's father, Richard Jacob (c. 1734–1810), the son of Joseph and Hannah Jacob of Waterford, was a staunch birthright Quaker, married to Thomas Greer II's daughter, Mary (d. 1815).[2] As a wealthy linen merchant trading with English and American markets, Thomas Greer II may have extolled the virtues of the prosperous southern port and his successful son-in-law's businesses, persuading Arthur Mason that Joshua would do well in Waterford.[3]

An established mercantile centre, Waterford City, the third busiest port in Ireland, was strategically situated in fertile countryside on the bend of the River Suir, which flowed through the city to the sea. The city's prosperity was manifested in stately public buildings; elegant Georgian houses graced the wide thoroughfares, such as the Mall, Merchants' Quay and Bridge Street.[4] Behind these fashionable avenues lay a maze of narrow alleys where poorer people struggled to survive.

The Religious Society of Friends reached Waterford City by 1655. The first Waterford Meeting House (1694–1893), where Joshua Mason and his family worshipped, stood at the heart of the busy city centre and now houses the Garter Lane Theatre. Present-day Waterford Friends meet in Newtown.[5] Although few in comparison with the Roman Catholic majority, Waterford Quakers established sound commercial networks across south-east Ireland. From 1783, the Quaker brothers George and William Penrose manufactured the famous white crystal Waterford glass; the Cherry and Strangman Quaker breweries also flourished. Proximity to the sea facilitated trade with Newfoundland and British ports. Goods for export, such as beef, pork, butter, corn and flour, were brought to the quays by water; hides and tallow came by road.[6]

With a well-established tallow-chandling and soap-boiling business, Richard Jacob had been nominated by the mayor for election as a freeman of the City of Waterford on 5 January 1778. Honoured and enfranchised, freemen were entitled to vote in municipal and parliamentary elections and were generally excused from customs duties to facilitate overseas trade in their products. At Jacob's King Street factory, the operatives and apprentices would have dealt with all the messy procedures. After Jacob moved the business to the prestigious Quay, fresh sea breezes blowing up the River Suir would have wafted the pungent odours away on the wind.[7]

Joshua Mason assuredly laboured steadily and found favour with his master. Learning to manage tallow-chandling and soap-boiling techniques was not glamorous, but there was regular demand for the products. Before gas and electricity transformed illumination, tallow candles lit homes, workshops and the streets, while expensive beeswax candles graced the churches. Tallow was rubbed into ropes used on sailing ships to increase pliability.

The use of fatty animal acids for soap making and tallow-chandling favoured joint enterprise.[8] Raw suet, containing a white crystalline substance called stearin which gave tallow its solidity, was extracted from livestock and bought from the city's slaughterhouses and bacon yards. Heated to remove all fibrous matter, the tallow was melted down, boiled again, cooled and poured into appropriate containers. Candle wicks were inserted before the final hardening. Soap was made by adding a liquid alkaline solution of potash hydroxide called lye, prepared from ashes variously mixed with water, familiar to Joshua from turning flax into linen. After boiling to remove impurities, the fats were cooled, causing any remaining detritus to sink below the solidified fats on the surface. Lye was then added and the solidified fats were boiled until a thick, frothy mass was formed. The soap was ready if there was no noticeable 'bite' when the operative placed the froth on his tongue! This pungent process produced a soft, brown, jellied soap which was stiffened with the correct proportion of common salt. Hard blocks of soap, easier to store and transport, were cut into bars or sold unwrapped by the pound.[9]

Political turbulence erupted in 1798. Inspired by the American fight for independence (1775–1783) and French revolutionary struggles (1789–1799), the United Irishmen, drawn from Dublin Catholic and Protestant groups, fought to unify and free the Irish people from the longstanding domination of the Protestant Ascendancy, composed of the powerful minority of British landlords and the established Church.[10] The rebellion reached Waterford in May 1798. Friends, true to their Peace Testimony of 1660, did not fight. Removing weapons from their houses, they worshipped as usual in occupied territories. Trusting in divine protection, they gave food and shelter to all who applied. Joshua surely joined with the Waterford Friends who organised soup kitchens and assisted those whose goods had been destroyed or seized.[11]

In 1798, Quaker education reached Waterford City. The Quarterly Meeting held upriver at Clonmell on 19 April 1796, attended by Richard Jacob, planned a Friends' school for fifty boys and girls from Munster province. Within two years, the Friends raised the funds to purchase an austere Georgian house on a spacious estate in Newtown, on the edge of Waterford. As at Lisburn, Friends believed in a sound practical education to transmit the truths of their faith and equip their young people for future work. Free places for poor children were agreed, with donations for clothes and apprenticeship fees. Developed from the same firm foundations as Lisburn School, Newtown School is flourishing today.[12]

Joshua Mason was destined to marry young. At the age of twenty-two, after serving for seven years, he won the heart of his master's firstborn daughter, Sarah Jacob, eleven months younger. As birthright Quakers they did not rebel against the formality of the Friends' marriage enquiries; 'Joshua Mason, son of the late Arthur Mason of Levaghery in the County Armagh & Mary his wife and Sarah Jacob daughter of Richard & Mary Jacob of the City of Waterford' declared their 'intention of taking each other in marriage before the Monthly Meeting of the People called Quakers in Waterford'. Having published their intentions twice, after due enquiries and with the consent of their parents and relations, their marriage was arranged.

On 6 July 1802, Joshua and Sarah appeared at a 'Public Assembly of the Aforesaid People in their Meeting Place in Waterford'. They took each other by the hand in turn, promising to be loving and faithful to each other 'until Death shall separate us'.[13] The ninety-six guests who celebrated a popular marriage witnessed the signing of their names. The Jacob family turned out in force. Joshua was supported by his brothers John and James with their sister, Hannah. Although Mary Mason was only fifty-four, she may have been unable to travel. Joseph Gough, who was present, may have represented her. Perhaps she *was* the mysterious 'Mary Mason who came here from —' who was subsequently recorded as having been buried in the Friends' Newtown cemetery after her death on 7 April 1803. If so, she sadly died aged only fifty-six, a month before Joshua and Sarah's firstborn son arrived on 6 May 1803.[14]

Richard Jacob probably established Joshua Mason in a new tallow-chandling and soap-boiling business to ensure the young couple's future. From 1802 to 1835, the Mason family lived in substantial premises with workrooms and 'out offices, situated on Summerhill, in the parish of Holy Trinity Without'. An 1835 deed confirmed that Joshua Mason was the recognised owner. An 1834 map shows that Summerhill was well-situated and conveniently edged by bacon yards run by local Quakers.[15] There was ready access to the river port below, past the Georgian houses in Bridge Street.

During thirteen years of marriage, Sarah and Joshua had eight children on Summerhill. All survived to adulthood. After her home education, Sarah Jacob would have gained valuable experience in helping her mother to look after and educate her seven younger siblings, two of whom died in childhood. Regularly attending meeting on First Day, bringing up and home-educating their family in the light of Quaker Truth would have been the Masons' shared priority.

After the birth of Richard Jacob (1803–1846), Joshua joined Sarah's brother, Joseph Jacob (1783–1827), in November 1803 to collect the Friends' annual subscriptions and record the amounts given to support the Munster Provincial School at Newtown. Clearly the Friends accepted Joshua and Joseph as honest young men.[16] As a second son, Joshua Mason's closest relationship seems to have been with his own second son, Joshua junior (1805–1846). Neither Mary (1806–1852), named for both grandmothers, nor Sarah (1808–post-1881) would marry. Hannah (1810–1876), named after her paternal great-grandmother, was succeeded by Arthur Newburgh (1811–1861), named for his grandfather. Huldah Jane (1813–1902) was born next, and Joseph, destined to live out his later years in Australia, was the last born in 1815.[17] While Charlotte may never have met her older half-brothers, she would certainly get to know Hannah and Huldah Jane.

In May 1807, Joshua suddenly realised that as a freeholder who owned or rented a property worth forty shillings, he could register to vote in the 1807 election, like Richard Jacob. Under the established Church's tight control,

Waterford Corporation was empowered to register freeholders as new voters. Alas, by procrastinating until the thirteenth day, Joshua missed his chance. Sir John Newport Baronet (1756–1843), the Whig sitting member, had already been returned after a knife-edge struggle on day twelve![18]

Joshua and Sarah welcomed the Friends' school at Newtown, accepting the puritan ethos for their sons. The school's superintendent, Richard Allen, from Cork, had been a pupil from 1798. From apprentice teacher in 1801, he rose to be superintendent in 1810 aged only twenty-four. He was well placed to uphold the school's traditional teaching and discipline until his retirement in 1854. Called 'Master', although everyone else used first names, he devised a catechism to teach the children the Friends' principles and expected them to address each other as 'thee' and 'thou' in plain language.[19]

The Quarterly Meeting approved each school admission. Admitted as a boarder aged eight on 19 October 1811, Richard Mason stayed until 1817. Joshua junior boarded at the school from 1814 to 1819.[20] Although girls were accepted as pupils, none of Charlotte's half-sisters attended Newtown or any known school. Joshua and Sarah must have preferred to educate them at home; both Mary and Sarah became teachers. This Quaker practice may have underpinned Charlotte Mason's late Victorian advocacy of home education.

Newtown School was supervised by a committee representing the nine Munster meetings. This gave parents a say in the running of the school, enabling them to make recommendations, such as daily walks or sea bathing. At each October AGM, the Quarterly Meeting appointed six Waterford members to serve on the school committee. In 1813, both Joshua and Sarah Mason represented Waterford. Joshua was re-appointed alone from 1814 to 1817 and for a further three years.[21]

The climax of the year was the annual examination of the boys' and girls' educational progress, notably in reading, writing and recitation. Each Monthly Meeting appointed a male and female Friend to set questions, suited to the children's ages and genders. Some Friends found it as hard to frame the questions as the pupils did to answer them. The male examiners checked the annual accounts; the women inspected the domestic arrangements. Their reports were generally favourable. After the tests, the 'whole family' joined in the 'religious opportunity' which closed the AGM.[22]

Charlotte's half-brothers wore jackets and waistcoats over a linen shirt, with a 'frock shirt' to protect their clothes; the girls wore 'stuff gowns' (frocks) over flannel petticoats. The youngest boys were taught by women. On First Day, the boys walked to the meeting house in ordinary boots, while the girls, nicknamed 'Piety in Pattens', wore pattens, which were shoes or clogs set on a raised iron ring to keep their feet clear of rubbish, horse manure and mud in the streets. As the children attended meeting in

Newtown School in spring.

the morning *and* afternoon, their Sunday dinner was served at the meeting house, where the Masons and other local children could glimpse their parents. Although boys and girls attended meeting and had their meals together, the superintendent had the quaint idea that the girls should not look at the boys or learn their names!

The sole annual holiday was in July and the school day was long. Reading and spelling began before the breakfast of bread and milk, or 'stirabout' in winter.[23] The superintendent read from the Bible, followed by silence. The boys also studied English grammar, geography, writing, arithmetic, book-keeping and useful branches of mathematics, up to their capacity. The girls were mainly taught domestic subjects, such as sewing, marking, knitting and how to make, wash and mend their clothes and those of the boys, who were expected to lay the tables for their substantial meals. The boys had gardens and could grow vegetables, such as radishes, although study occupied most of their day. The Friends purchased Bibles for each child. Lindley Murray's well-known *English Grammar* (1795) was used in lieu of James Gough's *A Practical Grammar of the English Language Tongue*. French and Latin were offered *after* students had mastered their English studies.

Puritan strictures preventing the children from reading frivolous fiction may have indirectly influenced Charlotte's later dismissal of 'twaddle'. Edifying poetry or books of travel or history might be perused if the content was true. Other literature included the Mason boys' great-grandfather's *History of the People Called Quakers* and their great-great-

Richard Allen, the superintendent of Newtown School from 1810 to 1854.

uncle James Gough's *Memoirs*; Robert Barclay's *An Apology for the True Christian Divinity* (1678); *A Testimony Concerning That Worthy Elder Abraham Shackleton*, founder of Ballitore School; Sarah Grubb's journal; Sophia Hume's *Exhortation to the Inhabitants of the Province of South Carolina* (1747); and a two-volume compendium of 'Sufferings' (recording goods distrained in lieu of tithes). While they did not participate in music or dancing, students could draw and colour pictures if they were informative and did not 'inflame the imagination'; embroidery and calligraphy were similarly permitted.[24]

The school library opened in 1806. As both Richard Mason and Joshua junior were appointed to the Library Committee of Six, they must have been selected from the most literate students. They had to ensure that the books were returned and checked. Still on the Committee of Six in 1817, Joshua junior had clearly satisfied the librarian as to his efficiency.[25]

The summer of general rejoicing in Great Britain and Ireland over the defeat of Napoleon at the Battle of Waterloo on 18 June 1815 and the end of the war with France was a desolate time for Joshua Mason and his family. Sarah's mother, Mary Jacob, passed away on 18 August 1815, ten days before Joseph was born. Then, on 15 September, Sarah died, only eighteen days after the safe arrival of her last-born.[26] Heartbroken, Joshua was left with the responsibility of bringing up his four daughters, aged eight, seven, five and two, and his two sons, aged four and two weeks, without any support from grandparents. No doubt Friends offered succour at this dark time. Joshua's first duty was the care and education of his children and, like his great-uncle James, to see them settled in life while he advantageously developed his business interests.

Two years later, Joshua Mason felt financially secure enough as a property owner and merchant to apply for freeman status from Waterford Corporation, based on his seven-year apprenticeship with the late Richard Jacob, who had died on 30 August 1810. Successful Quakers were not only accepted but permitted to affirm, rather than swear, the freeman's oath. Joshua applied for the coveted honour in a dashing hand, as if Richard Jacob was still alive:

To the Mayor, Aldermen, Sheriffs and Common Council of the County of the City of Waterford. The Petition of Joshua Mason of the City of Waterford- Mercht.-

Herewith

That your Petitioner served a regular apprenticeship to Richard Jacob of the City of Waterford Merchant who is a freeman of said city and is therefore entitled to his freedom. That your Petitioner residing in said city is ready to take the affirmation of a freeman to bring the usual and accustomed fees and to perform all other requisites usually required of freemen on their admission.

Your Petitioner therefore prays to be admitted to the freedom of said City-

Josh'a Mason.

The petition was granted. Joshua was accepted as a freeman and citizen on 3 October 1817.[27] As noted, the privileges included reduced rates of customs and tolls in the city and the right to vote in parliamentary elections. Did Joshua Mason cast a more punctual vote for Sir John Newport, again returned to Parliament in 1818? As mayor of Waterford from 1817 to 1818, he had signed Joshua's petition.

Although tallow-chandling and soap-boiling offered a steady income, Joshua registered as a tobacconist by 1824. As tobacco was one of the principal imports, there was a ready market in Waterford City and County.[28] He may also have dealt in corn from 1824. Exports of Irish corn had trebled by 1820; it was time to enter the fray. Corn mills were springing up across Co. Waterford and south-east Ireland.[29]

Richard Jacob Mason left Newtown School in 1817 and Joshua junior in 1819. As their father's apprentices, they were not required to pay fees.[30] No doubt they helped Joshua to strengthen his flourishing tallow-chandling and soap-boiling business as well as dealing in corn and bacon, unrecorded in the directories.

Sarah Leckey (1786–1836), destined to marry a chandler, was born in Candlemakers Row, Edinburgh, Midlothian. She was the first-born daughter of Irish Quakers, William and Blessing Leckey, who married at Forrest in Cork on 15 July 1784. After Dr Leckey graduated in medicine from Edinburgh University, one of the few universities open to dissenters, they settled in Co. Carlow by 1787. Their fourth child, William Robert (1790– 1867), would befriend Joshua Mason. Anna Jemima (1796–1881), their youngest daughter, would be Joshua's sister-in-law.[31] The Co. Carlow Leckeys were highly respected as resident landlords for the past 150 years, providing security for generations of Irish tenant farmers. William Robert Leckey leased the entire Ballinacarrig townland, owned by the powerful Tory, Colonel Henry Bruen (1789–1852) of Oak Park, where he rented out fields of light, gravelly soil at 21s per Irish acre.[32]

Friends may have urged Joshua to marry again and arranged for him to meet Sarah Leckey, aged thirty-three, in 1819. If Joshua Mason was thinking of acquiring property, joining the Leckey family, who owned substantial properties in Co. Waterford, would bring lands at Pickardstown, an Irish plantation at Ballydrislane, and nearby Rosemount House in the barony of Middle Third. While these rural lands and properties, a substantial part of his marriage settlement, promised prosperity and advancement, they probably confronted Joshua Mason with tithing for the first time.[33]

The *Waterford Chronicle* reported that a marriage had taken place at Carlow Friends Meeting House between Mr Joshua Mason Esq. and Sarah, daughter of William Leckey MD of Ballina Cottage, Co. Carlow, on 14 April 1819.[34] Joshua brought his bride back to Waterford. As a freeman of the City of Waterford, there was no question of him moving to Co. Carlow while Richard and Joshua junior were serving as his apprentices, eight-year-old Arthur was boarding at Newtown and the other children were in need of his care. At home on Summerhill, Mary was twelve, Sarah was eleven, Hannah was nine, Huldah Jane was five and Joseph was nearly four. Whatever the children thought of their new step-mother, her active presence in the house must have lifted a heavy burden from Joshua's shoulders.

Nine months later, Sarah Leckey Mason gave birth to Caroline (1 February 1820–3 June 1820), who died in infancy. Although deaths in early childhood were not unusual, if always a cause for grief, for Sarah it must have been a distressing start to her marriage. Fortunately, Emily (1821–1888) arrived the following year and Isabella Blessing (1823–1883), named for Sarah's mother, was safely born two years later. Their only son, William Leckey (1826–post-1842), was born when his mother was forty.[35] Aged forty-six, Joshua was providing for eleven children.

Joshua Mason left the Waterford Friends' school committee in 1820. Arthur Newburgh's school career lasted from 1819 until 1826. Joseph, a newborn when his mother died, boarded at Newtown from 1823 to 1830. Joshua arranged more salubrious apprenticeships in prosperous grocery shops for his two younger sons. Commended by Waterford Friends, they were warmly welcomed in Limerick. Arthur was apprenticed to Jonas Morris in 1826. On 24 February 1831, as Richard Jacob left for Dublin, Joseph was apprenticed to Joshua Hill, known as 'the Great Commander'.[36] It is likely that Charlotte's half-brothers met members of the Baylee family at Limerick Meeting. John Tyrrell Baylee was master of the Limerick school at 45 Cecil Street. Although he was nicknamed 'Terrible' for his severe dealings with miscreant pupils, many of them did well; others have claimed that his famed methods were milder than those of contemporary schoolmasters![37] His better-known son, Joseph Baylee (1808–1883), rejected his Quaker upbringing before Charlotte crossed his path in Birkenhead during the 1850s. Both Arthur and Joseph Mason survived the devastating Limerick cholera epidemic of 1832.

Joshua Mason gained a significant new family connection through his sister-in-law's marriage to Joseph Robinson Pim (1787–1858), a birthright Quaker from Dublin, at Carlow Meeting on 11 May 1831, after the Friends' usual enquiries. Like Sarah, as a second wife at the age of 34, Anna inherited a family of 5 daughters, before bearing 2 sons and 2 daughters of her own. Joshua Mason was undoubtedly impressed by Joseph Pim's large-scale entrepreneurial skills. He ran the Greenmount Milling Company, which employed 150 people producing paper, cotton and flour in mills, jointly powered by steam engines and water wheels. In 1841, the Pim family moved to Birkenhead, where Charlotte, her mother and her father would encounter them by 1852. More dubiously, Pim would possibly edge Joshua into his alleged financial ruin in 1848 and 1849.[38]

On 26 September 1832, as a freeman's son, Joshua junior, merchant, having affirmed the oath before Mayor Henry Alcock, was readily 'admitted and received into the Freedom of the County of the said City of Waterford'. Five days earlier Joshua Mason had approached Richard Cooke, the town clerk, for confirmation of his own freeman status since 1817. On 29 September, Joshua Mason and Joshua junior, a freeman of three days standing, appealed to Mayor Henry Alcock for further ratification of their freeman status, under the seal of his mayoralty, to secure specific trading rights with Liverpool freemen.[39] This could be the basis for Charlotte's alleged memory, 'My father J.H. Mason was a Liverpool merchant, a drysalter.' However, nothing is known of their ambitious Liverpool trading deals.[40]

Joshua junior, now twenty-seven, married Eliza Woodward (1810–c.1879) at Waterford Meeting on 19 December 1832. Born in Deptford, Eliza was the daughter of Joseph Woodward, a Quaker linen draper who had died of typhus the year she was born. Her mother, Mary, who then married Robert Adcock (1783–1854) of Linton in Cambridgeshire, died suddenly in Ware on 12 June 1820. Eliza, who, with her sisters and step-sisters, remained under Robert Adcock's protection, may have accompanied her step-father to Waterford as he explored investments in Irish lands and property. She probably met Joshua junior through the Friends. Both had lost their mothers at the age of ten. Eliza would prove to be resourceful in adversity.[41]

Marriage and children propelled the favoured Joshua junior into debt. He and Eliza had ten children in twelve years, losing Alfred at fifteen months. In 1835, Joshua Mason senior had decided to move to Staplestown Mills to ensure that Sarah, doubtless already seriously ill, could be near to her family at Ballinacarrig. This bold move, which would raise his standing, enabled him to hand the extensive Summerhill property over to his beloved Junior, who sold it lock, stock and barrel for £260 sterling to his step-father-in-law. Robert Adcock generously let them stay there, before Joshua junior and Eliza ambitiously took over Rosemount House, kindly lent by his obliging father.

Several of their children were born there.[42] Although the 1835 sale should have dramatically eased their situation, debt overshadowed their lives.[43]

After the Summerhill sale in February 1835, Joshua Mason's daughters lost their home. He must have enabled Mary and Sarah to set up the Academy School at 33 King Street; they probably lived there from 1835. By 1839, Mary Mason was registered as the teacher and owner.[44] She may have left Waterford by 1841 to run a boarding school for the daughters of Friends at Croydon in Surrey, possibly accompanied by Sarah, who would return to Waterford in 1846. If Joshua asked Hannah, now twenty-five, to stay with Joshua junior in Waterford to help Eliza with the children, as there is no evidence of her taking up teaching, she is likely to have felt rejected and jealous of Huldah Jane. Her father had chosen her younger sister to accompany him to magical Staplestown.

The die was cast. Having made the necessary arrangements for his older children, Joshua Mason was destined to be the gentleman proprietor of Staplestown Mills. Sarah's brother, William Robert Leckey (1790-1867), as a trusted leaseholder farmer, may have brokered the deal with Colonel Henry Bruen II. Joshua's daughter, Sarah, as junior clerk to Waterford Friends Women's Monthly Meeting, joined Thomas Jacob in commending their removal on 28 May 1835 after a satisfactory enquiry. Joshua and Sarah Mason, with Emily, aged fourteen, and Isabella Blessing, aged twelve, were welcomed into the compass of Carlow Friends with twenty-two-year-old Huldah Jane. Nine-year-old William Leckey was left behind at Newtown School, bereft of his mother's care and sisters' company.[45]

5.
Trouble at Staplestown Mills, 1835–1841

The springtime move to the historic Staplestown townland promised a fresh start for the Masons. The tall house, paved with stone flags, stood proudly beside the sparkling Burren stream, which powered the ancient water mill. The seventeenth-century antiquary, Thomas Dineley, made the earliest record of the triangular-shaped hamlet in 1680, when the mill was owned by Robert D. Lackey, possibly a Leckey ancestor. Merged with Staplestown, Ballinacarrig, where the Leckey family farmed, was known as 'the town of the rock'. Joshua must have hoped that this momentous move would restore Sarah Leckey Mason's health in the clear air, free from the pungent odours of bacon curing, tallow-chandling and soap-boiling pervading Summerhill. Seeing her family in Ballinacarrig every day would surely lift her spirits; attending Carlow Meeting for Sunday worship would welcome her home again.[1]

Fifty-six years later and with comparable aspirations, Joshua Mason's as yet unborn thirteenth child would retreat to beautiful Ambleside, nestling among lakes and mountains, to launch her educational projects with happier outcomes. At first, Staplestown seemed to promise new opportunities for her father – it was close to Carlow, which was advantageously situated on the Barrow River, and there were excellent trade links with Ross, Waterford and Dublin. By the 1830s, coaches halted daily in the townland, en route to these centres of population. The newly leased Georgian mansion had been built by a local Carlow architect, Joseph Fishbourne, in 1798, the year Newtown School was opened, but also the year that hundreds of United Irishmen were massacred by the military supporting the Establishment during the battle of Carlow on 25 May.[2] Ominously, the Masons also moved in during the month of May, thirty-seven years later.

Joshua had reached the age of fifty-five. Now a gentleman with local standing, did he have any inkling of the troubles foreshadowing that first, bright summer? Joshua junior's debts should have been cleared by the Summerhill sale and Hannah must have joined his household. Six of his older children were in gainful occupations and, hopefully, young William Leckey had settled at Newtown School. Happily, Huldah Jane was with her father at Staplestown. After forty years in Waterford, committed to Quaker Truth, Joshua Mason Esquire was a country mill proprietor. Was he prepared for this new field of endeavour? He had to meet the challenge of keeping an old-fashioned water mill going while doubtless pursuing new business opportunities alongside his Waterford interests.

During the 1830s, Colonel Henry Bruen II (1789–1852) of Oak Park Estate by Carlow town, a Tory MP, owned Staplestown Mills and vast tracts of land. Known as a neglectful landowner, who, as Joshua would painfully discover, had clearly failed to invest in the mill, Colonel Bruen would not have greeted his new proprietor in person, but required his agent, Captain Carey, to arrange the lease with Joshua Mason and William Leckey.[3]

Joshua and Sarah, Huldah Jane, Emily and Isabella were warmly welcomed by the Friends at the Carlow Monthly Meeting, held at Ballitore on the 12 June 1835, and visited at home. No courtesy was forgotten. The clerk acknowledged the Friends' regard; John Williams forwarded the certificate confirming their membership of Carlow Friends. Carlow Meeting had started as the New Garden Meeting in 1700; the Masons would have worshipped at the 1712 Carlow Meeting House.[4]

On 22 January 1836, Sarah Leckey Mason died. Carlow Friends read her burial notes. She was only fifty; the cause of death is unknown. Even if Joshua Mason was not as devoted to Sarah Leckey as his beloved first wife, her death was a serious blow. Again a bereaved widower, did he look to Huldah Jane for comfort? She was now twenty-six; Emily was only sixteen and Isabella Blessing nearly thirteen years old. In later life, Sarah Leckey Mason's daughters would choose to live near their Leckey relatives at Tramore.[5] Grieving for their mother, they apparently sought consolation from her Leckey family rather than from a preoccupied father.

In May 1836 came the welcome news that Joseph Mason had successfully accomplished his apprenticeship with Joshua Hill; his certificate from Limerick Friends confirmed that he had been true to his Quaker upbringing. He was warmly welcomed by Carlow Friends.[6] As an energetic 21-year-old, Joseph may have looked forward to helping his father keep the water mill in production. Did Joshua Mason sometimes leave Joseph in charge while he travelled on business trips in Ireland and England? While the 1835 Municipal Reform Act had rendered freeman status honorary, it still conferred beneficial standing.

> Ballinacarrig, otherwise Staplestown, contains 615 inhabitants. . . . The parish which is situated on the road from Carlow to Tullow comprises 2576 statute acres, as applotted under the tithe act, and valued at £2,200 per annum. Two thirds of the land are arable, and nearly one

third pasture or wet grazing land; there is little waste or unprofitable bog; the state of agriculture is improving. There are some quarries of excellent granite for building; and mills at which about 10,000 barrels of flour are annually made.[7]

Staplestown House,
'A very good gentleman's residence.'

The seventeenth-century Staplestown Mill was initially set with two water wheels; the original wooden bridge had seven arches. Was the respectable output of flour mentioned above by Lewis produced at Staplestown, or mainly by other nearby mills? Was the mill already declining by May 1835, fed by a winding stream which lacked the strong surge of the River Bann of Joshua's childhood?

Despite competition from more effective local mills, there was a ready market for milled products during the 1830s and an extensive corn and butter trade in Carlow. However, old-fashioned water-powered mills, such as that at Staplestown, were already becoming rare and would be superseded by four steam-powered mills in Carlow during the next decade.[8] At Staplestown, accumulated stones and gravel often impeded the uneven flow of water from powering the mill effectively, despite the deeper channel protected by higher banks close to Staplestown Bridge. Were Joshua and Joseph the struggling millers who reportedly blocked four of the six arches under the bridge to direct the stream with greater force through the two remaining arches in order to turn the mill wheels and power the grinding stones? Unfortunately too strong a head of water, surging through the two arches, tended to flood the fine quality pasture land, noted above by Lewis, on both sides of the Burren. Furthermore, during exceptionally dry summers there was too little water in the tortuous stream to power the millstones effectively. Whatever Joshua and Joseph initially achieved by sterling effort, their output of flour cannot have been high.[9]

The river Burren runs along the north boundary. There are several gentlemen's seats, a handsome parish church and a large flour mill. . . . The proprietor is Colonel Bruen. . . . The townland also contains two very good dwelling-houses, one called Staplestown

Lodge, which is the residence of Mr Watters, and the other called Staplestown House, which is the residence of Mr Mason, the proprietor of the flour mill at Staplestown Bridge.[10]

Lewis additionally referred to the seats of the three principal 'gentlemen' in Staplestown: Kilmeany, the residence of S. Elliott Esq.; Staplestown Lodge of H. Waters Esq.; and Staplestown Mills of '— Mason Esq.'.[11] Was Joshua Mason keeping a low profile, if his first name was unknown? Although he must have attended Carlow Meeting, only one reference to his active involvement with Friends' affairs has been found. In October 1837, the Monthly Meeting appointed Joshua to a committee of eleven Friends to investigate rising expenditure. After examining the accounts, the eleven reported back in November that they could find no effective way of cutting costs.[12]

Joshua Mason's social standing was further ratified by being placed in the prestigious section for 'Nobility, Gentry and Clergy' in the 1839 Carlow Directory. Listed with his gentlemanly neighbours, notably Samuel Elliott Esq., the local magistrate Henry Watters and his brother-in-law William Robert Leckey Esq., he was also ranked alongside his landlord, Colonel Henry Bruen II.[13] His occupancy of the tall Georgian house conferred comparable local status to that to be achieved by Charlotte upon moving to Scale How in Ambleside sixty years later.

Perhaps due to living grandly at Rosemount House in Co. Waterford, Joshua junior's confidence had soared. An esquire, like his father, he rashly joined the distinguished Waterford subscribers to Samuel Lewis's *Topographical Dictionary of Ireland,* Volume 1, in 1837.[14] Despite selling Summerhill to Robert Adcock in 1835, the beloved Junior, now thirty-two and the father of four children, was disowned by Waterford Quakers for 'having incurred considerable debts which he could not discharge'. The disappointment of the Friends, his public disgrace and their hopes for a better future were recorded by Waterford Monthly Meeting:

Whereas Joshua Mason Junr. who had his birthright and education among the people called Quakers by not attending to the limitation of Truth in trade and outward concerns, hath so far deviated from there as to incur Debts to a considerable amount which he was not able to discharge.

Now for the clearing of the Truth which we profess from the reproach brought thereon by such conduct, we feel it incumbent upon us to testify against the same, and hereby disown him, the said Joshua Mason Junr. to be a member of our religious society, until he may be brought to a just sense of his error. . . . Given forth at our Monthly Meeting held in Waterford on 27th of 7th month 1837. . . . Signed by Thomas W. Jacob Clerk.[15]

Eliza, Joshua junior's resilient wife, remained united with Waterford Friends; the children received a Quaker education. Woodward, Charles and Joshua Henry would board at Newtown during the 1840s; the three oldest daughters were educated at home. During the 1850s, Eliza junior, Gertrude and Arthur would join the children of Eliza's sister-in-law, Hannah, at Ackworth Friends' School at Pontefract in West Yorkshire, which offered the children of poor Friends a plain English education. Still active today, the school was founded in 1779 by John Fothergill (1712–1780), a physician, plant collector and philanthropist, the son of the Quaker minister John Fothergill (1676–1745) who had inspired James Gough.[16]

Joshua Mason probably established Richard Jacob in his own tallow-chandling and soap-building business before leaving Waterford. Poor Richard Jacob may have disliked returning to this odorous work after his Dublin break in 1831. Finding solace in the bottle, he was disowned by Waterford Quakers on 22 March 1838 for 'drinking to excess seriously affecting his health'. After moving to Liverpool, his final occupation would be as a white collar book-keeper.[17]

Had Arthur, Joshua's third son, also renounced his upbringing? He was probably the Arthur Mason from Tipperary who received a testimony of disownment on 31 May 1838 for 'having failed to make payment of his debts, bringing loss to his creditors'. His subsequent marriage in a church suggests that he remained disowned.[18]

On 10 August 1838, William Leckey Mason was welcomed into the compass of Carlow Meeting after only four years at Newtown School. Eleven years younger than his half-brother Joseph and alone at school, William had undoubtedly been desolated when the family left Waterford with his sisters and may have failed at school. Staplestown House was sadly bereft of his mother's presence.[19] William did not return to Newtown.

Did the devastating storm over Carlow, lasting three nights from Tuesday 27 until Friday 30 November 1838, symbolise the further dark days to come? The prolonged turbulence must have worsened the winter flooding in the pastures and pushed up extra gravel to form obstructive shoals in the Burren stream, reducing the mill's power and possibly damaging the ancient bridge.[20]

Joshua Mason did not apply to Lisburn School, under Ulster Friends' firm management since his grandfather's day, but sent his youngest son across the sea to a new Friends' school at Penketh village, near Warrington in Lancashire. Was he thinking of moving to Liverpool, where he and Joshua junior had established links with Liverpool freemen since 1832? The Pim family was nearby in Birkenhead.

Penketh Friends' School (1834–1934) was small, with only forty-nine children attending in 1839. William Leckey Mason was the ninety-eighth pupil to be admitted. He joined a class of nine boys and eight girls as the only Irish student. The religious and moral ethos was comparable to the Quaker schools already described. There were no servants; the school was run on the principles of strict economy that Charlotte would uphold at her future House of Education. The superintendent, William Thistlethwaite (1834–1846), was later master of Ackworth Friends' School. Joshua may have hoped the open-air lifestyle would suit William, if he had health issues or learning difficulties. The boys, working alongside their masters, undertook extensive manual employment, chiefly in agriculture. In 1842, William, aged sixteen, was listed as a school-leaver.[21] No further mention has been found; he may have stayed with his sisters or died soon after leaving school. William's half-sister, Huldah Jane, who may have initially escorted him to school, must have liked Penketh as she sent her three sons and two daughters there during the 1850s and early 1860s.[22]

Towards the end of 1839, Joshua faced a painful dilemma. Huldah Jane was being courted by Peter Doyle (c. 1814–pre-1871), also a member of Carlow Friends. She conceived a child before wedlock, replicating her grandmother Mary Gough's predicament of 1777. The 1841 British census showed that Huldah Jane's first son, Benjamin, was born by June 1840; happily he survived. To avoid the customary rigorous investigation by the Friends into their suitability for marriage, and doubtless to conceal the pregnancy, their solution was to 'marry out' speedily. By December 1839, they declared their intention of being legally married in a Church of Ireland church before a priest, a decision bound to lead to disownment. Joshua Mason was expected at the Friends' Monthly Meeting on 6 December 1839, held at Carlow, no doubt to discuss the proposed disownment. The minutes read, 'Joshua Mason is prevented from attending'. As the January and February 1840 Monthly Meeting minutes are lost, there is no further information.[23]

On 7 February 1840, Huldah Jane and Peter Doyle were married in a Church of Ireland church as planned, possibly at St Mary's, Staplestown. Attending his daughter's church wedding before a priest would have caused Joshua's disownment. He must have stayed away; no record of his disunity with Carlow Friends has been found. Three days later, Queen Victoria married Prince Albert wearing a train born by twelve maids of honour. Her hair was 'dressed quite plain'; the only ornament on her head was a tiara of brilliant diamonds.[24] Huldah Jane's marriage shook Joshua's firmly rooted Quaker foundations. On 6 March 1840, Carlow Friends recorded that a

> Testimony of Disunity with Peter Doyle and Huldah Jane Mason, now Doyle, prepared by the Friends appointed at the last meeting has been read and with one addition, approved. The same Friends are desired to share it with the parties and bring it to the next meeting with their objections if they should have any.[25]

After their marriage, the Doyles left promptly for Bangor, Caernarvon, in north Wales, perhaps at Joshua Mason's instigation. They may have moved into 41 Garth Village on Garth Point before Benjamin Mason Doyle's birth. Whatever his feelings, Joshua Mason probably set them up financially as the 1841 Bangor census revealed that Peter had 'independent means'.[26]

Did Joshua allow Emily, at nineteen, to manage the household with Isabella, who was seventeen? What did her half-sisters feel about Huldah Jane's precipitate marriage and sudden departure? For distraction, the Carlow Quarter Sessions were in full swing. On 4 April 1840, Joshua Mason and William R. Leckey, with eighteen other gentlemen, were sworn onto the grand jury for the disposal of the criminal business.[27] The Doyles returned in September 1840, surely to show off the new grandson and to receive Joshua's blessing. When the Friends finally delivered their Testimony of Disunity, Peter and Huldah Jane Doyle calmly raised no objections. The fact that Carlow Friends knew they were staying at Staplestown House shows that Joshua Mason was still attending meeting.[28]

Then news of another breach with Waterford Friends arrived. Rebellious Sarah Mason had associated with four other women who had

> at this time come under our solid consideration and a feeling of painful concern has prevailed on their account, believing that some if not all of these individuals have been in great degree led astray by the influence or example of others, yet as they have wholly withdrawn from the attendance of our Religious meetings, and have united with other persons in holding meetings in this city which have been disowned and disclaimed by accord of our Monthly and Quarterly meetings, having also manifested great disunity with their friends and repeatedly refused to receive any committee or communication from this meeting it is evident that there are no open occasions for further labour on our part and now feel it incumbent upon us now to declare that we no longer consider them as members of our Religious Society.

The declaration ended with the hope that by yielding to the influence of the Holy Spirit they would come to 'regret the separation . . . and be once more re-united'. Sarah would fulfil that hope by 1846. Disowned with the others on 8 October 1840, she may have promptly left Ireland, either with, or to join, her sister Mary, in Croydon.[29]

To quit Staplestown, a place of unhappiness, Joshua needed capital to clear any debts and support his children. With the consent of his brother-in-law, the memorial of an indented deed, dated 11 May 1840, recorded Joshua Mason's sale of the lands and property received under his second marriage settlement:

> lying and being in the Barony of Middle Third and County of Waterford together with all and singular houses, outhouses, advantages and appurtenances whatsoever to the said lands tenements hereditaments and premises belonging or appertaining together with all the Estate and interest of him the said Joshua Mason in or to the same and all the deeds papers and writings in the possession of the said Joshua Mason, Robert William Leckey or either of them or any person on their behalf.

Joshua's brother, James, may have put him in touch with a Quaker property owner from New Ross, Co. Wexford. Joseph Jeffares and his heirs were the recipients of the lands and property; the deal was affirmed on 24 November 1840. Joshua junior had also been planning to let or sell his extensive 7 Bridge Street dwelling house, corn store, kiln, shop and offices to clear his own and perhaps also Arthur's debts.[30] If Junior regretted leaving Rosemount and 7 Bridge Street for the small Mary Street house in July 1840, he may have hoped Eliza's obliging step-father, Robert Adcock, would help him rebuild his corn, chandlery and tobacco enterprises. About this time, Arthur Mason returned to Waterford and probably worked with Joshua junior.

It was time to leave Staplestown. The flour market was uncertain, the mill was failing and local tenant farmers doubtless blamed Joshua Mason for the water-logged fields. He was missing Huldah Jane. His brother-in-law was moving on. Elected as a Conservative poor law guardian on 3 October 1840, William R. Leckey left the Ballinacarrig farmlands for his new duties.[31] Did he welcome Emily and Isabella into his family? Nothing is known of their whereabouts until they joined their half-sister, Mary Mason, at her Croydon Friends' School by 1851.

During this dark time of despair, maybe in 1840 and no later than April 1841, Joshua Mason, now aged sixty-one, met Margaret Shaw (c. 1818–1858), a beautiful Roman Catholic woman thirty-eight years younger than himself.[32] Was she a local Carlow woman, possibly employed at Staplestown House? Or did Joshua meet her in Bangor, Birkenhead or Liverpool? Acute loneliness, aggravated by a sense that the foundations of his spiritual and temporal life had collapsed with his children's disownments, and despair over the failing mill may have propelled Joshua Mason into intimacy with a sympathetic young woman. Whether the affair lasted a while or was brief, a child was conceived in the spring of 1841. Joshua's thirteenth child would be Charlotte Maria, born in his absence, but destined to be co-founder of the Parents' (National) Educational Union in 1887.

Margaret may not have realised that she was pregnant. As an experienced father of twelve, Joshua might have sensed that she had conceived if he had spent time with her. As an honourable and responsible widower, he is unlikely to have intentionally left her in the lurch; this suggests that he was unaware of her predicament. Whether or not it was a fleeting encounter, sparse evidence indicates that Margaret knew the Doyles and how to reach them at Garth Point in Bangor.

Joseph had been true to his upbringing and a great support to his father. Was it his idea to sail to Australia, a land of opportunity? Friends' records show that Joshua Mason wrote from Staplestown House on the 27 May 1841 to consent to the marriage of his thirty-one year old daughter, Hannah, to Edwin Birchall junior (1819–1884), nine years younger. Born in Leeds, Edwin was the son of Edwin and Eliza Birchall (née Hardinge). The bridegroom's father managed Edwin Birchall and Sons, stuff manufacturers with warehouses in Leeds, where Edwin worked. The couple settled there after their marriage at Waterford Meeting House on 1 July 1841. Hannah was undoubtedly deeply hurt that her father did *not* attend. Joshua junior signed the marriage certificate.[33] Joshua senior and Joseph had probably quietly slipped away in June. A year later, on 12 August 1842, Carlow Friends' clerk recorded,

> We are informed by the Friends appointed last month that Josh. Mason one of our members sailed for Sydney about twelve months since but they have not been able to ascertain his present residence. They are desirous to keep the subject under their care and inform the Meeting when they obtain such information.[34]

In April 1840, the *Carlow Sentinel* had advertised a special offer on passages to Australia.[35] Joseph may have applied for the assisted passage to Australia scheme, backed by the governor of New South Wales in 1830 and funded by the British government to attract British migrants with a range of skills to the new colony. Irish people had been regularly emigrating to Australia since the 1820s. After 1840, emigration became more respectable as the transportation of convicts to New South Wales had officially ceased, although some boatloads persisted.[36] Convicts and free travellers had sent back enticing information about the beauty of the country and the opportunities it offered.

Joshua and Joseph's port of departure is unknown. There were numerous sailings to Sydney during 1841. They may have boarded one of the flotilla of cargo boats, rather than a fast clipper. The long voyage, which might last for weeks or months, depending upon the direction of the winds, was fraught with danger from stormy seas and icebound waters. Their quarters would have been rough; they would have had to bring all their food. Joshua Mason probably obtained introductions through Liverpool and Irish Friends' business associates. Well-known Friends had travelled in ministry to Australia. Meetings for worship were established in New South Wales.[37] If Joseph had obtained an assisted passage, he would have been tied down until the 'remittance regulations' had been met, while his father, who may have paid his own way from the proceeds of the 1840 sale, was free to return. Joseph settled in Australia; he died there true to the Friends.[38]

Having acquired the lease of Staplestown House, Mill and land valued at £118 from Colonel Bruen, Henry Watters did not work the mill after Joshua Mason left in 1841. In June 1846, Charles S. Ottley, a civil engineer, visited Staplestown to check the drainage and improvement of the Burren district lands. His comprehensive report revealed the insuperable problems confronting Joshua and Joseph. Without massive investment, keeping the ancient mill working would have foiled the most experienced millers' best efforts. Ottley ordered the historic mill be dismantled. Too late to benefit Joshua, the Burren stream was diverted from its tortuous course.

> It is in short an artificial site where no natural facilities exist for the establishment of useful mill power. . . . The fact of the mill being so long idle, in the vicinity of such an important and improving town, as Carlow is, affords sufficient proof that its value to the public is by no means commensurate with the injury it inflicts upon the lands.[39]

The mill was demolished in 1847. No trace of it remains today, apart from a modern house erected beside the stream.

6.
Charlotte Mason's Mysterious Childhood, 1842–1852

In this chapter, the unusual circumstances of Charlotte's birth in Bangor, her parents' marriage in Dublin and their move to Birkenhead by 1852 will be explored. Surprisingly, Charlotte was born to parents from different generations and antithetical Christian traditions. While Charlotte's Anglican church attendance for the sake of her schooling promised a *via media*, her parents would draw apart by 1855. Almost certainly her mother's only child, Charlotte definitely knew some of her father's family connections, notably the Doyles, the Birchalls and the Pims. Whether she met any of the others is not known.

In February 1840, Peter and Huldah Jane Doyle probably sailed to Holyhead from the port of Dublin. After crossing Anglesey Island, they would have driven over Thomas Telford's suspension bridge (constructed in 1826) to reach Bangor, an expanding seaboard city with a population of 7,500 by 1841. Bangor may have been chosen for its proximity to Ireland. By April 1841 the Doyles were definitely living in Upper Bangor at 41 Garth Village on Garth Point, beside the Menai straits. The house was occupied by Thomas Jones, aged thirty-five, a master mariner, with his wife Martha, aged thirty, their four-year-old daughter, Margaret, and their son, Thomas, aged one, a companion for Benjamin Mason Doyle who was now ten months old. Huldah Jane told the census officer that she was twenty, not twenty-eight. Aged twenty-seven, Peter Doyle had independent means.[1]

While Joshua and Joseph were being whirled across storm-tossed seas from an unknown port of departure to Sydney, Margaret Shaw discovered that she was with child. If Irish, and almost certainly reared as a Roman Catholic, the majority population in Ireland, she faced being labelled a 'Magdalene'. Without resources, she could have been despatched to a local convent to work in the laundry under the punitive conditions imposed on girls in trouble, followed by the agony of handing over her precious baby for adoption by a carefully chosen Roman Catholic family. Aghast at the prospect of ignominious disgrace and moral condemnation from the local priest and her relatives, if any, to whom could she turn?[2]

Margaret must have appealed to Huldah Jane Doyle, her link to Joshua Mason or, perhaps, though this is less likely, through Peter's Roman Catholic relatives. Letters announcing their safe arrival in Sydney would have surely reached Joshua's beloved daughter by the end of 1841, enabling them to keep in touch. Did he ask the Doyles to look after Margaret and her unborn child? If so, Margaret Shaw would have fled from Ireland to Garth Village in time for the birth of her child with huge relief. Did Huldah Jane feel responsible for her father's mistress? In 1840 she had left him in the lurch after avoiding a comparable disgrace.

Although all births, including illegitimate births, were supposed to be registered in England and Wales from 1837, no secular record has been found of Charlotte's arrival. The Isle of Man had no compulsory registration until 1878. Extensive searches for Charlotte's birth in England, Wales, Ireland and the Isle of Man over two decades yielded no Church of England or Roman Catholic baptism certificates, nor any Quaker record. Irish census records for 1841 and 1851 have not survived.[3]

Longstanding confusion about Charlotte's date and place of birth, mentioned in Chapter 1, has been partly explained by census records indicating that her half-sister, Huldah Jane, was living with her family in Bangor around the time of Charlotte's birth, said to be on 1 January 1842. Charlotte may never have had a birth or baptism certificate. Until sometime between 1861 and 1871, when somebody, surely Huldah Jane, suggested that she had been born in 1842, Charlotte believed that she had been born at Douglas, Isle of Man, in 1841.[4]

Although her little daughter was born out of wedlock, as a God-fearing Roman Catholic, Margaret would have wanted Charlotte Maria to be promptly baptised. However, there had been no dedicated Roman Catholic church in Bangor for 300 years. In 1827, Bishop Peter Collingridge (1757–1829), Vicar Apostolic of the Western District of England, had launched a mission in South Bangor for the tiny handful of poor Roman Catholics living there.[5] Father E. Carbery from Chester may have been the first resident priest. He celebrated Mass in houses in the southern district of the town, some distance from Garth Village in Upper Bangor. The first Roman Catholic church in Father Carbery's time, dedicated to 'Our Lady', was not built until 1844. No records from the 1840s have survived. All early Roman Catholic church records, stored at the priest's house, were burnt in 1856 because one of the priests who succeeded Father Carbery died of the plague.[6]

Charlotte Maria may not have been baptised by a priest. If raised as a Catholic, Margaret would have believed that baptism was necessary for salvation, but as an unmarried mother, she was vulnerable; she had fallen from grace in the eyes of the Roman Catholic Church. After a hard first labour, she probably lacked the physical strength or effrontery to enquire for a priest soon after Charlotte's birth. Although both were disunited, Huldah Jane was a birthright Friend who did not believe in sacramental baptism; Peter probably shared her view although he may have been baptised as a Roman Catholic before joining the Friends. Garth villagers may not have heard of Father Carbery's seventeen years of ministry in South Bangor or known how to find a priest. If Margaret realised that, in the absence of a priest, a lay person could baptise a baby, usually only *in extremis*, by performing the rite of pouring water over the infant's forehead while making the sign of the cross and saying, 'I baptise you in the Name of the Father, and of the Son, and of the Holy Spirit,' she may have secretly christened her baby daughter to save her immortal soul. Whether or not a priest later confirmed that the baptism had been performed, Charlotte Maria could not be baptised twice.[7] Without a certificate, Charlotte may never have been certain of her true date of birth or how, when, or if she had been baptised.

Little Charlotte Maria, who is likely to have spent her first two years lovingly swaddled in her mother's arms, would have been impervious to doctrinal conflicts over her birth and baptism. As her mother's first and probably only child, Charlotte may have felt especially singled out; the style of her later life as a cosseted invalid suggests a lifelong yearning for the safety of her mother's loving embrace. 'Mother was beautiful – always an invalid. . . . One pleased Mother.' Grown-up, Charlotte delighted in using baby-talk with friends' children until she was roundly criticised by her publisher, Charles Kegan Paul, in 1886.[8] As she grew up, she may have met puzzling expressions of disapproval from her Quaker relatives hostile to Roman Catholicism. Living with this tension may have powered her determination to find her own way through religious disputations. Decades would pass before she dared to acknowledge her Roman Catholic mother by adding Shaw to her name.

Huldah Jane gave birth to Sarah Harriett in Bangor in 1843. If Margaret and Charlotte stayed on with the Doyles in Bangor, for lack of any alternative, Charlotte must surely have played with her half-niece. Life in a crowded shared house on Garth Point with young children to play with suggests that little Charlotte was not lonely. Towards the end of 1843, the Doyles returned to Ireland, where their three younger children were born, probably in Dublin: Charles in 1844, Joshua F. in 1846 and Hulda Jane in 1847.[9] By January 1844, Margaret Shaw was definitely living in Wellington Street, St Mary's parish, Dublin.[10]

Whether or not Joshua Mason had planned to stay in Australia with Joseph, delayed news of the birth of his thirteenth child called him home to Ireland. Hopefully Joseph's Australian future was secure. As an experienced merchant, Joshua Mason was unlikely to have returned from the New World empty-handed. Having survived the outward journey in 1841, he overcame the rigours of the return voyage without Joseph's support. Did he dock in Liverpool or sail straight into Kingstown, the port of Dublin, in time for his sixty-fourth birthday on 3 January 1844?[11] Notwithstanding her background, Margaret may have possessed a special quality of character or vulnerability that attracted an unhappy, older gentleman merchant, who responsibly returned from Australia to marry her.

Joshua Mason was staying in Kingstown, in Monkstown parish, where the Quaker community had been established since 1830. Quakers had constructed the railway from Kingstown to Dublin in 1834. Did he call on Joshua Mason Chaytor (1790–1857), at Heathville in Monkstown, who had served an apprenticeship in Waterford? A successful wholesale butter merchant and shareholder with the Pims' and Perrys' joint stock companies during the 1840s, Joshua Mason Chaytor might have been connected to Charlotte's father through relatives of the eighteenth-century Clonmell bookseller, Joshua Mason.[12]

Did Joshua voluntarily resign from membership with the Friends after resolving to marry Charlotte's Roman Catholic mother before a priest? 'Marrying out' was another ground for disownment. Regret over disunity from the Friends would not have been an ideal start to this hastily arranged third marriage. Despite the critical disparity in their ages and religious backgrounds, Joshua was clearly determined to put things right. If Margaret was lively and intelligent, with a sense of humour comparable to her daughter's, he may have been delighted that this beautiful young mother wished to be his wife.

For Margaret, the marriage promised a return to a brittle respectability. For this couple, their legal marriage before 1845 had to be conducted in a Church of Ireland church, the compromise chosen by the Doyles. No doubt as soon as Joshua reached Dublin he promptly arranged the marriage by special licence for Thursday, 25 January 1844 in the galleried, early-eighteenth-century church dedicated to St Mary (1702–1986). No banns were called; the marriage licence enabled the quiet ceremony to be promptly arranged as Margaret was resident in the parish. With no doubts as to the legality of the marriage, Joshua Mason did not pay the customary monetary bond to the diocesan Bishop of Dublin.[13]

St Mary's parish in central Dublin, north of the River Liffey, was named after the medieval monastery, St Mary's Abbey (1139–1539). Arthur Guinness (1724/5–1803), founder of the Guinness brewery, married there in 1761. Theobald Wolfe Tone (1763–1798), doomed leader of the United Irish uprising of 1798, was baptised at the church. George Handel (1685–1759), lodging nearby in Abbey Street, practised regularly on the early eighteenth-century Renatus Harris organ. In arranging their wedding

[Page 45]

MARRIAGES solemnized in the Parish of St. Mary
in the County of the City of Dublin in the Year 1844

Michael Healy of St Bridget's Parish
residing in Peter St
and Fanny Jones Swift of St Mary's Parish
residing in Mount Joy St
were married in this Church by Consistorial Licence with consent of
Parents & Guardians this Twenty fifth Day of
January in the Year One Thousand Eight Hundred and forty four
By me [illegible]
This Marriage was solemnized between us { Michael Healy / Fanny Jones Swift
In the presence of { Benj Swift / [illegible]
No.

Joshua Mason of Monkstown Parish
residing at Kingstown
and Margaret Shaw of St Mary's Parish
residing in Wellington St
were married in this Church by Licence with consent of
Parents & Guardians this Twenty fifth Day of
January in the Year One Thousand Eight Hundred and forty four
By me Daniel Mooney
This Marriage was solemnized between us { Josa Mason / Margaret Shaw
In the presence of { Joseph [illegible] Bradley / [illegible]
No.

Thomas FitzGerald of this Parish
and Frances Neill of this Parish
were married in this Church by Publication of Banns with consent of
Guardians this 28th Day of
January in the Year One Thousand Eight Hundred and 44
By me Jas. Howie
This Marriage was solemnized between us { Thomas FitzGerald / Frances Neill
In the presence of { Julia [illegible] / [illegible]
No.

The notice of the Mason marriage.

ceremony, Joshua and Margaret would have been amazed if they could have foreseen that this historic church, made redundant in 1986, would one day be transformed into a glittering bar and restaurant, dominating the oldest unaltered church interior in Dublin.[14]

Did Margaret drive in style to her wedding from lodgings in Wellington Street, now replaced with modern housing? Joshua and Margaret were joined in wedlock by the perpetual curate, the Revd Daniel Mooney; he had ministered at the church at least since 1840. Joseph H. Bradley witnessed Joshua's hastily scribbled signature; Margaret's witness was Jane M. Wheeler. They may have been friends, acquaintances or parishioners.[15] Did the Doyles attend? If Huldah Jane was looking after the children, she would have been unable to witness the marriage of two people who had not met for nearly three years and whom she may have brought together.

Dublin may have been their first base, as Mrs Groveham indicated. Did Joshua Mason take his new young bride and thirteenth child home to Waterford to see Junior and his grandchildren? It is not known.

On 21 April 1846, Arthur Newburgh Mason, bachelor and cashier, married Mary Woodward (c. 1806–1865), a spinster of no occupation, by banns in a church at Linton in Cambridgeshire, her step-father Robert Adcock's parish. Older than Arthur by five years, she was the older sister of Eliza Mason (née Woodward). Joshua junior witnessed the marriage.[16] He and Arthur were surely working together at this time. In 1846, Junior was listed as an insurance agent, tallow-chandler and tobacconist at 7 Bridge Street. Arthur acquired land at Gibbet Hill, off Bridge Street, near their former Summerhill home, and an office and land at Pickardstown in the Drumcannon parish, in a sense winning back the Leckey properties his father had sold off. By 1856 he was running the family businesses of tallow-chandling, soap-boiling and marketing and manufacturing tobacco from prestigious premises at 42 Merchants Quay. Arthur and Mary had no children.[17]

Sarah Mason returned to Waterford and her 'native land' in 1846. She appealed for reinstatement to membership with Waterford Friends in June, deeply regretting 'speaking some years since in your Mo. Meeting in the heat of intemperance', and was reunited with the Friends on 27 August 1846.[18]

Richard Jacob Mason, aged forty-three, still disunited from the Friends, died of cholera on 22 July 1846 at 15 Rathbone Street, Mount Pleasant, Liverpool, attended by an illiterate woman called Margaret Derry. It is not known if he had kept in touch with the family.[19] A month after Richard's untimely death, Joshua junior, of 51 Merchants Quay, died on 19 August 1846, aged forty-one. Still disunited from Waterford Friends, he died a month before his youngest son was born.[20] Junior may have left Eliza with few resources. Arthur Mason probably paid for the three older boys' Newtown schooling and subsequent apprenticeships while supporting his sister-in-law, Eliza, and the six younger children. Her last-born, Arthur, was named for his uncle.

The dire effects of the Irish famine were causing starvation. By November 1846, Waterford Friends were raising subscriptions to supply the poor with beef broth on four days a week. Probably at Sarah Mason's suggestion, on 25 February 1847, Eliza obtained a certificate of removal to Kingston, England, for herself, her five daughters and baby Arthur to join Mary Mason at her well-established boarding school for the daughters of Friends in Croydon, Surrey, founded by Mrs Wigton.[21] Mary welcomed her sister-in-law, nieces, nephew and half-sisters to the school. By 1851, Emily and Isabella Blessing were also teaching there. Now an annuitant, Eliza managed the school as Mary's health was failing.[22]

> South-End House, Croydon, Surrey
>
> This Establishment, hitherto carried on by MARY MASON, will, at the ensuing quarter, be transferred to her sister, ELIZA MASON, by whom it will in future be conducted. M Mason takes this opportunity of acknowledging her gratitude for the confidence so freely reposed in her, and hopes that the same favour may be extended to her sister.[23]

On 30 December 1852, aged only forty-six, Mary died in Croydon.[24]

Did Joshua Mason invest in the Waterford family businesses and take over Joshua junior's insurance business from 1846? This might explain why the insurance agency at 51 Merchants Quay in Slater's National Commercial Directory of Ireland still bore the name Joshua Mason in 1856, ten years after Junior's death.[25]

Joseph Robinson Pim was a versatile merchant, banker, insurance broker and company director. Joshua Mason probably kept in touch with the Pims after they moved to Birkenhead sometime before 1841. While the Pim businesses were flourishing, the nine children from both marriages were grandly brought up at Oakfield House in Claughton, Birkenhead. Then Pim made some risky investments. Too heavily involved with brick-making, he was disowned by the Friends, presumably for debt, on 26 October 1843. Five years later the Liverpool and Manchester Saw Mills and Timber Joint Stock Company collapsed on 15 December 1848. If Pim had persuaded Joshua Mason to invest in this company on return from Australia, the crash might have caused the latter's alleged financial losses of 1848 and 1849. Bankruptcy proceedings were issued against Joseph Pim and published on 20 November 1850 in *The London Gazette*. This disgrace would have prejudiced Pim's financial recovery as well as reunion with Birkenhead Friends.[26]

Before 1851, the Pim family downsized to Exmouth Street in Holy Trinity parish. Anna Pim and the children stayed within Hardshaw West Friends' compass, perhaps attending the Beckwith Street Meeting.[27] Two of her daughters had married during the 1840s; in 1853, Elizabeth died and Margaret, the eldest, left for Lisburn, leaving Mary, twenty-four, Hannah, seventeen, and Anna, fourteen, whom Charlotte *must* have known, in Birkenhead. The Pim sons, Joseph and William Leckey, aged seventeen and fifteen respectively, returned to Dublin for apprenticeships by 1849.[28]

The Doyle family left Ireland for Birkenhead during 1848; Benjamin started at Penketh Friends' School in 1849. By 1851, they were living at

62 Oliver Street in Holy Trinity parish, near the Pims. Peter was a clerk in the Liverpool cotton business.[29] Not recorded in the 1851 British census, the Mason family probably remained in Ireland until later that year. They certainly stayed at Douglas, Isle of Man, for a time as Charlotte believed she had been born there. Her parents doubtless educated her at home, as she later wrote,

> I knew a girl whose parents devoted themselves entirely to training her; they surrounded her with care and sufficient tenderness; they did not make much of her openly, because they held old-fashioned notions about not fostering a child's self-importance and vanity. They were so successful in suppressing the girl's self-esteem that it never occurred to her that all their cares meant love until she was woman-grown and could discern character, and, alas! had her parents no more to give them back love for love. The girl herself must have been unloving?[30]

An intelligent girl, Charlotte must have learnt to read, write and study the Bible; she may have escaped into stories. We can only guess what books she read: perhaps Layard's exotic *Nineveh*, *Aesop's Fables* in Henry Butter's famous spelling book or *Robinson Crusoe,* the book Rousseau chose for *Émile.* She may also have browsed on seventeenth-century literature. While there is no evidence for Charlotte's alleged memory, 'I think I was a dull, silent, uninteresting and not very observant child,' it rings true.[31] Age discrepancy, religious differences and Margaret's health problems may have surfaced more intrusively in Birkenhead. While the odds were stacked against an enduringly happy childhood, Charlotte's early education prepared her for school.

Did the Birchall family's arrival in Dublin during 1851 precipitate the Masons' move to Birkenhead? Edwin Birchall was a carriers' agent for Pickford's in Dublin following the collapse of his father's business in Leeds. Hannah may never have forgiven her father for missing her wedding. Joshua's Roman Catholic wife was eight years younger than her, a cause for smouldering resentment. Facing old age outside the Friends' compass, Joshua Mason, now seventy-one, may have felt more relaxed with the Doyles and the Pims. Perhaps the Masons lodged nearby or with the Doyles at 62 Oliver Street, in a terraced brick house within Holy Trinity parish.[32]

Birkenhead, formerly Birchen Haven, once surmounted by a Priory, was founded in AD 1151 by the Norman nobleman, Haman de Masci. Bounded by the vast Wirral forests on one side and by Liverpool across the Mersey on the other, Birkenhead remained a small hamlet until nineteenth-century industrialisation brought substantial growth.[33] Rising to 8,000 by 1841, the population was swelled by a huge influx of Welsh and Irish incomers seeking work in the shipyards or docks. The steam ferry services across the Mersey gave good access to Liverpool. As the working classes flooded into Birkenhead, their middle-class counterparts moved out to Oxton village, set on a high ridge from which merchants could watch their cargo boats sail in.[34]

Birkenhead had the advantage of the beautiful park, designed by Joseph Paxton (1803–1865) of Crystal Palace fame. Opened in 1847, it spread over 125 acres of marshland. This 'pleasing variety of landscape gardening, adorned with picturesque lakes, flower beds, rockeries, sloping mounds, sculpture, ornamental bridges, serpentine walks and lodges, in various styles of architecture' may have enchanted nine-year-old Charlotte. Was she taken to the bustling Old Market opened in 1845 to gaze at the motto engraved on one side of the clock, '*Ubi Fides Lux et Robur*: Where there is Faith, there is Light and Strength', which anticipated her later mission?[35]

Holy Trinity Church, Birkenhead.

Inner city church building was gaining momentum during the Victorian religious revival. A future sanctuary for Margaret Mason, St Werburgh's Roman Catholic Church in Grange Road opened in 1834; it is still active today. By moving to England, Margaret had joined the unpopular Roman Catholic minority, shown by the Religious Census of 1851 to comprise only 3.5 per cent of those attending church.[36]

Holy Trinity, Price Street, the second Anglican church in Birkenhead and Charlotte's future parish church, where her Anglican life would begin, was opened on 13 November 1840. The building held 950 souls for a district of 6,274 people. The main entrance was 'by a deeply recessed, elaborately ornamented doorway'. Inside, the roof was supported by stone figures of angels. The nave was divided from the aisles by five lofty arches supported by 'clustered iron pillars of extremely delicate proportions', painted red and blue; the rest of the church was drab and brown. There was a 'fine-toned organ'. The east (actually north) window was fitted with stained glass. This extraordinary edifice, demolished in 1975, aroused mixed feelings:

> The church is very peculiar and by no means of an ornamental structure. . . . The belfry is separated into divisions by dwarf windows from the corners of which wild looking figures present themselves. Very wild looking and remarkable indeed. Round the entire church

> below the cornice runs a band of sculptured faces of the most distorted and ludicrous character comparable only to a set of inferior pantomime masks . . . ridiculous monstrosities.[37]

There would be plenty there to distract the eye and scare a self-conscious young girl during Sunday services at 7:30am, 10:30am, 3:00pm or 6:30pm.[38]

Charlotte's incumbent, or perpetual curate, was the Revd Joseph Baylee (1807–1883). He was the fifth child of Joseph Tyrrell Baylee, the Limerick Friends' schoolmaster whom Arthur and Joseph Mason undoubtedly met at Limerick Meeting. A highly intelligent, ambitious and maverick personality, Baylee trounced his Quaker upbringing by stating he was *self-educated* when he applied to Trinity College, Dublin, in 1828. After marrying his Limerick bride, Matilda Collis, in 1832, he began his evangelising ministry at the Achill Island Mission.[39]

In 1842 he arrived in Birkenhead ablaze with zeal. A master of many languages, he engaged with prestigious local dignitaries to set up various parochial and charitable endeavours. He achieved his MA in 1848 and his Doctorate of Divinity in 1852.

> But Baylee's heart was in Merseyside, filled with longing to reach the untaught and untended poor in its crowded streets and courts.[40]

The Church of England National Society for the Education of the Poor in the Principles of the Established Church was founded on 16 October 1811 to set up a church school in every parish in England and Wales. It was the largest of the national voluntary educational societies to receive government grants from 1833 onwards.[41] Determined to educate the poorest children, Baylee started Sunday schools at Holy Trinity, followed by a 'ragged school' in Brook Street, later called Trinity Free School.

In 1843 he opened the Holy Trinity National-Society-sponsored day schools for boys, girls and infants in Trinity Street, where Charlotte would start her school education around 1852. Adequately financing and equipping these schools and providing accommodation for the teachers remained a perpetual challenge.[42] On 2 September 1845, Baylee dashed off an appeal to the National Society representative, the Revd Wm Harrison at Christ's Hospital, for £1,500 to fund a new infant school building:

> I enclose an application for an Infant School which will I hope meet your kind support. . . . My church is only capable of accommodating 1,000 so that I have necessarily a small congregation to call upon for the support of three schools in addition to the many local charities.
>
> The present infant school is erected on part of the same site as the boys' and girls' schools. We are anxious to provide over it residences for our Mistresses. But unless your Society help us by a liberal grant we

> must give up the idea. Such residences would be a material benefit to the Schools. . . . I can truly assure you that I have not come before the Society until I had given my best exertions in my district.

Having ended the letter by promising to preach annually in support of the National Society, he obtained a grant for the infant school, where Charlotte would teach when needed and may have resided with the mistress.[43]

The setting up, supervision and funding of National Schools was a demanding commitment expected of Victorian Anglican clergy, crucially dependent upon effective support from the school managers and clerk. As incumbent, Baylee was chairman of the three schools' committee. He met with fourteen gentlemen and two clergymen on the first Monday of every month at the school. All but two of the eight weekly visitors at Holy Trinity National Girls' School, led by Mrs Matilda Baylee (d.1864), were wives of committee members. Mrs Gladstone would have known Charlotte well; she was still regularly visiting the schools in 1863.[44]

> When they were in Liverpool they were attached to St Aidan's Church of which she frequently spoke.[45]

Enthusing about her church life at 'St Aidan's Church' with Lizzie Pendlebury, Charlotte was clearly referring to the close link between Holy Trinity Church and St Aidan's Theological College, founded by Joseph Baylee (1847–1970). The College was named after the Anglo-Saxon saint, Aidan (d. AD 651), acclaimed by Bede for working with the sick and poor. No other St Aidan's Church was opened in Birkenhead or Liverpool before 1860.[46] Distressed by the lack of clergy serving inner city communities, Baylee's innovatory strategy was to prepare non-graduate, urban-dwelling candidates, notably business men, clerks and merchants, for holy orders. Emphasis was placed on training for parochial visiting. The students visited local families on three afternoons a week, keeping a journal to be handed to Baylee on Saturdays. They saw at first-hand the poverty and degradation assailing poor people living in crowded conditions.

Described as a fiery biblical literalist, Baylee set the syllabus for the academic two-year course himself, without external inspection to cramp his style. The students studied the Greek Testament and Latin texts, ecclesiastical history, the Bible, liturgy, the Thirty-Nine Articles of Religion and evidences, including Paley's work. In spite of the impressive curriculum, negative comparisons were made between Baylee's non-graduate ordinands and Oxbridge clerical graduates, usually destined for quiet rural livings. Fears were expressed that the former would weaken the church's links with influential groups in society. Baylee, who prudently enlisted the great and the good in support of St Aidan's Theological College, was mindful of these ineluctable social class distinctions.[47] They were remarked upon decades later by H.G. Wells (1866–1964), who described a fictional confrontation between his heroine, Ann Veronica, and the prison chaplain, who failed to raise his hat:

> 'Are you a special sort of clergyman', she said after a pause, and looking down her nose at him, 'or do you go to the universities?' 'Oh!' he said profoundly.[48]

'One pleased Mother.'[49] Charlotte's mother may have wished her to attend a Roman Catholic school. However, the first St Werburgh's Roman Catholic school did not open until 1857.[50] Joshua may have investigated the local schools and resolved to accompany his daughter to Holy Trinity Church by 1852, perhaps believing that respected Anglican membership would give her a better start in life. Margaret may have decided to return to her Roman Catholic roots and started attending St Werburgh's Church. Doubtless advised to conceal her unacceptable mixed dissenting and Catholic religious background, Charlotte's acceptance at Holy Trinity National Girls' School would have depended upon regular church attendance.

Charlotte probably started attending Holy Trinity by 1852. Did she really gaze out of the window at 'lots of children' following 'a tall lady with a dark shawl'?[51] If so, this 'tall lady' could have been Miss E.A. Toby, the certificated mistress of the girls' department of Holy Trinity School in Trinity Street, or Miss Macbeth, who taught in the infants' school. If funds were low, Joshua would have been relieved that the weekly fee was only 2d, believed by Her Majesty's Inspector (HMI), the Revd J.P. Norris, to be 'quite too low for a place like Birkenhead'.

> An admittance fee of 1s would, I think, help to check the capricious attendance; and with the same view, the children should be induced to buy their own books. Active and systematic visiting among the parents would also help to remedy the evil. Until it is remedied the school cannot reach a satisfactory state of efficiency.

Miss Toby, the mistress, had recently obtained her teacher's certificate and 'was taking great pains' in running the school, assisted by a pupil-teacher. The school had greatly advanced since 1851. The needlework had improved. At this time many Irish families were pouring into Birkenhead. As most of the girls had joined within the past twelve months and very few had moved up from the infant school, Charlotte would not have been the only Irish new girl.[52] If Joshua Mason's manifest concern for practical education, surely engendered by his Quaker grandfather's endeavours and his involvement with Newtown School, led him to ensure his thirteenth child's attendance was regular, unlike most of the newcomers, it would explain why she achieved the required standard for pupil-teaching in under three years.

Charlotte must have missed the Doyle family when they crossed the Mersey to Everton by the end of 1853. Sarah Harriett, Charlotte's contemporary, was ten, and her siblings Charles, Joshua and Hulda were nine, eight and six respectively. Charles would join Benjamin at Penketh in 1854. By the time Sarah Harriett left for Penketh in 1855, Charlotte was a second-year pupil-teacher. By 1861, Peter Doyle was a landholder; the whole family was living together at 29 Woodville Terrace in Everton. Benjamin was a commercial clerk, Sarah was teaching, Charles was apprenticed on the railways and Joshua was an optical apprentice.[53]

Charlotte recalled her delight in browsing old volumes of the *Spectator* and in exciting stories, perhaps read to her by her father:[54]

> We wonder does any little girl in these days of many books experience the joy of the girl of eleven we can recall crouching by the fireside clasping her knees and listening as she has never listened since to the reading of *Anne of Geierstein*?[55]

Anne of Geierstein (1829) by Sir Walter Scott (1771–1832) was a dramatically romantic tale to feed Charlotte's imagination and aspirations as well as love for an elderly father. Anne is beautiful, as agile as a goat on the mountain, courageous, wise and successful in all her adventures, as well as skilled in keeping house for her uncle. Her mother has died; her mysterious father turns out to be Count Albert of Geierstein. Arthur, who came secretly to Geierstein with his father, the Earl of Oxford, is nobly born; he marries Anne after proving himself worthy through many ordeals. Elsie Kitching said that Charlotte's father had read to her and introduced her to Sir Walter Scott's Waverley novels, notably *Anne of Geierstein* (1829). Was this the last time her father read to his special eleven-year-old daughter with a distinctive Irish accent, thereby intensifying her memory of the occasion? In later life, Charlotte 'always had "some Scott" the last thing at night', even if *Anne of Geierstein* was never read again.[56] The book may have been borrowed from the Holy Trinity Church lending library, open on Monday mornings, or from the Church Institute's reading room, which opened in 1853.[57]

Whether or not teaching was Charlotte's true vocation as claimed in *The Story*, her 'mission' to teach would be launched at Holy Trinity's girls' school. As shown by her half-sisters, she would be following in her Quaker family tradition. Emulating her great-grandfather's training as an usher, she would become a pupil-teacher apprentice. If not as yet bored by standard school readers, she may have been a model pupil, earning a few pence as class monitor, as hinted in *The Story*.[58] Her few years at school, never mentioned or described, were essential preparation for her future pupil-teaching apprenticeship.

7.
Pupil-Teaching at Holy Trinity School, Birkenhead, 1854–1859

All that Joshua Mason had invested in his older children's futures had been dashed by death, disownment and distance. In Birkenhead, his strongest desires may have crystallised into clear aspirations for his last-born, thirteenth child. Eight years after Dr James Kay-Shuttleworth (1804–1877) launched the pupil-teacher scheme in 1846, Charlotte Mason began her apprenticeship at the Holy Trinity School in August 1854, aged twelve years and eight months. Attendance at Holy Trinity Church, linked to St Aidan's clergy training college, offered a challenging introduction to mid-Victorian Anglican evangelism. The unknown 'E.A.B.' who gave Charlotte William Paley's *Natural Theology* (1802) for her birthday in 1857 and Thomas Girtin's *Physiology* (1855) in August 1859 recognised Charlotte's intellectual potential, perhaps engendering an early interest in the physiological sciences in the wake of Paley's treatise on the inter-relatedness of God's designed creation.[1]

Kay-Shuttleworth was the first secretary (1839–1849) to the Select Committee of the Privy Council (Committee of Council) on Education, which administered the government grants extending state education. The new pupil-teacher system was intended to raise the baseline set by the monitorial system instituted by Andrew Bell (1753–1830), whereby the instruction was passed on from older to younger pupils in vast galleried schoolrooms. While gaining practical teaching experience, pupil-teachers were prepared for the Queen's Scholarship examinations to win free admission to a 'normal school', the contemporary name for the growing number of teacher training colleges.[2]

Prospective pupil-teachers, aged thirteen or older, were selected from the best elementary scholars. As the apprenticeship was not intended for privately educated middle-class applicants, pupil-teaching became synonymous with lower-class status. Here is a primary reason for Charlotte's later concealment. However, her hero, Matthew Arnold (1822–1888), poet and lay HMI, described pupil-teachers as 'the sinews of English public instruction'. Apart from the HMI reports, there are no extant descriptions of Holy Trinity School in the 1850s.[3] The school has since been demolished.

As shown, Joshua Mason had arranged his sons' apprenticeships and doubtless established his unmarried daughters as Quaker teachers. Enabling his thirteenth child to apply for a government-funded pupil-teaching apprenticeship would have relieved all anxieties about her future. Believing in the value of sound practical education, he set her on the same sure path as his grandfather and great-uncle. As Charlotte's father, or 'next friend', Joshua would have acted as the surety on her pupil-teacher indenture – her formal contract with the certificated mistress.[4] The incumbent, Dr Baylee, should have confirmed that she had been punctilious in her religious observance. Frenetically busy, he may have delegated this duty to an assistant curate or to the school managers' clerk. Although National School pupil-teachers had to be baptised in the Church of England, many 'slipped through the net'.[5] While Dr Baylee's belief in the sacrament of baptism was manifested by his strong record of baptising at Holy Trinity Church, as a former Quaker he knew Friends did not accept baptism.[6] If Charlotte had been regularly attending church, he may not have enquired about her baptismal status; alternatively, he and Joshua Mason may have come to an understanding.

As Joshua was absent when Charlotte was born, Margaret may not have dared to reveal her daughter's baptismal status. Without a birth or baptism certificate, Joshua Mason may not have known Charlotte's precise date of birth. As an invalid and a Roman Catholic, Margaret Mason was probably excluded from the apprenticeship negotiations. If Charlotte began pupil-teaching in August 1854, after the HMI's annual visit, as laid down in the regulations, her father must have informed the school authorities that she was thirteen. As a bright, well-read girl, she may have seemed older than twelve. As shown, in 1861 Charlotte gave her age as twenty.

Charlotte's future adherence to the evangelical wing of the Church of England was determined in Birkenhead; she discarded her Irish Quaker roots and her mother's Catholicism. As a National School pupil-teacher she had no choice about attending church services. Later, Charlotte enthusiastically discussed her church life with Lizzie Pendlebury at College. Holy Trinity, with its close association with St Aidan's, must have been a significant early influence. She may have been fascinated by the ordinands' trial sermons; some were former merchants like her father. While Baylee's dynamic preaching could have perplexed her, his passion for education may have uplifted her spirits.

Previous rebuffs arising from his Irish Quaker background may have fired Dr Baylee's determination to establish St Aidan's in a grand building, with a prestigious board of trustees. His practical training model was comparable to that of the non-graduate Church teacher training colleges, established to meet the urgent need for practised, professional teachers in the National Schools, such as the Home and Colonial Schools Society's Training Institution, founded in 1836, where Charlotte would study the craft of teaching. The excitement engendered in Holy Trinity circles by the opening of the prestigious College building in Claughton on 4 November 1856 may have left Charlotte with lasting impressions.

Did Baylee's controversial views on Roman Catholic dogma and papal infallibility persuade Charlotte to reject her mother's devotion to sacramental Roman Catholicism, as she earnestly studied her Bible and the Catechism?[7] As a new evangelical Anglican, Charlotte was struggling at the start of a religious pilgrimage that owed much to her father's yearning for the Light.

> 'Only believe', the writer was told as a girl, to her great anger and soreness of heart. If 'only fly' had been said, she could not have flown, but anyway she would have known what definite thing was expected of her; but 'only believe' carried no meaning. Of course she believed that yesterday was Wednesday, the 5th October, say. . . . Of course she believed in God in that way, but how could it matter? She was aware that such belief was no part of her life, and she knew no other way of believing.[8]

There are no extant Holy Trinity Church records before 1928 to establish if, and when, Charlotte was confirmed. In Ambleside, she would be accepted as a lifelong communicant member of the Church of England.[9]

The annual pupil-teacher stipend was sent directly to Charlotte's post office account by the government at the end of each successfully completed year, under Article 143. Starting at £10 5s, rising to £17 10s in the fourth year and to £20 for the remainder of the apprenticeship, her stipend would have conferred a certain independence.[10] Did her father start her off with respectable clothes and books, covering her first year's modest living costs? Not known as a skilled seamstress in later life, she may have been obliged to cut out and sew suitably neat dresses. Saved up monitor's pence would not have gone far.

The Committee of Council's stringent moral standards laid down that pupil-teachers had to live in an approved household.[11] Would her parents' lodgings have met these strict requirements? If they had parted by 1855, Charlotte may not have been allowed to live with her Roman Catholic mother, already frail. As the Doyles had moved to Liverpool, did the Pims take Charlotte in? Mary, now twenty-five, may have been teaching; Hannah, eighteen, and Anna, sixteen, were also at home.[12]

Charlotte Mason's strong distaste for state control must surely have begun with the moralistic entry qualifications for the apprenticeship. The engagement of the pupil-teacher, reviewed each year by the regional

Dr Joseph Baylee, Principal of St Aidan's College and Charlotte's parish priest.

HMI representing the Committee of Council, began and ended with the month fixed for the annual inspection, apart from the final year, which always ended at Christmas. On application, pupil-teachers were carefully assessed by the HMI and approved by the school managers and the parish clergyman. Charlotte's usual HMI was the Revd J.P. Norris, a Fellow of Trinity College, Cambridge, who inspected Holy Trinity Schools on 10 August 1854. In the girls' school, he noted,

> School-room, playground, discipline, instruction and fitness for training apprentices good. Offices fair. Desks still against the wall. Furniture sufficient. Books well supplied, except that the Bibles are worn out. Registers fairly kept. Apparatus, one large black-board in a stand, and a smaller board with easel. Organisation, five classes for all subjects on parallel forms, under a mistress, one apprentice and two monitors.

Committee membership may have declined and the managers' meetings lapsed when Charlotte began pupil-teaching, as the Revd. J.P. Norris, the HMI, criticised the declining standard of managerial support for the teachers from 1854 onwards. However, he was pleased that all three schools had improved under difficult circumstances. As the first principal, Baylee's attention was focused on St Aidan's. Unlike the more worldly-wise St Aidan's students, National School HMIs were ordained Anglican upper-class Oxbridge gentlemen. The annual inspections were a time of tension for all concerned. Whether or not Charlotte was overawed, Mr Norris's August visit was the right occasion to appoint the new apprentice who, by starting in the second half of the year, would serve for five and a half years until Christmas 1859.[13]

Charlotte had to present a certificate of punctuality, diligence, obedience and attention to her duties from the mistress. For her entry test before the HMI, Charlotte had to read aloud with fluency, ease and expression, and write neatly from dictation a simple prose narrative, with correct spelling and punctuation. She had to take down from dictation sums in 'the first four rules of arithmetic, simple and compound', to work them correctly and to know the table of weights and measures. She had to identify the parts of speech in a simple sentence and display an elementary knowledge of geography. One of the Holy Trinity clergy would have tested her ability to repeat and understand the Catechism and her knowledge of Scripture history. She had to be able to knit and sew neatly. The most challenging test might have been teaching a junior class to the satisfaction of Mr Norris, although Charlotte may have gained preliminary experience as class monitor. The academic standard for boys was higher as they might be additionally examined in simple Latin and the 'Use of the Globes'.[14] Charlotte's application would have been dismissed if she was observed to be suffering from any of the following diseases:

> Scrofula, fits, asthma, deafness, great imperfections of sight or voice, the loss of an eye from constitutional disease, or the loss of an arm

or a leg, or the permanent disability of either arm of leg, curvature of the spine, hereditary tendency to insanity, or any constitutional infirmity of a disabling nature.[15]

Beginning her apprenticeship in the second six months of 1854, our healthy heroine faced stiff competition for entry into a normal school. In 1855, nationally, Charlotte was one of 2,413 female pupil-teachers. By 1859, there were 7,005 girls and 8,219 boys, totalling 15,224 in all. Governmental anxieties about the rising expenditure on pupil-teachers and teacher training would surface well before 1860.[16]

Pupil-teaching was tremendously hard work; the days were long. On the five school days, supervised by the certificated mistress, Charlotte had to assist as under-teacher, officially for only forty scholars. Simultaneous teaching alongside four other noisy groups, taught by the mistress and monitors crowded into one large schoolroom, must have been tough, although accepted as the norm. Standards may have slipped, especially during the more relaxed autumn period after the annual inspection. Pupil-teachers were sent to the pupils' homes to enquire after absentees and collect their weekly pence. After the children had gone home and the clearing up had been done, the mistress, who received an extra £5 in her annual salary for this responsibility, was expected to instruct the pupil-teacher for one and a half hours in the art of school-keeping and prepare her for the annual pupil-teacher examinations, more exacting each year.[17]

Did the managers enable Charlotte to receive regular issues of *The Pupil Teacher: A Monthly Journal of Practical Literature* (first launched in 1857)? This journal, anticipating the guidance to be given by the new Pupil-Teachers' Centres from the 1880s onwards, not only published lists of historical dates, mathematical problems, grammatical tests and guides to drawing with perspective, but also explicated potted versions of geography, literature and philosophical topics such as utilitarianism. The editorial team welcomed and rigorously criticised answers sent in by pupil-teachers, commenting, for example, that a piece of work was not up to fifth-year pupil-teacher standard. The journal developed a 'Notes and Queries' section which Charlotte may have adapted for *Parents' Review*.[18]

If Mr Allen, the certificated boys' schoolmaster, gave Charlotte instruction, the mistress acted as chaperone. Fearing that female pupil-teachers would grow up ignorant of simple housewifely skills, the Committee of Council decreed that girls should clean the schoolroom by scrubbing the floors and desks. Kept late at school by these duties, Charlotte faced further study and the required hour of evening housework. At weekends, Charlotte may have had to help the mistress with church duties, from Sunday school classes to cleaning and tidying up. Boys had a far easier time. No doubt she felt wrung out like a wet rag when the holidays came round.[19]

> 'My Hiding Place.' – A friend tells me the following story of her girlhood. It so happened that extra lessons detained her at school until dark every day during winter. She was extremely timid, but, with the unconscious reserve of youth, never thought of mentioning her fear of 'something.' Her way home lay by a riverside, a solitary path under trees – big trees with masses of shadow. The black shadows . . . filled her night by night with unabated terror. She fled along that riverside path with beating heart; but quick as flying steps and beating heart, these words beat in her brain, over, and over, and over the whole length of the way, evening by evening, winter after winter: 'Thou art my hiding-place; Thou shalt preserve me from trouble; Thou shalt compass me about with songs of deliverance'.[20]

This expressive passage written by Charlotte must surely have been autobiographical, although no waterway on any route near the school has been identified, unless she hurried home from her school duties through Birkenhead Park in the evening. By this admission, she never lost her fears of dark, lonely places.

The HMI's 1854 report suggests that Charlotte was apprenticed to Miss Toby, the only certificated mistress in the girls' school. R.R.W. Lingen, who succeeded Kay-Shuttleworth as secretary to the Committee of Council in 1849, had insisted in an earlier circular to the HMIs, on 15 June 1855, that the moral contract between the pupil-teacher and the teacher and managers was mandatory, not voluntary.[21] Whether the supervising teachers lived up to this dictat is questionable considering the pressures they faced. The prestigious school managers' external commitments often enticed them from their school responsibilities. In 1853, the HMI had said the boys' school had to be improved if they were to take pupil-teachers. Luckily for Charlotte, by 1854 he thought the girls' school was suitable for pupil-teacher training. As The Holy Trinity Schools had further improved by 6 August 1856, the managers must have responded to the HMI's criticisms. That year they received a grant of £393 16s 8d for pupil-teachers. Charlotte may have been the only girls' and infants' pupil-teacher; the HMI reports from 1854 to 1859 failed to mention pupil-teachers.[22]

On 19 December 1857, Lingen required the HMIs to recommend the interchange of girl pupil-teachers between girls' and infants' departments to extend their experience. Pupil-teachers who had *only* taught infants were advised to sit the Queen's Scholarship for a college specialising in infant teaching. In 1859, noting how few ten-year-old scholars stayed on at school, the Committee of Council reported that infant schools could do much more for neglected lower-class younger children.

> If the instruction be not pushed beyond that of the perceptive faculties, and if the discipline be sober and kind, in order not so much to teach

> children as to prepare them for learning. Doubtless the infant school is only an artificial, and therefore, an inferior substitute for domestic instruction but it is evident that the home of the ordinary working man cannot supply such instruction.[23]

Officially apprenticed to the girls' school, Charlotte doubtless gained experience with infants, as this minute recommended. From 1854, Miss Toby's sister had been running the infants' school, where the average attendance was seventy-two. The HMI reported,

> Buildings and the ability of the mistress good. Playground common to girls. Furniture, books and apparatus sufficient. Discipline and instruction fair. Lessons on objects moderate. General efficiency of the school very fair. I was pleased with an original lesson on the elementary forms of letters given to the gallery on the blackboard.

A large number of children, 132, had joined the girls' school and 215 infants had attended during the past 12 months. These numbers fluctuated wildly. While 95 girls and 125 infants had been present at the August inspection, the daily average attendance for girls was only 71 and 72 for the infants.[24] With well over 100 on the registers of each of the three schools, the teachers never knew how many pupils would arrive each day. A chronic shortage of books and equipment was reported between 1855 and 1860 and there were frequent staff changes. Matters were never as neatly organised in schools as envisaged by the Committee of Council; teachers had to improvise to compensate for poor buildings and the lack of educational resources and equipment. Notwithstanding the Pestalozzian influence expressed by 'object lessons', the syllabus may have been limited by lack of resources.

In 1857, Miss Mary Ann Sprackling was mistress of the girls' school. In 1856, she had gained a second-class certificate after training at the Home and Colonial Training College, popularly known as the 'Ho and Co'. Miss Fanny Ormsby now taught the infants. By 1859, the efficient Miss Selena Stevens arrived from the Ho and Co without a certificate. However, 'having secured firmer control over the scholars', she had 'with spirit and ability' improved the girls' skills in reading and writing, although 'the supply of books' still needed attention. She would gain a third division certificate via the examination for teachers in charge of schools in 1863. Charlotte's supervision by two teachers trained at the Home and Colonial Training College would have been infused with Pestalozzian principles and methods. As her training was incomplete, Selena Stevens may have had some difficulty in thoroughly preparing Charlotte for the Queen's Scholarship examinations.[25]

Where did Charlotte live from 1854 to 1859? When the Doyles left Birkenhead for Everton across the Mersey, by 1854, did Charlotte and her mother move into the Pims' house in Exmouth Street near to the school as she began pupil-teaching? In 1855, Gore's Birkenhead Directory listed

Joshua Mason, gentleman, at Exmouth Place, 48 Watson Street, near the Pims' residence. This house, owned by Mrs Mary Ann Watson and her married son, Henry, contained three flatlets designed for single people. Number 4 housed Joshua Mason and a Mr Charles McErithy.[26] Having arranged Charlotte's apprenticeship and set her on course for a teaching career, was Joshua's paternal duty done? Perhaps he was already displaying symptoms of the degenerative disease from which he would die. Anna and Mary Pim may have asked Mr McErithy to look after Joshua if he was too frail to live alone. Clearly there was no room for Margaret and Charlotte in the small flat.

By 1856, Joseph Pim's health may have been failing. The departure of Anna Leckey Pim and her daughters, Hannah and Anna, for Ireland was recorded by the Friends on 17 April 1857; still disunited, Joseph Pim died in Ireland in 1858. Mary Pim, probably teaching, stayed in Birkenhead until February 1860 before moving to Cork. Perhaps she befriended Charlotte. After Joseph's death, Anna Leckey Pim and her youngest daughter settled in Tramore in Co. Waterford where her brother, William R. Leckey from Ballinacarrig, resided at Beechmount, Newtown, Tramore. Other Leckey family members, such as Jane (1798–1880), gathered there with Charlotte's half-sisters, Emily and Isabella Blessing. Isabella married Alfred Clark at Ballitore Meeting, Co. Kildare, on 18 June 1856; after his death she rejoined Emily at Tivoli Cottage, Tramore. The sisters had chosen to be near their mother's Leckey relatives. By 1881, Emily had achieved her father's standing, listed as a lady among the nobility, gentry and clergy.[27]

During 1856, Margaret Mason, an invalid for as long as Charlotte could remember, probably needed more care than the Pims could provide. If she had returned to her Roman Catholic roots at St Werburgh's Church in Grange Road, she may have asked to move into a Roman Catholic household. Since 1851, or earlier, Dr Baylee had been the visitor at an establishment at New Brighton 'for the purpose of affording accommodation at a low charge for poor women whose state of health renders sea bathing desirable'. In view of the allusion in *The Story* to Margaret Mason's delicacy, need of sea air and love of swimming, did Dr Baylee's committee place her at New Brighton for the sake of her health?[28] By now, illness and Roman Catholicism may have separated Margaret Mason from her fourteen-year-old daughter. Yearning cries from the heart surface in Charlotte's later writings:

> This girl would watch her mother about a room, walk behind her in the streets – adoringly. Such intense worship of their parents is more common in children than we imagine.
>
> But, dear mother, take your big schoolgirl in your arms just once, and let her have a good talk, all to your two selves; it will be to her like a meal to a hungry man.[29]

Towards the end of 1856, the Birchalls arrived in Birkenhead and settled at Oakfield Villas, Conway Street, within Holy Trinity parish. Conway Street crosses the junction of Watson and Exmouth Streets where Exmouth House stood, before the present modern development. Having left Ireland for Burley Grove, near Leeds, after her marriage in 1841, Hannah may have hoped to see more of her father when Edwin was posted to Dublin in 1851, after his father's firm collapsed. If so, she would have been aggrieved by Joshua's departure for Birkenhead during 1851, even if she had upset him by criticising his third wife.

In 1856, Edwin had obtained a transfer from Dublin to Pickford's Liverpool office, again as a carriers' agent. Highly intelligent, Edwin was destined to rise from this lowly position to become a well-known scientific naturalist and entomologist. He identified new species and published controversial articles on scientific and theological topics. He corresponded with Darwin and Wallace on the origins of British lepidopterous fauna in the Isle of Man. Edwin and Hannah's first child, Edwin Howard, was born in 1846, when Hannah was thirty-six; Arthur arrived next in 1847, followed by Oswald in 1849. Before they left Dublin, Hannah, aged forty-six, gave birth to Diana Florence. Like numerous contemporary baby daughters, she was named after the Lady with the Lamp, Florence Nightingale (1820–1910), Charlotte's heroine, who returned from her Crimean crusade in the summer of 1856. In that year, Edwin Howard (1846–c. 1906) and Arthur (1847–c. 1913) began boarding at Ackworth Friends' School (founded in 1779 and still active today) until 1861 and 1862 respectively, presumably because Edwin's father had served on the Friends' Provincial Committee supporting the school. Oswald went to Ackworth from 1860 to 1864.[30]

Surely it was no coincidence that Joshua Mason, gentleman, now seventy-seven, had moved to Victoria Road, Oxton, by 1857? He was now domiciled outside Holy Trinity parish and beyond the brand new St Aidan's College, off Howbeck Road, in Claughton.[31] His move seemingly coincided with the arrival of the Birchalls and the departure of the Pims.

Essex Cholmondeley told me that Charlotte had lived with an 'uncongenial relative' after her parents died – or, more probably, after they separated.[32] As relatives, the Birchalls were indubitably respectable, notwithstanding their dissenting Quaker background. Not listed as members of Hardshaw West Friends, they may have attended Holy Trinity Church. If their home was approved and they took Charlotte in, surely she would have played with Oswald, aged seven, and baby Diana. Did Edwin introduce his half-sister-in-law to the delights of observing nature directly, while walking in Birkenhead Park on leisured days?

Exhausted after late childbirth, Hannah, thirty-two years older, may have off-loaded excessive household chores onto her timorous half-sister. In 1917, Charlotte Mason sent 'Evelyn, With Xmas Love' a copy

Birkenhead Park in pleasant sunshine.

of *Little Mother* by Ruth Brown MacArthur, published that year. It tells the heart-rending story of an orphaned girl sent to live with rich relatives, who treated her like a skivvy, calling her 'little orphan Tannie' instead of her proper name. The father is sympathetic to the unhappy orphan; gradually, the snooty mistress of the house is won round by Tannie's affectionate personality, domestic skills and ability to keep the children happily amused. Did this old-fashioned American tale resonate with Charlotte's actual experiences with her half-sister in Birkenhead?[33]

Between 1859 and 1869, Eliza Mason left Croydon to run a private lodging house at 203 Euston Road with her younger children, offering one or two ladies 'a large airy bedroom with every comfort of a private house' on moderate terms. As she lived near the Home and Colonial Training College, did Charlotte ever meet her? Hannah Birchall was close to Eliza from their shared Waterford years. Eliza's daughter, Eliza junior, visited the Birchalls in Birkenhead during April 1861.[34]

Parted from her parents, the next three years were a desolate time for Charlotte; she may have found consolation in teaching lively young children. Margaret Mason probably suffered severe pain. Laudanum could have afforded some relief, unless, as a repentant Roman Catholic, she was expected to meet her maker without any such easement. For her healthy young daughter, her mother's never-to-be-forgotten wearisome illness presented Charlotte with a model of womanly suffering and weakness appropriate to the Victorian ideal of feminine demeanour. She, herself, would adopt this lifestyle in Ambleside, after taking her mother's surname and, in some fashion, coming to terms with her memory.

All we know for certain is that when Margaret died prematurely at the age of forty on 16 September 1858 of a 'corroding ulcer of the uterus', she had been ill for at least eighteen months. Nothing is known of other pregnancies or miscarriages, confining her to a sofa. Her death certificate confirmed that she was the wife of Joshua Mason, a retired merchant.[35] Joseph Heighisway, a Welshman from Flintshire, aged thirty-seven, attended her death. A master joiner employing one apprentice, he lived with his family at 15 Whetstone Lane, where Margaret died. His house and shop were just round the corner from St Werburgh's Church in Grange Road. It is hoped that Anne Heighisway, aged thirty-four, from Upton in Cheshire, nursed Margaret tenderly through her last illness, although she had three young daughters, aged ten, six and one, to look after in 1858. Her younger sister, Elizabeth Evason, aged thirty-one, probably assisted.[36]

Was Charlotte allowed to see her mother before she died? Although mourning dress was expected, Charlotte, beset by unrequited longings, was unlikely to have been permitted to attend her mother's Roman Catholic funeral at St Werburgh's Church to say farewell. Margaret's burial certificate confirmed she was a Roman Catholic; the priest, Father George Clegg, stated that she was in communion with Holy Mother Church and had received the last rites. Margaret had had time to confess her sins before the priest and receive absolution, relieving residual guilt about her troubled past. No gravestone marks her resting place in St Werburgh's churchyard.

> Anno 1858 die 16 mensis Septembris Margarita Mason ex Birkenhead aetatis 40, in communione S. Matris Ecclesiae animam Deo reddidit Sacramentis munita cujus corpus die 18 mensis Septembris sepultum est in Cemeterio Sta Werburgha Georgius B Clegg.

In translation:

> In the year 1858 on the 16th day of the month of September, Margaret Mason of Birkenhead at the age of 40, in communion with Holy Mother Church gave up her soul to God, fortified by the Sacraments, whose body was buried on the 18th day of the month of September in the churchyard of St Werburgh. George B. Clegg.[37]

The winter of 1858–1859 was a miserable time for the motherless seventeen-year-old sitting her fifth and final set of pupil-teacher exams. Her father had moved even further away. He had crossed the Mersey and was living fairly near the Doyles in Woodville Terrace, Everton. Joshua survived Margaret by only five months. Aged seventy-nine, he died on 15 March 1859 at New Road, Tue Brook, in the West Derby district of Liverpool.[38] Peter Doyle was present at the death; Huldah Jane would have been at hand. Did Hannah and Charlotte have the chance to say goodbye to their father?

The Doyles may have been attenders at Hunter Street Friends' Meeting in central Liverpool. If Joshua was able speak coherently during his final months, his words would have been laden with regret for his disunity with the Friends. At peace at last, Joshua Mason was laid to rest among Friends at the Hunter Street burial ground on 19 March 1859. His death certificate simply recorded that he was a former merchant. Huldah Jane must have told Hunter Street Friends about her father's gentlemanly Staplestown life. His burial note stated that he was *not* a member of the Religious Society of Friends but had been a miller at Staplestown.[39]

For the seventeen-year-old Charlotte, there was no light to illuminate the darkness of her loss. How did she cope? Although neither of her parents left a will, the prospect of the final year's rise in her allowance to £20 may have spurred her to quit the Birchall household, if she had not left before. Lizzie Groveham told Elsie Kitching that Charlotte had lived with a friend, who had died.[40] If Miss Stevens or a lady visitor, such as Mrs Gladstone, perceived Charlotte's distress, they may have arranged for her to move in with Miss Ormsby, in the residence funded by Baylee's 1845 appeal to the National Society. Unfortunately, Miss Ormsby's health also declined during 1859.

In spite of having to study hard for the scholarship, Charlotte may have run the infants' school and undertaken other duties unsupervised. If so, she had sixty-nine boys and forty-six girls to teach with monitorial support in Miss Ormsby's absence. To keep order, firm control of large classes was essential. At this critical juncture in her life, Charlotte not only lost a valued colleague but had to brace herself for the Queen's Scholarship exams. It redounds to Charlotte's credit that although an icy chill may have settled on her heart, she got on with her work and faced her final HMI inspection in July 1859. The Revd S.J.G. Fraser HMI, new to Charlotte, found the infants' school to be in a very satisfactory state, although

> The standard of instruction has somewhat gone back; owing I believe partly to the illness of the mistress.

At Christmas 1859, Miss Ormsby died. After Charlotte had left Birkenhead, Mr Norris recorded at his next inspection on 25 June 1860 that

> The Infants' department has fallen off in efficiency during the year, owing partly to a change of teacher, the former mistress having died at Christmas. Much is needed to restore the school to its former position.[41]

Although he failed to acknowledge any pupil-teacher contribution during the previous autumn, if Charlotte taught the infants while Miss Ormsby was ill, she did remarkably well to keep the school going. With a brave face, she got ready to travel to London to sit for the Queen's Scholarship after some unbelievably hard and distressing years.

8.

'A Bud to be Unfolded': At the Home and Colonial Training Institution, 1860–1861

In December 1859, Charlotte Mason left the northern seaboard town of Birkenhead for the bustling London metropolis to take the 1859 Queen's Scholarship examinations at the Home and Colonial Training College on Gray's Inn Road. Did a friend, A. Wilson, see her off at Liverpool station with a book and a lunch basket, as a signed volume in her collection might suggest?[1] The orphaned pupil-teacher had successfully passed over five years of teaching experience with girls and infants. Fearful of new challenges, excessive scrutiny of her work and the competitiveness of colleagues, Charlotte would absorb the Ho and Co's Pestalozzian mission to teach poor children while succumbing to the 'serious illness' that would circumscribe her later lifestyle. The evangelical influence of the training master, Robert Dunning (1805–1892), would be a treasured possession.

Eliza Mason's guest house was near the Ho and Co, and yet there is no record of contact between the half-sisters-in-law. Charlotte allegedly lost touch with her half-sisters and their families – even Huldah Jane, who had surely known her from infancy. Charlotte probably knew little of the circumstances of her birth before wedlock and her parents' marriage, or even the reasons for their separation.

The highly regarded Home and Colonial Infant School Society's Training Institution was one of the earliest and largest but not 'the first and only' training college in the country, as Essex Cholmondeley averred.[2] Founded in 1836 as a mixed Anglican foundation, but unattached to a diocese, the college was now training women. In 1857 there were 11 voluntary training colleges for schoolmistresses serving 4,199 student teachers; by 1860 there were 35 colleges for men and women.[3] In 1860, the Ho and Co was selected for a special report by the Committee of Council which praised

> the excellence of the system where it is thoroughly carried out. Here no material improvement is to be expected, no point of importance

> has been neglected, no principle overlooked, no practical application has been untried. Managers and officers, lecturers and teachers have steadily co-operated in the work of forming practical and intelligent teachers.[4]

Johann Heinrich Pestalozzi was a deeply religious Swiss educational reformer. His innovatory writings on early childhood education and teacher training influenced the English infant school movement.[5] Pestalozzi opened schools for poor children and his Yverdun training college (1805–1825). Impressed by Jean-Jacques Rousseau's widely read novel, *Émile* (1762), he published educational treatises in a series of letters, suggesting that by reducing knowledge to its basic elements, anyone could teach children by means of developmentally ordered exercises. He rejected Rousseau's rationalism; for Pestalozzi, religion was a matter for the heart, not the head. Love was the key. Although his school education, like Charlotte's, had been rooted in Protestant Christianity, he followed Rousseau in showing that children should begin by learning from the natural world. Early Enlightenment philosophers from Francis Bacon (1561–1626) to the Czech John Amos Comenius (1592–1670), who subsequently impressed Charlotte, had opened up a new rational spirit of scientific enquiry, discerning the natural laws of intellectual, physical and moral development to guide education. Pestalozzi was writing *How Gertrude Teaches Her Children* (1801) while Wordsworth was composing *The Prelude* (begun in 1798), 'dedicated to Nature's Self and the things that teach as Nature teaches', as they faced the nineteenth century with a new reverence for innocent young children.[6]

The Revd Charles Mayo (1792–1846), an Oxford classical scholar, spent a year from 1818 to 1819 as chaplain to a party of British youths studying at Yverdun. Initially critical of observed contradictions and experimentation, he gradually perceived the beauty and harmony of Pestalozzi's method and brought it to England. Mayo ran Pestalozzian schools for the higher classes at Epsom and Cheam from 1821 until his death. His sister, Elizabeth Mayo (1793–1865), shared his enthusiasm and part of the teaching. Developing their own version of Pestalozzian method, they produced influential textbooks, including Miss Mayo's *Lessons on Objects* (1831), *Model Lessons for Infant Schools* (1848–50) and *On Religious Instruction* (1849).[7]

John Stuckey Reynolds (1791–1874), a retired Treasury civil servant and banker who had opened infant schools in London, met Charles and Elizabeth Mayo. They inspired him with Pestalozzi's educational principles. Reynolds invited Charles Mayo to join the committee launching the Home and Colonial Infant School Society's new training institution. From 1 June 1836, Miss Mayo, the first woman employed to train teachers in England, taught three students in Southampton Street. By 1837, the committee had promptly established the institution in extensive premises on Gray's Inn

Road. Queen Victoria graciously became the Society's first patron.[8] By 1838, model and practising schools for about 600 children were opened in the densely populated St Pancras neighbourhood. Miss Mayo, a dynamic presence, led the educational department in Charlotte's time. As treasurer, John Reynolds visited the Home and Colonial Training College daily in 1860, 'regarded virtually as the principal'.[9]

The Home and Colonial Training College in early days.

The voluntary British infant school movement exercised a beneficial influence upon National Society elementary schools, dominated by repetitive instruction in galleries.[10] The Ho and Co endeavoured to incorporate Pestalozzian individualism within formal schooling. The debate turned on whether children were qualitatively different from adults or merely smaller and less experienced. The Ho and Co's Christian evangelical, Pestalozzian ideal of blending behavioural and moral habit training, considered necessary for lower-class children, with the progressive naturalism derived from a pre-evolutionary concept of developmental stages, was easier to uphold in principle than in practice. Compromise proved necessary in the early infant schools. Pressure from parents induced the utopian reformer Robert Owen (1771–1858) to start reading lessons in his infant school at an earlier age than planned. The Mayos were criticised for promoting mechanical interpretations of the free spirit underlying Pestalozzian principles.[11] Rote learning, which fostered order and discipline, would take a greater hold during thirty years of 'payment by results' (1862–1897). The enduring question was how to educate all children without excessive cost.

The abstract core of the Swiss educationist's philosophy was *Anschauung*, meaning 'the immediate experience of objects or situations'.[12] This was crystallised into the 'object lesson' taught at the Holy Trinity infant school in Charlotte's time. The aim was to develop the 'faculties' by means of progressive physical and sensory impressions through sight, touch, smell and hearing. Charlotte would subsequently maintain that training the faculties separately emphasised the *method* of learning at the expense of *knowledge*. Applying an individualist method, based on the intimate ambience of Gertrude's kitchen, to noisy galleries packed with poor children easily diverted the pupils from imaginatively describing chosen objects such as leaves, a piece of glass or a bat into a droning, mechanical repetition of names, numbers and attributes. The submissiveness instilled into their pupils under the watchword 'Holiness unto the Lord', promoted by the 'earnest inculcation of pure evangelical truth', may have discouraged Ho and Co graduates from falling into Pestalozzi's temptation of delivering a sudden cuff to the ears of recalcitrants, but at the price of attentive interest to the scrutinised object.[13] Ho and Co staff earnestly endeavoured to awaken their students' grasp of the harmonising principles underlying Pestalozzian practice, notwithstanding the difficulties.

> He stimulated the pupil to use his own efforts in the acquisition of knowledge, and thus secured the assimilation of the knowledge acquired so that it really became his own; but beyond this and involving this, he distinguished between instruction and education, propounding that the latter must proceed on the principle of organic development. 'A child', said Pestalozzi, 'is not like a mineral, which increases only by a process of mechanical accretion. He is like a plant which grows by the continual expansion of those organs which lie folded in the germ. He is a *bud to be unfolded.* Every leaf must be expanded, and each must fit into its place. So must the teacher keep in view the organic development of all the pupil's faculties, moral, intellectual and physical, not singly, but simultaneously and harmoniously. The great means of moral development is love. A teacher must be a parent to his scholars, not a martinet; for moral education does not consist in preventing immoral actions, but in cultivating dispositions, forming principles, and establishing habits. The great means of intellectual education is to teach by things and realities, rather than by words and signs. Take nature for the school manual. Let the first lesson lead the scholar to observe with accuracy; the second to express his observations with correctness. The cultivation of the senses and bodily powers is essential to that complete system of education which secures, not mere skill in the accomplishments of a school, but fitness for the duties of life.'[14]

Charlotte Mason, a small, thin young woman with piercing blue-grey eyes and hair 'the darkest possible shade of brown, verging on black', believed she would be nineteen on 1 January 1860.[15] Since 1854 she had passed five sets of annual pupil-teacher examinations and practical teaching tests before the HMIs. Entry to the Ho and Co depended upon gaining the Queen's Scholarship.

The HMIs held the annual Queen's Scholarship examination at the colleges under inspection. Although it was open to any suitable applicant over eighteen, pupil-teachers had the best chance of passing. As mistress, Miss Stevens must have certified that Charlotte had successfully completed her apprenticeship and was expected to pass the examinations. Undoubtedly recommended by Miss Stevens, Charlotte's choice of the Ho and Co was assuredly determined by the institution's justifiably high reputation. All female candidates sat the same examinations.

The Committee of Council's minute of 24 April 1857 decreed that applicants from infant schools were only eligible for the second-class Queen's Scholarship worth £17, presumably because of the lower academic standard. As shown by her subsequent certificate, Charlotte applied for the usual two-year course rather than the new one-year infant school teachers' course initiated by the Ho and Co. She was not classed as an infant-school pupil-teacher.[16] First-class scholars were awarded an additional £3 personal allowance. Men received a higher rate; their first-class scholarship was worth £23 per annum with a £4 personal allowance. Although the basic £17 Queen's Scholarship was lower than the final pupil-teacher stipend, government grants funded the full cost of board, lodging and laundry at the Ho and Co. With her living expenses covered, Charlotte only needed clothes and books, such as Thomas Girtin's *Physiology*. In 1860, the Ho and Co admitted 124 Queen's Scholars, receiving a government maintenance grant of £2,357 for their upkeep, which contributed a quarter of the total cost.[17]

Ho and Co officers probably asked first-year students to look after nervous candidates during examination week. Selina Healey (1839–1911), a journeyman baker's daughter from Hammersmith, was three years older than Charlotte. She may have introduced Charlotte to Elizabeth Pendlebury (1841–1930), a pupil-teacher from St Thomas's National School, Preston, later Mrs Groveham and destined to be Charlotte's life-long friend. Selina gained a first class in both annual examinations, with a prize for drawing competency in her final year. We may imagine that the tremulous charm of the dark-haired, blue-eyed, vulnerable Irish orphan girl touched her heart.[18]

Anne Clough, the sister of the poet Arthur Hugh Clough (1819–1861), had taken up teaching after her father's businesses failed. During the winter of 1849, she visited London and tried her hand at teaching very unruly and energetic children at the Borough Road school before spending time in the Ho and Co schools. She recorded,

> I found the classes [at the Home and Colonial] very interesting. The teachers and the pupil-teachers were mostly very pleasant, and they all seem happy and comfortable together. Mr Dunning the head master is a good kind of man apparently, but rather over religious. The school is much stronger that way than at the Boro' Road. I should fancy the teachers had not so much in them, nor so much mechanical knowledge as the Boro' Road people, but they understand things better, and that from their lesson [the children] would acquire a greater love for information.[19]

When Miss Clough sought a teacher for her Ambleside school, Eller How, opened in 1852, perhaps she asked Mr Dunning, by then the College's training master, to recommend a student. Selina Healey joined Miss Clough's school in 1861, taking it over in 1862 when the latter left Ambleside to live with her widowed sister-in-law.[20] The Ho and Co committee had

> sought for a training master and were so happy to find in Mr Dunning a man ready to grasp, and to hold firm the principles they were all labouring to inculcate. The teachers sent forth from the Institution were of acknowledged superiority.[21]

First, Charlotte had to win a Queen's Scholarship. Each of the nine daunting examinations lasted three hours. Useful summaries from *The Pupil Teacher* would undoubtedly have helped. Geography questions included, 'Describe the river system of Great Britain' or 'Write a short history of Hindustan, its most striking natural features, variances of climate, political divisions and productions.' A history question asked, 'How was Ireland governed until the completion of the legislative Union?' Or, 'Write out from British History any narrative which you think would interest children aged 8 to 10 years on <u>one</u> of the following points: a) courageous perseverance under difficulties; b) readiness to suffer on the side believed to be right; c) uncertainty of fortune.' Religious knowledge included the Old and New Testaments and the Catechism. After years of dynamic sermons by Dr Baylee and his curates, Charlotte was well versed in the Bible and Christian doctrine. She would have been able to 'Write out a short account of the book of Ruth', 'Quote a text from the New Testament to prove the existence of angels, and mention some occasions on which they have appeared', 'Write out some of the texts in which the Holy Ghost is promised and state the offices attributed to him', or 'Give a short account of the institution of the Sacrament of the Lord's Supper, with the circumstances connected with it'. The question 'Give reasons for infant baptism and explain why the Church of England requires god-parents' might have perplexed a Friend's daughter who may have 'slipped through the net'.

There was no literature paper. Well attuned to grammar, Charlotte faced questions on paraphrasing and the correction of ungrammatical sentences that 'violated the rules', such as 'the slate was broke when you give it me.' 'Define the term "parenthesis", parse fully, and explain the syntax of the words: "it being withal the greatest perfection of our nature and the noblest privilege to do so."' Music questions included, 'Write down the diatonic major scale on the treble staff, in two positions, with the names of the notes and repeat in the bass.' A hard question, if Charlotte could not play the piano. For the taxing drawing exam, free hand sketching of an object and geometric measurements were two of the five tests. Neither Charlotte nor Lizzie passed drawing.

The arithmetic paper offered puzzling conundrums reminiscent of The Gough, such as 'If 18 horses eat 37 quarters, 7 bush. 3 pks of corn in 45 days, in what time will 50 horses eat 25 quarters?' After drumming it into her pupils for years, Charlotte could have recited the table of weights and measures backwards. As the boys took Euclid, algebra and geometry, they were excused the domestic economy paper. Here, varied questions included, 'Describe, step by step, the process of washing, ironing and drying. Mention common faults and give practical rules.' Or, 'Explain the methods you would adopt for teaching needlework to thirty girls aged from 7 to 14 years and explain the meaning of and use of the following: hemming, sewing, felling, running, gathering, whipping, stitching, back-stitching and herring-boning. Add illustrations.'

Female candidates were asked what was meant by a 'drain'. 'Why is a house unhealthy if it has no drains or is near to open ones?' Or, 'What is vaccination? What is the object of it?' Or, 'Name the most common vegetable and mineral poisons. What course would you adopt in the case of a person who had taken poison?' A telling question directed at working-class life asked, 'What is to be said for and against the mother going out to work? Illustrate your answer by money reckonings.'

On school management, all candidates were asked how they would arrange a class in parallel desks and to discuss their advantages and defects. Or, 'Explain your method of obtaining silence in a gallery, and recalling (from time to time) the inattentive to order.' There were questions about poor ventilation, teaching reading and writing, as well as organising the day: 'What registers and time tables are necessary for a school of 100, with two pupil-teachers, and how many classes should there be?' and 'What games can you play at and, if necessary, teach?' Charlotte and her fellow applicants must have been shattered when the nine exams were over; they had covered vast ground.[22]

In 1858, the Revd F.C. Cook, HMI for women's training colleges, was concerned about the shortage of trained teachers in National Schools. He wanted to ensure that eligible applicants who received training did not 'wastefully leave the course of life for which they have been specially educated'.[23] Yet by 1860, when Cook was reporting on the Ho and Co for the Committee of Council, he fretted over the high cost of funded Queen's Scholars and the obstacles preventing privately-funded higher-class students from being trained, as their 'habits and qualifications would make their admission desirable'.[24] At the end of 1860, the total cost of running the Ho and Co was £8,140 7s 8d for that year.[25]

Competition was stiff. Charlotte showed sterling courage in facing up to the ordeal. At Christmas 1859, a total of 159 Church of England female candidates obtained a first-class Queen's Scholarship; only 14 were not pupil-teachers. Second-class scholarships were awarded to 275 female candidates; 33 of these were privately funded.

In the list of second-class Church of England Queen's Scholars, published for all to see in *The Pupil Teacher* and class lists, Lizzie Pendlebury gained 70th place, above Charlotte's position of 141. Listed as National School pupil-teachers, their second-class scholarship was not, therefore, due to infant school pupil-teacher status. Did that 71-place gap subtly influence Charlotte's relationship with her friend and other more successful colleagues, although 134 women were behind her and 9 not placed?[26] As Cook sought a higher proportion of private students, the flexible Home and Colonial Training College accepted those who had passed the exams creditably; they saved on cost and raised the cultural *tone* of the institution.[27]

In 1860, Charlotte's year, the Ho and Co accommodated 140 first- and second-year students; 121 were Queen's Scholars and 19 privately funded. Successful candidates were listed in order of merit. Did this determine their places at the table and in the dormitories, as at the Borough Road College (founded in 1804)? In view of Charlotte's strong antipathy to competition, this seems likely.[28]

On 25 March 1860, the quarter day known as 'Lady Day' (the Feast of the Annunciation to the Blessed Virgin Mary), Cook reported that there were 124 Queen's Scholars and 16 others in residence at the Ho and Co; 83 Queen's Scholars and 16 non-government funded students had left.[29] It is not known where Charlotte stayed awaiting admission, unless she had to return to Holy Trinity School. More fortunate, Lizzie Pendlebury came from a settled Preston family. Her father, Jeremiah, aged 44, was a millwright. Ann, her mother, was 39 when Lizzie left for London at just 18. In 1860, Lizzie's older sister Mary was 20, her younger sister Ann was 13 and her brother Richard was 10. Her maternal grandfather lived with the family.[30]

The non-government students, 'qualifying to become governesses and teachers for private families and superior schools', lived in a separate house 'a little distance from the Institution', attending for classes and teaching practice with their designated governess. The training of middle-class women had been recommended by Mrs Frances Buss, Frances Mary's mother.[31] No doubt this select group was better fed and more smartly dressed than the Queen's Scholars; their families had paid for their tuition, board and residence. Glimpses of these privileged ladies probably aroused mixed feelings in Charlotte and her fellow students.

Frances Widdowson has described the Spartan life at the training colleges, borne out by Spencer's experiences at Borough Road in 1892.[32] Charlotte probably boarded with Lizzie at 11-17 St Chad's Row, in one of the Ho and Co's Georgian houses. By 1861, Lizzie was living there with fifty-one fellow students. Harriet Williams, aged fifty, was the superintendent head of the household; five Ho and Co schoolmistresses lived in the block with two superintendents in charge of the schools, two cooks, four housemaids

The children's playground at the Home and Colonial Training College.

and one kitchen maid. The junior chaplain lived next door at 18 St Chad's Row.[33] Women students were usually expected to undertake strenuous domestic chores to prepare them to run a schoolhouse and instruct future pupils in housecraft. With cooks and maids in residence at St Chad's Row, Ho and Co women doubtless had more time for study, exercise and rest than students at smaller colleges.

Cook's report, describing Charlotte's year, noted that the Ho and Co dormitories were spacious and airy. Curtains may have protected the students' privacy in place of stuffy, wooden-partitioned cubicles. There was space for a single bed, a small chest of drawers, a wash-basin and chair. The day began early with study before prayers and breakfast. Classes took up most of the day; the students prepared the next day's work in the large classroom, supervised by a governess. They only returned to their sleeping quarters at specified times.

To ease the students' highly structured sixteen-hour day, Cook allocated four hours for exercise, recreation and household chores. There were eight hours for lectures and lessons, including school observations and practice teaching, needlework and music, leaving two hours for private study. The three meals took up two hours, leaving eight hours for sleep.

There was no garden apart from the school playground. The previous year, Cook had boldly advised shortening the lectures to allow more time for walks and relaxation, recommending two daily walks of three quarters of an hour rather than one hour's exercise. He regretted that 'owing to the conditions of the property in that crowded locality, the students have not sufficient opportunities for exercise and recreation on the premises or in the immediate neighbourhood.'[34]

St Bartholomew's Chapel on Gray's Inn Road, built in 1811, was consecrated as the district church by the Rt Revd A.C. Tait (1811–1882), Bishop of London, on 13 February 1860. The Revd E. Garbutt had been the evangelical vicar since 1849.[35] The students probably attended Sunday morning services but were free in the afternoons. Lottie and Lizzie may have met William Huston (1811–1880) at church. A Protestant bachelor in his fifties from Kilrea in Londonderry, he was a Scripture reader, or verger. Lizzie recalled his friendly invitations to Kentish Town:

> Mr Huston – very much attached. Dear old man seemed to live for others. Chose ½ dozen girls to come to tea. She kept up her acquaintance with him, 'a charming friend for eternity'.[36]

Did Charlotte, the needy orphan, reach out for a spiritual father figure? She wrote to Mr Huston after leaving London. Although he addressed two letters to Charlotte as 'My dear niece', there is no evidence that they were related. Sally, later Dr Coleman's wife, Charlotte's other longstanding friend, may have joined the tea parties.

In 1859, Cook commissioned Dr J. Pidduck MD, the College physician since 1839, to investigate the students' health and wellbeing. Dr Pidduck examined the 1860 'freshers', including Charlotte, twice: at admission and at the end of the year. He recommended less animal food and more fruits and vegetables, which he had found effective in improving children's health in a servants' school. The students' daily diet was solid and plain. No jam, fresh fruit or vegetables appeared on the menu. Breakfast consisted of bread and butter with tea or coffee. The main meal was dinner; on Sundays, cold salt beef or pork and fruit pies were provided. On other days there were meat pies, roast or boiled beef or mutton. Irish stews appeared from Wednesday to Saturday with bread pudding on Tuesdays. Rice pudding followed the main course daily, except for treacle puddings on Thursdays. Tea was served with bread and butter and cake. There was no mention of supper; maybe the students retired early to get their eight hours sleep.[37]

Reviewing the effect of mental training upon the students' bodily health, Dr Pidduck thought it a mistake

> to suppose that a large amount of bodily exercise is needful to counteract the effects of mental labour; the truth is that persons whose minds are much exercised do not require and cannot bear a great deal of bodily fatigue. I have seen more injury to the health from very long walks on Saturday afternoon and Sunday than from study during the week.

Moderately exercising the arms and upper body in 'pure air' was 'undoubtedly conducive to health'. While deploring the dangers of poor ventilation, he was opposed to opening windows over the hot water pipes lining the classroom walls, claiming the incoming cold air could cause catarrhal and rheumatic complaints by preventing the expulsion of stale air. 'No plan has been devised that is equal to an open fire and wide fireplace.'

> Formerly the practice was to send persons in delicate health to be trained under the erroneous impression that the duty of a schoolmistress was comparatively light and, therefore, suitable for delicate and even deformed young persons. Experience has corrected this error in judgement and proved that a strong sound constitution is requisite to form an efficient teacher.

Pupil-teachers, inured to scholastic discipline, coped better with the mental training required. Dr Pidduck discovered that thirteen students out of seventy-nine who were initially marked 'not strong' were rated as 'strong and in good health' after three months of training. Was Charlotte one of these? As most pupil-teachers came from poor homes, the plentiful food built up their physical strength.

However, excessive mental effort might engender 'erethism', a state of abnormal mental excitement of the nervous system. Symptoms ranged from an inordinate appetite for food to headaches, enteric irritation, stomach pain, 'gastro-blurred' sight and other visual problems and various neuralgic affections. 'Rest and a little medical discipline' effected a cure. When previously healthy students suffered from nervous dispositions, Pidduck concluded that cephalic, thoracic or gastro-enteric irritation was caused by mental anxiety because of family circumstances or fears of examination failure.

Students with intractable physical diseases, such as tuberculosis, would be dismissed from College. Recognising psychological causation, Dr Pidduck accepted that women could study hard and teach well without ill effects. He made no reference to 'overpressure'. Government incentives encouraging women to work hard for their qualifications led to healthier states of body and mind; there were fewer 'disorders of female health and their concomitant hysteria'.[38] A little wholesome neglect was proving effective.

The Ho and Co training master was Robert Dunning (1805–1892). There were two chaplains. The Revd James Joyce Evans was both secretary and general superintendent; he also lectured on religious subjects. The other chaplain, Mr Fleming, taught history and teaching. Of the six governesses, two trained prospective infant schoolmistresses. Seven lecturers taught arithmetic, geography, history, domestic economy, natural history, penmanship and drawing, while eleven teachers were employed in the model and practising schools under Miss Mayo's watchful eye. The Revd J.G.C. Fussell, who inspected the Ho and Co in 1859 with Cook, found that

> The students receive excellent instruction in all subjects. Due care is taken to give them clear and scientific instruction in the principles of education, as regards the formation of character, the development of the faculties and the systematic communication of necessary and useful information. The students are thoroughly grounded in all elementary branches of knowledge and the results of written examinations have been entirely satisfactory for some years. The system of professional training is remarkably complete and efficient.[39]

Born in Ayrshire in Scotland, Robert Dunning lived in Islington with his wife and daughters. He had taught infants in Belfast in 1839 before he was appointed headmaster of the Home and Colonial Training College's model school by the time Miss Clough made her approving visit in 1849.[40] A very experienced training master and master of method, he was one of the permanent fixtures on the staff, writing occasional articles for the Ho and Co's educational paper. Meticulously supervising their work, he knew all his young women students well. By 1860, Mr Hassell was assisting Mr Dunning in the training department.

Cook and Fussell inspected the Ho and Co in July and October 1860. They found the managers had spared no expense in supplying everything the students needed for their training. While deploring the congested streets, Cook saw the advantage of proximity to numerous local poor children who could attend the Ho and Co schools. The model schools were always open to the general public. There were five model classes for infants under eight years and three or four classes for infants and juveniles, taught by a mistress and pupil-teacher in one large room, as in country village schools. The older children aged twelve to fifteen were taught in the model school to

> begin to seek knowledge from books . . . not as recitations, but by getting information which will enable them to answer any question put by the teacher on the subject. In each juvenile section they are accustomed to reproduce in writing the lessons they receive. Morally, they are thrown, to a great extent, on their own responsibility, and accustomed to self-government.

Only second-year students practised in the model schools, where the older children were encouraged to develop habits of attention and independent study. First-year students started in the practising schools, which included four infant galleries and six juvenile classes spread over five separate rooms. Local children were initially admitted to the practising schools. As most of their lessons were given by the student teachers, progress was slower than in the model schools, although they shared the same lesson plans. Jones explained that the aim for infants was 'not to communicate knowledge, but to form good impressions and correct habits . . . to cultivate attention, the power of accurate expression, and, by storing the mind with ideas suitable to the infantine period of life, to lay the foundation for future progress'. Diligence, good conduct and punctual attendance enabled practising school children to upgrade to the model school on quarter day. In each school, the children's work was subject to intense scrutiny.[41]

Fussell described the five steps in the students' two-year training course, rigorously supervised by Mr Dunning. Inbuilt criticism fostered progress at each stage of the daunting work programme. During Step One, from Lady Day to Midsummer 1860, the first-years were lectured on the necessity and advantage of training and shown how the full range of elementary subjects, such as reading and numbers, were to be taught according to the Ho and Co's Pestalozzian method. They then observed a model lesson delivered in the model school, followed by close observation of at least eighteen further lessons on all subjects, noting the steps taken to teach the subjects effectively. Mr Dunning was invariably present to explain the principles upon which each lesson was founded. The full notes each student had to make of her observations were entered into a journal which was then scrutinised by Mr Dunning and his assistants, who made any necessary revisions.

After studying model lesson 'sketches' (plans) on each subject, the students had to write their own lesson sketch along the same lines, to be examined and revised by Mr Dunning and his team. In class 'the faults and excellencies' in each student's record were criticised in turn by the student group, a tough ordeal for anxious students such as Charlotte. There were lecture courses on general teaching, such as the difference between gallery and class instruction, the art of questioning and sketch writing and lessons on all elementary subjects.

At Step Two, lasting six months, the challenges increased with the first important step in practical training. Observation was replaced by six months of teaching in the practising schools for three quarters of an hour on three days a week, exactly reproducing the lessons learnt at Step One. While gaining practical teaching experience under supervision, the students had to concentrate very hard to remember everything they had been taught. Mr Dunning, Mr Hassell, the three practising schools mistresses and the governesses of their class supervised these lessons. They wrote reports on the successes and failures of each student. At the following class, Mr Dunning discussed errors of method with the whole group.[42]

As Charlotte struggled with the intense, if outwardly benign, scrutiny of her practice before confident first-class fellow students, she manifested symptoms of illness. Lizzie recalled these bouts: 'So brave – wake up put all away – Kate Webster, Miss Mason, wishing to be with her at any time.'

Was Charlotte afflicted by the nervous states described by Dr Pidduck? Catherine Webster, aged twenty-four, was the youngest of the three housemaids at St Chad's Row. Did she look after Charlotte with Lizzie, soothing her into sleep? Splitting headaches or indigestion would have been worrying; hyperventilation or palpitations might have been perceived as incipient heart disease.

Charlotte passed the first-year examinations. She was intelligent; the lectures and training had been exceedingly thorough. The class lists have been lost, but none of the Ho and Co students failed. A delighted Cook reported that the results had exceeded all expectations and justified the present system of elementary teacher training.[43] Charlotte must also have passed the first two steps in practical teaching. Yet Lizzie recalled that Charlotte was 'too delicate for the work. . . . Too ill to take the certificate – could have taken it well enough. She was advised to leave after about a year.'[44] Later she allegedly recalled that Charlotte spent her holidays in College as she had no relations. If true, isolation and anxiety would have made her holidays very dreary, with only Kate Webster for company.[45]

At Step Three, in the fourth quarter of the year, from January to Lady Day 1861, those who had passed Step Two class teaching and the infant school teaching had to give lessons on all elementary subjects to be fully criticised by their colleagues, under Mr Dunning's supervision. During the Step Two teaching practice, Cooke observed that the students' lessons were

> remarkable for good arrangement, happy illustration and a clear perception of what children would hear with interest and retain with advantage. The cultivation of the faculties and the inculcation of sound principles both of thought and feeling are rightly held more important than the information which is, however, of intrinsic and practical value.

He was especially delighted with the natural history lessons.

Each student had to prepare a private half-hour lesson to be criticised by a training officer. Then every student had to devise between twelve and fourteen separate sketches of private half-hour lessons, corrected by Mr Dunning, Mr Coghlan, a professor in the art of teaching, or Mr Hassell. If they were dissatisfied, the student had to re-write the sketch to be re-checked *before* delivering the lesson. The training in the art of writing effective lesson plans was extremely thorough.[46]

Mr Dunning, who had successfully trained young women teachers for many years, was caught off guard by our heroine's distress in flunking a Step Three ordeal. An experienced pupil-teacher, did she baulk at her fellow students' criticisms? Although it would have been inappropriate to see her in person, Mr Dunning felt obliged to respond to her acute distress. Tears could be harbingers of disease.

Friday Afternoon

My Dear Miss Mason

I was very sorry indeed this morning when I found that giving a lesson was too much for you. When I saw you first I was exceedingly pleased thinking you were better and strong and not nervous in giving a criticism. Indeed, I felt as if you had lost all fear of me as a critic and regarded me as a friendly genius sitting there to do you a good turn. But oh you naughty girl – it was your own spirit and resolution that would not give way even before disease – that would discharge a duty at whatever it might cost you. You must not attempt another. I shall not let Mr Hassell approach you any more. You can teach well and need only only [*sic*] to study our principles. I liked your lesson much. I trust the good Lord will spare your life and permit you to work in his vineyard a while here. If however his sovereign will – to depart and escape this world and its snares wd. be more for your real and eternal happiness. Do not you love the Saviour, dear Miss Mason and so to behold his face will be glorious. I hope yr affliction does not lead you to repine. You may be young in years but rich in experience and to <u>suffer</u> perfects more and faster than to <u>do</u>. Thus you are brought to be more like the Saviour. May the Lord's presence be with you in all the riches of his power and love and give you when the summons comes an abundant entrance into his everlasting kingdom, which is a kingdom of glory, not of suffering. . . . [This section of the letter has been cut out.]

I could not leave comfortably without scribbling this note. I was so grieved.

Affectionately R. Dunning[47]

Mr Dunning was shaken by Charlotte's reaction. At first unsure what was wrong, he concluded Charlotte was dangerously ill. His letter, written in the expectation that she was not long for this world, may have shocked Charlotte to the core, although she may have escaped many classes through illness. Rising to teach an elementary subject to her fellow students, Charlotte manifested perturbing symptoms; perhaps she fainted or wept. Mr Dunning had already lost two daughters and was gloomily pessimistic about signs of disease in women, convinced that Charlotte might die young.

In the cut-out section of this letter, Mr Dunning may have intimated that Charlotte might have to leave the Home and Colonial Training College at Lady Day. Those too ill to finish the course were required to go. Study was still regarded by some, notably Mr Dunning, as injurious to women. Mr Dunning's precious letter, retained for life, set Charlotte apart as a special person, an unfolded bud, whose sufferings had brought her closer to her Saviour. His 'over religious' assumption that the patient suffering her mother had endured led to perfection would haunt Charlotte all her days.

Charlotte missed Step Four, which involved three weeks of intensive observation and reporting on the teaching in the model schools, followed by the final certificate exam. In the first quarter of 1862, she would miss the final step, Step Five, which included first assisting and then running one of the nine small practising schools under the supervision of a mistress, lectures on the mental and moral constitution of children, the professional training of pupil-teachers and school organisation and much further study.

The Committee of Council insisted on ensuring value for the monetary outlay on Queen's Scholarships. Lingen's letter to the HMIs on 2 June 1856 directed that the renewal of a student's Queen's Scholarship for the second year depended upon the principal's confirmation that the first year had been successfully passed *and* that the second year would be completed to the Ho and Co's high standard.[48] No doubt a conference was held between Mr Dunning, the governess, Dr Pidduck and the principal to decide Charlotte's future. With the thoughtful care they showed towards all their students, they may have considered the detrimental effects of urban congestion and study upon her health, her orphan status and Mr Dunning's assurance that she could teach well.

The kindly Ho and Co officers found her a post at a well-established infant school with Ho and Co connections in Sussex. Leaving her friends behind on Lady Day 1861, Charlotte travelled to Worthing as the new mistress of the William Davidson Infantine School in the Broadwater parish district.

9.

Mistress of the Davison Memorial Infantine School in Worthing, 1861–1873

> Allow me to inform you, my dear E that I am at present bearing a higher honour than you can ever hope to receive. I am the Mistress of the first infant school that was ever established in the British Empire. How I wish you could see my children – Some are such sweet little cherubs, and some such noble little Washingtons, and some such tiresome little monkeys. . . . I should like to send you one of my children to London in a bandbox. She would be like a week in the country to you all, she would refresh you so much. She gives herself the name of 'itta Loui', and is the most loveable little lisper that I think I ever knew.[1]

The move to Worthing by the sea, far from London congestion and Birkenhead miseries, was exactly what Charlotte needed. Only nineteen, Charlotte had left her training prematurely but, like Miss Stevens, she was now in charge. Her great-grandfather, John Gough, had taken over the Cork Friends' school at about the same tender age. Remaining in Worthing for twelve years and eight months, she would enjoy excellent health inherited from her father, gain the certificate and win respect for her capabilities as a professionally qualified headmistress. An influential friendship would engender new dreams.

On census day, 7 April 1861, Charlotte was settled in lodgings at 39 High Street in central Worthing. Her landlady was Mrs Fanny Redford, a 70-year-old widow. The other lodger was a 21-year-old painter and glazier called William J.C. Collins. Her initial salary of £35 per annum with the £10 lodgings allowance promised independence with blessed freedom from domestic chores; there was no schoolhouse.[2]

Created as a town in 1803, Worthing had clean water and main drainage thanks to the efforts of Thomas Shaw Brandreth (1788–1873), Justice of the Peace and first chairman of Worthing's Board of Health from 1852 to 1858. The population rose from 9,744 inhabitants in 1861 to about 12,000 by 1874 as Worthing developed as a pleasant seaside resort. The new pier was completed by April 1862; the royal baths on Marine Parade offered warm, cold and medicated vapour baths; there were bathing machines on the beach. During the 1860s, lectures, concerts and public meetings were held in the two large halls; the libraries provided daily papers and general periodicals. The smooth sands lying below the shingle stretched for 4 miles. On summer evenings, Charlotte could stroll along the promenade or take a turn in Steyne Gardens.[3]

The Revd William Davison MA (1779–1852) was the first chaplain serving the Worthing Chapel of Ease. Passionately concerned about the education of poor children, he energetically opened his first school in a barn in 1812 and is warmly remembered for founding the Davison Infantine School in 1817. His determination to establish National Society and free schools in Worthing and Broadwater anticipated Dr Joseph Baylee's zeal; his achievements are highly valued today.[4]

Taking on the established infant school in Chapel Road was a tough challenge for the new mistress. The Committee of Council regarded infant schools as 'public nurseries for children from the very earliest age at which they are able to walk alone and speak, up to the age of seven'. For those 'a little advanced beyond helplessness of the first stage of infancy', the teachers 'impart the sort of instruction which in the wealthier classes of society is conveyed almost imperceptibly by constant intercourse with educated persons'. As men worked from 6:00am to 6:00pm and mothers were busy with domestic tasks, 'the house is not furnished with objects which awaken intelligence, nor has anyone the leisure to form the manners and temper of the child'. Infant schools filled these gaps; they kept poor children off the streets and protected them from injury. The report added that teachers impart 'knowledge, which although apparently small in amount, is of high value and habits of docility and submission to discipline which are of still higher importance'.[5]

The Chapel of Ease was the first Anglican church in the Worthing district of Broadwater parish. Facing Chapel Road, the elegant Doric portico had four columns. Consecrated in 1812, this proprietary chapel was not a mission church, like Holy Trinity, but served the upper and middle classes, who purchased or rented pews. Profitable collections for the parish schools were taken twice yearly by titled ladies and gentlemen holding plates at the door.[6]

High boxed-in pews filled the main body of the chapel. The gallery, with three tiers of pews, ran round the upper walls of the church, supported on Doric pillars. On holy days, Charlotte and her pupils perched at the west end of the gallery, discreetly accessed from the porch. They could gaze down on the Beadle's three-cornered hat and blue coat with a gold collar and large gold-trimmed pockets, as he preceded the chaplain in stately manner up the aisle holding a black staff with a brass crown. Or they could stare across at the preacher in the three-decker pulpit. At Sunday services Charlotte listened

Returning Health *by Thomas Falcon Marshall (1818–1878).*

intently to the sermons, some perhaps verging towards the liberalism of the 'broad church'.[7] The metrical psalms favoured by Protestant worshippers may have been chanted. In due time, *Hymns Ancient and Modern* (1861) replaced the private collection of thirty-six hymns. Closed in 1996, the former chapel has been conserved as an events hall and café.[8]

The Revd William Read MA Cantab. (1799–1884), manager of Davison School, ministered at Worthing Chapel of Ease from 1852 until 1882 under the Rector of Broadwater's oversight. A late entrant to the ministry, Read was ordained priest in 1846, after his Manchester diaconate. Accepting a modest stipend of £150 per annum, his move to Worthing in Chichester diocese was dictated by his wife's poor health. Mrs Sarah Read died on 14 May 1853. Their daughter Mary (1829–1877) kept house for her father, assisting with their charitable endeavours and the management of Davison School.[9]

> Although considered pompous by many, he [Mr Read] could at times unbend and become quite frivolous (in an overbearing way), his manner and bearing were such as to crush any bad conduct of rough lads and others he might meet in the street, he always taught them to pay due respect to those over them. . . . He was a deep thinker with a great and wide-ranged knowledge of theological writers and the English classics as well as astronomy and microscopy.

The polymath chaplain used to work the lathe while delivering lectures on mechanics and kept up his scientific studies; the wide horizon gave clear access to starry skies.[10]

Mr Brandreth joined the Reads on the Memorial Committee which planned the new single-storey Davison Infantine School in Chapel Road, based on the Home and Colonial Training College's model infant school design. A small classroom adjoined the galleried main room. Gallery teaching with monitors was still taught and practised at the Ho and Co in Charlotte's time. Re-established in the new building in Chapel Road in 1854, the school was run by a certificated mistress from the Ho and Co and an assistant mistress, teaching the children needlework, knitting and straw plaiting, the three Rs and Christian principles.[11] As with other National Schools, fundraising was an ongoing preoccupation. The children of respectable tradesfolk attended the Davison Infantine School. From 1861, the rebuilt Christ Church girls' and infants' school, situated to the south of the church, accepted the poorest children in Worthing.[12]

The intellectual guidance of the well-read chaplain was of immense benefit to Charlotte, who won his respect. Mr Read made a substantial contribution to the cultural life of Worthing. Preaching at the highest level, he had

> the most unusual, but most excellent practice of recommending books to read. He was constantly doing this from the pulpit. He recommended such books as Watts' *Logic*; the Duke of Argyle's *Reign of Law*, Locke's *Essay on Human Understanding* and other books which train the mind to think and raise it above the humdrum or butterfly condition into which it so frequently drifts.[13]

Mary Read was a model of efficiency and intelligence, masked by womanly decorum, as she guided the mistress in the day to day running of the school. She regularly taught the children.

> One could not help being struck with that absence of obtrusiveness and ostentation which was such a distinguishing feature of her character, so quickly did she move that she was working when no one saw her work. . . . Most of us can bear witness to her gentle persuasiveness, the grasp of her intellect . . . to her possession of every characteristic which belongs to a woman as she should be, to her capacity for dealing with questions which do not usually engage the thoughts of the honoured sex. Few knew the accuracy of her estimates for carrying on the work of the schools during the coming year – the exactness which invariably accompanied the banking transactions which necessarily devolved on her.[14]

Regarding her with awe, Charlotte absorbed Miss Read's quietly effective approach. Father and daughter gave kindly encouragement. Louisa Hubbard (1836–1906), an Anglican deaconess promoting the training of ladies as elementary teachers, graphically illustrated the humble standing of the elementary school teacher:

> Where the mistress of the parish school is really a lady, there is little fear but that she will be very soon recognised as such by her equals of either sex and respected by her inferiors. She ought at least to be able to reckon upon the Christian Courtesy and good breeding of her clergyman and his wife, and among the few friends of the quiet society befitting her modest position, she may suffer less from isolation than a governess in a private family, besides the valued privilege of having time to herself when the duties of her day are over.[15]

Charlotte took comfort from sharing her innermost thoughts with Lizzie Pendlebury in weekly letters:

> I am all alone here; there is no one with whom I can seek that sympathy which is such a craving of my nature. I live within 5 minutes walk of the sea, and yet until this evening I have not even been there. . . . This evening, however, old Mrs R took me in hand, and after a great deal of persuasion . . . I got into a retired part of the beach and stood watching the sea, half inclined to cry, half inclined to laugh, and more than half-inclined to scream with a strange wild joy, and throw myself in, and join with the mad gambols of the waves. . . . I cannot tell you how passionately, how intensely I love the Sea.[16]

Aflame with indecorous 'early Victorian' emotionalism, perhaps overlaid with repressed childhood memories of the seaside, this letter, omitted from *The Story,* exposed powerful yearnings. Dear Lizzie could be trusted to understand her friend's turmoil; she also warmly encouraged Lottie to study for the certificate:

> Thank you very much for your advice respecting my studies. I will try to follow it as closely as possible, though as you will easily believe, studying for a certificate after a hard day's teaching is not without its difficulties. With one hour's intermission, I teach from 9 till 4. But yet, I am happy in my work and should not let its being hard, prove a hindrance to me. I have some very sweet characters among my children, some that I love much already. One pretty general feature is a strict honesty and uncompromising faithfulness. Is not that encouraging? . . . Fancy! I have been here four weeks today.[17]

While Charlotte's Pestalozzian training inhibited her from wielding the cane, she must have forcefully raised her voice many times a day to calm disruptive children. For the Centenary celebrations, a former pupil recalled joining the infants' school, seemingly unchanged since Charlotte Mason's day. She stood by

> the old tortoise stove awaiting instructions and being directed up the wooden steps to sit on long wooden forms arranged in tiers at one end of the room and from which sixty of us gazed with longing at Class 1

already old enough to sit in the real desks (long wooden benches with seats) and really to write and do arithmetic. . . . A noisy screen was pushed back and forth after morning assembly and at night to separate Standards 1, 2, 3, and 4 (all in one room with two teachers) from the big girls, under another assistant and the Headmistress.[18]

As the strain was beginning to tell, Charlotte poured out her anxieties about her certificate studies and being a bad teacher to Mr Dunning.

My Dear Miss Mason

Although your last letter reached me in due course, two months and more have elapsed since. . . . You must think that I have forgotten you & have given me up as a faithless correspondent and Friend. Pray do not think anything of the kind. Since I returned home affliction upon affliction has come upon me like so many rolling waves in the storm. I have lost one of my dear children, a daughter. My second, a girl of 22, not long since apparently strong & healthy & sure of long life. My own health has also been very indifferent & my poor wife still ill. – My visit to Scotland did me very little good. – But the Lord has declared that in life's troubles he will be with us in lessons that teach us. Bless His name, my hope is in him. And believe me dear girl, I consider your case a far more trying one than mine. An orphan, alone & a stranger and a woman too. Ah, I would rather close the eyes & adjust in the coffin the last of my dear daughters than leave them orphans to weep for me and their once comfortable home without any in a cold world to be their protector and guide. My heart is always very tender towards the orphan. Within seven years, I have buried three & have now only two left. . . . They all died in the faith of the Gospel.

I do hope dear child that your mind is more at ease & comfortable than it was when you wrote in August. I do understand how very wicked you may feel in your heart & yet be a Christian. It is 'Christ in us' the hope of glory, not a pure and sinless heart in us the hope of glory. Paul called himself a wicked man. Are you lower than that? If you can say 'with the mind I serve' – then you are safe. . . . Without any hesitation I say to you if you are still hesitating – go on. Yes surely go on & go on consciencioulsy [*sic*] oh yes and cheerfully, & thankfully. But do not without a Doctor's advise [*sic*] attempt trying for a certificate. Let your lawful desire to occupy the ground of a certificated teacher be put aside. God speaks to you in disease these words. Do not excite the brain and central nervous system or you are a dead or useless woman. Is it not better to work without a certificate than to possess a certificate and be unable for work afterwards. I sympathise with you in yr desire but teach & improve yourself steadily but gently & perhaps at Xmas 1862 you may be strong enough. I hope your pride is not an unworthy pride.

> If I were near you when you talk about sinning against the souls of the children I fear that I should scold or do something worse. You can only use the means of spiritual good not the good itself. I do not believe a word about your want of wisdom & love. And as to your moods, I am prepared to hear that you go through all the moral moods and tenses too & yet you should when you get into the indicative assert without reserve all you know and feel of the best love and like to God. Glorious parsing. . . . And so I must say the Lord bless you and keep you in his sure keeping in his own arms. And though with carefulness, firmness, kindness and love as you said, I must subscribe myself, yours very affectionately R. Dunning.[19]

Mr Dunning's two letters were preserved as guiding lights. An excellent training master, immersed in grammar, who genuinely cared for the wellbeing of the student teachers, he preached an uncompromising gospel of affliction which reinforced Charlotte's weak, inferior status. More than anyone, he understood the overwhelming demands of crowded classrooms, yet he clung to the old-fashioned belief that excessive study could perilously endanger the health of his delicate former student. Charlotte's gaze was fixed on heaven; Mr Dunning's concern, overlaid with his own morbid distress, authoritatively confirmed that she *was* as seriously ill as her College friends believed.

Recalling Charlotte's weekly letters sent from Worthing during the 1860s, Mrs Groveham told Miss Kitching in 1923, 'What I set great store upon are the Sunday Letters – precious and numerous – and, who knows, but they may find an echo in your Sunday afternoon gatherings, where, She being dead, yet speaketh.'[20] Charlotte wrote to Lizzie, probably during this first year of teaching.

> I believe for spiritual growth, I would rather receive affliction than blessings – the latter bring so many temptations with them. But then all things work together for good to them that love God. We had a sermon tonight on I Cor.2 v.9. 'Eye hath not seen nor ear heard, neither hath it entered into the heart of man, the things which God hath prepared for them that love Him.' I always thought the passage referred to the joys of a future state, but the clergyman who preached tonight proved from the context & from the passage from which it is given that this language is used to denote only those joys which godliness will bring to its possessor in this present life.[21]

Like other earnest evangelical women of her generation, Charlotte's quest for personal holiness would be lifelong. In seeking the light to guide her to the next world, Charlotte was developing a personal ministry embedded in her paternal heritage, with Lizzie as the only member of her flock. Esoteric advice from their kindly old friend, Mr Huston, was passed on:

> 'Choose no friends but those whose society you would wish to enjoy through Eternity.' Is it not a beautiful thought? The business of making that eternity a happy one belongs to ourselves and under God to each other.[22]

Charlotte advised Lizzie

> that it is for our temporal as well as spiritual growth to be much in prayer with our God. Often in our prayers at the fag end of the day and tired out, we often mumble a set of words. . . . I cannot help thinking that in this way, many draw down curses instead of blessings. So to remedy, so far as in me lies, this great evil, I have made up my mind as soon as tea is over, when I feel quite fresh, I will devote half or ¾ of an hour to Bible reading & earnest prayer. I think that by thus 'seeking first the Kingdom of Heaven' I shall be sure to – nay, I will say no more, lest I receive my answers in this life and may Heaven keep me from that.[23]

As Lizzie's December examinations approached, Charlotte masked her own fears with sanctimonious advice:

> 'The Lot is cast into the lap, but the whole disposing thereof it is of the Lord.' Such is the text I have chosen for your support and comfort in this week of trial. . . . Trust in the Lord. When you have not answered questions as you could have wished, do not worry & murmur & chide with yourself, for in so doing, you murmur against our God, and forget not that he is a God 'unto whom all hearts are open'. . . . [R]emember that the whole disposing of thy lot is of the Lord, that the victory cometh not by might, nor by power but only through the Spirit of the Lord. Get all the strength you can for this emergency – be much in prayer – struggle against a weary body & still weary mind. Try to carry a calm strong heart, 'Strong in the strength which God supplies through his eternal Son.'[24]

Well-prepared, Lizzie achieved a first-class certificate, minus the five drawing competencies.[25] The friends spent Christmas together. A lifelong monarchist, Charlotte returned from church on Sunday saying, 'I have some sad news – the death of the Prince Consort.'[26]

Mr Read, a scrupulous mentor, expected the best from Charlotte, undeterred by fear of pressurising her. He introduced her to psychology and encouraged wide reading. His favourite maxim was 'Throw perfection into all you do'.[27] Having sent for the examination syllabus for teachers in schools from the Committee of Council by 1 November 1862, he confirmed that Charlotte would sit the examination in December, supported by his recommendation and two favourable reports from the HMI. The published class lists show that Charlotte took the second-year papers at Christmas 1862, the earliest permitted time.[28]

The exam questions covered the same broad range. Religious knowledge included questions on the Catechism, liturgy, Church history, doctrine and the Old and New Testaments, such as, '1. State the doctrine of our Church upon two or more of the following points, as defined in the Articles, and prove it by plain declarations of Holy Writ – The Person of Christ, the Godhead of the Holy Ghost, the sufficiency of Holy Scripture, Original Sin and the Justification of Man.' Or, 'State the conditions on which sins are forgiven, and the privileges of the Christian Covenant are secured. Quote texts.' Other papers for female candidates were on history, geography, book-keeping, music, school management, drawing and grammar. For example, for geography, 'Give some account of the physical features and natural and artificial productions of the eastern counties of England,' and for history, 'Which institutions of the Saxons have left the most permanent effects upon our history and laws?'

The arithmetic paper included 'What is the meaning and object of a profit and loss account? Is it different from an income and expenditure account? Give an example.' Or, 'A person's weekly expenditure is £15.5s. What must be his daily income that, at the end of eleven years, he may have saved £425.18s.8d., supposing that the first year is leap year?' For domestic economy, there were practical, class-related questions such as, 'Calculate the cost of clothing [for] a girl sixteen years old. State the materials you would recommend, and justify your calculations.' Or, 'Give clear directions to a young cook as to the faults to be guarded against in common culinary processes.' A third demanded, 'Write a short letter of advice to a girl about to take the place of kitchen-maid or nurse-maid.' A fourth question asked, 'On what principles would you recommend a particular way of investing money or effecting insurance, in the case either of a labouring man or a young school teacher?' Finally, 'Prepare notes for one or two lessons on some of the following subjects: 1. Habits injurious to health and strength. 2. The treatment of some common maladies, including symptoms and best modes of prevention. 3. The folly and sin of showy and expensive clothing.'[29] Fortunately Charlotte had heard sermons announcing 'on at least one Sunday out of four' that 'habit is ten natures'.[30] Preparing for these questions offered a baseline for future writings.

Charlotte trumped the competition. Successful candidates were listed alphabetically. She won a first division place with one other teacher, Sarah Grant, also from the Ho and Co, ahead of seventeen in the second division, thirty-one in the third division and twelve in the fourth. Like Charlotte and Lizzie, most teachers failed drawing. Sarah Grant got two competencies; another teacher obtained one.[31]

Certification ensured government funding for half of Charlotte's salary. Formally certificated in July 1863, Charlotte had won headmistress status, a salary rise to £50 per annum and a lodgings allowance of £13.[32] After only

Charlotte's first thrilling visit to Ambleside in 1864.

one year's training, her certificate could not be confirmed within the usual two years. She would have to wait five years at the same school for the upgrading of her certificate, backed by five favourable HMI annual reports. A change of school would have delayed ratification of her first-class status.[33]

The Revd R.L. Koe, HMI for the south-eastern district, who was said to provide 'an invariably prompt, friendly and efficient service', regularly inspected Davison Infantine School. On 25 November 1863 he recorded Charlotte as 'Mistress 1/1' in the log book, presumably signifying a first-class certificate after one year's training. For the next seven years he inexplicably recorded that Charlotte was '3/1'; did that mean gaining the certificate three years after starting the training? It is not known. Tied to Worthing, she had to wait *eight years*, until certificates were re-classified under the New Code of 1871, to be duly affirmed as a first-class teacher in the first division (1/1) by Koe's colleague, Mr Knocker. The strain of waiting and the taxing annual inspections put her off governmental regulations for life, although Koe always acknowledged her capabilities.[34]

Charlotte first visited Selina Healey at Ambleside in 1864. That year, Selina moved Miss Clough's school, opened in 1852, to Loughrigg View. Charlotte spent several holidays there and helped in the school; Herbert Bell (1856–1946), later a gifted photographer, recalled Charlotte taking classes in 1865.[35] After Selina married John Fleming, a local architect, the school was based at Fairfield View from 1868 to 1880. The Flemings had no children.

Studying with Mr Read had extended Charlotte's intellectual aspirations, and spiritual development. Inscribed with 'his kindest ever remembrances' in February 1866, Mr Read gave her a treasured copy of Dean Goulburn's *Thoughts on Personal Religion* (1861), a treatise on devotional reading, prayer, the spiritual life, the high prerogative of suffering and the public service of the Church.[36] Associating with local Oxbridge clergy and the gentlemen and lady visitors to the school and observing the superior classes attending the Chapel of Ease enabled Charlotte to develop the social graces and pleasing manner facilitating her rise through the rigid social structures keeping elementary schoolteachers in their place.

Robert Lowe's Revised Code (1862) came into force on 1 June 1863. In 1861, the Newcastle Commissioners had expressed concerns about the irregular attendance of children at school and low attainment in the three Rs following their investigation into the state of popular education in England. Value for money was paramount; the outcome was a complex performance-related system of grant funding. Infants aged 2 to 6 were too young to be tested by 6 new standards measuring fixed levels of attainment in the three Rs. The few Davison School children aged over 7 were annually assessed by the HMI. Examination failures and poor attendance forfeited specific grants, such as 6s 6d for each absent child under six or an unsatisfactory general report on the school. Average attendance throughout the year could win or lose 4s per child. Scholars who attended over 200 morning or afternoon sessions and passed the tests earned 8s each, but forfeited 2s 8d for every subject failed by the HMI. Fortunately for Charlotte, Miss Read competently supervised this bureaucratic piecemeal funding system.

The minimalist six standards for the three Rs were linked to age and ability. At Standard I, pupils were required to read monosyllabic words, write upper and lower case letters from dictation and count up to twenty. By Standard V, pupils had to show that they could read some lines of poetry from a school reading book, write one sentence slowly dictated from a reading book used in the first class and solve a sum in compound rules (common weights and measures). By Standard VI, pupils were expected to read a passage in a newspaper, write a short piece from dictation and solve a 'sum in practice or bills in parcels'.[37] The funding system pressurised managers to attract new pupils, boost attendance figures and retain those who had started school but were kept at home to help with lodgers or work in the fields during the summer.

From 1863, certificated teachers could instruct working adults and children over the age of twelve for 1½ hours. Attendance at twenty-four evening classes brought in 2s 6d per student and 5s for each annual test passed; 1s 8d was deducted for each failure. Charlotte ran an evening school for two winters.[38]

> We have recommenced our Night Sch. & got a few fresh pupils. I am having a terrible struggle to get my School under foot & am in hopes I shall succeed. Will it not be a good thing? I have as usual been making wonderful resolutions about what I shall do when we begin school again. I mean to be so firm, so kind, so loving, so altogether admirable. I really feel half-inclined to fall down at the feet of what I 'mean to be' & say 'Stand there & be my admiration – & my praise.' Alas! I may do so, for 'what I mean to be' is the only part of myself that I shall ever be

> able to admire. How are Mother & Father, Sisters and brother & the dear little stranger? . . . I should like to see you before you go to your School. . . . Who knows, if I change my school, I shall certainly try to get one up north. And now Love I think I have given you a sufficient dose of very 'small talk.' Your ever most loving friend Lottie.[39]

Objections to the restrictive Revised Code were raised by the Home and Colonial Training College and the poet Matthew Arnold, a highly experienced lay HMI (1851–1888) for non-conformist schools. Payment by results fostered mechanical instruction by rote to the detriment of developing children's intelligence through learning languages, history and geography. By 1867, the Code enabled pupils to earn grants from passes in 'special' or 'higher' subjects, notably geography and history. Skills in singing, drawing, knitting and needlework were assessed as part of the overall efficiency of the school.[40]

Keeping the log book was compulsory. Tantalising glimpses of life at the Davison contained within leave much to the imagination. The mistress had to make brief factual daily entries about the ordinary progress of the school, staff appointments and illness. Attendance was recorded in the school registers. The Ho and Co added extra guidance, based on the model schools' best practice, recommending the description of punishments and visits by managers and clergy. Although Charlotte always had pupil-teachers and one or two assistant mistresses, apart from mentioning one failing pupil-teacher, she recorded nothing about their capabilities.

On the first day, she wrote, 'Monday June 1st 1863. Children re-assembled after Whitsun holidays, rather unsettled and a good deal of marching and drilling necessary.' Managing order and noise levels was a constant challenge; some monitors could not control their classes. The girls were idle at needlework. Once, the infants took their slates home to do written exercises. Past efforts could not be reviewed as slates were wiped clean for the next day's written work.

Despite two fireplaces, the schoolroom was cold in winter. The grimy black dust in the playground brought complaints from parents about their children's dirty clothes and boots. Troublesome boys climbed into the playground and damaged school property. Some children were punished after misbehaving in chapel on Ash Wednesday. Tired by the end of the week, the children had to be cajoled into learning something, from infants struggling to master the names and shapes of capital letters to older girls bemused by multiplication tables. Standard I children improved rapidly when reading from boards. 'On June 10th 1863 the children were a little unsettled owing to the introduction of new books, with which they were greatly pleased.' An older girl monitor read a little story to the babies, which they enjoyed. In 1864, Charlotte selected *The Irish Second Book* for

Standard II and Nelson's *Step by Step* for Standard I, probably from very limited choice. The first class of the infant school (seven-year-olds) read the Psalms for Sunday and apparently wrote out the Collect, which the mistress said should be done every Friday. Victorian children were expected to understand the King James Bible and the Book of Common Prayer without interpretation, a practice accepted by Charlotte.

In 1865 a visiting clergyman was greatly struck by the healthy appearance of the children. Otherwise, the children caught the usual illnesses, from coughs and colds to epidemics of mumps and scarlet fever. Absenteeism was caused by bad winter weather or very hot summer days. The mistress sent a pupil-teacher out if children arrived without their weekly pence or to chase up absentees. The annual holiday on Coronation Day, 28 June 1864, was enjoyed. Any public event excited the children, such as the yearly regatta off the beach or the grand demonstration honouring the Prince of Wales on 9 November 1863.

> Tuesday January 12th 1864. Admitted several girls into the middle school and spent the morning receiving the parents.

There had been plans to extend the school since 1862. The steady admission of girls with ages ranging from seven or eight to ten or eleven meant that a new classroom was urgently needed to relieve overcrowding. Funds were raised. Charlotte's girls' 'middle school' was a second classroom with glazed, diamond-patterned windows, added to the building by 25 July 1865. Everyone was relieved when the disruptive building work ceased. At the grand opening there was a lavish tea, with prayers, singing and addresses by Mr Read and the Revd Henry Beverley, MA Cantab., his curate from 1865 to 1868, who also took classes.

The admission of older girls, eligible to take the standards, boosted the government grant, replacing those moving to elementary schools and the need for night school pupils. Charlotte expressed concern about the *tone* in the girls' class; Miss Read hoped that when the new scholars had settled in, the children would be as nice as ever. On 16 May 1865, Charlotte wrote hopefully,

> Find that the Girls' School causes many more respectable children to attend the infants and leads it to be generally held in higher repute.[41]

Attendance numbers for the girls and infants, usually recorded in spring, remained high. Starting with 120 in 1862 and rising to 180 by 1863, the numbers fell to 161 in 1867 but rose again to 180 in 1872, reaching 210 by May 1873.[42]

Mr Read visited the school to hear the girls reading or to give a moral talk. He advised the girls on the importance of self-culture and reproved the infants for their dirty boots. Miss Read took reading, writing, dictation, arithmetic, singing and needlework. A Miss Cholmley taught singing and gave a natural history object lesson on the bat. There were visits from Management Committee members, subscribers and representatives from the Diocese of Chichester. Close links with the Ho and Co were upheld.[43]

Copy registers listing admissions from April 1865 to January 1874 show that the older girls' parents were respectably employed as sailors, labourers, pleasure men, a sea captain, footmen, ostlers, butchers, bakers, fishermen, carpenters, builders, gardeners, bricklayers, publicans, coach builders, shoe makers, painters, porters, plumbers, ironmongers, rag dealers, shopkeepers and engineers. The few single mothers were lodging-house keepers, dressmakers, seamstresses, washerwomen and housekeepers and one schoolmistress.[44]

The HMI arrived in winter when the children were more likely to be absent with coughs or colds. Hopefully, they were *not* dragged from their beds to be present at the inspection, as reputedly happened elsewhere. The staff carefully prepared the children. On 8 November 1864, Miss Read tested the older girls' arithmetic; they wrote practice exams on Scripture, geography and history. As school manager, Mr Read summarised the HMI report on 2 March 1865:

> This is worked as a Girls' and Infants' School in one large room, with two classrooms, the whole under the management of Miss Mason, two assistants and one pupil-teacher. Much skill and judgement are shown by Miss Mason in the management of so large a number of children, all of whom seem to receive a due share of her attention. The scripture lessons are remarkably well given.

Koe commended Miss Mason's ability and integrity in conducting the school. Although 'the weak point was numeration in the second standard', threatening grant withdrawal in 1866, he noted Miss Mason's 'industry and assiduity'. In December 1867, Koe reported that 'the School is conducted by Miss Mason in a thoroughly conscientious manner and with very creditable results'. In October, Miss Gaston from the Ho and Co was pleased with the orderliness of the school and the children's attainments.[45]

Charlotte followed Pestalozzi's directive that love is the best means of communication. In January 1868, Flora Lindup, a star pupil born on 6 September 1860 who was the daughter of a painter from Alfred Place, joined the girls' class after passing Standard I in 1868. She gained Standard II in 1869, Standard III in 1870, Standard IV in 1871, Standard V in 1872 and Standard VI in 1874 before leaving school in May 1875. At the Centenary celebrations in 1912, she recalled,

> Miss Mason was my teacher. She was very nice. She taught me to knit and took me home to tea, so I must have been good. I didn't like history but I liked all the other things we did.

Flora Lindup shone as the *only* girl to pass Standard V by 1872.[46] Although the girls were taught and tested in subjects such as history, geography and religious knowledge as well as music, drawing and plain needlework, passes in the higher subjects were only achieved in 1867 and 1873, illustrating the difficulty of achieving results under the Code.

After 1862, Lizzie married a Somerset man, John Groveham (1831–1882). He was ten years older and a gilder. Lizzie's marriage probably prevented her serving the two years full-time teaching in a government-funded school to confirm her first-class certificate. She opened a private ladies' school in 1866.[47]

Championed by the Ho and Co, middle-class education for girls was emerging as the new crusade thanks to steady campaigning by Miss Buss, Miss Beale and Miss Clough, who were amongst those who gave evidence to the Schools Inquiry Commission (Taunton Commission) (1864–1868) investigating secondary education. A viable national system addressing the separate requirements of the different social classes and genders was urgently needed; the Commission identified only thirteen secondary schools for girls. 'It cannot be denied that the picture brought before us of the state of Middle Class Female Education is, on the whole, unfavourable.' The commissioners sensibly recognised that 'girls could attain the same level of intellectual education as boys', taking gender differences into account. The value of early liberal education was emphasised:

> Clearness of thought is bound up with clearness of language, and the one is impossible without the other. When the study of language can be followed by that of literature, not only breadth and clearness, but refinement becomes attainable.[48]

Charlotte and Lizzie, now Mrs Groveham, had planned to open a middle-class girls' school in Bradford. Mrs Groveham took a house, 17 Derwent Street, and had brochures printed; then Charlotte said she could not go! In 1923 Mrs Groveham told Miss Kitching that Charlotte had been 'the pioneer of a new movement by founding' a privately funded 'girls' Middle School in connection with the Infant School'. In reality, the girls who joined the new Davison class in 1864 paid the same weekly pence, from 6d to 8d, as the infants.[49] Miss Kitching realised that Mrs Groveham was still feeling hurt by Charlotte's withdrawal. Was the unauthenticated letter, headed 'House of Education' in Miss Kitching's hand, ending, 'I long to know that there is a Middle School in Bradford conducted by you', a post hoc apology to Mrs Groveham on behalf of their late dear friend? An unreferenced section of another letter was attached to a genuine excerpt in *The Story*, incorrectly claiming that Charlotte had independently founded a private girls' school in Worthing 'charging a guinea a quarter.'[50] In another authentic letter, Charlotte again declined Lizzie's invitation as pompously as Mr Read:

> Besides, darling, my duty lies here at present. There is a work to be done in Worthing that I feel that it is possible for me to do – indeed one of the very few things that I am at all fitted for. The tone of intellect and feeling here is very low. The people want to be raised, forced if need be to a higher level. The tradespeople being almost the only class resident, give tone to the town – & that tone is narrow, coarse and illiberal. Well dear, we know that if the young women of any district be elevated, they will raise the rest. So pet, my work is by means of our school for tradesmen's daughters to refine and cultivate the young women.[51]

Charlotte's persistent refusals to join Lizzie in Bradford were probably rooted in her longing to be a fully qualified, salaried professional teacher. Contented in Worthing and perhaps unwilling to be subservient to her competent, married friend, she blamed poor health instead. Mr Huston advised,

> Your health and not the manner of Mr and Miss Reid [*sic*] should be the great consideration. If you were sure that it would not be improved by change then every consideration would be in favour of your remaining. . . . I am your affectionate uncle, Wm Huston.[52]

Later misrepresentations about Charlotte's girls' 'middle school' were partly derived from Victorian terminology describing separate classes as 'schools'. In old age, Charlotte added an extra gloss to her Worthing teaching experiences:

> I had an Elementary School and a Pioneer Church High School at this same time so that I was enabled to study children in large groups.[53]

By such means myths are spun and upheld. The girls' school, attached to the infants' school until about 1907, did not qualify as a secondary Church high school until 1928. However, if the older girls' class had not been grafted on to the infants' school in 1864, the flourishing Davison Church of England Technical High School for Girls, rebuilt in Selbourne Road, Worthing, in 1961, might not have triumphantly developed into the twenty-first century as a living memorial to William Davison, acclaiming Miss Mason as the first headmistress.[54]

Charlotte misrepresented her states of health to her friends. Mrs Groveham believed she suffered bouts of *serious* illness, later mentioning a nervous breakdown to Miss Kitching. The school log accurately recorded that the mistress was 'indisposed' for *a day* on 16 November 1863 and for three days from 3 May to 6 May 1864 – hardly a breakdown as suggested in *The Story*.[55] However, one mysterious 'illness' lasted from 14 February 1867, when she took 'a rest of some weeks', until 29 April 1867, possibly spent at Selina Healey's school in Ambleside. Miss Maslen was summoned from the

Ho and Co to run the school in her absence but the assistant, Mary Acons, had to take over. Although often utterly exhausted at the end of long school days, Charlotte failed to succumb to her pupils' infections or catch the fever resulting from the floods of 26 October 1865. There was no other record of 'illness' until 1873.[56]

In January 1868, Charlotte's salary rose to £65 per annum plus £20 lodgings' allowance, enabling her to buy books, notably John Milton's *Paradise Lost* (1667) and John Gill's *Textbook on School Education* (1865).[57] By 1871 she had left the bustling High Street for more spacious and sociable lodgings at 4 Sussex Place. Her landlady was Mrs Elisabeth Goble, a widow with four daughters: Kate, aged 22, a 'lady governess'; Emma, aged 20, an 'assistant mother'; Ellen, aged 17; and Sarah, aged 14, both scholars, all living at home. Two other respectable lodgers were Mr William Sibley, a 63-year-old bachelor clothier, and Miss Ann Sims, aged 60, an annuitant. Ideas on education were doubtless aired over tea in the evenings. Revelling in their companionship, Charlotte may have encouraged the girls to help her in various ways.

For the 1871 census, Charlotte changed her status from 'governess' in 1861 to 'school mistress'; as noted, she was twenty-nine and had been born in Bangor.[58] Had Huldah Jane contacted her young half-sister, revealing that her mother's maiden name was Shaw and implying, out of respect for their father's honour, that his third marriage had taken place in 1841? If so, she may have sent news of the forthcoming marriage of Charlotte's former playmate, Sarah Harriett, to James Carey Morris (1838–c. 1911), a professor of natural philosophy, on 14 September 1868 at St Anne's Church in Dublin. The log showed that Charlotte did not attend. Or did the Birchalls, living in Leeds by 1871, encounter Charlotte in Bradford when visiting Edwin's parents, who had settled in Little Horton Lane by 1867?[59] Was Hannah the reason for avoiding Bradford? Assurance of legitimacy and paternal honour was essential to rising in the world, although like Eliza Bennett, Charlotte could say with equal confidence, 'I *am* a gentleman's daughter.'

From 1868 onwards, a life-changing friendship with Miss Emily Brandreth (1829–1893), Thomas Brandreth's unmarried daughter, enhanced Charlotte's social standing, nourishing aspirations beyond school teaching. The son of a Liverpool physician, Mr Brandreth was descended from a noble family listed in *Burke's Landed Gentry* (1826). A Fellow of the Royal Society, he had practised as a barrister and was a classical scholar, a brilliant mathematician and an ingenious inventor. In 1822 he married Harriet Byrom, the daughter of Ashton Byrom, also from Liverpool; they had two daughters and five sons. During the 1830s, Mr Brandreth brought his family to 15 Steyne, an elegant Georgian house facing Steyne Gardens in Worthing. He published a definitive *Dissertation on the Metre of Homer* in 1844 and a blank verse translation of the *Iliad* in 1846.[60]

Mr Read was well acquainted with Mr Brandreth, whose sisters-in-law, the Misses Byrom, served on the Davison Management Committee. The Revd Walter Lewis, the first vicar of St George's Church, who temporarily replaced Mr Read as school manager and first visited the school on 13 January 1868, may have asked Emily Brandreth to visit Davison School. She had donated £10 to the school in 1867 and visited the school four times during 1868. On 18 February she gave the 'upper girls' a knitting lesson, followed by a needlework lesson on 26 February and a further session on 12 March. At her last recorded visit on Monday 9 November she gave all the children a present. Her visits may have ceased because she was nursing her mother who died in 1869.[61]

From 1869, Charlotte's friendship with Miss Brandreth blossomed through helping her to look after her god-daughter, Harriet, aged five, Sam, aged four, and Edgar, who was only a few months old. They were the children of Miss Brandreth's brother, Colonel Ashton Milnes Brandreth (1836–after 1893) and Esther, his Indian wife, with whom he was currently on a tour of duty in India.[62] Visits to 15 Steyne enabled Charlotte to savour the culture and comforts of upper-class life, converting her to the merits of home education. Holding the brilliant Mr Brandreth in respectful awe, she saw value in Miss Brandreth's life spent with imaginative children, not missed opportunities.

The Brandreth connection enabled Charlotte's further development as a lady of culture while offering creative ideas on home education. While not a friendship based on equality, Miss Brandreth, some twelve years older, was clearly pleased with Charlotte's intelligent assistance. Addressed as Miss Brandreth, she referred to Charlotte as 'C.M.'. The children shone brightly by comparison with the duller Davison infants:

> My child friends supplied the answer: their insatiable curiosity showed me that the wide world and its history was barely enough to satisfy a child, who had not been made apathetic by spiritual malnutrition.[63]

Years later, Charlotte recalled Harriet's sensitive distress over the plight of a tramp, just like a character in one of the morally uplifting novels of Charlotte M. Yonge (1823–1910):[64]

> While still a young woman I saw a great deal of a family of Anglo-Indian children who had come 'home' to their grandfather's house and were being brought up by an aunt who was my intimate friend. The children were astonishing to me; they were persons of generous impulses and sound judgment, of great intellectual aptitude, of imagination and moral insight . . . illustrated one day by a little maiden of five who came home from her walk silent and sad; some letting alone, and some wise openings brought out at last between sobs – 'a

> poor man – no home – nothing to eat – no bed to lie upon' – and then the child was relieved by tears. Such incidents are common enough in families, but they were new to me.[65]

Their disciplined home education with their aunt epitomised an ideal of early education, where the alert child

> brings to the higher school . . . habits of attention, obedience, of order, neatness and exactitude, cultivated in him by watchful care from day to day, and only requiring further development and encouragement as he advances in age to become fixed and permanent.[66]

Charlotte had been drumming grammar into her young pupils for years. In 1871 Miss Brandreth insisted that Harriet and Sam, then aged eight and seven, could not understand grammar *per se*. Recalling Mr Dunning's passion for parsing, Charlotte wrote a grammar for them, ruefully discovering that Miss Brandreth was right.

> I was allowed to give the lessons myself with what lucidity and freshness I could command; in vain; the Nominative 'case' baffled them; their minds rejected the abstract conception of grammatical terminology.[67]

The grammar was faithfully preserved and published after Charlotte's death.

When Ashton and Esther Brandreth returned to take their children back to India, Charlotte handed the accolade to their aunt:

> Who does not know of the heart-burnings that arise when Anglo-Indian parents come home to find their children's affections given to others, their duty owing to others; and they, the parents, sources of pleasure like the godmother of the fairytale, but having no authority over the children. And all this, nobody's fault, for the guardians at home have done their best to keep the children loyal to their parents abroad.[68]

Miss Brandreth's comfortable lifestyle influenced Charlotte's longing for an easier life.

> Heigh-ho my Lizzimins! The ornament of a meek and quiet spirit is I think the change I wish most for just now. You wish to know dear friend what change I propose making in my way of life. Well, I did think of making a grand change at Xmas.

Charlotte was thinking of taking up part-time peripatetic English teaching in Sussex.

> Miss Read went up to the Ho & Co today. Saw dear Mr Dunning and asked him about it. He says there is an immense demand for women teachers in that way. . . . You see I don't want to teach more than three days a week if I can manage it.

Part-time teaching in Bradford was not an option: 'It would be coals to Newcastle for me to come.' As Mrs Lewis, the wife of the rector of St George's, advised waiting a year, the plan was dropped.[69]

In 1867, seven children passed in higher subjects; the HMI's report was very satisfactory. By 1872 the six standards were nationally upgraded, requiring a higher level of attainment. The summarised HMI reports for the next three years are missing from the log, presumably because Mr Read was ill. Charlotte also let the log entries slip. In 1871 and throughout 1872, she hit on the convenient but unlawful plan of writing weekly summaries instead of a daily record. Arithmetic was weak that year. Koe reduced the grant by one tenth and threatened withdrawal of the whole grant if the log book was not duly kept and the register called at the specified time under Article 23. This was Charlotte's worst inspection.[70]

Ideas about a new type of school surfaced at this restless time. From 4 Sussex Place, Charlotte drafted three undated letters, discovered in an old blotter after her death. They reveal an ambitious post-Taunton-Commission (1868) scheme to bring liberal culture to the lower orders in a remodelled National School with a transformed teaching force. In grasping the business potential of a profitable educational scheme, Charlotte allocated £200 per annum to the head teacher. Her mixed-class and mixed-gender model school would cater for 110 poor children, 20 better-class children and a superior class of 4 to 6 boarders up to secondary level to 'give tone to the school'. Better off children, benefiting from the National School education to which Charlotte remained loyal, would be charged on a sliding scale of fees related to parental income, effectively subsidising poorer pupils. Emergent class tensions would be quashed by requiring all children to 'be expected to make companions of their own order to prevent toadying and other evils'. Teachers of recognised social standing offered school-based teaching practice and *a few months* at a training school would replace unsatisfactory staff. Liberal training would equip a new class of genteel teachers, drawn from superior pupils, for work in National or private schools or as family governesses.

> [Pupil-teachers], chosen with reference to their homes, should be educated with all the usual accomplishments . . . but the <u>principle</u> of the thing being that 3yrs pupil-teachership (at 15 or 16) is the best kind of 'finish' – *giving* the mental culture to be had by working mind to mind with a cultivated person besides as an opportunity of doing useful work in the world itself on education.[71]

The former Bradford industrialist, Liberal MP and disunited Quaker son-in-law of Dr Thomas Arnold (1795–1842) of Rugby, W.E. Forster (1818–1886), was vice president of the Committee of Council on Education. He steered the Elementary Education Act (1870) through Parliament. The Act established school boards in all areas lacking schools to plug the gaps in educational provision and, controversially, granted the right of withdrawal from religious instruction on conscientious grounds, even in Church schools. The Act did not abolish the Revised Code. Familiar with the Taunton Commission report from the Ho and Co papers and the debate around training genteel surplus women for elementary school teaching, in the letters, Charlotte regretted that 'the discrepancies of class and class increase . . . & altogether things get more & more wrong every year'. Children should acquire 'habits of veneration, trust and graciousness' instead. These cherished letters, outlining her first thought-out, part-costed educational plan, anticipated her future aspirations. It is not known if, or to whom, they were sent.[72]

Mr Brandreth died on 27 May 1873 at the age of eighty-four. Suddenly Miss Brandreth was relieved of all her responsibilities. Mr Brandreth had willed £4,000 apiece to his four sons and two daughters. Left in possession of 15 Steyne, Emily Brandreth was leaving Worthing.

> Dear Mr Brandreth has gone to his rest. Miss Brandreth is going abroad for a couple of years, so your friend is taking the opportunity to break loose from Worthing for the present & make a new way of life for herself. I have fully pondered, dear & shall always be grateful for the kind & wise & loving letter you wrote me when I told you before of my teaching schemes. . . . I cannot just now think of my life so little responsible & I ache with responsibility so, if the way opens, I mean to try. My plan is to leave here at Xmas. Sit for the Cambridge Women's exams.

Two further truncated, undated letters describe Charlotte's search for an opening. Pleading illness, she avoided seeing a local doctor and visited her College friend, Sally Coleman, in Manchester. She explained, 'I wanted to see Dr Coleman. . . . He makes me surer than ever that I must get less work. Worthing is terribly dull without dear Miss Brandreth – still there is plenty to do.'[73] Charlotte continued to look for work anywhere but Bradford. She visited some London schools, which did not strike her 'as very excellent'. Unknown hosts escorted her to the Grosvenor Gallery in Park Lane, built to display the first Earl of Grosvenor's paintings. Here is Charlotte's first essay in picture study:

> One by Gainsborough was very generally admired. It is a portrait, I believe, called 'The Blue Boy'. The dress is of a peculiar blue, most difficult to paint & it is said to be wonderfully well done but this was not the great charm for me. It was the figure standing out so boldly and substantially from the canvas. The face is full of the present boy & the future man. So beautiful in its purpose-like earnestness. . . . Some of the landscapes were beautiful – exceedingly.[74]

Where next? There was a vacancy for a senior governess at the re-opened Bishop Otter Memorial Training College in Chichester. The first Ho-and-Co-trained applicant had been asked to leave after three months. Miss Read may have praised Charlotte's abilities and cultural knowledge. If so, perhaps Mr Dunning confidently recommended his former student to redeem the Ho and Co's dented reputation.

Fortunately Charlotte's final 1873 inspection was encouraging. The Education Act (1871) had directed that infant schools should be separated from elementary schools. On 28 November, Koe reiterated that the Davison girls' and infants' schools should be segregated. The total grant of £103 8s was the largest awarded in Charlotte's time, including £1 10s for passes in special subjects for the second time. Miss Read would have been highly relieved.

> The Children are under good moral influence, and are fairly instructed by Miss Mason in the usual subjects. As at present organized, the School is a difficult one to work. It would in my view be better to form two wholly separate departments.

On Friday 10 October 1873, the log recorded that 'Miss Mason went away yesterday for a few days change on account of illness' from Monday 13 October to Friday 17 October 1873. Returning on 22 October, she was absent again on Friday 24 October. These absences gave her time to prepare to give lectures at Bishop Otter Memorial College on three successive Fridays: 1 December, 8 December and 15 December, subsequently sanctioned by the Davison managers.[75]

Peripatetic work, even if she could have earned half a guinea a session, was too uncertain. The Worthing years had given Charlotte essential stability and excellent health. Teaching infants and girls, running the school, supervising her teachers, her church life and mingling with the superior classes, notably the Brandreths, had enlarged the range of experience on which she could build her future aspirations. Lecturing to gentlewomen students at Bishop Otter Memorial College was exactly the kind of new challenge that she was well-equipped to meet, provided no one mentioned her past pupil-teacher apprenticeship.

10.
Senior Governess at the Gentlewomen's College in Chichester, 1874–1878

In January 1874, at the age of thirty-two, Charlotte Mason began her new career at the Bishop Otter Memorial College in Chichester, which had re-opened the previous year as a training college for gentlewomen.[1] Here was her 'grand change'. As senior governess, she was moving up a class to teach lady students. Class status *mattered*. Necessity obliged ladies to train for the alien world of elementary school teaching. Although Charlotte Mason was charming, intelligent, well-trained and practised in teaching all elementary subjects under the Revised Code, she needed to fine tune her knowledge of education, human physiology and hygiene to hold her own with superior, home-bred gentlewomen from strikingly different backgrounds to her own. Bringing a disciplined reticence into play, she would endeavour to prevent the students from prying into her background.

William Otter (1768–1840), Bishop of Chichester from 1836 to 1840, had charged his clergy to place 'the education of the people' at the forefront of their aspirations to develop the achievements of the National Society. Like St Aidan's, the new diocesan training college for elementary schoolmasters opened modestly in 1840. By 1850 'an elegant building of stone in the collegiate style of the late fifteenth century' had been erected in Bishop Otter's memory. Renamed University House after its incorporation with Chichester University in 2005, the College building stands today much as it was in Miss Mason's time, although the chapel has been replaced.

Bishop Otter Memorial College closed in 1867. The Revd Matthew Parrington MA Cantab. (1807–1882), the third principal from 1847 to 1867, had failed to recruit enough male students to keep the College open. Having landscaped the gardens, planted a magnificent cedar of Lebanon and ornamented the interior with decorative wood carvings, assisted by his students, he lingered on in the principal's rooms as a canon of Chichester until 1872. Miss Mason probably had rooms behind the principal's residence. From the upper floors, she could look out over the gardens to open agricultural farmland offering a pleasant aspect beyond the spacious lawns, flower beds and stately cedar tree.[2]

The 1870 Education Act vastly increased the demand for teachers in the new schools opened by local school boards and religious denominations. Less costly than schoolmasters, there were too few qualified women teachers to fill all the vacancies. As the Taunton Commission had shown, the few secondary schools and university colleges established by campaigning pioneers, such as Frances Buss, Dorothea Beale, Anne Clough and Emily Davies (1830–1921), founder and first mistress of Girton College, Cambridge, in 1869, exemplified the widespread need for higher education and professional training for women. Various strategies were adopted in deference to the prevailing domestic ideology. Decades would pass before the wealthier upper-classes generally accepted higher education and professional occupations for their daughters. After training young ladies as domestic governesses in her Tiverton school during the 1860s, Mary Porter gave evidence to the Taunton Commission. She said that 'a governess was concerned with the social and moral development of her pupils as well as the simply academic, and her qualifications were not merely of the academic variety but were part of her birthright as lady'.[3] Charlotte Mason would concur with this view.

The philanthropic heiress, Angela Burdett-Coutts (1814–1906), the first woman peer in 1871, campaigned for the honourable employment of the so-called 'surplus' middle-class ladies as teachers to enhance respect for lowly elementary school mistresses.[4] Louisa Hubbard (1836–1906), a former Anglican deaconess and wealthy, upper-class spinster from Leonards Lee, near Horsham in Sussex, was also actively campaigning for better education and work for indigent gentlewomen. She published pamphlets and corresponded with Sir James Kay-Shuttleworth. He agreed the need for a new institution; all the country's nineteen women's training colleges were over-subscribed. As Miss Hubbard published her pamphlet, *Work for Ladies in Elementary Schools*, the notice of the re-opening of Bishop Otter Memorial College for Ladies appeared in *The Queen* on 18 May 1872 and also in *The Times* and other newspapers. A major fundraiser and donor, Miss Hubbard was closely involved with the re-launch and management of the *first* exclusive training school for middle- and upper-class women, linked to Chichester diocese.

The Rt Revd Richard Durnford MA Oxon. (1802–1895) was Bishop of Chichester from 1871 to 1895. He echoed Bishop Otter's original charge of 1838 in looking forward to the time when the Anglican Church would do as much for middle-class education as for the poor. Fundraising and management committees were established by 1872. Bishop Durnford was appointed College visitor and chairman of the General Committee until he died. To preserve the domestic atmosphere suitable for young ladies, Miss Hubbard advised that no more than fifty students should be admitted.[5] In October, Charlotte Mason's heroine, Florence Nightingale, wrote approvingly to Miss Hubbard from her bed, announcing that it was 'one of the most useful plans I know – it will be of inconceivable advantage if sensibly carried out.'[6]

Miss Fanny Trevor.

Private students were to be charged fees of £35 a year or £20 for six months. The third prospectus announced that the College would give preference to the daughters of clergy and professional men; it was not intended for pupil-teachers. However, due to the shortage of female training places, Queen's Scholars were permitted to apply for the two-year course and charged £20 for full residence.[7]

Miss Hubbard attended the General Committee at the National Society's office in Westminster on 30 October 1872 when Miss Sarah Frances Trevor (c. 1818–1904) was appointed the first lady principal, a position she held until 1895. Formidably intelligent, Miss Trevor, a canon's sister, came from Milverton in Somerset. Apart from experience of Somerset schools, she apparently had no formal qualifications. The post had been advertised as 'lady superintendent', resonant of housekeeper status, but Miss Trevor firmly took the title of lady principal and proudly declined the £100 annual salary. As a lady of independent means and property, she clearly wished to be acknowledged as a gentlewoman of equal standing to Miss Hubbard.

Bishop Durnford formally dedicated the new College on 19 February 1873, when thirteen students were installed. He said, 'the little knot of students who have come hither, attracted, one scarce knows how, to prepare themselves by labour and discipline for the Profession of Elementary Teachers may be the vanguard of a great army. . . . There is surely an art of Teaching, and it is a difficult art. . . . All must be trained for this special work.'[8]

The idea that gentlefolk could transform the rough open world of elementary schooling by instilling cultural and moral standards and obedience alongside basic education was predicated on a bland ignorance of the realities of working-class life, which Dr Baylee had encouraged his ordinands to explore. Would elementary education give the lower orders too strong a voice? Fears were also expressed that the independence of college life would attract ambitious, under-bred, lower-middle-class girls who might dilute the pure atmosphere, hence Miss Trevor's reluctance to admit former pupil-teachers.[9]

With hindsight it seems clear that Charlotte was both indebted to and over-stretched by the indomitable first lady principal, who had difficulty in retaining her staff. Miss Trevor's style of managing a small, exclusive training college and practising school, imbued with the cultural and religious atmosphere appropriate for mid-Victorian gentlewomen, would profoundly influence the way Charlotte Mason ran her House of Education eighteen years later. Difficulties arising from the unsettling first year were succeeded by interpersonal tensions and two disruptive periods of building work overshadowing her time Although she was praised by the Inspectorate and commended by the General Committee, Charlotte would resign after four years because 'she found the work at the College too trying'.[10]

Miss E.J. Steventon, the first senior governess recommended by the Ho and Co, and two junior governesses had been asked to leave in 1873. Determined to take no more risks, Miss Trevor needed someone who could cope with a greater influx of students.[11] Although awareness of Charlotte's background in pupil-teaching could have made her hesitate, Miss Trevor needed a governess who could hold her own. On Thursday 18 December 1873 the College's Sub-Committee authorised payment of £3 to Miss Mason for the instruction she had given on trial and confirmed her provisional appointment with Miss Trevor's agreement. The Brandreth connection and her practical teaching experience, gracious manner and wide reading would all have counted in Charlotte's favour. Her first salary was £75 per annum with board and lodging. On 12 January 1874 the Davison log recorded, 'Miss Mason resigned the school at Christmas in consequence of having accepted the post of Senior Governess at the Chichester Training College.'[12] Miss Trevor probably insisted on recording her merely as 'governess' on the front of the 1874 Annual Report while she was on trial; this modest appellation was raised to 'senior governess' the following year as proof of Miss Mason's competence.[13]

In October 1876, Mr Huston, her trusted acquaintance from his Sunday tea parties for Home and Colonial students, addressed the acknowledged senior governess as 'My dear Miss Mason' instead of 'My dear niece'; he signed off, 'I am yours very kindly' instead of 'Your affectionate Uncle'. This formality acknowledged his young friend's welcome rise in status.[14]

Bishop Durnford recommended the Revd Cecil Hook as the first non-residential chaplain. His annual stipend of £120 was higher than the salary offered to the lady principal. The chaplain was not only asked to take daily services and give an hour's daily religious instruction to the students but had to keep the general accounts, see to the college correspondence and deal with admissions. These overlapping duties demanded close co-operation between the chaplain and the lady principal. Miss Trevor, a strong and uncompromising character, cannot have given way over matters she felt were her concern. Mr Hook resigned after four months. The Revd Richard Espinasse MA Oxon., vicar of Westhampnett from 1868, was appointed the second chaplain in August 1873. He survived for four years before quitting on account of 'weak health'. Ensuing tensions between the chaplains and the lady principal were partly resolved by 1878, when the Committee allowed Miss Trevor to take over the role of chief officer and *de facto* secretary, limiting the chaplain's duties to religious matters.[15] Was Miss Mason swept up into the role conflict between the chaplaincy and lady principal? Accustomed to clergy, she may have soothed Mr Espinasse during their shared four years at the College. Nevertheless, when Miss Mason opened her House of Education in 1892, it was years before she appointed a personal chaplain. The local vicar taught divinity while she assumed the mantle of principal and religious leader.

Miss Trevor described Chichester as 'a very dead-alive, out-of-the-way place'.[16] Charlotte Mason concurred:

> Like most Cathedral towns, Chichester is very quiet; it has four straight streets, which meet at the market cross; and parts of the old walls remain, a pleasant walk from which the red roofs and gardens of the city may be seen. Chichester stands upon quite flat ground and the cathedral is the only striking object which rises between the Downs and the Sea. The city owes its cathedral, or a great part of it to the Normans as may be seen in the round shape of many of the arches. The campanile or bell tower stands by itself, apart from the Church.[17]

At the heart of the Anglican diocese, Chichester was a busy market town. The London-Brighton railway offered easy access to Worthing eighteen miles away. The city was pleasantly laid out with well-built houses and clean, paved streets lit by gas, not tallow. Chichester Cathedral was, and is, a noble edifice, containing interesting monuments and painted glass windows. Surely Miss Mason was invited with the students to the fifteenth-century Bishop's Palace by Bishop and Mrs Durnford in 1876?[18] Chichester offered myriad opportunities for exploration and discovery.

As the chaplain had the cure of a parish, Bishop Otter staff and students may have worshipped at the cathedral on Sundays. The solemn high church ritualism and soaring choral music may have seemed strange to the young lecturer, accustomed to evangelical fervour at Holy Trinity and scholarly sermons at Worthing Chapel of Ease. Bishop Durnford was said to be a churchman of the old school of pre-Tractarian, 'high and dry' Anglicanism, but one caring more for the things of God that the orderly sequence of ritual symbolised than the ritual itself. The first dean in Miss Mason's time was the Very Revd Walter F. Hook MA Oxon. (1798-1875). He had ventured beyond the 'high and dry' into Tractarianism, derived from *Tracts for the Times* published between 1833 and 1841. Led by John Keble (1792–1866), the Tractarians believed that worship had become too plain. They sought a revival of the traditional mediaeval liturgy – poles apart from the quiet meetings of Charlotte Mason's Quaker forebears.

Whether or not Anglo-Catholic worship at the cathedral broadened her vision of churchmanship, Charlotte may have first discovered John Keble's popular volume of religious verse, *The Christian Year* (1827), in Chichester. She received the precious book for her birthday on 1 January 1878. Her notebook listing walks in Hampshire described her pilgrimage to Keble's former village parish. The Tractarian leader, who had ministered in Hursley for thirty-one years, was said to live with his family in a household marked by 'gaiety and gravity' as well as by the plain living and high thinking that Miss Mason would introduce at Ambleside.[19]

A new dean, the Very Revd John W. Burgon MA Oxon. (1813–1888), succeeded Dean Hook in 1876. Also a poet, he was famous for the line from his Oxford Newdigate Prize poem, 'Petra', describing the ancient city in Jordan as 'a rose-red city half as old as time', perhaps evoking Miss Mason's longing to compose religious verse and to travel in the east. An erudite theologian and high churchman in the same pre-Tractarian vein as Bishop Durnford, he was vehemently opposed to the radicalism of *Essays and Reviews* and preached vigorously against the new biblical criticism, declaring,

> Either, with the best and wisest of all ages, you must believe the whole of Holy Scripture; or, with the narrow-minded infidel, you must disbelieve the whole. There is no middle course open to you.

This message would have spoken volumes to Charlotte Mason, who trusted fervently in the veracity of Holy Scripture and abhorred controversy. Edward Meyrick Goulburn MA Oxon. (1818–1897), Dean of Norwich in 1892, who shared his doctrinal views, brought out a two-volume biography of Dean Burgon in 1892. Goulburn's *Thoughts on Personal Religion* and his *Holy Communion* were both treasured by Miss Mason.[20]

Aged over eighteen, the Bishop Otter students were being prepared to teach elementary subjects to the Code's standards, a tough call for home-educated ladies. The 1874 annual report noted that in 1873, twenty-five unmarried students and a widow, aged between eighteen and forty-two, were resident, some for six months and some for the year. Most subsequently obtained work as teachers or in a related profession. Their fathers were mainly middle-class professionals: naval officers, land agents, school teachers, solicitors, a clergyman, a musician, a university professor, a commercial traveller, a mill director, an Indian civil servant and a hosier.

Of this first cohort, eleven were orphans like Miss Mason. Contemporary commentators criticised Bishop Otter Memorial College for its insistence on exclusivity, contending that the daughters of officers and clergymen attended other colleges, notably Whitelands, founded in 1841.[21]

Bishop Otter's gentlewomen students were spared most of the obligatory domestic chores believed to be undertaken by the allegedly *lower-class* women students attending other cheaper training colleges. Unobtrusive servants looked after the young ladies. While average college expenditure was £30 per woman student, Bishop Otter fees were raised to £50 per head, enabling Miss Trevor to provide a more comfortable residence. In the dormitories, each young woman had a wooden cubicle with a door facing the central aisle to ensure complete privacy; most had access to a window. However, as water was not laid on, all had to take turns at the pump. At the height of Victorian reverence for the matriarchal sphere, Miss Trevor wished to show, by example, that womanly women could be capable managers as well as teachers; her training should be no bar to marriage. If her students married, as many did, they would be well-prepared to supervise their households efficiently.[22]

By May 1873, as advised by the HMIs, the Committee decided to build a model practising school within the College grounds to provide in-house teaching practice. During the first year, the students' teaching practice had been supervised by Miss Bowren, the Mistress of the Chichester Central National School for Girls. The elementary school teachers thought the superior lady students were unsuited to teaching in local elementary schools because they had not been pupil-teachers and lacked experience of working-class children.[23]

The first two years were an ordeal for Miss Mason as she got to grips with adjusting to the principal's demands, preparing lectures and coping with staff changes. The noise and dust caused by completing the hurried building of the Flintstone School on site, followed by the construction of the new College wing by 1876, would have been considerably more disturbing than the erection of the new Davison classroom. In March 1874, Miss Mason lost the support of the new junior governess, Miss M. Spencer, who was appointed mistress of the new College practising school on a salary of £60 per annum. The school opened in April 1874. Lasting one term, Miss Spencer resigned in August; by then there were twenty-two students at the College. During Miss Mason's four years, five junior governesses and six practising school mistresses departed after short stints.[24]

Apart from Miss Trevor's courses, much of the lecturing had been covered by non-resident staff from local Chichester schools. From the outset, Miss Mason undoubtedly had a heavy teaching load, although Mr Stevens, master of the Chichester Central National School for boys, taught arithmetic. Mr St Clair, headmaster of Richmond House Private School, was the College's choirmaster and taught the students music, adding grammar to his workload after Miss Spencer left.[25]

Because the College was small, Miss Trevor was convinced that all the students should belong to the same Anglican Christian denomination. When giving evidence to the Cross Commission (The Royal Commission to Enquire into the Working of the Elementary Education Acts) of 1888, Miss Trevor responded to a question about denominational religious teaching: 'It is necessary when you are living in a household that you should all be of one mind in the house.' She did not believe the 1870 Education Act's conscience clause, enabling students to opt out of Anglican daily worship, would

> work well where you live together in a small community. Possibly it might in large colleges, but we are like a family, and I think it would cause a great deal of dissension and controversy which would be very objectionable in so a small college as ours.[26]

Miss Mason would adopt a similar practice at her future House of Education.

Fanny Williams, a clergyman's daughter, was a Queen's Scholar. As she entered Bishop Otter Memorial College at the age of twenty-six, she is unlikely to have served a pupil-teacher apprenticeship. Her recollections suggest that she had no previous teaching experience. As a future member of Miss Mason's inner circle, Fanny's later memories were infused with loyal admiration:

> Miss Mason had become so well known in the neighbourhood that she was appointed Lecturer on Education and Teacher of Human Physiology. In 1876 I went to Otter College as a student and thus came under dear Miss Mason's influence. Unlike her, I was not a born teacher, I was simply anxious to do some useful work and help my family (my father was a clergyman and an invalid and I wished to help him retire). Under dear Miss Mason's teaching, my views of life changed; I saw that teaching might be a noble profession instead of a mere trade, and I too longed to put her theories into practice. I am sure that many old 'Otters' would gladly testify to the help and enlightenment they received from Miss Mason's lectures on Education. I remember she told us that the true teacher must be prepared to lay down her life for her pupils.

As it happened, Fanny's father remained active in ministry. Aged fifty-two in 1871, he was vicar of Otterton in Devon, and at seventy-two was rector of Fyfield in Hampshire in 1891.[27]

Miss Mason also taught hygiene. Her prepared notes for all three subjects would provide material for lectures to Manningham ladies in 1885. Other subjects were covered, notably geography and history. After leaving

Miss Trevor with her family of students.

Chichester, she produced a series of geographical texts for schools. Volume I, *Elementary Geography*, was warmly dedicated to the 'Otters':

> The writer begs affectionately to inscribe these Books to Teachers trained at the Otter Memorial College, in memory of very pleasant hours spent with intelligent and responsive classes.[28]

Essex Cholmondeley claimed that Miss Mason 'later became Vice-Principal of the college'.[29] There was no such post until 1886, when the 'energetic and thoughtful' Miss Elizabeth Davy, Miss Mason's former student from 1874 to 1876, was appointed vice principal. She succeeded Miss Trevor as principal from 1895 to 1897.[30] However, as Miss Trevor had manifold responsibilities, including teaching in the College and practising school, as senior governess, Miss Mason may have occasionally acted as *de facto* vice principal when visitors or distinguished lay and clerical committee members required attention.

In 1874, the General Committee ruled that the chaplain was responsible for all religious instruction given in the practising school. Miss Trevor could only teach these lessons in his absence. All the prayers used and religious books studied had to be approved by the school's Management Committee. Although Miss Trevor and Miss Mason gave religious instruction to the students from 1874 until 1877, in that year the Committee decreed that the chaplain should take it over. They could only teach under his direction. All the books used had to be submitted for his approval, with the right of appeal to the Committee if Mr Espinasse blocked their suggestions. Miss Mason would have sorely missed independently teaching religious knowledge, her favourite subject. Significantly, all seventeen students passed religious knowledge with a first or second class in December 1874, after a year of Miss Trevor's and Miss Mason's classes. At the end of 1875, twenty-one students passed the religious knowledge examination, with four third-class passes. The figures for 1876 and 1877 could not be found.[31]

Miss Mason was rated as a gifted and effective lecturer during her four years at the College, as correctly recalled by Fanny Williams. In the face of constant challenges, she displayed sterling qualities. In February 1875, the Sub-Committee raised Miss Mason's salary to £80, backdated to January 1874 when she started lecturing. By August 1874 there were twenty-two first- and second-year students in residence; more were expected. Although the average number stayed around thirty until 1878, the workload was unremitting.[32]

In 1875, the Committee decided to extend the College to accommodate forty students by adding another lecture room, another dormitory for twelve students and some smaller rooms. Up to 1900, the College had no library or sitting-room. At Ambleside, Miss Mason's students would also lack a sitting room in which to relax. Early in 1876, the new wing was finished, to everyone's relief. A connecting passage linking the main building with the chapel protected staff and students from rainstorms.

Miss Hubbard, still closely involved at this stage, claimed that the residential staff of two could easily cope with more students. Canon Tinling HMI disagreed. Since June 1875 he had been pressing for a second residential governess. From 1876 onwards, Miss Trevor adopted the usual practice of recruiting staff from qualified Otters. This was not always successful; a Miss Davison, appointed junior governess in February 1876, lasted two months to be replaced by a second Otter in April. In 1877, the highly competent Miss Elizabeth Davy took over as junior governess.

At the annual College assessment in October 1876, the HMI reported that the lesson given by Miss Mason was very good. The students had done well. The first twelve students to complete the two-year course had successfully obtained teaching posts, as well as two one-year students, although they were initially promised no assistance in finding posts according to the disclaimer in the new terms of admission to the College. In contrast, at her future House of Education, Miss Mason would arrange all her students' posts to ensure that they exemplified the value of her training.

Feedback from the HMIs and diocesan inspectors was very favourable. The precise figures for 1877 have been lost with the missing annual reports from 1877 to 1880. However, the April 1877 finance report recorded that the Committee had raised the senior governess's salary to £100 per annum, backdated to January. This second rise confirmed the Committee's warm appreciation of Miss Mason's lecturing abilities as well as the overall success of the College during the first five years.[33]

The model practising school enabled the students to have in-house supervised classroom experience with middle-class children, thus avoiding exposure to poorer children in the Chichester elementary schools. The weekly charge was 6d to 8d, as at the Davison. In claiming that there were sufficient places for poorer children at local National and Lancastrian schools, the Committee assuredly believed they had a better chance of establishing a model school with middle-class children, to enhance the standing and popularity of the College as a training centre. The school cost £1,000, raised by public subscription. There was room for 130 pupils. Now no longer used as a school, the Flintstone building survives to the present day. Miss Mason's former HMI, the Revd N.L. Koe, inspected the school on 4 November 1874 as recorded by the manager, Mr Espinasse:

> The children attending are socially above National School Children. The standard of attainment is low – many of the older children are being presented in the First Standard.

The school was run by the mistress with an assistant mistress and monitors, but *no* pupil-teachers. By April 1874, forty-six girls aged between four and fifteen had enrolled in the school; average attendance would rise to eighty by 1878. The curriculum included the three Rs, religious instruction, grammar, English history, geography, needlework, singing and freehand drawing. For additional fees, extra lessons in French and music were offered. There were future plans to establish a kindergarten for the infants and a boarding house for girls preparing for entrance to the College, to bypass the pupil-teacher system, heartily disliked by Miss Trevor. Both government and diocesan inspectors assessed the school. The initial HMI reports revealed many challenges still to be addressed. The frequent changes of mistress inhibited the upward rise to model school status before 1900.

At her future Ambleside practising school, Miss Mason would follow Miss Trevor's practice of sending two students to take classes for a week at a time on a rota basis, facing regular 'criticism lessons' of their teaching. No record has been found to establish that Miss Mason was mistress of method in the Bishop Otter practising school as claimed in *The Story*, a role equivalent to Mr Dunning's position at the Ho and Co. The lady principal taught regularly in the school, introducing domestic economy as a subject in 1877, and shared the role of mistress of method with the current mistress. The school's log book, begun on 14 September 1874, recorded only four visits by Miss Mason. On 15 October 1874 she took the first class in Holy Scripture, as Miss Trevor was away. Miss Hubbard visited the school on that day. On 7 December 1874, Miss Mason took care of the school as the mistress was absent; this time the visitor was Bishop Durnford's wife. On 16 December 1874, the entry read, 'Weather very stormy. Only seven children present. These were sent home and the school closed for Christmas by Miss Mason.' Finally, on 16 October 1877, Miss Mason took Standards IV, V and VI to enable the mistress to examine Standard III pupils in dictation and reading.

The log book recorded the students' teaching practice. On 10 November 1875, Miss J. Frances Hall was teaching in the school when the HMI, Canon Tinling, arrived for his inspection. Fanny Williams and a Miss Davison gave lessons on the 'Motions of the Earth and Rivers' on 6 October 1876. In April and May 1877, Miss Williams shared three criticism lessons with a fellow student. On 11 October 1877, Miss Rosa Westmorland, a first year, gave a criticism lesson on 'Coffee' to Standard II and Miss Williams, now a second year, gave a lesson on 'The Squirrel' later that month.[34]

Criticism lessons would be Miss Mason's priority at Ambleside. In Miss Trevor's absence, she *may* have chaired the Bishop Otter students' criticism lessons, attended by all the staff and students. The school log only recorded those students teaching when 'Crits' were held but *not* the staff or students who were present. This view is partly substantiated by Deaconess Rosa Westmorland's memories of Miss Mason:

> I was there in 1877–78. I can remember her personally quite well – her wonderful kind face – her lectures on training children, were, I feel sure, very helpful, specially her classes in the Practising School. . . . I think she must have left <u>for more appreciated work</u>.[35]

Rosa Westmorland had sensed Charlotte's discontent during her last year at Bishop Otter Memorial College. Mary Read's premature death at the age of forty-eight on 10 January 1877 distressed her deeply. Exhausted and ill at Christmas, Miss Mason had gone to Manchester to see Dr and Mrs Coleman. Planning to stay with her former landlady, she left for Worthing too late to see Miss Read.

> Many of the inhabitants of Worthing will regret to hear of the death of Miss Read, daughter of the Rev W Read, Chaplain of the Chapel of Ease. . . . The deceased lady caught a cold a fortnight ago, which led to her being seized with acute rheumatism, the malady affecting her heart, produced death on Wednesday evening last. Miss Read was highly esteemed by all who knew her, and they were many.
>
> At the Chapel on the Sunday following her death a great number of the congregation were in mourning. . . . The Funeral took place on Monday [15 January 1877] the first part of the service being read at the Chapel and the sacred edifice, whose pulpit etc had been bright with emblems of Christmastide, are now draped with black, was packed with an overflowing congregation, comprising most of the clergy of the district.[36]

Charlotte opened her heart to Lizzie in a touchingly forthright letter:

> My dear Lizzie
>
> Many thanks for your nice long letter which was to have had a nice long answer directly I got to Worthing, but in the first place S.C. kept me by various kind devices such as locking up my clothes, writing to Mrs Goble, a week longer than I meant to stay & you know what grievous news greeted me when I got here. I can hardly tell you what a shock and pain it was. I counted Miss Read among my dearest, truest friends & now she is gone, find I cared for her even more than I thought. . . . What she was as a daughter no one can tell – her life was so utterly devoted to her father – so merged in his that no one saw it was devotion or thought it possible she could have any pleasure apart from him. . . . The poor will miss her terribly. . . . Her poor father is at present keeping up with what I fear is unnatural brightness. . . . Then I go on to London to Miss Brandreth. I had been looking forward to my week here, to the sea air – the quiet sight of old friendly faces and above all to seeing a good deal of Miss Read. . . . She has left nothing but her bright example & do pray dear that I may try to follow it for, for every fault of mine I think she had the opposite virtue.

Lottie added that Sally Coleman's home was 'prosperous and happy and I tell her it is time she & her husband got over their honeymoon – but that is the way with you married people.' She lovingly ended the letter by asking after Lizzie and her three daughters, her godchildren.[37]

After visiting Miss Brandreth, who was staying with Sister Maria D'Arcy in Hoxton, Miss Mason returned to Chichester for the new term, financially well rewarded for her final year. In May 1877 Miss Brandreth wrote to 'C.M.' in an informal, colloquial style from the family house near Lucerne in Switzerland, on the slopes of Mount Pilatus above a lake. Once again, she was enjoying looking after Ashton's children, Harriet, fourteen, Sam, thirteen, and little Edgar, eight years old.

> We have such a lovely summer home I only hope I shall not grumble much when I go into winter quarters wh. must be small indeed in comparison. Whether my sister [Esther Brandreth] comes now or in the spring they purpose taking their chicks for 4 years but my sister is too kind in hoping I will always stay lc &c [*sic*].

Signing herself 'my best love. . . yr affec. EB', she asked Charlotte Mason to send a message that 15 Steyne was <u>not</u> to be let again. This joyful news foretold her return to Worthing and may have triggered Miss Mason's secret yearnings to leave Chichester to see the world, or at least Europe.[38]

Miss Kitching recalled Miss Mason saying that, at Bishop Otter, she 'came into touch with the minds of young women and she found them very little different from those of the children except their powers were not so fresh'![39] Low-spirited throughout 1877, Miss Mason may have felt out of kilter with her over-confident students from comfortable middle-class homes, especially when comparing her hard-pressed life with that of Miss Brandreth, caring for those special children. Hearing that the Grovehams had travel plans was no comfort. During the summer holidays, did she take refuge at Lincoln Farm, Otterbourne, because the famous novelist and friend of Keble, Charlotte M. Yonge, lived at Elderfield in the village?

> Dearest Lizzie
>
> Do not think dear that I have forgotten you because I have not written sooner. The fact is my head has been so good for nothing that I have barely been able to do quite necessary work & now have removed here for a rest which I hope will so far set me up so that I shall be able to go on until Xmas. Do not be uneasy dear. I am bodily quite well & mentally too now that I am in this beautiful country. I find the work at the college too trying & have settled to give it up at Xmas and take a rest. Now don't go proposing all sorts of wild adventures in Germany and elsewhere for the pyramids but at present I can make no such plans. So heigh ho for the pyramids. I shall return to the College next week, where write.
>
> Your very loving Lottie.[40]

In Worthing Miss Mason could relax in her lodgings when her school day ended. As the College was run on familial lines and living in residence, Miss Mason and the junior governess were doubtless expected to take meals with the students and supervise their studies. The students' curiosity about their lecturers would have strained Miss Mason's powers of reticence to the limit. Secure in the principal's house, Miss Trevor may have seemed remote, leaving the governesses exposed to student banter.

Elizabeth Davy, the former Otter, who had given a 'Crit.' on physical geography in the practising school on 10 June 1875, was now junior governess. Observed by Canon Tinling HMI to be 'energetic and thoughtful', she would return as senior governess in 1880. Already familiar with 'physiography' in 1882, Miss Davy helped to develop the new training in science teaching at Bishop Otter, recommended by the Devonshire Report on The Royal Commission on Scientific Instruction and the Advancement of Science (1875). No longer her student but a highly intelligent colleague, Miss Davy's competence may have threatened Miss Mason's hard won self-confidence. If the Devonshire Report was discussed at Bishop Otter Memorial College, Miss Mason may have fretted about her lack of experience in teaching elementary science and the potential conflict with dogmatic theology. These developments may have further strengthened Miss Mason's decision to quit.[41]

As the lady of the house, Miss Trevor faced down any challenge to her authority or opinions, as her forthright evidence to the Cross Committee revealed in 1886. She ran the small College 'like a family', acting as adviser and mother to the girls. Her fierce prejudice against pupil-teachers must have profoundly affected Miss Mason. Miss Trevor informed the Cross Commissioners in 1886 that she had not been able to 'cater for a higher social class than ordinary Training Colleges' and had accepted middle-class girls, explaining she had 'been obliged in the last two years to take a few pupil-teachers who are not quite of the class we would wish. The private students, paying £50 per annum, are of a very superior class.' When asked if she had the daughters of shop-keepers or artisans, she responded, 'I do not think we have ever had anyone of so low a class as that. . . . We have had two or three large farmers' daughters.'[42] She said that few pupil-teachers came from 'educated and good' homes. She believed 'any parents of better position' would do their best to prevent their own children 'from going through the drudgery of pupil-teachership'. Pupil-teachers were less receptive. Their training reduced their efficiency. Her aim was to get 'a higher tone and getting more thoroughly educated people into the schools to teach the children'. Miss Trevor claimed her educated-class students 'were very much more intelligent than the pupil-teachers, but they have not the same amount of mechanical knowledge; they cannot do sums as well as the pupil-teachers'.

> We cannot do much with them; they go out very nearly as they came in, beyond having learnt a little more by cram. . . . Very much less efficient and very much less physically fit. The strain on their bodies is very great, poor girls.[43]

Miss Trevor was right to raise the issue of health. Policy makers organising the pupil-teacher system had scant grasp of the pressures put on the girls even by the 1880s. Miss Trevor asserted that, by the end of the training, her educated-class students had mastered the elementary subjects; many achieved first-class certificates. With entry at a later age and support from pupil-teacher centres, the apprenticeships would be less gruelling by the end of the century. Evidence from the Cross Commission's Minority Report led to a much fuller enquiry by the Department of Education in 1896. Miss Trevor's negative preconceptions about pupil-teachers may have given her senior governess further notions about taking liberal education into elementary schools, first explored in *The Blotter Letters*.

Hard-pressed throughout the four years she spent there, Miss Mason suddenly resigned from her post as senior governess at Bishop Otter at Christmas 1877, doubtless determined to keep her pupil-teachership a secret forever. The 1877 annual report, now missing, read and approved at the annual meeting of subscribers in May 1878, referred to her departure: 'The Committee greatly regret that the College had lost the valuable services of Miss Mason, the Senior Governess, who has resigned owing to weak health.' She finally left in March after working her required three months' notice by giving 'occasional instruction' for which she was paid £10, instead of her usual £25 salary.

At the AGM in May 1878, the lady principal's valuable contribution to the success of the College was warmly acknowledged. There was no reference to Mr Espinasse or to Miss Mason's efforts. In May 1878, having found the College to be satisfactory, Canon Tinling was very critical of the 'weak and occasional' teaching power. He recommended a larger staff of women resident teachers and felt things only improved when three governesses were appointed by 1880.[44]

Charlotte Mason made two enduring friendships, with Fanny Williams and Frances Hall, who finished the training at Christmas 1877. Frances Hall was appointed mistress of the practising school in January 1878 but left the following November to marry Mr Washington Epps. Miss Williams replaced Miss Mason as senior governess in March 1878. A Miss Brown, later described as 'painstaking and well-informed', who was appointed junior governess in July 1878, was upgraded to senior governess in September over Miss Williams, who was demoted to junior governess but stayed until December 1879 for confirmation of her government certificate.[45]

In 1890 Miss Mason asked Mrs Frances Epps to write about Bishop Otter Memorial College for *Parents' Review*. Mrs Epps described it as an excellent, delightfully situated training college for gentlewomen, offering 'a very happy and profitable time, full of interesting associations, new ideas and mental growth'. On the life of an elementary schoolmistress, she suggested,

> In the first place she must be 'gentle' not 'genteel'; she must be robust in health, both in body and mind to stand the physical fatigue and anxieties that belong to the profession. . . . Added to this she will need enthusiasm for the work with an interest in matters affecting the working classes and a humble belief in the principle that that which acts most powerfully on the condition of the school is the character of the teacher.[46]

Miss Mason's mixed experiences at Bishop Otter left her at a crossroads in 1878. Although her stresses and strains were translated into depression and anxiety, these four years were definitive. The idea of being the principal of an exclusive Church of England training college and practising school for indigent gentlewomen lay dormant. Meanwhile, on 12 March 1878, with no clear way forward, she left Chichester, an inspiring lecturer and emergent writer, prone to 'weak health'.

11.
The Breakthrough in Bradford, 1879–1888

Anxious and exhausted, Charlotte was perplexed about her future. Applying for a high school post in Chester suggests reluctance to relinquish professional teaching. To meet the urgent need for middle-class secondary education, the Girls' Public Day School Trust (founded in 1872), was developing high schools for girls of all ages, modelled on Miss Buss's North London Collegiate School (opened in 1850). Extending girls' education beyond mere instruction and accomplishments enabled them to understand their *relations* to the wider world and pass exams, notably the Cambridge locals, which Charlotte had thought of taking.[1] Yet, taking lunch at home with time for 'home duties' in the protected domestic sphere failed to allay all upper-class fears about 'over-educating' girls in large impersonal groups.

> Girls' high schools, we are told, make the scholars ugly and sickly and we are referred to a golden age in the past . . . when English girls . . . at least learnt to extract essences and distil lavender water.[2]

Charlotte finally wrote to Lizzie in March. Illness had delivered her into 'dear Miss Brandreth's . . . delightful care'. Feeling poorly in Chester, she had called on Dr Coleman who 'said I must have perfect rest for six months'. Perplexed by her symptoms, Dr Coleman took Charlotte to Birmingham to see Professor Balthazar Foster MD FRCP (1840–1913) on 31 January 1878.[3] Foster had studied valvular heart disease but decided that she was 'suffering from overwork'. As Charlotte needed 'absolute rest for some months', he could not 'sanction her doing any educational work for the present'.[4] Rest was the usual treatment for feminine overpressure, a vague catch-all diagnosis.

> The image of the perfect lady, in time, became the image of the disabled lady, the female invalid.[5]

Charlotte preserved his medical note, although heart trouble was not mentioned. She told Lizzie,

> Therefore I gave up the Chester School – went to Chichester for a little to fill a gap tho' against advice & since then I have been here with dear Miss Brandreth, who certainly does possess the secret of rest. Our next move is to Lucerne whither we go in a fortnight & stay for two or three months as the case may be. Another lady travels with us – a Miss D'Arcy – otherwise Sister Maria, the lady with whom Miss Brandreth went to work the Hoxton parish & who is now done up & like somebody else in need of rest. How am I? will be your next kind ? Very well, when I am doing nothing – but knocked up by the least effort – the least attempt to bring myself together & attend to anything. However the Birmingham man promised me that if I would take the 'absolute rest' he commanded, I should be quite well and longing for work when it was over – & so I try to keep in good heart but it is not always easy.[6]

Frailty spared Miss Mason from working her three months' notice at Bishop Otter Memorial College full time. Fanny Williams indubitably offered loyal support. Now Miss Brandreth was providing comforting care *and* more extensive European travel than the Grovehams' Paris trip. After three days in the 'very gay French town', Boulogne, they spent a pleasant week in Paris.

> We did not go to the hotel you . . . stayed at but at the Louvre Hotel which is miles big & very comfortable, more comfortable a good deal than smaller places, the rooms are so many & so large that we do not get in each other's way.

Troyes was 'a quaint old town with narrow streets, overhanging storeys & a very fine gothic cathedral'. Their next stay was at Basle, where, 'think of it dear, the Rhine flowed under the windows of our hotel, flowed with such force as I had never seen before between banks on which the buildings were grouped in a picturesque way beyond description'. This grand tour of 1878 would be the prototype for Miss Mason's future European journeys. Pampered in deference to her invalid status, she travelled like a *grande dame*, tiresome anxieties smoothed away by her patroness's devoted attentions. Her descriptive letter is pregnant with intimations of an emergent writer of geographical texts and the enthusiasm of a Heidi for the Alps.

> And the mountains! The glorious Alps, snow covered now most happily, and delighting us every hour with endless play of colour and apparent change of form.

Lying in bed recovering from the journey, Charlotte closed her letter with a plea, often repeated in later life: 'But I must not write you a long letter now dear as letters are an effort beyond me.'[7]

Returning home through France, Charlotte painted a glowing picture of their visit to a prestigious girls' boarding school in Auteuil, Western Paris, 'as big as the Ho and Co', after the pleasure of seeing the Grovehams who had travelled out there in the rain, generously leaving her more money.

> And on the whole are you pleased with your visit to Paris? & has it done you good? I believed it has thoroughly refreshed you both – you were looking a world better.

The Grovehams left before Madame Rey's grand school fête. Prizes were presented to each girl; all were crowned with coloured wreaths: a white wreath 'for diligence in working with the poor' and pink for *sagesse*. Champagne flowed at an interminable dinner followed by a dance and then bed. Charlotte added that 'the night annoyance . . . has never happened to me since'.[8] Obscure troubling symptoms would periodically dictate complete rest between bouts of frenetic activity.

Back in England during 1878 and 1879, presumably relying upon her savings while seeking safe havens, Miss Mason taught at Selina Fleming's school in Ambleside.[9] She also stayed with her former Davison assistant mistress, Mary Acons, headmistress of Alton National School in Hampshire. She shared the schoolhouse with her assistant mistress, Jane Smith, whose nephew's wife, Winifred Smart, recalled,

> Miss Mason was at that time not well and came home very tired after her country walks. She used to lie on a little sofa (you know the kind with a head piece and no arms) to write up her notes. She must have been a brave spirit.[10]

Preparing a history of the counties of England, Miss Mason pencilled in a notebook, 'The writer hopes that the indefatigable walker will not be aggrieved because she asks him to sit down and ponder . . . and trusts she may be forgiven for endeavouring to see and write a few things rather than to see everything.'[11] It is not clear how much journeying around England Miss Mason actually achieved; she travelled by train and took walks in Hampshire, Surrey and Yorkshire. Much of her material was undoubtedly drawn from Bradshaw and other guide books.

Did Charlotte return to 15 Steyne in early August 1879, just after Arthur Brandreth visited his sister Emily? Stationed in India during the so-called 'Indian Mutiny' (1857–1858), Arthur was aide to Sir John Lawrence (1811–1879), later Lord Lawrence (1869). After Lawrence's deal to end the conflict was rejected in September 1858, he sent forces to quell the Punjab uprising. Concerned about the condition of the British Army during the Indian struggle for independence, Florence Nightingale proposed a new Commission of Enquiry in 1867 into the

British Army's health in collaboration with Lord Lawrence.[12] On 30 July 1879 Florence Nightingale thanked Arthur Brandreth for writing to *The Times,* describing Lord Lawrence's valiant service:

> Sir, I am a stranger to you but not to John Lawrence. . . . Your contributions to his story in [*sic*] the Mutiny is precious beyond words. It is priceless. Could you not publish now soon before the mass of people have forgotten him in the rush of the present day. . . . But what an immeasurable advantage you have, above Macaulay, being the sharer in those great deeds of which you write. . . . Give us his spirit in a sketch by you of the deeds wh. it inspired & which you shared while his name may still be made one of England's and India's 'good words'. . . . We do so want a hero to reverence.[13]

Like her bedridden heroine, Miss Mason set a high value upon the British Empire, which rose to its zenith in 1876 when Queen Victoria (1819–1901) became Empress of India. Did Arthur leave the letter lying about? Somehow the precious missive fell into Miss Mason's hands and stayed there, treasured for life. Did its disappearance cause a breach with her wealthy patroness? There is no record of any contact between them from 1879 onwards. After giving up the Worthing House, by 1881 Miss Brandreth had moved to 1 Bexley Villas at Clewer near Windsor, with Sister Maria, her chosen companion.[14]

By 1881 John Groveham was a commercial traveller; Lizzie had borne him three daughters: Annie E., later Edith Müller (b. 1865), Mary E. (b. 1870) and Mabel Ernestine (b. 1876), later Mrs Curjel. Their faithful cook and domestic servant was Sarah Pendlebury.[15] Alongside family responsibilities, Lizzie had successfully opened her Bradford Girls' Middle-Class School by 1866, at 17 Drewton Street, *without* Charlotte's assistance. The prospectus offered the daughters of the middle classes 'a thoroughly sound practical English Education, which will not be lost when their school days are ended but will tend to make them intelligent and useful members of society. Special attention is given to those subjects that will be the most use in after life. A careful religious training is made the groundwork of the education given.' An exclusion clause, setting the annual fees at six guineas for the seniors, £3 18s for the juniors and £2 5s for the preparatory class, ensured the school was 'beyond the reach of those for whom other schools are provided'.[16]

In contrast to sleepy Chichester, Bradford was a flourishing industrial 'worstedopolis' with a growing population of 197,190 by 1880. Surrounded by desolated moorland, it was cold in winter. The Bradford Library and Literary Society, established in 1774, held 17,000 books, making it a wonderful resource for an aspiring writer. Though dominated by the Lister Mill, a brewery and quarry, Manningham was a pleasant suburb, inhabited by bankers, German manufacturers and respectable tradesfolk. Nearby, Lister

Park, with attractive wooded areas, stretched invitingly over 54 acres.[17]

The Grovehams' upward move to Manningham offered better prospects. The success of the Drewton Street School and John Groveham's commercial transactions clearly enabled the launch of Mornington House Ladies' School at 2 Apsley Crescent, adjacent to Mornington Villas. Mrs Groveham had merely 'conducted' the previous school; the new brochure announced she was principal. The senior, junior and preparatory divisions and a Froebelian infants' division, introducing kindergarten games and object lessons, enabled her to accept middle-class girls of all ages.[18]

2 Apsley Crescent in Manningham: the Grovehams' house.

After parting from Miss Brandreth, teaching middle-class girls with Lizzie was Charlotte's final option. Without a regular income, she needed security. As a prospective writer, was she less wary nervous of her friend's manifest competence? If Charlotte arrived in August 1879, was it her idea to change the name to 'The Ladies' Collegiate School'? In the revised second brochure, the Kindergarten Division became the 'Lower Preparatory Division'. Senior girls could take French, German and Latin as well as book-keeping with the three Rs, Holy Scripture, natural science, history, geography (physical and political), English grammar, composition and literature as well as drawing, vocal music and calisthenics. There was a school library. As the girls went home for lunch and 'proficiency in plain Needlework' was advertised with classes for 'Fancy Needlework' on Saturday mornings, domestic femininity was upheld.

> While bearing an altogether private and select character, this School possesses the advantages of a public High School. It is conducted by Mistresses holding high-class Certificates with an efficient staff of assistants and visiting masters. Instruction is given upon the most modern methods. . . . The pupils are prepared for the Cambridge Local Examinations.[19]

If competent Lizzie demonstrated how to run a highly successful private middle-class school, set fees, retain staff, attract suitable pupils and devise curricula for different age groups while caring for her husband and daughters, Lottie added the sparkle. In 1879, Edith was fourteen, Mary was nine and Mabel was only three. Safely settled in her own room, Charlotte was invited to take a form and teach for two hours daily.[20]

On 3 March 1885, the *Bradford Observer* reported that two girls from The Ladies' Collegiate School had passed the Cambridge locals. High school standards were being achieved.[21] Mrs Groveham recalled that Charlotte had taken part 'in the actual teaching of the school', adding a parent's commendation:

> We shall ever retain most grateful recollections of the benefit our children have received in your excellent school, especially the thoroughly good religious instruction and reverence for sacred things inculcated. We have also a keen appreciation of Miss Mason's good influence. Our girls think & speak of her with much affection.[22]

In 1887, Mrs Groveham took over 1 Apsley Crescent; she may have run the school until 1900. By 1901 she was living in Grassington in the Yorkshire Dales. In 1911 she settled in Woodbridge, Suffolk, near her widowed, youngest daughter, Mabel Curjel.[23]

Had Charlotte really lost touch with her relatives? There is no record of any reaction to the death of her half-sister, Hannah Birchall, on 13 March 1876 at her youngest son Oswald's Ilkley house. Poor Hannah died of marasmus, a devastating weight loss caused by five years of diarrhoea, at the age of sixty-six. Charlotte certainly knew Oswald as a small boy in Birkenhead. Now he and his wife, Elizabeth, were living at Moorbank, Clifton Road, Ilkley, in Wharfedale, where their four children would be born and where they would stay until after 1901. After Hannah's death, Edwin Birchall and their daughter, Diana, later an art student, moved to Douglas, Isle of Man. An indefatigable naturalist, Edwin studied lepidopterous fauna and other species until he died on 2 May 1884 in Douglas, attended by Diana. Widowed before 1871, Huldah Jane had moved to Lewisham to help her daughter with her six children. She stayed on to keep house when Sarah died after her son Isidare's birth in March 1880. Huldah Jane eventually succumbed to 'senile decay and cardiac failure' in 1902.[24] Who knows if Charlotte kept in touch with the half-sister who had known her from birth?

Fanny Williams had fallen under Miss Mason's spell. Summoned to Bradford after Christmas 1879, she was later said to have adopted all of Miss Mason's teachings to the letter: 'We talked it, she lived it.'[25] She recalled, 'I wished to teach in a school and through Miss Mason's influence, I was appointed Headmistress of a Higher Grade Board School in Bradford. I did not succeed very well in this position; the little success I did achieve was due to Miss Mason's advice.' Fanny was mistress of the girls' department of the Belle Vue Boys' Higher Grade Board School (founded in 1877) in nearby Lumb Lane, under the dynamic leadership of the first headmaster, Richard

Miss Fanny Williams is summoned to Bradford.

Lishman, who served the school until 1919. These hybrid schools had emerged in piecemeal fashion after the 1870 Education Act to remedy the lack of secondary education for bright elementary school children up to fourteen years. They offered 'higher subjects' including science.[26] Both Fanny and Charlotte fell ill at Christmas 1881.[27]

In 1882, John Groveham suffered from peritonitis for eight days. His untimely death at the age of fifty-two on 25 October 1882, in Lizzie's presence, may have altered the delicate balance of the relationship between the three women in his house.[28] Twenty years would pass before appendices could be safely surgically removed, as in the case of King Edward VII in 1902. The sudden loss of her husband of eighteen years may have drawn Lizzie closer to Lottie, excluding Fanny from their longstanding friendship. Although Fanny was an indispensable support to her former lecturer, her 'hearty ringing laugh which greeted every discomfort and turned every annoyance into a joke' may have grated on the ears of the grieving widow and her three daughters. Soon after, Miss Williams left Bradford and was appointed headmistress of the London Orphan Asylum School in Watford, which was founded in 1813. By 1890 she was superintendent of the women's training college in Kildare Street, Dublin.[29]

Early in 1880, Miss Mason had sent *A History of England*, renamed *The Forty Shires,* to Hatchards of Piccadilly. The Preface stated that the book was designed for pleasant holiday reading 'in the hope it may prove to have a certain educational value'. Mr Hatchard, a philanthropic supporter of new writers, commended the book, although there were 'already two or more of the kind published. . . . We have glanced at your MSS and like the easy style of it very much.' On 19 March, Hatchards' reader declared,

> The manuscript is full of interest of a special kind and if such books as *Dear Home* in competition with the modern school books still find a ready sale, this will, I think, command success. The treatment of the different counties is somewhat unequal.[30]

This delightfully old-fashioned book, set with twenty-one charming woodcut illustrations, was enlivened by local stories and legends as well as facts. Charlotte's unequal treatment of some shires was not remedied.

For example, 'Of Essex, also, little need be said' was merely followed by a brief page of text. With striking detachment, Charlotte did not expand on places she knew well. Worthing was reduced to a sentence and Birkenhead omitted. Yet Liverpool's grand buildings, ports, trade and 'merchant princes' were glowingly described:

> The ships from Ireland bring not only butter and eggs, pork and bacon but a constant stream of Irish people. Many of these settle in Liverpool, which has a large Irish population, mostly poor folk who have no clear way of getting a living; but many just come to take their places in the emigrant ships which carry them all over the ocean to find a home, and work, and wages in the New World.[31]

As a child she had followed that stream of Irish people to Birkenhead. Her merchant father, who died in Liverpool, had connections with Liverpool freemen. Richard Mason and her half brothers-in-law, Peter Doyle and Edwin Birchall, had all worked in the city.

Charlotte was a published writer! She sent copies to her friends; 840 copies were sold by June. Delighted with *The Forty Shires*, Mr Read wrote that he would 'not fail at every possible opportunity to express my favourable opinion of whatever you propose to effect: for I am sure it will be most satisfactorily performed'.[32] On 9 December 1880, Mr Stanford forwarded a kindly note from Arabella Buckley (1840–1929), a well-known writer of scientific books for children which would be used for forty years in Charlotte's future correspondence school. She had seen a 'nice little notice of Miss Mason's *Shires*' in *St James's Gazette*'s Christmas books list and said, 'I think that book ought to do.'[33] Although well-reviewed in at least ten papers, notably as 'one of the best books for children we have seen this year', *The Forty Shires* was expensive to produce and lost £105. Miss Mason received £10 for her pains.[34]

On Mr Hatchard's advice, Miss Mason approached Mr Stanford, who undertook to publish her *Geographical Readers for Elementary Schools* at his own expense, on certain conditions. He would pay Miss Mason a royalty of 5 per cent or 7 per cent depending upon the price of the copies sold. Stanford's London Geographical Series included notable works by the late A. Keith Johnston (1804–1871), Fellow of the Royal Geographical Society, a well-travelled explorer and the first exponent of physical geography, Miss Davy's speciality.[35]

Miss Mason's five *Geographical Readers* came out between 1881 and 1884. Stanford's anonymous reader thought Volume I, *Elementary Geography* (1881), dedicated to the 'Otters', and Volume II, *The British Empire and the Divisions of the Globe* (1882), were too difficult for Standards I and II and should not be published. He preferred the 'eminently bright and pictorial style' of the last three volumes. The descriptions of 'the English Counties and some European countries' surpassed anything he had seen before.

Boldly listed as a separate book, Volume III, *The Counties of England* (c. 1881), was a shortened version of *The Forty Shires*. Volume IV, *The Countries of Europe, their Sceneries and Peoples* (1883), was intended for middle-class *and* elementary school children taking Standard V. An expanded version of Volume II, the fifth volume, *The Old and the New World* (1884), was for Standard VI children. Stanford's reader's eldest daughter wished *her* school used these books. The literary style of the *Geographical Readers for Elementary Schools*, mingling history with legend, soared above dull lists of physical phenomena. Unrevised, the books would be recommended texts for Charlotte's future correspondence school.

Thomas Godolphin Rooper, a humane inspector of schools.

Alas, the inappropriate Victorian imperialist racism in Volume V would cause consternation in 1937 over unfortunate innuendoes about American leaders' misbehaviours. Worse still, the Turks of the towns were said to be 'debased and corrupt', the Bedouin described as 'an inferior being . . . utterly lawless, shifty, untrustworthy', the Chinese as 'a nation of gamblers & fortune tellers' and the Bengali as 'weak and cringing'. Miss Mason's loyal followers had failed to consider that the critically outdated, imperialist readers were an obstacle to children learning 'to sympathise from their earliest years with people of other countries'.[36]

The readers brought contact with Thomas Godolphin Rooper MA (1847–1903). As the HMI for the West Riding of Yorkshire, he 'breathed a new spirit into the methods of English education. Always exacting a high standard, he rose above formalism and routine by throwing himself into every movement likely to interest teachers in their profession and humanise their approach.'[37] Rooper failed to introduce Charlotte's readers into his schools; funds were short and horizons limited.

> It is, I am afraid, the tendency of bad books like bad coin to drive out good. The Art of Bookmaking under the New Code is something fit to amuse Gods and men. Even our old friend *Horatius* has to be garbled to suit the market. The text – easy as it is – is too hard for children under the Code.

Rooper's gloomy assertion that the fault lay with a state educational system that failed to encourage pupils to read big books would lodge in Miss Mason's mind. His request for a sixpenny pamphlet on Yorkshire for the schools went unheeded.[38]

By 1885, fresh aspirations were lifting Miss Mason out of the schoolroom. She rented a pew at St Mark's Church in Grosvenor Road, near Apsley Crescent. A new evangelical church, St Mark's, was consecrated in 1875, serving a parish of 7,061 souls. The Revd Edward Wynne MA (d. 1892), a TCD graduate and an experienced evangelical vicar, ministered at St Mark's from 1878 until 1889. As at Worthing Chapel of Ease, Wynne's parishioners came from the higher classes; pew rents raised £200 per annum. For Charlotte, acclimatised from childhood to Holy Trinity's eccentric ornamentation, entering St Mark's through the decorated narthex may have seemed natural. Inside, there were six 'peculiarly striking' stained glass windows. The choir was paved in encaustic marble, the font was 'a handsome work composed of variously coloured marbles' and the pulpit 'an elaborate composition in marble, alabaster and metal work'. The church was demolished in 1956.[39] Miss Mason led St Mark's young women's Bible class and was a lady parish visitor to cottage mothers. She attended Mrs Wynne's gatherings, where Shakespeare's plays were read. She joined the Bradford Philosophical Society, founded in 1865. Linked to the Browning Society, it promoted the study of science, literature and art.[40] Mr Wynne thanked her warmly for *The Forty Shires*:

> I shall always esteem it very highly as a present from its gifted authoress. . . . I have looked into 'The Forty Shires' and find it a most instructive little book, comprising a very large amount of information in a compact form and presenting it in a simple, readable style. . . . Mrs Wynne is delighted with the book and means to read it to the women at her Mothers' Meeting as she is sure it will interest them.[41]

Like other urban centres, Bradford was caught up in the Victorian Christian revival. In 1879 the alert American consul in Bradford had remarked, 'It is astonishing what a movement is abroad preparing for the new advent of Christianity – the selfish and luxurious are shaking in their shoes.'[42] At St Mark's, larger premises were needed for this nationwide call to mission. Church members were drawn into the fundraising effort which successfully established a new Parochial Institute and Sunday school building shown on an 1890 map. There was a bazaar and a concert series; a large crowd attended the concert given by Miss Groveham and Milly Müller.[43]

The proverbial cry of the school teacher, 'Oh that children were born without parents', demanded a remedy. In offering to deliver a course of eight lectures to local ladies to raise church funds, Miss Mason's new cause was parent education. Her researches took her to the ladies' benches of the British Museum Reading Room in August 1885; no doubt she discussed her ideas with Mrs Frances Epps, the former Otter with whom she stayed in Bloomsbury.[44]

> In giving lectures to ladies preparing to teach in elementary schools, the extraordinary leverage which some knowledge of the principles of physiological-psychology gives to those who have the bringing up of children was brought home to me. . . . During . . . years of educational work, literary and other, a single idea was taking shape. . . . What if these two or three vitalising educational principles could be brought before parents?[45]

If humble Gertrudes sitting in cottage kitchens lacked the scientific principles to train their offspring, much was awry among the higher classes. Governesses were poorly educated, nurses ignorant and parents heedless of their responsibilities. Earnest late Victorian parents were obsessed with the importance of education in an increasingly competitive age while preserving the ideal of orderly domestic life. Upholding civilisation, education was seen as a liberating and modernising force, combating fears about the passing of the old order, the rise of secularism and the decline of Christian belief. Post-Darwinian anxieties about mankind's ape ancestry found expression in anxieties about moral decline or the forceful campaigns for workers and women's rights to education and employment. Greater awareness of children as lively persons in their own right fuelled concerns about their upbringing.[46]

Mrs Wynne attended all of the eight lectures, eagerly discussing the points with her husband. After reading Lecture VI on 'The Will and the Conscience', Mr Wynne commented,

> You go into the heart of the matter & deal with the whole question in a thoroughly practical way. I have been greatly struck with some of the counsels you lay down for the religious training of the child, knowing them to be opposed to the ordinary practice of worthy Christian parents but convinced that they will be adapted to develop a healthy spiritual character. . . . I am satisfied that the publication of these lectures would be an immense boon to the cause of Christian education. There is a widespread dissatisfaction with the system of cramming which goes under the name of education. But we want someone to point out the right direction in which the true educator should proceed.[47]

Emboldened by Mr Wynne's praise, Miss Mason added an introduction and despatched *Home Education* to Kegan Paul and Co. Ltd, known for publishing serious books. Did the Groveham girls make the fair copy and offer ideas as 'girls of the period'? The Revd Charles Kegan Paul (1828–

1902) corrected the page proofs. Sympathetic to an emergent woman writer, he noted, 'this book is an excellent and very sensible one.' Finding few faults, apart from the author's use of 'baby talk' and excessive praise of monochrome engravings, he queried whether it was intended for the less well-off classes or for the very rich.[48]

The remarkable assurance with which the lectures were delivered infuses the original version. Convinced of her duty to restore the moral compass to late Victorian home training, Miss Mason was neither married nor a mother, but, as an onlooker who saw most of the game, she had the advantage of being an experienced, professionally trained schoolteacher, unlike her public school counterparts. Several papers offered favourable reviews. The *Reading Mercury* encapsulated the heart of the matter:

> Of the making of books about education there has been no end. The author has availed herself of the rich harvest of thought and experience of the past but has, by the way, gleaned new grain and fresh flowers for her readers. . . . A commendable feature . . . is her employment of physiological and psychological teaching – the latter perhaps a little too much from one school of writers – to enforce the care of the body and culture of the mind. On some of the many details . . . opinions will inevitably differ and rightly so. . . . However . . . this volume . . . will prove helpful and suggestive to many parents and instructors of youth.[49]

There is a widely held belief, engendered by reverential PNEU disciples, that Miss Mason's educational ideas were entirely original. This was never the case; she drew upon wide-ranging sources from Locke to Rousseau and Pestalozzi as well as from nineteenth-century physiologists, as the *Reading Mercury* reviewer remarked. Although her timely lectures, fresh in tone, were published in the wake of a vast and varied range of women's writing on motherhood, education and women's place, she ignored eminent past women writers.[50] Instead, Miss Mason sought authenticity from leading male theorists from the seventeenth century onwards, daringly including secular evolutionists such as Thomas Huxley (1825–1895) and G.H. Lewes (1817–1878) to support her view that parents should master the new physiological science of education.

> Whoever has closely studied the evolution of the faculties, will see the folly and wickedness of leaving children to the care of ignorant servants and vulgar companions at a period when impressions are most indelible – a period when, as we know, the germs of the future character are deposited.

The impetus for *Home Education* was *Mental Physiology* by Dr William Carpenter (1813–1885), a sequel to his magnum opus, *The Principles of General and Comparative Physiology* (1839), praised by Herbert Spencer (1820–1903).

He offered a scientific basis for well-established seventeenth-century advice on habit formation and character training, derived from *Some Thoughts on Education* (1693) by Dr John Locke, already embedded in Victorian upper-class upbringing. Locke's ideas had influenced the 'new educationists', notably Rousseau, whose widely read *Émile or On Education* (1762) had informed Pestalozzi's naturalistic, down to earth teaching methods, familiar to Miss Mason from the Home and Colonial Training College.[51] Miss Mason gracefully blended the fashionable 'new education' recognition of the child as a self-acting, self-developing being – not Locke's *tabula rasa* – with a Wordsworthian romantic vision of angelic little children 'trailing clouds of glory' from God in heaven.

She felt that parenthood should be considered a profession: 'That work which is of most importance to society is the bringing-up and instruction of the children.' The distinguished atheist and bachelor Herbert Spencer had declared in *Essays on Education Etc.* (1861), 'The training of children, physical, moral and intellectual is dreadfully defective.' Parents were not educated for parenthood, the 'gravest of responsibilities'. Charlotte Mason commended Spencer's idiosyncratic take on non-coercive upbringing, parental defects, good health and the sound Pestalozzian education in which she had been trained.[52] Unlike Spencer and Locke, Carpenter was a family man who played the organ regularly at St John's Wood Unitarian Church. A physician, zoologist and physiologist, he was also a keen scientific naturalist. Reared on Paley's theories of intelligent design, Miss Mason explained that, while much could be learnt from the scientific laws presented by Carpenter, the basis of natural law was that

> the universe of mind, as the universe of matter, is governed by unwritten laws of God; that the child cannot blow soap bubbles or think his flitting thoughts otherwise than in obedience to Divine Laws; that all safety, progress and success in life come of obedience to law, to the laws of mental, moral, or physical science or that spiritual science, which the Bible unfolds.
>
> All our Great Educational Reformers have been men. The reforms of women have taken the direction rather of practical application than of original thought. This is worth thinking of in connection with the theory that the home training of children is the mother's concern. Happily, it does not fall to each of us to conceive, *for the first time*, the principles which underlie our work. But when we take the conceptions of other minds into ours so that we are able to work them out – to handle them as the skilled artisan handles his tools, to *produce* by their means – why, then, we do originate?[53]

In that sense, *Home Education,* her most engaging book, was an original treatise.

Reluctant to 'pander to the child worship to which we are all succumbing', Miss Mason insisted on the discipline of habit training. Carpenter's discovery that habit training left permanent traces in brain tissue confirmed Locke's view that character was formed by early training in good habits. Therefore, habit training was a matter of great urgency as, after physical maturity had been reached, 'both the Intellectual and Moral Character have become in a great degree fixed'.[54]

Carpenter's 'valuable educational hints' based on his physiological findings explained how to uphold domestic order and control behaviour. They confirmed those repetitive Worthing sermons proclaiming that 'habit is ten natures'. Habit training, the central plank of Miss Mason's rational educational philosophy, was said to ensure that once the child had mastered physical habits, such as shutting the door every time, keeping clean and neat, tidying up toys and regularly practising sports or music, these would be permanently retained, *provided* the mother did *not* falter in her training, which, Miss Mason claimed, was *not* laborious!

> It is necessary that the mother be always on the alert to nip in the bud the bad habit her children may be in the act of picking up from servants, or from other children.[55]

Reflecting the puritan tradition of moral and religious inculcation which demanded education from the cradle, habit training appealed to puritanical evangelicals poised to eradicate evil from fallen human nature.[56] Habit training also appealed to evolutionists who believed in mankind's progress. Carpenter's physiology anticipated theories of sub-conscious mental functioning integral to Freudian psycho-analytical method. Influenced by the personal struggle of J.S. Mill (1806–1873) with the determinist doctrine of human automatism, Carpenter argued that, duly organised, habit-training could control the forces of instinct and irrational thought processes suggestive of man's descent from ape ancestry. These were associated with the contemporary bogey, human automatism, defined as 'the performance of actions without conscious thought or intention and typically without awareness'.[57] R.L. Stevenson (1850–1894) made automatism terrifyingly explicit in *The Strange Case of Dr Jekyll and Mr Hyde* (1886).

To illustrate the key relationship between the human will and the guiding light of conscience, 'the law giver', Miss Mason explained that parents could not rely on the interventions of 'Divine grace' if they chose to leave their children's will power 'undeveloped or misdirected':

> 'I AM, I OUGHT, I CAN, and I WILL' are (as has been recently well-said) the only firm foundation-stones on which we can base our attempt to climb into a higher sphere of existence.

Changing the order of her future mantra, by accident or design, to 'I am, I can, I ought, I will', Miss Mason upheld the right of parents to maintain their authority in training their children for future life; she sanctified the phrase by attributing it to St Augustine.[58]

Further developing these ideas in Lecture VI on 'The Will and the Conscience', which had fascinated Mrs Wynne, Miss Mason challenged her great-great-grandmother's puritanical view that the child's 'will' should be broken, and spoke of '*willessness*' rather than *wilfulness*. Habit training the will-less child to exercise will power was as important for intellectual development as forming the moral conscience. Conscience, developed from the right application of will power, was encapsulated in Carpenter's paradigm. Character was the result of conduct, regulated by will and developed through powers of attention leading the child into the way that he should go. As Charlotte had personally discovered, an individual had the power to form his or her own character. In emphasising the importance of acquiring the habit of attention early in life, Miss Mason followed Locke's recommendation that teachers should secure the pupil's attention and engage interest, noting that 'What the mind is intent upon and careful of, that it remembers best', which resonated with Pestalozzi's views on securing attention.

Miss Mason's call to ministry was manifest in her reflections on 'Divine Life in the Child'. To bring their children to a knowledge of Christian teaching, mothers were advised to select a 'few quickening thoughts' because out 'of the vast mass of the doctrines and precepts of religion . . . there are only a few vital truths', such as 'Our Father in heaven', that will have meaning for the young child. A mother should read 'the beautiful stories of the Bible' without commentary and without selecting verses for the child to learn by grind. The idea was to give the child the idea of joy in belief 'as one lights a torch at the fire' to enable him or her to grow in religious understanding.[59]

In Lecture II, 'Outdoor Life', Miss Mason creatively expanded ideas from Locke, Rousseau and Pestalozzi in offering children myriad ways of observing and experiencing nature. Lecture V, 'Lesson as Instruments of Education', offered a flexible, wide, liberal curriculum for home schoolrooms for children up to nine years, which Miss Mason would later develop further. She suggested that before learning to read, children should listen to stories to acquire new, fruitful ideas from worthwhile books, not the 'weak literature' she called twaddle. Recommending short, interesting lessons to secure attention, Miss Mason extolled the study of natural objects out of doors with plenty of time for imaginative play, games and exercise. To uphold interest, formal history lessons should be varied by heroic stories from Plutarch's *Lives* and geography from observations during walks. Following Rousseau's and Spencer's progressive theories of education through self-discovery, she advised that empirical investigation into botany, literature and the arts should be taught by experts if mothers lacked the knowledge.

Two topical lectures on 'The Home Education of the Schoolboy and Schoolgirl' and 'Young Maidenhood' were the most highly praised by contemporary reviewers. For boys, Miss Mason held that thorough training in the classics at public schools prepared them for future empire building, although intellectual development was inhibited by 'cramming' to pass competitive examinations. Girls should not be mentally idle, despite fears of 'overpressure'. As school was the dominant force in children's lives, she felt that the home, as in Ruskin's romantic ideal, should offer a liberal cultural atmosphere and moral training to compensate for mechanical school teaching. 'The liberal soul deviseth liberal things,' declaimed the pedagogic lecturer, giving her remarks the aura of biblical authority as well as Matthew Arnold's 'sweetness and light'. To get children through 'the awkward age' to acquire good manners, Miss Mason recommended *Evenings at Home* liberal culture with music, aesthetics, elegant table talk and the reading aloud of *good* literature, not twaddle. Sunday readings should be chosen to suit the holiness of the day.[60]

Continuing these themes in Lecture VIII, Miss Mason said that while grown-up daughters at home should assist their mothers with domestic duties, they needed time for study, exercise and sports. Young maidens should read 'earnest *intellectual* works' to develop sound opinions on matters of public concern, such as the threat of revolution arising from 'these times of dangerous alienation between class and class' and the dark decline of belief in Christianity.

> Women have been clamorous for their rights, and men have, on the whole, been generous and gentle in meeting their demands. So much has been gained that we have no right to claim immunities which belong to the seclusion of the harem. We are not free to say, 'Oh these things are beyond me; I leave such questions to the gentlemen.'[61]

Not all protected daughters would marry; those who had to earn their living needed recognised training.

> It is not necessary to specify the lines for which women may qualify by thorough training – art, music, teaching, nursing, loftier careers for the more ambitious and better educated; but may I say a word for teaching in elementary schools – a lowly labour of quite immeasurable usefulness. . . . May I urge, too, the advantage of training for work which has been too long the refuge of the destitute – I mean, the truly honourable, and often exceedingly pleasant post of governess in a family.[62]

Planning her own future projects, Miss Mason had unerringly struck a contemporary chord by offering practical solutions to the educated classes' anxieties about their daughters.

The publication of *Home Education* would bring its author a definitive and delightful new friendship. Emeline Steinthal (1856–1921), known to Charlotte as Lienie, had married Francis Steinthal (1854–1934) on 5 April 1882 in Rochdale. Mr Steinthal, a worsted merchant, was son of the patriarchal Carl Gustavus Steinthal, a German Jew, who came from Frankfurt in 1844 to found the Little Germany wool manufacturing colony in Bradford. A naturalised British citizen, Francis was a Christian like his wife and the epitome of the upright Victorian gentleman with a courteous respect for royalty and the conventions of polite society. After his father's death, he took over and expanded the family firm.

Lienie, eldest daughter of George Petrie, came from a well-known Rochdale family. With a lifelong concern for the poorer classes, she took Sunday school classes and collected up the wildest ragged boys from Rochdale streets to hold meetings with them; many grew up to be sound citizens. She was an artist and gifted sculptor, regularly exhibiting sculptures and miniatures at the Royal Academy and later taking up watercolours and brush drawing. Her marble bust of John Bright (1811–1889), Quaker radical statesman and family friend, was placed in Oldham Town Hall.[63]

In November 1886, the Steinthal family moved to 2 Walmer Place, between Apsley Crescent and Manningham Lane. Early in 1887 Lienie read a newspaper article about *Home Education* and discovered that the author lived nearby. Lienie was bringing up three young children: Paul Telford (1883–1930), Dorothea (1884–1978) and Francis Eric (1886–1974). Her fourth child, Paul Cuthbert (1888–1979), would be Charlotte Mason's godson.[64] Seeking guidance, Lienie wrote to the author of *Home Education*. They met in the spring; their warm friendship lasted her lifetime. Miss Mason took wholeheartedly to this enthusiastic young mother:

> That so charming a woman, so full of vitality and many interests, should be prepared to go so deeply into thought about education was a surprise to the writer. So sympathetic and so full of understanding was she that a project nursed for years (and that had taken form in 'Home Education') was divulged to her and she threw herself heartily into the aims and hopes of what was to be the P.N.E.U.[65]

Lienie, in whom the urge to reform battled with her artistic temperament, possessed great force of character and a loving ability to draw the best out of people. Delighted with Miss Mason's 'bubbling ideas', 'vitality and enthusiasm', she and her new mentor talked for hours as they paced round 'those Manningham squares of which we wore out the pavements'.[66] Lienie needed an outlet for her mental energies to complement her domestic responsibilities, as she was not free to study further as a sculptor. Lienie's mother had been reading *Home Education* exclaiming, 'Why didn't someone tell me these things? I could have brought you up so much better!' Lienie wrote from Germany, 'It was nice for us that we found you. It has often comforted me. With fondest love, Your ever loving and grateful Lienie.'[67]

Charlotte, an orphan painfully at odds with her past, was driven by intense yearning for the ideal home and family life epitomised in *Home Education*. Her charismatic dynamism knew no bounds; her inspirational mission was fired by Lienie's urge to do good. She responded with true affection to Lienie, her family and her concerns. Lizzie Groveham's unfailingly generous support was assumed. Like Florence Nightingale's favourite aunt, Mrs Mary Smith, Charlotte became 'Aunt Mai' to the Steinthal children. Dorothea recalled,

> We loved 'Aunt Mai,' with her slow smile and gentle voice, and every Christmas brought a batch of books with a personal inscription for each one of us. A bright-coloured illustrated 'Chaucer for Children' and another, 'Queen Victoria's Dolls.' I remember specially that Miss Mason liked to teach her dolls as a child.[68]

Mrs Steinthal and Miss Mason planned to start a propagandist society to bring those 'two or three vitalising educational principles' before a wider audience of parents 'without appearance of presumption'. Energised with anticipatory zeal, Miss Mason addressed Selina Fleming's school leavers in Ambleside. Alice Burn (née Gates) recalled her magical spell:

> A very ordinary looking little lady sitting in the midst of us, motioning us to draw up closed round her . . . a voice so quiet that one must concentrate if one wanted to listen, a smile that took us all with one sweep into a very confidential partnership. This was no dictator – no lecturer – no superior being talking down to us from a height, rather she seemed a fairy godmother with a wand which touching lightly many quite ordinary thoughts and facts made them glow with colour and mysterious light, giving a hint of hidden treasure within. . . . Speaking to us who were 'leaving' there was no oration on the subject – that too well-worn theme – of what we were going to do with our lives, to become, to train, to work at, no warnings against this or that. . . . Rather with that confidential smile, that hidden wave of her wand, she showed us what wonderful even charming creatures we were with just one boundless outlook, one limitless possibility and opportunity. . . . We were women – each would become a mother or aunt to children somewhere, children with their personalities – sacred ground.[69]

'Just before the summer holidays' in 1887, Mrs Steinthal opened her drawing room at 2 Walmer Place 'to discuss a scheme for a Parents' Educational Union'. A drawing room meeting was the accepted setting for launching a new society. There were only about a dozen present, including Mrs E.P. Arnold-Forster, Lienie's longstanding friend; Mrs Gates, the County Court judge's wife and Alice's mother; Mrs Priestman, a Quaker; Mrs Carter Squire, the headmistress of a small girls' school; Mr Rooper; and the Revd William Keeling, headmaster of the famous Bradford Grammar School. Mrs Groveham was not present. Miss Mason addressed the gathering from hastily pencilled notes on 'a simple sheet of foolscap paper'. The outcome seemed unclear. Eventually, it was hazarded that parent education was the aim rather than reform of the educational system.[70]

Lienie Steinthal, co-founder of the Parents' Educational Union.

A former tutor, Mr Rooper understood upper-class liberal home education: 'From the first inception of the idea he was with us . . . he went straight to the principles of the Union and embraced them with great warmth and insight.'[71] Rooper had studied under T.H. Green (1836–1882) of Balliol, the model for Gray in Mrs Humphry Ward's best-selling novel *Robert Elsmere* (1888). Subsequently troubling to Miss Mason, the novel described how Gray's intellectual argumentation destroyed Robert Elsmere's religious belief.

In August 1887 Miss Mason lectured on 'The Bearing of Home Education on Technical Education' at the British Association meeting in Manchester, where she met the Revd Hardwicke Rawnsley (1851–1920), later a canon of Carlisle, Lakeland poet and co-founder of the National Trust with Octavia Hill (1838–1912). The wife of Professor Munro, the conference organiser, recalled, 'I remember Miss C.M. Mason very well. . . . [T]he outstanding feature was her vivid personality, her clear presentation of her thesis and the marvellous effect of her inspiration on everyone.'[72]

In the autumn of 1887, invitation cards were sent to 200 locally influential citizens to launch a prototype Bradford PEU for parents *and* educationists at the Bradford Grammar School. The details of the meeting, described here, were later recorded in *A New Educational Departure.* Miss Mason outlined the Walmer Place deliberations, explaining that the aim was to raise parent education to the level of scientific physiological and psychological research. After much discussion, it was resolved that while every parent needed modern scientific guidance, the practical wisdom of experienced parents and 'young earnest-minded parents full of purpose for their children' would give the new society credibility in educating public opinion. Fathers were invited to join because they shared upbringing responsibilities; their presence at meetings would confer 'vigour and power'. However, young people, the parents of the future, were excluded because they could be 'lynx-eyed in spying inconsistencies, and might be quick to think, if they did not say, that theory and practice failed to jump together'.

Mrs Steinthal and Mr Rooper insisted that parents of all classes should be included. Others present disagreed because 'while there was common ground on which rich and poor should meet together . . . the details of home training and culture are not the same for people who have nurseries and artistic surrounding and those whose lot is cast within narrower lines.'

Accordingly membership was restricted to educated- and upper-class parents and teachers, to present ideal, rational parenthood, combining the best traditional methods with modern scientific findings. Compromise on the class issue was addressed, but not resolved, by the decision to attend the 'usual meeting places' of members of the artisan class and work through existing organisations, such as guilds, mothers' meetings and temperance halls. Eighty members enrolled on the spot. As a working model, the programme seemed modest by comparison with Miss Mason's soaring aim of educating public opinion nationally. Between four and six lectures were planned for the winter with two or three summer field excursions for mothers and children, led by a naturalist.[73] At Mrs Steinthal's insistence, a meeting for artisan parents was held at the Temperance Hall. In the first year, there were four working mothers' meetings, two mixed parents' meetings and three meetings for nursemaids. Lienie, later a gifted speaker, made her debut.

> My very dear Miss Mason
>
> . . . You deserve every good thing and every success. I am only afraid that you may have too much to do. I must confess that I was very nervous about that first meeting . . . and I dreaded your letter about it – that has done more to cure my foolish nerves than anything else could and now I feel quite brave about the future.[74]

In November 1887, Miss Mason heard from Mary Hart-Davis, the wife of the vicar of Dunsden, near Reading, and a daughter of Sir Thomas Dyke Acland (1809–1898), parliamentarian and educationist, who would delight in sharing seventeenth-century writings with the 'brilliant' pedagogue.[75]

> I owe you so much gratitude for your book, *Home Education*. . . . I have read and re-read it so many times, that much of it is a possession for life, and I can truly say it has given me inspiration, strength of purpose,

> guidance and courage which has made a real difference to me in health. I can never remember feeling so light-hearted and joyous after reading some of it. . . . I have 8 children between the ages of three and thirteen and the problems of life & education are very hard to solve sometimes. We are far away from High Schools and many modern advantages are quite out of our reach, but your book has made me feel what can be aimed at and accomplished in Home Education.[76]

Approbation from a stranger emboldened Charlotte Mason to despatch a red-bound copy of *Home Education* to the Countess of Aberdeen (1857–1939). Lord Aberdeen (1847–1934) and his wife, Ishbel, who married in 1877, were earnest, evangelical, philanthropic reformers. Lady Aberdeen had founded the Onward and Upward Association (1882), providing correspondence courses for isolated women farm servants on her husband's Haddo House Scottish estates. As Lady Aberdeen had borne five children between 1879 and 1884, home education was a priority. She commented privately, 'I am v. pleased with a new book, "Home Education" by Charlotte Mason; really sensible, rather on the lines of Herbert Spencer.'[77] Miss Mason received a gracious response on 12 December 1887:

> Will you allow me to send you a line of sincere thanks for your book 'Home Education'. It cannot fail to be most helpful & productive of much good. May I also venture to ask if you know of any governess, either foreign or English, who is imbued with the ideas expressed in this book and whom you could recommend for three children . . . one too who would wish to work with the mother.[78]

Ishbel Aberdeen was a highly intelligent aristocrat. Her commendation opened up exciting possibilities. Mrs Boyd Carpenter was chosen as the PEU's first president. In 1883 she had married the silver-tongued Bishop of Ripon (1841–1918), beloved of Queen Victoria, and was bringing up eight children by his first marriage with three of her own.[79] The four Bradford winter lectures, held during 1888 and 1889, included Mrs Boyd Carpenter's presidential address and a talk by Lady Aberdeen.[82] Membership doubled in the second season.

The Bradford PEU was Miss Mason's 'open sesame' into an expanding universe. The price was the relegation of Lizzie Groveham's unstinting love and sacrifice to the shadows. In the spring of 1889, the Steinthal family moved seven miles out of Bradford to St John's, a spacious house at Wharfemead with beautiful views. Lienie kept up her clay modelling and brush drawing Saturday classes at the Girls' Belle Vue School.[80] In 1889 the faithful Wynnes left for the Forest Gate parish in London's East End. Bradford was losing its charm.

12.

'Education is an Atmosphere, a Discipline, a Life', 1888–1893

If Charlotte felt 'fettered' in Bradford like her great-grandfather in Dublin, she had inherited the Gough brothers' missionary fervour. The price of her frenetic educational propaganda campaign was periodic physical prostration. Perturbing conflicts with the committees beset the three-year journey to the formal constitution of the Parents' National Educational Union in June 1890. Lack of income powered Miss Mason's resolve to start remunerative Ambleside educational projects, enabled by Selina Fleming's generous hospitality.

Lady Aberdeen invited Miss Mason to address upper-class mothers at Hamilton House in London on 5 June 1888, hosted by Lord and Lady Wimborne, saying 'I could not for a moment consent to your not speaking first and we hope that you will speak for half an hour.' Invited to bring her friends, this meeting heralded the 'coming out' of Charlotte Mason and the new Union. Her lecture was published in *Murray's Magazine*.[1]

Using Lady Aberdeen's name as her introduction, Miss Mason wrote to numerous dignitaries. The choleric Archbishop Benson (1829–1896) withheld his patronage, finding her aims unclear.[2] With Miss Clough she struck gold. Invited to Newnham College, Cambridge, from 8 to 11 November 1889 to talk things over, she scribbled her plan for the new Union, oddly named the 'Draft Proof', on the train. Miss Clough, who had 'a sort of happy way of managing suggestions which had the force of commands', introduced her to, among others, Frances Buss; Helen Gladstone; Louise Creighton, the wife of Mandell Creighton (1843–1901), future Bishop of London; and the Hon. Mrs Lyttelton, the wife of the cricketer schoolmaster, Revd Hon. Edward Lyttelton (1855–1942). Canon B.F. Westcott (1825–1901) shared Miss Clough's conviction that Miss Mason should restrict her energies to 'local effort, small beginnings, quiet working and steadfast effort'. Observing that Miss Clough was overly deferential to Canon Westcott in her own drawing room, Miss Mason felt

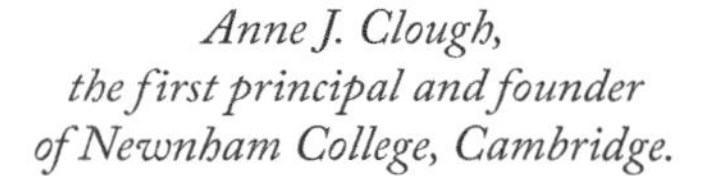

Anne J. Clough, the first principal and founder of Newnham College, Cambridge.

Oscar Browning invited Charlotte Mason to tea and chapel at King's.

their advice did not play with her global ambitions! Quietly spoken, Miss Mason inspired Miss Clough's distinguished guests with her mission to raise child upbringing to new heights.[3]

> She [Miss Clough] united in a unique way the old and the new. She understood and believed in parents of the sort who educated their children quietly on the lines of Evenings at Home etc.![4]

In Cambridge Miss Mason took tea, followed by chapel, with the ebullient Oscar Browning (1837–1923), a fellow of King's College.[5] In 1891, with Miss Clough's encouragement, 'the great O.B.' would co-found the Cambridge University Day Teacher Training College with Henry Sidgwick (1838–1900). He was the first principal from 1891 to 1909.[6] Unaware of any taint of Etonian scandals, Miss Mason, who zealously guarded her own secrets, enjoyed his eccentricity.[7] Both had a lively sense of humour; they got along famously. After her enlivening Cambridge visit, a modest local society was out of the question. Besides, Miss Clough had agreed to form a Cambridge committee.[8]

Printed as a propaganda pamphlet in 1889, the 'Draft Proof' was amended in 1892 to emphasise the personhood of every child and the new mantra for the Union, 'Education is an atmosphere, a discipline and a life,' attributed to Matthew Arnold, but unreferenced. Notwithstanding stringent comments on the draft, now lost, proffered by Miss Clough, Oscar Browning, Professor Sully (1842–1923), Canon Henry Liddon (1829–1890) and Sir Joshua Fitch HMI (1824–1903), the critics found the aims of the manifesto too vague.[9]

On 5 December 1889, Miss Mason wrote from Bradford to O.B. and other followers, explaining that the meeting of the Central Council had been held in the Indian music room of Lord and Lady Aberdeen's London house. Describing the successful launch of new branches in London and elsewhere, she implored her correspondents to give 'wise and weighty counsel' at the next Central Council meeting. 'A serial publication' was planned. 'The Parents Union Magazine, a journal of Home Culture for Educated Parents' would be issued monthly from 'February next'.[10]

Academic educationists dominated the next meeting. They promptly constituted themselves into an 'informal Central Council' with powers to appoint a provisional Central Executive Committee, chaired by Canon Evan Daniel (1837–1904), principal of the historic Battersea Teacher Training College from 1866 to 1894. Lord and Lady Aberdeen accepted the presidency. Canon Daniel had expert knowledge of elementary education and educational theorists. His staunch defence of the 'power' conferred by pupil-teacher training to the Cross Commission of 1888 had set him at odds with Miss Trevor's opposing evidence. At this delicate stage in her new career, Miss Mason clearly felt ill at ease with Canon Daniel, although as a former pupil-teacher she was living proof of the *power* acquired.[11]

The first (provisional) Executive Committee met on 18 January 1890 at the Graham Street High School in London. Canon Daniel took the chair. As proposed by Mrs Boyd Carpenter and seconded by the Revd T.W. Sharpe (1829–1905), chief HMI, Miss Mason was elected honorary secretary. Others present included Mrs Hart-Davis and her sister, Mrs Anson, Mr Keeling, Mrs Steinthal and Mortimer Margesson Esq. (1861–1947), cousin to Emily Shirreff (1814–1897) and Maria Grey (1816–1906), co-founders of the Girls' Public Day School Trust and the Froebel Association in 1874. The society was duly named the Parents' National Educational Union; the draft constitution was agreed.[12]

The Revd Robert Quick (1831–1891), whose innovatory Cambridge lectures on education history were published as *Essays on Educational Reformers* (1868), hosted the first PNEU Central Council Meeting at the College of Preceptors on 18 February 1890. Those present included Mrs Steinthal, Mr Wynne, Miss Shirreff and L.T. Meade (1854–1914), a well-known author of stories for girls. Miss Clough, despite her gloomy prognostications, arrived untypically but 'exquisitely dressed in rich black silks, fashioned to suit her own dignified personality'.[13] The two aged educational pioneers, Miss Shirreff and Miss Clough, commanded the fine tuning of the PNEU constitution, insisting on fathers' full participation. With Mr Quick's support, Miss Clough won an important motion to broaden the ethos of the society from 'Christian' to 'religious', a significant amendment.[14] Ratified by this august assembly, the constitution was agreed.

The P.N.E.U. Constitution

Objects:

a) To assist parents of all classes to understand the best principles and methods of Education in all its aspects, and especially those which concern the formation of habits and character.
b) To create a better public opinion on the subject of the training of children, and, with this object in view, to collect and make known the best information and experience on the subject.
c) To afford to parents opportunities for Co-operation and Consultation, so that the wisdom and experience of each may be made profitable for all.
d) To stimulate their enthusiasm through the sympathy of numbers acting together.
e) To secure greater unity and continuity of Education by harmonising home and school training.

Central Principles:

1. That a religious basis of work be maintained.
2. That the series of addresses and other means employed by the Union shall be so arranged to deal with Education under the following heads:- Physical, Mental, Moral and Religious.
3. That arrangements concerning Lectures, etc., be made with a view to the convenience of fathers as well as mothers.
4. That the work of the Union be so arranged so as to help parents of all classes.[15]

Without direct reference to *Home Education*, these broad PNEU principles and objectives remained open to variable local interpretation.

Parents' Review, reclassified by the co-editor, Mrs Steinthal, as 'a monthly magazine of home training and culture', first appeared in February 1890. Influential friends joined the Board of Directors; others were persuaded to invest in the new journal. Funds were sought for propaganda expenses; Miss Clough generously sent £5.[16]

> The Society struggled into birth without its own magazine, but it was felt . . . that such a society without an inspiring organ would be a mere tool to the hand of every educational faddist who had a theory to advance.
>
> How one remembers the 'fearful joy' of the first number of the P.R. . . . to fetch it from the publishers at the moment of issue, to carry it to the nearest A.B.C. shop, to ponder its pages . . . now with joy, now with anxiety, now with doubt, again with rejoicing.[17]

An angel bearing a torch and standing on the globe beside the tree of knowledge was depicted on the front cover of the early volumes. 'Wisdom is better than rubies' was inscribed on the globe; underneath was written, 'See that ye despise not one of these little ones.' Contemporary societies needed a journal to disseminate information. A *different* Charlotte Mason, who founded a 'house of rest' for tired Christian Bible women in 1866, edited a magazine called *Rest and Reaping*; the Froebel Society, founded in 1874, published *Child Life*. *Parents' Review* remained in print, albeit in altered format, from 1966 to 1986, before the World-wide Education Service (WES) of the PNEU closed in 1989.[18]

The risky venture succeeded brilliantly due to the loyal support of the *Parents' Review* trustees and because it was imaginatively conceived. Mrs Boyd Carpenter had tried to dissuade Charlotte from publishing 'a high-class educational magazine appealing to a public of parents and not in the least popular'; another 'influential friend' remarked, 'it will bring you to the Workhouse.' Devoted supporters from the Steinthals to the Aberdeens and Anna Swanwick (1813–1899), an educational philanthropist, kept the *Review* afloat, although sales did not cover costs. Lienie's editorial assistance was invaluable. Friends passed the *Review* around; a second fund was raised when closure threatened. James Gordon, manager of the Bradford Old Bank, the Bradford PEU treasurer and trusted neighbour from Mornington Villas, proffered financial advice. When the circulation finally reached 2,300 by May 1900, the *Review* was self-supporting. Having borne the risk for eleven years, the tolerant directors and shareholders received their *first* dividend.[19]

Editorship of *Parents' Review* not only gave Miss Mason a platform for her views and control of the content, but also conferred prestige. It was a daringly clever move. She told Oscar Browning, 'The *Review* is the pivot upon which a great scheme of education turns.' Miss Clough, who had been cajoled into sending in 'Thoughts and Suggestions on Early Education' commented, 'It is a great thing the *Review* answers and I hope it may continue to succeed.'[20]

From her own experience, the editor understood the pleasure experienced by budding writers on seeing their work in print. New contributors, such as parents, were as useful to the *Review* as well-known writers from L.T. Meade, Oscar Browning, R.H. Quick and Dorothea Beale to Ruskin's secretary, W.G. Collingwood (1854–1932), an artist, who contributed 'The Fesole Club Papers', an art correspondence course. Thomas Rooper's addresses to PNEU branches made excellent copy.[21] When material was short, the editor added anonymous writings or borrowed instructive essays such as Madame Necker de Saussure's *L'Éducation Progressive* (1828). Charlotte had a marvellous capacity for tossing off brief articles, sentimental poems and chatty moral tales. Mrs Steinthal edited the children's section, 'Aunt Mai's

Budget', from 1893. 'Notes and Queries', perhaps borrowed from *The Pupil Teacher Monthly,* offered space for comments and advice to worried parents. 'By the Way' contained news snippets. By agreement, 'Our Work' and 'Notes' reported on PNEU activity. Within the broad framework of upper-class liberal culture, medical and educational discourses and practical advice, the imaginative cornucopia of variable articles was eclectic and erudite, while lacking a dominant theory of education. No one could have accused the *Review* of faddism; its regular appearance was a remarkable achievement.

The Steinthals were startled by a strangely violent poem in Issue 3. An allegory for every thoughtless mother, the verses ended with the beheading of a neglectful mother by 'a strong man, Ivàn Ivànovitch, blessed with clear inner light'. She had let wolves snatch her three sons and devour them:

'A tale to haunt you, I grant, but wide of our talk, for, here
Is the tale of a sin we could not; our children are over dear;
We spoil them rather'. 'Agreed, if only such as these
Are the wolves that be on us! Think; does no woman, for ease,
In this high civilisation of ours, leave her offspring a prey
To wolves that eat out the vitals – gnaw the good heart away?'
'What, the mere faults of a child?' 'Aye the faults of a child, let be,
Run down the man to his ruin:– waste o' breath to impugn the decree!'

The poem was signed 'M. Shaw'. Lienie blundered in asking,

> But who is M. Shaw? Is it not Paul's Godmother? We could not go to bed last night but read it and re-read it over and over again. Francis says that alone is worth the 1/- for the magazine. The reasons we have been suspecting you are; 1. It is so artistically reflective. 2. The last few words are like you. 3. Only an enthusiast like you could bring out the last fine point. 4. It is the most . . . wonderful sermon and poem we have read for a long, long time. If you will write back, 'My Dear Lienie, ask no questions,' I shall understand; but I shall ever tremble before you and be if possible more humbly grateful that we know you.[22]

What are we to make of this chilling poem signed 'M. Shaw'? The reference to Charlotte's long-lost Catholic mother remains obscure. The sensitive Lienie had touched a nerve; closed shutters blocked out explanatory light.

Attracting readership from the poorer classes proved unsuccessful. Miss Mason failed to produce the planned eight-page tract for cottage mothers, 'The Parents' Friend', containing 'brightly written tales by an able writer' to illustrate aspects of home training. Offering Lady Aberdeen's *Onward and Upward* magazine and its children's supplement, *Wee Willie Winkie*, to cottage mothers also proved impracticable.[23]

The first PNEU AGM was held at London House, St James Square, Piccadilly, on 3 June 1890, by kind invitation of Dr Frederick

Temple (1821–1902), Bishop of London and former headmaster of Rugby, who presided. Praising the *Review*, Lord and Lady Aberdeen sent apologies. Overwhelmed with commitments and troubled by scrutiny, Miss Mason was also absent. Confirming that the Union was needed, Canon Daniel closed his long discourse on parents and education by acknowledging Miss Mason's contribution:

> This movement . . . largely owes its conception and inception to Miss Charlotte Mason [applause], who began the movement in Bradford by establishing a small, local Union which, I believe, has done a great deal of good there. Accounts of her work spread there, and she has been invited to help in the establishment of similar Unions in other places. . . . Money will be required . . . and I trust that a sympathetic public will now come to our support.

Dr Temple closed the meeting with a 'pleasant reference to Miss Edgeworth's "Parents' Assistant" . . . and other books of an earlier generation which dealt not unsuccessfully with the problems of home education'.[24]

Trouble loomed. Canon Daniel's AGM address heralded the centralisation of the Union in London; this decision would stand despite Miss Mason's objections. Often absent, Miss Mason did attend the Executive Committee on 4 June 1890 but missed a critical meeting on 9 July when Miss Sharland, the London organising secretary, proposed re-organising the Executive Committee to give preference to London residents. Inexplicably, the next meeting was delayed until 3 April 1891. At a stormy session the PNEU books were found to be overdrawn by £3 6s 9d! Miss Mason had not presented her accounts for a year. Resignations were tendered but deferred; an urgent Council meeting was planned to receive Miss Mason's financial statement and discuss the Union's immediate dissolution.[25]

After visiting Mrs Groveham in Bradford in July 1891, Mr Wynne wrote to Charlotte Mason:

> I would be glad if you would let me know how the case stands as I would make a point of being present at this meeting and try to see that right is done. This circular has a very suspicious look as if Miss Sharland's object is to crush the Union. Put me in possession of the facts of the case & I will make a fight for it. It is too bad that those who profess to be warm friends of Education should allow petty jealousies to influence them and try to thwart a movement that has been so successfully inaugurated.[26]

Perilously close to the emergency Council meeting, Miss Mason activated support. She implored Oscar Browning to attend and stand for the Executive Committee:

> A series of erratic communications from my co-sec [Miss Sharland] will probably prevent many members from attending. . . . This notion of 'dissolving' the Council appears to emanate from her solely. Do . . . help to lick the Society into shape – the organisation seems to answer admirably with regard to the branches – some of which are doing splendid work – but the centre unhappily started with dissension & we have never got on well. I think things may be better now that the 'Opposition' secretary is retiring. . . . Do you remember saying in Bradford that only two or three people believe in education? The remark is profoundly true & the object of the society is just this – to get people to believe in education – Do Help![27]

Only four members attended the decisive Council meeting on 10 July 1891. Miss Sharland had left for Devon. Miss Mason stayed away. The balance of £10 18s 7d was now 'in favour of the treasurer'. Mr Wynne and Oscar Browning joined the Executive; Canon Daniel, Miss Shirreff and Mrs Anson retired from the fray. In spite of failing health, Mr Wynne took over as the London organising secretary; he died the following autumn, a great loss to Miss Mason.[28] The deaths of Miss Clough and Mr Quick were also mourned that year.

Although the Executive Committee did not reconvene until 8 April 1892, the Union survived, thanks to contemporary zeal for ideal upbringing. Eighteen prestigious vice presidents, including six bishops, Miss Buss, Miss Beale and Miss Shirreff had been appointed. The Central Council had acquired sixty-one citizens from the ranks of the great and the good, including Miss Mason's Bradford supporters. As general organising secretary, but weary of committees, the Union's acknowledged founder left the Council.

Miss Mason's propaganda was inspirational. Eight London meetings had been held and five branches were opened. An Australian branch was started; interest was expressed in America. Miss Buss promoted the north-west London branch; the Wynnes backed the Forest Gate branch. Invited by Dorothea Beale, who started a Cheltenham branch, Miss Mason addressed parents, teachers and nurses at Cheltenham Ladies' College in 1890. From September 1890 to February 1891, Miss Mason criss-crossed the country: from Sheffield to Cambridge, from Cheltenham to Bournemouth and from Birmingham to Bradford and Kendal, summoning parents and teachers to the cause of education.[29]

Mrs Dallas Yorke, an enthusiastic aristocratic ally, had invited Miss Mason to lecture on the training of children during Lent in 1891. In May, her daughter, the Duchess of Portland (1863–1954), hosted a drawing room meeting for 'ladies in society'. It was chaired by Sir Douglas Galton, a GPDST supporter, who said the planned House of Education offered a desirable training for high school leavers. His medical colleagues, notably Helen Webb MB (d. 1926) and Dr Alfred T. Schofield (1846–1929), were captivated by Miss Mason's mission. Helen Webb joined the Executive Committee; she gave expert lectures to the branches on health, habit-training and the conserving of nerve force, later published in the *Review*. She recalled,

> I have always remembered the impression then made upon me by her gracious personality, and great charm of voice and manner.[30]

Dr Schofield, a PNEU Council member, commended the House of Education as if it was already in existence, adding,

> the development of Mr Matthew Arnold's definition: 'Education is an atmosphere, a discipline, a life' offers a very scientific and practical idea of education.

Receiving his warm approbation for the *Review*, Miss Mason promptly appointed him as honorary examining physician to the House of Education to enable prospective students to qualify for the National Health Society diploma in Physiology, Hygiene and Fitness.[31] As an expert on nineteenth-century physiology, Dr Schofield had doubtless read Carpenter. The additional appeal of the Union lay in the opportunities for disseminating National Health Society propaganda through its networks. While he paid lip service to the campaign for higher education for women, in reality he hankered after 'the fragrant memory of the unemancipated, yet gentle and loveable, early Victorian woman', like the gracious Miss Mason and comparable to the aristocratic ladies he treated at his Harley Street practice with gentlemanly decorum. Subscribing to the contemporary ideology of motherhood, he believed

> that the development of the mother instinct of woman into true motherliness is one of the greatest achievements of feminine culture and the root of altruism in her.

The new dominant type of committee woman was not to his taste: 'To attain a truly . . . legitimate end, a woman may use means that would offend the conscience of a man.'[32] Miss Mason commented, 'The gain to the movement in the adhesion of so able and active educationist and man of science is very great.'

To Miss Mason's relief, Dr Schofield took over as executive chair on 8 April 1892. The amiable and adaptable Henry Perrin Esq., another Council member, succeeded the late Mr Wynne as London organising secretary.[33]

The House of Education was eagerly awaited. The 'Draft Proof' had devised plans to give women 'of some refinement and education' a special training in the bringing up of children. The idea of training governesses, *not* teachers, had been sanctioned by Lady Aberdeen. Ambleside was pleasingly remote from London. Set beside Lake Windermere, the magical setting was constantly transformed by the changing seasons and unpredictable weather.

> By the way, what a pleasant village, or rather town, Ambleside is – built of the dark blue-grey rock of the slate mountains, and standing in an open valley with towering mountains round it. . . . That rock, looking over the little lake is 'Wordsworth's seat'; and on the slope of the fell is Rydal Mount which was the home of the Lake Poet.[34]

In April 1891 Miss Mason addressed the Ladies' Committee for Boarding Out Pauper Children in Ambleside on 'The Principles of the Parents' National Educational Union'. Returning to Bradford to lecture to the PNEU branch on 'Punishment', she finally left the Groveham family and the Bradford Union, no longer listed in PNEU annual reports after 1892. No letters have survived to throw light on the parting of the longstanding friends. By now Mrs Groveham was accustomed to Charlotte's frequent absences. Her loyalty never faltered; her daughters' reactions are unknown. The PNEU had brought Miss Mason prestigious new friends and delightful places to visit, such as the Steinthals in Wharfedale or Highfield House, Ilkley, a favourite resort for intellectual and poetic natures.

Ambleside had the right *atmosphere* for the *discipline* of developing the liberal cultural education to which Miss Mason would devote her *life*. Popular as a holiday centre, it was alive with naturalists, artists and writers. Wordsworth had visited Harriet Martineau (1802–1875) at the Knoll; the Clough family lingered in local memory. The Arnolds had stayed at Fox How since 1831. John Ruskin, a fount of liberal ideas, was secluded at Brantwood on Coniston Water, supported by William Collingwood, his secretary and an artist.[35]

On census day, April 1891, Charlotte M.S. Mason aged forty-nine, author and editor, was visiting John Fleming, aged fifty-three, a local Ambleside surveyor and architect and his wife, Selina, aged fifty-one, now mistress of Belle Vue Boarding School on Kirkstone Brow, with forty boarders. Mrs Fleming's younger sister, Bodina Healey, was housekeeper. Miss Mason stayed at Belle Vue until the end of the year. Did she seek assistance with her exacting projects from Selina and her three governesses, teaching art, English and French? Dependent upon the hospitality of generous friends, the persuasive and determined Miss Mason could not have achieved success without massive support. Was Selina's goodwill stretched to breaking point during 1891? No records of their thirty-year friendship were kept; contact apparently ceased after Charlotte settled independently in Ambleside. In 1894, Mrs Fleming retired from teaching. She and her husband moved to Rothay Garth, now a hotel, which John Fleming had built for her retirement.[36] After she died in 1911, her students installed a plaque in St Mary's Church, which acclaimed her teaching prowess.

Miss Mason was wondering whether to educate nurses, governesses or the whole family. To please her aristocratic patronesses, an advertisement in *Parents' Review* in 1891 explained that 'women of some refinement and education' would receive a year's training in '*the enthusiasm of childhood*. . . . [T]he need for co-workers in their labour of love is grievously felt by mothers, especially by some of those of the upper-classes whose engagements press heavily upon them.'[37] A superlative 'Angel in the House' was evoked. This 'gracious vision', referred to as 'Tante', believed 'in the sanctity of the little bodies she tends . . . and that every woman who is not a mother should hold it a privilege to serve an apprenticeship to motherhood'. Unfortunately, as Tante's training and a six-week summer school for all the family were advertised at short notice, both projects were cancelled due to lack of response.[38]

In contrast, Miss Mason was on to a winner with the *Parents' Review* School (PRS), hastily launched at half-term on 15 June 1891. Teaching children was her métier; she desperately needed an income. Before the month was out, the editor reported in the *Review*, 'We receive great credit for this "brilliant idea",' described as a unique education whereby pupils kept school hours at home. Profitable to Miss Mason, the PRS offered an imaginatively organised home-schooling curriculum for the higher classes, costing less than private school fees.

> No school advantages can make up to a child for the scope for individual development he should find at home, under the direction of his parents, for the first eight to ten years of his life. . . . Most children of the educated classes, boys and girls, get their schooling at home. . . . Girls of the highest class are rarely sent to school.[39]

Mary Hart-Davis had alerted Miss Mason to the plight of rurally isolated mothers struggling to educate large families at home on moderate incomes. Wealthy matriarchs were troubled by the inadequacies of poorly educated private governesses and nurses. Joining 'cottage children' at village schools was out of the question; upper-class parents opposed their daughters being 'crammed' to pass exams at the high schools.

> Oh well, high schools are simply fearful. . . . It's the number perhaps. . . . Treating the gels like soldiers. Like a regiment. D'ye see? No individual study of the gels' characters.[40]

'F.L.B.' may have shocked *Review* readers by a graphic description of her obstreperous, yet sensitive son, too young to be sent away to school, but in sore need of domestic discipline:

> Indoors he is miserable. At Christmas I bought him ten shillings' worth of toys, all the kinds he wanted. He never played with one of them. . . . He teases the little one, worries the nurse, and is selfish and quarrelsome with

> his gentle elder sister, who gives up everything to him. . . . He seems to have no tastes; he likes tops and marbles and running wild. . . . His father is a busy man and says it is woman's place to look after children.[41]

Her story was a godsend for the PRS.

Boldly conceived under the transposed motto 'I am, I can, I ought, I will', the PRS offered programmes – Miss Mason's term for curricula – previously outlined in *Home Education*. With the development of excellent postal services, correspondence courses were flourishing, such as the National Home Reading Union founded by Dr Paton (1830–1911) in 1887 to bring method into home study.

The PRS was designed for children aged six to ten and older girls at home. 'Highly qualified professional teachers' selected the books for the programmes. To register, parents had to state if their children were baptised, draw round their hands, give chest measurements and answer detailed questions on physical and intellectual attributes, interests and levels of attainment in reading and observation. 'Is his chest expanded, his head well carried? Test his power of attention, his powers of observation and his accuracy by asking him to say, after one hearing: "Down from the stars sailed the wooden shoe/ Bringing the fisherman home" or a similar unknown couplet. Try him again in an hour – Result?'[42] The liberal PRS was the antithesis of the outmoded Revised Code's stifling curriculum. Sent out each term, the programmes timetabled short morning lessons on the usual subjects, including arithmetic from Pendlebury's *Shilling Arithmetic*, but not The Gough, and Latin and modern languages for older children.

Afternoons were kept for the Pestalozzian nature walk to observe and collect botanic specimens and for free play, outdoor games or activities such as handicrafts, drawing and music according to the child's bent and the weather. Non-competitive half-yearly examinations, lasting a week, tested the child's individual 'intelligent knowledge'. Those too young to read or write were examined orally by parents taking turns. The papers were individually marked by Miss Mason and her team; there was no competition between the far-flung pupils.

New ideas and books suggested by PNEU associates were absorbed, such as the tonic sol-fa (1841) method of sight-singing popularised by John Curwen (1816–1880) and an Italic script devised by Monica Bridges, the wife of Robert Bridges (1844–1930), later Poet Laureate. Miss Mason expected children to be inspired by meeting 'great minds' through 'great literature', from the novels and poems of Walter Scott (1771–1832), to *Aesop's Fables* and Sir Thomas North's translation of Plutarch's *Lives.*[43].

Bruised by her debacle with the PNEU Executive Committee, Miss Mason kept the financial management of the PRS firmly under her personal control. Initially, one child or a family of children aged under ten were charged one guinea per annum; fees for older children ranged from three to five guineas. Overheads were low as Miss Mason and her assistants managed all the administration. George Middleton and Sons, local Ambleside printers, produced the programmes, leaflets and examination papers.

By 1892, 150 children had joined the PRS, rising to 300 by 1899. As only one nearly empty notebook containing details of PRS transactions in 1892 has survived and subsequent accounts are missing with the actual numbers of children participating from 1900 until 1923, Miss Mason's precise rate of profit remains unknown. In 1923, records revealed that PRS fees were worth £2,590 2s 7d. Peggy Lane-Roberts recalled, 'My grandmother spoke of Miss Mason's flexibility in business. She never let a small obstacle deter her progress.'[44] The PRS, renamed the Parents' Union School (PUS) in 1907, gave Miss Mason essential financial security. Unquestionably, this brilliant idea was one in which she was especially well qualified to succeed.

> She . . . tenderly shielded those who worked for her from any anxiety as to ways and means; and such times of difficulty were not infrequent for she bore the financial responsibility entirely alone and went on with faith and courage when many a lesser spirit with a life so frail would have quailed.[45]

The editor published deferential articles in the *Parents' Review*: 'Parents as Inspirers', 'Parents as Rulers' and 'The Parent as Schoolmaster'. These were reissued in her next book, *Parents and Children* (1896), to attract pupils into the PRS, at home or overseas, and to remind parents of their responsibilities.[46]

At the 1897 PNEU conference, Mrs Steinthal assured the audience that all her children had been most satisfactorily educated in the PRS; her eldest son was doing well at Rugby. Mr Underhill, the first 'practical schoolmaster' to use the programmes in his boys' preparatory school in 1897, said the PRS was the most useful agency of the whole Union. It provided boys with leisure interests, which were 'a tremendous safeguard in . . . idle time'.[47] In 1899, Florence Parsons (1864–1934) said the PRS

> Provides against grooviness, lax ways, absence of good methods and good books and the general mental stuffiness to which private education is so exposed.[48]

The plan to train nurses was dropped. Emily Ward (née Lord) (1850–1930), a Froebelian, founded the Norland Nurses' Training Institution in 1892. To address their uncertain social status, she advised, 'Nurses, take your silver-backed brushes to impress the servants'![49] Governesses' ambiguous standing did not trouble Miss Mason, who believed it a privilege to live in a gracious house. Her governesses would be trained to use the PRS programmes in cultured home schoolrooms instead of teaching large classes in elementary schools, now free to all.

In January 1889, Miss Mason had met Mrs Eliza Parker and her daughter, Violet, at the Wynnes' Forest Gate vicarage. By 1891, as self-appointed principal of the House of Education, Miss Mason had secured sixteen peeresses and seven PNEU matriarchs as patronesses, with the help of Mrs Dallas Yorke, whom she appointed the lady visitor.[50] In 1892 Mrs Parker rented Fairfield House in Ambleside to enable Miss Mason to quit Belle Vue and open the House of Education. After three months, Mrs Parker took over the vacant Springfield House, furnished and managed it, until she retired to Walton Cottage. By then Miss Mason could afford the rent and buy back the furniture. She annexed the big room on the right at the top of the stairs.[51] Starting from comparably small beginnings, Miss Clough had opened Newnham College in Cambridge in 1871 because Henry Sidgwick (1838–1900), a supporter of women's higher education, took a house on her behalf.

On 15 January 1892, Miss Mason, aged fifty, warmly welcomed Violet and three colleagues who arrived in Ambleside on a snowy night. For the first three years, the students lodged in the village. The lecture hall, erected in 1854 in St Mary's Lane by Robert Crewdson and John Fleming, was a godsend for the new principal, who spent the mornings teaching education and psychology to her first four students, based on *Home Education*. In afternoons Miss Mason sometimes accompanied the students on walks or excursions. Violet Parker allegedly recalled that Miss Mason often overtaxed herself; while said to be fighting off 'serious illness', she never referred to her health.[52]

The three experimental years leading up to December 1894 were characterised by plain living, high thinking and concentrated study on a wide range of subjects, both practical and theoretical. The students rose at 7:00am and studied for an hour before breakfast. Before leaving for the morning lectures they made their beds and tidied their rooms. From 1893, working in pairs for a week at a time, they practised on small groups of about four children of variable ages to emulate teaching families in home schoolrooms. Dinner was served at 1:30pm, followed by rest and recreation outdoors until tea at 4:00pm. The early evening was spent studying languages and doing needlework or manual training. As well as Mrs Steinthal's arts and crafts courses, the students were taken on natural history and geology walks. They attended County Council lectures on hygiene and botany as well as Oxford Extension lectures in the village on physical geography, geology and other scientific subjects. The vicar taught religious knowledge. Assembling a competent staff was no small achievement; how they were financed is not known.

Mrs Julia Firth, of Seathwaite Rayne, a longstanding friend of John Ruskin, gave the students a weekly artistic picture talk at her house from 1892 to 1908, initially attended by Miss Mason. Enjoying Mrs Firth's comfortable chairs, they followed Ruskin's method of studying monochrome

Miss Mason's bairns grapple with basket-making.

reproductions of Italian masters line by line. 'Picture study' became integral to the PRS programmes. Mrs Steinthal continued to instruct the students on 'home arts', such as basket work and clay modelling.[53]

> I must mention two or three of our visiting teachers. There were two sisters who lived at Rydal. One came in a bath chair drawn by a donkey, once a week, and took us for class singing. Her sister taught physiology. I remember her coming once with a bullock's eye, which she dissected in front of us! Most of all we loved Dr Johnson, who took us for hygiene. He could never resist a joke, and if Miss Mason chanced to enter the classroom . . . he always had a funny remark for her, and she was always ready with a reply. What fun we all had![54]

The annual fees and lodgings' expenses were raised from an initial £10 to £35-£55, according to means, which did not fully cover costs. By 1893, student numbers rose to thirteen, stabilising at around twenty-two by 1894 when the training was extended to two years and the fees were a more realistic £50 per annum, payable in advance.

By 1894, to cover the extended syllabus, Miss Mason had assembled fifteen lecturers and instructors to teach languages (presumably French and German), natural history and fieldwork, Japanese paper-folding, human physiology and Swedish drill, drawing, primary piano, arts and crafts, singing and geometry, clay modelling, Euclid and Latin. Miss Mason taught the theory and practice of education, mainly from *Home Education*, while the local vicar, the Revd

Brush painting in 'blobs' on the terrace.

C.J. Bailey, gave the divinity classes and Mrs Firth taught picture study. The district nurse instructed the students in bandaging and hygiene.

Mr Rooper undertook the first external, unofficial inspection to validate the first year's training. A former tutor to the Duke of Bedford, he prefaced his remarks to the students, 'When I was a governess':

> Miss Mason's intention is to train ladies who will teach in a family, not those who intend to teach in a school. . . . The training of the Governess for the family is thus quite different from that of teaching for the school.

The principal of the Borough Road Training College examined the four students' written papers. Violet Parker gained the only first class; she and a colleague were rated 'extremely good' and the other two 'the better for their training'. Developed from her Bishop Otter experience, Miss Mason had made an excellent start. Rooper added,

> It is right that those heads of families who seek the advantage of assistance in rearing their children should enquire into the social position of those whose help they require. The ladies who are trained at the House of Education are daughters of clergymen, officers in the army, professional men and merchants.[55]

The education of mothers already had a long history. Radical thinkers, such as Rousseau in his book *Julie or La Nouvelle Héloïse* (1761), or Mary

Wollstonecraft in her *The Vindication of the Rights of Women* (1792), had argued for an educated motherhood to improve child upbringing. Now modern scientific knowledge was required in addition to divine inspiration.

The Mothers' Educational correspondence Course (MEC) was launched through the *Parents' Review* in June 1892. Intended for mothers with children in the PRS, the MEC was designed to remedy historic deficits in girls' education by helping them to teach their children and supervise their nurses and governesses effectively. In 1890, 'O.O.' had complained in the *Review* that as a busy mother and vicar's wife in a 'wild parish', she rarely saw a new book or met an educated person. As she was losing 'all power of comprehending anything more improving than the daily paper', she was afraid of being unable to meet her children's intellectual needs as they grew older. Mary Hart-Davis said the ideals set out in the *Review* made a PNEU mother feel even guiltier about her time being 'frittered away by the pressure of small things' due to constant interruptions.[56]

The aim was to equip mothers for all their responsibilities to their children. For one guinea a year and 5s for each examination taken, the mothers were invited to take all, or some, of the four courses: Divinity, Physiology and Health (from the National Health Society's syllabus), Mental and Moral Science and Education, and Nature Lore and the Elements of Science. They could enter or avoid the half-yearly examinations, to be taken at home in their own time without recourse to the books. Miss Mason estimated that a year's work could be covered by reading one hundred pages a week.[57]

For most mothers, apart from Mrs Kinnear, a paediatrician's wife who 'had a large experience of examinations', the MEC was their first experience of specialised academic study and tests.[58] The questions were taxing. At the end of their first year's study, mothers were asked,

> Show how Christ's sacrifice is an atonement for us. How would you present this thought to children? Show the danger of mere verbal acquiescence.

From Paley, Miss Mason set,

> What difficulties present themselves in Natural Theology and how should a Christian meet them?

Other questions, encouraging the development of opinions, included,

> What do you consider the crux of modern thought? Show how 'our' definition of the functions of education meets the difficulty.

In an old-fashioned Spencerian vein:

> Show why no clothing is either warm or cool in itself. Describe in detail what you consider the best clothing for a boy and girl of eight, showing the principles on which you select each article.

Under Mental and Moral Science:

> Sketch briefly a) the sum of what a child is as a human being b) What has he become through 'heredity' c) what parents may reasonably expect to effect by education. Give illustrations from your own family.

Further questions on this topic included,

> Give Richter's theories as to the education of girls.
>
> Show how the action of immaterial thought on the material brain is the key to Habit. What part does the formation of habits play in education?
>
> Describe the nerve mechanisms of the child. Account for and describe 'nerve-storms' and show the importance of 'Suggestion' in education.

On Nature Study:

> Give the Characteristics of insects and spiders. Write out talks upon the dog, the caterpillar, the oyster and the earth-worm.[59]

Even Beatrice Wolrych-Whitmore, a star pupil from the dominant Belgravia branch who had seven of her answers on topics ranging from 'The Will' and 'The Imagination' to 'Nutrition' and 'Habit' published in *Parents' Review*, complained that 'the standard of intelligence required seems to me to be rather high. . . . I have sometimes mistaken the meaning of the questions.'[60]

In her 1897 survey of British female education, C.S. Bremner praised the MEC warmly. As 62 mothers had taken up courses by then, 'the significance of the movement can scarcely be overstated; the idea it embodies is bound to spread.'[61] However, as girls' secondary level education was improving, only up to 170 mothers, at most, took all or some of the courses during the 22 years before it effectively ceased operating in 1914.[62]

Presenting the MEC at the 1897 PNEU conference, Mrs Anson, the sister of Mary Hart-Davis, proclaimed the merits of sustained study as a stimulus to the mutual development of mother and child. She had commissioned letters from mothers which abounded with excuses for failure to start, complete the reading, obtain the books or take the examinations. One was nursing a sick child, another had too many children, a third could not afford the fees, and a fourth pleaded the demands of the London season. The perplexing questions, the academic reading list and the socially constructed feelings of intellectual inadequacy compounded by the pressure of domestic demands may have combined to make all but the most confidently intelligent mothers feel daunted by the MEC. As Mrs Anson remarked, 'If is true, as has been said, that a "mother is only a woman but she needs the love of Jacob, the patience of Job, the wisdom of Moses, the foresight of Joseph, the firmness of Daniel," we mothers are greatly in need of support.'[63]

Lacking the social spurs powering Miss Mason's intellectual development and surrounded by myriad responsibilities, most mothers probably felt that they needed the super-powers of five Old Testament giants to tackle her erudite questions. By raising the level of the tests by which Miss Mason chose to remind the mothers of their grave responsibilities to the coming generation, she did not defer to their social standing. However, the MEC responded to a pressing contemporary need which lessened as higher education and opportunities for women opened up during the early twentieth century.

The PNEU AGM in June 1893 confirmed that the Union's chief aim was educating parents to bring up their children. As chairman, Lord Aberdeen said 'that when the movement was set on foot there was a fear that the objects of the society were somewhat too vague for practical purposes'. Experience showed that if it had achieved nothing else, the *Parents' Review* articles had been most worthwhile. More positively, Lady Aberdeen moved a resolution pledging the meeting to support the PNEU, the *Parents' Review*, the House of Education and the PRS. She said that 'the Union owed its existence' to Miss Mason and her 'admirable book, *Home Education*. Half the difficulties in the education of children lay in the imperfect understanding of children by their parents. . . . The Union aimed at proper training: intellectual, moral, spiritual and physical of children. [Cheers].' This encouraging endorsement of her hard won achievements enabled Miss Mason to extend her Ambleside projects, relieved of the central organisation of the PNEU by the efficient Henry Perrin.[64]

In July 1893, Winifred Kitching had been awarded a first-class certificate after one year's training.[65] That summer, Miss Mason stayed with her family in Bognor, Sussex. Needing a break, she revisited Bishop Otter Memorial College to recruit assistance. She persuaded Miss M.H. Schofield, a governess, to run the House of Education for a few months.[66] Winnie's mother, Mrs Kitching, was keenly interested in education and had often spoken on the upbringing of children. Her younger sister, Elsie, aged twenty-three, had recently passed the London University intermediate arts examinations, but was at a loose end at home.

'There was something nervous in her make-up which through her growing years seemed to cause strain.' After 'two severe illnesses', Elsie felt she had no future. She needed someone to give her life direction and meaning. Both sisters attentively helped Miss Mason with her letters in the evenings. When Mrs Kitching asked for advice about Elsie, Miss Mason promptly replied, 'Let me have her,' and so it was that Elsie was given her work and the devoted friendship of a lifetime. She travelled back to Ambleside with Miss Mason and there she spent her whole life. Elsie reflected, 'After years of High School work the life at Ambleside seemed to me to open a new world of hope and possibilities.'[67]

Her immediate acceptance of Miss Mason's invitation set the tone for a symbiotic, yet unequal, relationship between the two. It depended upon Elsie's lifelong habit of keeping in the background and upon 'that astonishing devotion to labour in the service of others, which was just the expression

Elsie Kitching holding the fort with the students.

of herself'.[68] In 'Kit Kit', her nickname for Elsie, Miss Mason perceived a sound, practical intelligence, a useful knowledge of Latin, mathematics and music, a docile, loving nature and an energetic capacity for immensely hard work. Overwhelmed by myriad responsibilities, she needed a younger disciple who would serve her unquestioningly. Plain in appearance and astounded to be singled out by this gracious educational reformer, Kit Kit's devotion to her charismatic leader was the crowning experience of a life spent in unstinting service to Miss Mason's cause.

> She was a young woman then, quick as a flash of lightning in all she did, comprehending in her scope the most varied assortment of occupations from arranging the flowers to setting the examination questions and reviewing books. She kept all the College and Practising School records and accounts, and attended to all the details of Miss Mason's personal comfort and wellbeing.[69]
>
> As 'the Dear Dragon', her devotion, her self-effacing vigilance guarded Miss Mason literally day and night, year in, year out.[70]

The constancy of Kit Kit's generous service sustained the radiant atmosphere that the PNEU's acknowledged founder bestowed upon her disciples. Intelligently well-informed, Kit Kit became a keen observer of nature and birdlife. Significantly, her prompt arrival enabled Miss Mason to take a long break during the winter.

13.

The 1894 Challenge and the Mason-Franklin Alliance, 1894–1897

Green Bank, the elegant white house with the graceful veranda, had been vacant since Mrs Benson Harrison died in 1890. Here Miss Mason would gather her scattered 'bairns' under her guiding light. In this chapter, it will be shown that in facing down an unexpected challenge to her burgeoning leadership of the PNEU from Belgravia in 1894, she would reject the popular, progressive 'new education' theories presented in *Home Education* to focus PNEU thought on physiological habit training. An intense new alliance with Mrs Henrietta Franklin would protect Charlotte from external tensions, placing her at the heart of the Union.

Miss Schofield arrived from Chichester and took over the House of Education for three months while Miss Mason travelled to Italy with Mrs Julia Firth. Essex Cholmondeley's claim that grief over Emily Brandreth's death on 18 November 1893 caused Charlotte's alleged breakdown in health that winter is unsubstantiated; there is no record of contact since 1879. Lienie Steinthal ran the PRS and edited *Parents' Review* with Lady Isabel Margesson and Henry Perrin.[1] The timing was not ideal. As Lord Aberdeen had been appointed governor general of Canada with compulsory residence from 1893 to 1898, Lady Aberdeen's support would be missed. Reginald Le Norman Brabazon, thirteenth Earl of Meath (1869–1949), an Anglo-Irish soldier and a PNEU vice president, acted as president until their return.[2]

Helen Webb recalled,

> In Florence I came upon Miss Mason and her friend, Mrs Firth, standing by Giotto's Tower, and together we studied his beautiful medallions. I shall always especially associate with them that of the woman weaving on the loom which Ruskin copied when he revived hand-weaving in the Lake Country.[3]

Helen Webb MB, 'the wise and witty' Irish Quaker, known as 'Wai', was a pupil of Dr (later Dame) Mary Scharlieb (1845–1930), who was a

Aspiring to Green Bank for the House of Education.

forceful campaigner for women doctors and a PNEU Council member. Affectionately nicknamed 'B.P.', after St Luke the Beloved Physician, Miss Webb advised Miss Mason about her health.[4]

Visiting Florence with a cultured gentlewoman, imbued with Ruskin's acclaimed views on art, was a momentous inspiration. Of lasting significance for Miss Mason's spiritual development and expounded for the rest of her life was her 'deep and living impression' of 'the vaulted book' frescoes, enlightened by Mrs Firth's exposition of Ruskin's interpretation in his popular guide, *Mornings in Florence* (1881). These fourteenth-century frescoes, on the left wall of the Spanish Chapel at the Santa Maria Novella Dominican Church in Florence, are now attributed to Andrea di Bonaiuta. They portray the descent of the Holy Spirit upon the minds of men. Within his light stand the Apostles and the prophets; below St Thomas Aquinas is centrally enthroned. Above him float the seven virtues and at his feet sit the fourteen 'knowledges' or sciences, accompanied by their greatest exponent.

> The Great Recognition that God, the Holy Spirit, is Himself personally the imparter of knowledge, the instructor of youth, the inspirer of genius, is a conception so far lost to us that we should think it distinctly irreverent to conceive of the divine teaching as co-operating with ours in a child's arithmetic lesson. . . . But the Florentine mind of the Middle Ages . . . believed . . . that every fruitful idea, every original conception whether in Euclid or grammar or music, was a direct inspiration from the Holy Spirit.[5]

Miss Mason ordered a monochrome reproduction of the frescoes to be hung in a prominent place to inspire successive generations of students with this medieval illumination of educational harmony. This vivid experience confirmed her new mission as educational visionary and spiritual leader, infused with the inner light that had sustained her father and the Friends.

Lady Isabel (née Hobart-Hampden) (1863–1946) had married Mortimer Margesson (1861–1947) in 1886. The daughter of Lord Hobart, Earl of Buckinghamshire, she was descended from the parliamentarian John Hampden (1595–1643) and a long line of ancestors pre-dating the Norman conquest. Greatly influenced by her husband's cousins, Emily Shirreff and Maria Grey, leading founder of a successful teacher training college, active from 1878 to 1976, Lady Isabel was bringing up her three young children on Froebelian lines, assuredly guided by Emily Shirreff's treatise, *The Kindergarten at Home* (1876).[6]

Highly intelligent and well-informed about educational theories, Lady Isabel was already the Belgravia branch secretary. She joined Mortimer on the PNEU Executive Committee in December 1892. Her paper advertising 'training lessons' for mothers appeared in *Parents' Review* in 1893, affirming that PNEU teaching could not replace 'that individual study' of 'the science of education' detailed by 'Herbert Spencer, Locke, Sully, Froebel, Pestalozzi'.[7]

Anxious not to be labelled a faddist, Miss Mason had warmly commended these training classes. Besides, a broad spectrum of educational thought pervaded *Home Education*. Preoccupied at Ambleside, she failed to anticipate an intellectual challenge to her developing leadership. The core theoretical basis of the PNEU was unclear; in revising the 'Draft Proof' in 1892, the Executive Committee had affirmed that the doctrine of habit was merely a third part of education, despite Object A's emphasis on habit formation. Nobody had suggested issuing Miss Mason's paper, 'PNEU Philosophy' (1892), as a pamphlet. In it, she had set the scientific physiology of habit training within an evangelical religious framework.[8]

On 18 December 1892, the Executive Committee resolved to tell Miss Mason that Lady Isabel's pamphlet, *What is the P.N.E.U?*, should appear on the front page of the *Review*, replacing the advertisement for Mother Siegel's Syrup.[9] In two pages, not deviating markedly from *Home Education*, Lady Isabel put the progressive case for responsible professional parenthood:

> A reproach is levelled against the Parents' Union that it claims to have made a discovery and to call 'new' things that were known long ago! This is a misunderstanding. The so-called 'New Education' is only a recognition that as a child's nature is threefold: physical, intellectual and ethical, so all true education must deal with those three sides of his nature. . . . The 'New Education' further recognises that without the understanding . . . and the guidance of his parents, the child's education will lack harmony and adaptability to its individual requirements. All this was, of course, understood by the gifted few, the wisest and best parents and teachers from Plato downwards.[10]

If Miss Mason was perturbed by Lady Isabel's focus on 'new education', the irony lay in the obvious fact that she had welcomed Herbert Spencer's educational recommendations with those of Pestalozzi and other 'new' educationists in *Home Education*:

> Looking for guidance to the literature of education, the doctrines of Pestalozzi and Froebel were exceedingly helpful to me as showing the means to secure the orderly expansion of the child's faculties.[11]

In 1904, these names, apart from Spencer's, would be expunged from the revised *Home Education*.

Lady Isabel was one of the aristocratic patronesses of the House of Education. In April 1893, the Executive Committee agreed to her proposal that former students should pay five guineas out of their first year's salary as governesses for two years' PNEU membership and publications. Although their contributions would give Miss Mason the extra financial backing she needed to acquire Green Bank for the House of Education, a rebuttal against this interference was required.[12] At the AGM on 7 June 1893,

> Miss Mason . . . spoke of the success of the teachers they had trained and said that all the students who came there had a vocation to work in the true sense of the word. They did not train 'lady nurses' or 'mothers' helps' or 'nursery governesses' . . . people who could speak their mother tongue imperfectly, and were therefore thought fit to teach young children; but they trained ladies to be good teachers, whether of young or of older children (applause).[13]

While Miss Mason sojourned in Italy from January until April 1894, Lady Isabel seized the initiative at the Executive meetings; the chairman, Dr Schofield, was powerless to stem the surging tide of her reforms. As in Miss Sharland's strategy, all PNEU operations were to be transferred to London. Miss Ethel Forsyth, former principal of the Forsyth Technical College, was proposed as the first paid PNEU organising secretary on a salary of £75 with 25 per cent commission on all advertisements obtained by her for *Parents' Review*. A London office was established at 86 Victoria Street for a rental of £45 per annum. Lady Isabel wanted the PNEU to take over the *Parents' Review* and fund London office expenses from the journal's capital assets, provided the *Review* trustees guaranteed the amount. On 1 February 1894, the Executive Committee approved her plans.

A finance sub-committee was formed to transfer all funds from James Gordon, Miss Mason's former Bradford neighbour, to a London PNEU treasurer. Miss Forsyth was appointed secretary to the Belgravia branch, which paid the PNEU £15 to use the central office for branch business. The affiliation of the PNEU with larger bodies, from the Froebelian Norland Institute to the Anglican Mothers' Union (MU), was also mooted.

The PNEU was small by comparison with the MU (founded in 1876), which had benefited from the diocesan networks spanning the world-wide Anglican communion since 1885. The final proposal to affiliate PNEU satellite branches with the London centre to support a housewifery school run by Miss Forsyth and a *second* House of Education was unthinkable.

Controversially, Lady Isabel won agreement to vary the PNEU constitution 'to suit the altered conditions of working caused by the establishment of the Central Office'. Six Executive Committee members with the lowest attendance would have to resign before the AGM, thus effectively expelling Miss Mason's Bradford supporters. Unchallenged, the Belgravia branch had already revised the Union's Object A by inserting the names of key 'new' educationists. Meanwhile, Lady Isabel produced her leaflet on PNEU principles, to be advertised in the *Review*. Fortunately for Miss Mason, the Committee learnt at the meeting on 2 May 1894 that the *Parents' Review* company had *not* as yet agreed to transfer their capital reserves to fund central office expenses.[14]

Belatedly, Miss Mason grasped the extreme threat to her position. Dr Schofield's allegiance was indispensable, if they were to avoid being sidestepped by a strong-minded aristocrat. She graciously received Lady Isabel and Miss Forsyth at Springfield in May. Ablaze with azalea blossom, Ambleside was at its loveliest.

My dear Dr Schofield

What a comfort you are! The two ladies, Lady Isabel and Miss Forsyth have been here and departed – a most pleasant visit not unaccompanied by discussion. . . . I like Miss Forsyth much – she is a *Lady* – refined and enthusiastic . . . but she is easily led and at present Lady Isabel is *her* Committee and *her* P.N.E.U. . . . Lady Isabel is charming, her ardour and enthusiasm a pure delight – but the rush with which she takes things is appalling. I well understand it must leave the Committee panting. The situation seems to be this – the Froebel people have got hold of Lady Isabel & are endeavouring to use her, & our Society through her, as an agency to advance KG principles and work. For a whole day we contested the point – ! The discussion was a little feminine and droll.

At one moment it was – that I had drawn all our P.N.E.U. teaching out of Froebel & was to be honoured as an interpreter of that great sage – The next moment, I had not read, did not understand Froebel & that was why I held aloof!

I think the talk did some good . . . but they both cling to Froebel as a mystic who has said the last word on Education. In fact I think they rate him with Wagner and Ibsen amongst the 'eternities & immensities'. . . . We managed to agree a sentence to be submitted to the Committee – 'Herbert Spencer & Froebel supplemented by the progressive scientific thought of the day' – though personally I should rather we boldly claimed to originate our own school of educational thought, hanging on, not to the educational reformers – but to the physiologists of today & the philosophers of all time, but I trust all to the Committee – only we must be on the alert.

Miss Mason firmly quashed the idea of *another* House of Education supported by wealthy London branches; 'both ladies agreed that it would be impossible to secure elsewhere the elements of our success here and P.N.E.U. *must not* give sanction to a second rate project must it?' To avert the looming threat, Miss Mason was anxious to secure the lease of Mrs Benson Harrison's empty mansion, purchased by W.L. Mason, a local estate agent and architect.

One thing more – the trustees will not let me have the big house I spoke of unless the Committee will be party to the contract – At first I utterly declined to propose this but seeing that the Society derives an income of £100 or more from the students (22 at present) & that there is every human possibility of my being able to pay the rent for the seven years lease, even if our numbers do not increase, I think the Committee might venture to do this for us.– Rent £150. Could you bring this before the Committee? The residence in different houses is a most serious drawback –

Most truly yours [signed] C.M. Mason[15]

With the instincts of a successful general, Miss Mason sought a strong London-based disciple. Enquiring discreetly, she persuaded Mrs Whitaker Thompson, whom she had enthused at Highfield House in 1887, to visit Mrs Henrietta Franklin (1866–1964), a wealthy Anglo-Jewish mother, taking a copy of *Parents' Review*.[16] Mrs Franklin joined the Hyde Park and Bayswater branch, chaired by Dr Schofield. Persuading her husband Ernest Franklin (1859–1950) to spend a short May holiday in the Lake District, Netta answered the call to Ambleside for a momentous meeting.

I made my pilgrimage one afternoon to visit Miss Mason. Years afterwards she used to say, 'I looked out of the window and I saw a young person in a holland frock approaching the hall door.' Only that it sounds silly I would say we fell in love with each other at first sight. Miss Mason did say quite often that, with my arrival she had found her long-awaited and predestined 'chela'. If that was true on her side, it was still truer on mine. I had found the 'guru' or sage and teacher of whom I stood so much in need. I can only give you a very faint idea of the inspiration of her personality.[17]

For those familiar with the formidable presence of the Hon. Mrs Franklin CBE (1866–1964), a brilliant organiser and doyenne of forty-two committees in later life, her initial adoration of Miss Mason is startling. Aged twenty-eight, Mrs Franklin, the eldest of eleven, born into and married within the liberal Samuel Montagu family banking dynasty at nineteen, was in the throes of early motherhood. The two women spontaneously recognised a complementarity in the other, answering deep-felt needs. Miss Mason required loyally effective support in London. In the face of prevalent anti-Semitism, a leading position within a primarily Christian society would open doors for the young Jewish matriarch. The softly spoken Charlotte had the gift of making her visitors feel treasured; her inspirational ideas spoke to contemporary concerns.

> I think it was the intellectual and religious basis that attracted my eager young mind. Without the religious basis her teaching would have meant nothing to me. Though she was an earnest Christian and I a no less earnest Liberal Jewess, she accepted me with her wide tolerance.[18]

Recalling Netta's frankness about *schwärmerei,* or girlish passions, at school, it was an intensely loving friendship which developed into an enduring affectionate alliance, masking implicit rivalry.[19] These two dynamic daughters of Christendom and Judaism, from different generations and rival creeds, symbolised the complementary yet opposing forces of *Hellenism* and *Hebraism,* conceptualised by Matthew Arnold in *Culture and Anarchy* (1869). He defined culture as the study of perfection which sought to do away with classes, to 'make the best that has been thought and known in the world' current everywhere, to make all men live in an atmosphere of 'sweetness and light'.[20]

> We may regard this energy driving at practice, this paramount sense of the obligation of duty, self-control and work, this earnestness in going manfully with the best light we have as one force (Hebraism). And we may regard the intelligence driving at those ideas which are the basis of right practice . . . as another force (Hellenism). And these two forces we may regard as in some sense rivals – . . . Hebraism and Hellenism – between these two points of influence moves our world. But their methods are so different. . . . To get rid of one's ignorance, to see things as they are, and by seeing them as they are to see them in their beauty, is the simple and attractive ideal which Hellenism holds out before human nature . . . full of what we call sweetness and light. . . . Hebraism – and here is the source of its wonderful strength, has always been severely pre-occupied with an awful sense of the impossibility of being at ease in Zion.[21]

In planning an assault upon Lady Isabel's seemingly impregnable position, Miss Mason had to affirm the originality of PNEU teaching in spite of her dependence upon the age-old wisdom of 'new education' fathers. She had

Netta Franklin, a sketch by Fred Yates.

Matthew Arnold.

been immersed in Pestalozzian principles during her definitive Ho and Co training; her sole objection was his faculty training method. Mary Hart-Davis was again her emissary, as Oscar Browning, now an unreliable ally, had declared at the 1893 AGM, 'Rousseau, Pestalozzi had created almost a revolution in education.' Twelve years later he and Miss Mason would be at loggerheads over the theories of child development described by Dr Maria Montessori (1870–1952), whom Browning greatly admired.[22]

Miss Mason missed the Executive Committee meeting on 6 June 1894, when six out-of-town members, notably Mr and Mrs Keeling, were voted out under the new Rule 8 to be replaced by six new names, happily including Mrs Franklin. Mrs Hart-Davis read Miss Mason's paper outlining the history and aims of the Union to support the motion proposing the retention of the original PNEU objects. It was carried unanimously. Lady Isabel's alternative pamphlet was discussed 'with some warmth'! After Dr Schofield left early, Lady Isabel persuaded everyone, apart from Mrs Hart-Davis, to defer withdrawing her leaflet until a majority vote of the full Committee resolved the issue. Helen Webb seconded her proposal.

On 8 June 1894, Lord Meath chaired the AGM as incoming president. Elected as fourth honorary organising secretary alongside Mrs Steinthal, Mr Perrin, and Miss Mason, Lady Isabel's triumph was brief. In the 'unavoidable absence' of Miss Mason, the conciliatory Dr Schofield endeavoured to placate everyone:

> They were to be congratulated on the remarkable progress they had made in the last twelve months. They had got a central office in London, where the affairs of the Society could be transacted. . . . [T]hey had obtained the services of a Secretary of great ability. . . . With

> regard to the Society generally, people said that its aims were rather undefined and that they just did not understand what its principles were. . . . But whilst desirous of greater definiteness, they did not want a narrower platform.[23]

Mrs Hart-Davis read what Dr Gladstone tactfully described as 'the very philosophical paper of Miss Mason'. Skilfully designed to please upper-class traditionalists, her paper posited that Froebel's progressive educational theory of the development of the faculties was only suitable for 'ignorant or otherwise deficient children'. Pestalozzi's method only applied to poor children.

> Generations of physical toil do not tend to foster imagination. How good then for the children of the working classes to have games initiated for them, to be carried through little dramatic plays. . . . Thus education naturally divides itself into education for the children of the *lettered* and education for the children of *unlettered* parents.

Matthew Arnold, whose perception of the ameliorating power of culture infused *Parents' Review*, had suggested in *A French Eton* (1864) thirty years before that 'The education of each class in society has, or ought to have, its ideal, determined by the wants of that class, and by its destination.'[24]

Miss Mason claimed that the scientific doctrine of heredity proved that cultivated PNEU children had a head start; 'the child of intelligent parents is born with an inheritance of self-developing faculties. . . . This class question which we are all anxious to evade comes practically into force in education.' Cultivated parents had to train their children in right habits and 'nourish' them 'daily with loving, right and noble ideas', allowing 'time and scope for the workings of nature and of a Higher Power than Nature'.

> We lay no claim to original ideas or methods. We cannot choose but profit by the work of the great educators. . . . We are progressive. We take what former thinkers have left us and go on from there.

But where? The PNEU task was to bring 'educational ideas into more just relations with each other' to 'advance educational truth'. Later she would decide the child was the adjudicator, able to take or reject the ideas presented:

> We are altogether catholic in spirit, free to take of the best whenever we find it, as a bee ranges from flower to flower, but having our own definite ideas on the lines of which we advance.[25]

Miss Mason's veiled diatribe against kindergarten play-way methods failed to perturb the socially secure Belgravia enthusiasts for child-centred progressivism. Old fashioned habit training lacked appeal. The shackles of mid-Victorian authoritarian upper-class upbringing, like the backboards on which refined young girls like Netta Franklin had been daily positioned for hours, had poorly served the developmental and intellectual needs of young mothers who were finding a voice through new societies such as the PNEU and the Froebel Society. On 3 July 1894, the Belgravia branch circulated Lady Isabel's proposed alteration of Object A:

> The Voluntary Association of parents in an Educational Union is a means of compassing two ends; first, to assist all who are interested in children to understand the principles and methods of the 'new' education as set forth by Pestalozzi, Herbert Spencer, and Froebel, and other educational philosophers . . . and to apply them to individual character, aiming at the harmonious development rather than the mere instruction of the child; second, to establish a ground of meeting for the mutual advantage of theory and practice between parents and educationalists, thereby securing unity and continuity in home and school training.[26]

Dr Schofield took legal advice to see if Object A could be altered. On 9 July 1894, Miss Mason circulated her leaflet, incorporating the solicitor Geo Gatey's opinion that the objects could not be altered without the consent of 'a preponderating majority of *all* the members', because the Union had been formed for the specific purposes listed in the five objects under Rule 3, set in stone.

> If fresh objects are sought to be introduced, or the old ones varied, the present Union should be dissolved and a new one formed.

Miss Mason's leaflet maintained that PNEU education existed to encourage scientific, physiological habit formation and 'the presentation of the Idea which is the all-important initial step in the formation of every Habit'. She added, 'it cannot be said with justice that *absolute vagueness* is to prevail.' The teaching set out in 'the little manual . . . covers the whole scope of Education in every aspect'.[27]

Supported by Dr Schofield and Mrs Franklin and a majority of loyal committee members, the battle was won by 18 July 1894. They accepted the legal advice and withdrew Lady's Isabel's pamphlet. Without addressing the contradictions in *Home Education,* their crucial resolution froze the PNEU constitution in its 1890 format. Seven Belgravia members resigned. The Margessons wrote to Dr Schofield to express regret about 'serious . . . differences of opinion which unfortunately exist between the Founder . . . and ourselves'. Others agreed with Mr and Mrs William Borrer that Lady Isabel had not been fairly represented.[28] Mrs Borrer, who had desired 'our dear Queen' to be the patron of the PNEU but had lost touch as 'since my marriage I have been rather out of the Court', wrote forcefully to Miss Mason:

> I like Lady I & am sorry for her but I should have respected her more if there had been a real difference otherwise than what the politicians call an 'animus'. . . . Your views, so far as they are explained in P.R. & the Union are the views we held long before we ever knew you. I speak of general views & principles. In methods of carrying out those views & in several smaller matters as well as on several educational points I am and so is Mr Borrer largely in debt to the Union – We certainly do not intend to leave the Union. . . . [H]ad there been anything behind so that we were tied to some hitherto unexplained principle on the Physiology of Habit being the only point (& in your leaflet you did use some rather strong expressions there) we perhaps could not honestly have remained on the Council – but I now see your leaflet was not meant to sum up the entire objects of the Union – it was in answer to an alteration of the objects which excluded that thought and weakened it.[29]

In August Lady Isabel scribbled a letter to Miss Mason:

> It would surely be undesirable to continue to spread the principles of the 'New Education' as those of the Union when I had been obliged to withdraw from the centre on account of those principles! . . .
>
> My soul is burning with the enthusiasm that comes from gratitude to the 'New Education' principles. They seem to be a gospel that is of the widest importance to the welfare of the country. I could not work freely when I knew that the Centre, from which I ought to get guidance and help, was holding opinions that appeared to me to cover a small proportion of the field of Education.
>
> I am very sorry to have been obliged to withdraw from the Union – it has been the means of discovering the 'gospel' to me & I shall always be grateful to you for it. I think the difference of opinion was bound to come sooner or later as the work grew. . . . I have held my views strongly for a long time . . . and can see no reason why they should be considered right for a Branch and not for the Centre. . . .
>
> Yours truly,
>
> Isabel Margesson[30]

The irrepressible Lady Isabel redirected her energies into setting up the Froebelian Sesame Club in 1895 as a platform 'for various forms of progressive education'. She was pro-Boer during the war, in favour of votes for women and a supporter of the Women's Institute (founded in 1915). An enthusiastic person of high principles, sadly she became morbidly gloomy in old age.[31]

Victory reinforced Miss Mason's belief in her personal mission. Having betrayed the Pestalozzian mandate to teach poor children and the reformist ideals of beloved fellow travellers, notably Lienie Steinthal and Thomas

Rooper, 'new educational' ideas would be quietly practised at Ambleside, from the object lesson and kindergarten games to the nature walk. By ostensibly rejecting the 'new psychology' of child study and developmental stages, PNEU upper-class liberal education was cut off from the progressive educational advances of the twentieth century explored by Dr Maria Montessori (1870–1952) and John Dewey (1859–1852), those who, like Rousseau, perceived childhood as a separate stage from adulthood.[32]

The Executive Committee backed the acquisition of Green Bank.[33] Here was Miss Mason's Staplestown House moment! Helen Webb paid her first 'never to be forgotten' visit to Ambleside in September 1894. Relief brought abounding energy. They met with the architect to plan alterations and improvements.

> As we walked up the drive, the sun shone brightly, and in front of the house we stopped and turned round to gaze on Loughrigg and Wansfell, with Windermere between, and said to each other, 'Just think, Wordsworth stood here and looked at all that!'[34]

Miss Mason took Helen Webb to Harriet Martineau's house, the Knoll, close by Springfield. They had tea at Grasmere and visited the graves of the Wordsworth family before entering Mrs Melrose's shop, where she had sold the famous Grasmere gingerbread for fifty years. On Sunday afternoon, they climbed the hill to see Mrs Firth at Seathwaite Rayne. Ruskin had helped to lay out her garden, calling it 'the most beautiful nest in the world'. On 17 September 1894 the two ladies perched on the box seat of the Keswick coach. Trips to Elterwater and Langdale were arranged; in the evenings friends came in for coffee at Springfield. Around this time Miss Mason doubtless met the three Armitt sisters, who had moved to Rydal Lodge in Rydal village by 1894.[35]

Just after her fifty-third birthday in January 1895, during a bitter winter when Lake Windermere froze for three weeks, Miss Mason settled her staff and students into the renamed house, Scale How. Mrs Steinthal sensibly diverted Miss Mason from calling Scale How 'the House of the Holy Spirit'. The propitious move confirmed Miss Mason's matriarchal standing as head of her substantial House of Education household, with student 'bairns' as obedient surrogate daughters, as at Bishop Otter. Her elegant mansion offered a haven for a protected life, guided by her mantra, 'Education is an atmosphere, a discipline, a life.' A portrait of Matthew Arnold adorned the drawing room.

> The whole atmosphere of the house of education was so extraordinarily good – nothing ignoble seemed natural within its doors. . . . [T]he actual surroundings, the books, the pictures (reproductions of old masters), the simple furniture and *wild* flowers for decoration everywhere were a

> revelation in themselves in those days when the world lived in a crowd of ancestral treasures or the unutterable hideousness of the Victorian age when prosperity had to be apparent.[36]

The artistic lady visitor, Mrs Dallas Yorke, who had introduced Miss Mason to her aristocratic patronesses, devised the motto 'For the children's sake' and designed the students' leaving certificates, extolling the Lakeland setting during twice yearly visits:

> The House of Education is . . . in the true sense of the word a *home* for the students, who must look back on their student life as something at once practical and full of hard work, yet suffused with a radiance due, not only to the high aims and ideals of the College, but also to the glorious setting of the life in its 'house – beautiful'.[37]

The spacious house brought the docile bairns together; the protective Victorian atmosphere kept them safely within bounds. The ethos of plain living and high thinking justified the Spartan conditions. Friends had vigorously advised against the financial risk, but there was no turning back.

> With all her financial power, Miss Mason had a curious detachment from money and material possessions of any kind. She never worried, as many people do when resources are strained to the utmost. . . . The plain living and high thinking which governed her life made an atmosphere in the house which could be felt, and traditions which are still dear to those who had the privilege of living near her. . . . With the help of her auditor, Miss Mason kept the accounts in her own hands and each year she paid her way – *just.*[38]

The house was cold; the bairns were asked to bring woollen combinations, as baggy cardigans were deplored. With scant heating and no electricity upstairs, three or four students shared a bedroom, lit by small oil lamps. Long hair was obligatory to ensure the 'right' future posts. Hats were worn outside, even for mountain nature walks. Formality ruled the day; seniors and juniors did not mix. They had to address each other as 'Miss'. Walking partners were pre-arranged; no bairn was allowed visitors as a general rule or to venture out alone, even to the post box. On Swedish drill days, the bairns wore gym tunics over their long skirts, nicknamed 'double-deckers', to avoid showing the sergeant their knees! As at the Ho and Co, all study was done in the classroom; there were no easy chairs in which to loll. As at Bishop Otter, regardless of their previous Christian denominations, Sunday worship at St Mary's Anglican Church was compulsory.

Dorothea Beale, Ruskin's friend, visited Scale How in 1895 and lectured to students on geometry, saying that it could be as energising to the soul as gymnastics and mountain climbing to the body. Thoroughly approving

The students' Swedish exercises with the sergeant.
Dr Pidduck had advised that 'moderately exercising the arms and upper body in pure air was undoubtedly conducive to health'.

of the Christian underpinning of Miss Mason's training, she may have recommended Dante's humble, regenerating *rush* as a suitable badge for the Old Students' Association. In 1896 former students launched their journal, *L'Umile Pianta* ('the humble plant'), to keep in touch with each other and the Ambleside fount of inspiration.

Study, piano practice and daily prayers began the day. Up by 7:00am and in bed by 10:30pm, the students' packed timetable was creatively designed for teaching family groups with the PRS programmes. Domestic duties, lesson preparation, monitorial duties and music were fitted around six hours of lectures and afternoon nature walks. No study was done on Sundays. To foster attention, all work had to be completed within the brief allotted time. Nature notebooks were adorned with pressed flowers and found plants, rapidly painted in a style called 'blobs'. Apart from languages, picture study and all elementary subjects, a smattering of Greek, astronomy, practical handicrafts, cooking, leather work, carving, needlework, basketry, pottery, Slöyd cardboard models, flower arranging and 'child piano' were added to equip students to respond to most eventualities as governesses. Scouting activities, sports, entertaining visitors and nurturing the botanical garden were achieved with sterling effort.[39]

Miss Mason rarely missed the weekly criticism of the students' practice teaching at the Beehive Classroom in the grounds. Supervised by the mistress, two students taught there for a week at a time, as at Bishop Otter. 'Crit.' lessons were held in the classroom and delivered to spruced-up children by nervous students in turn, keenly observed by all the staff and students, as at the Ho and Co. This free school was attended by up to twenty local children of varying ages from six to seventeen.

Miss Mason's Criticism lesson in the garden.

Miss P.M. Bowser (CMT 1914) recounted her alarming first 'Crit.' in detail:

> My first Crit. – a lesson on Squirrels to Form IIB. . . . A long mirror was set behind the table. About half-way through the lesson the children, unbeknown to me, began to make faces at each other in the mirror. Suddenly Miss Mason's little bell tinkled. A gentle voice said, 'We will stop the lesson please, Miss Bowser dear, for four minutes – until the children have learnt to attend.' – Dead silence. Miss Mason and the staff behind me, the students at desks facing me – the longest four minutes I have ever known. Then a quiet voice said, 'Now please, Miss Bowser, continue your lesson.' This I somehow managed to do and surprisingly received a Very Good for the lesson.[40]

Although usually kindly, Miss Mason sometimes made caustic remarks. During a geography lesson, a hapless student watched the children colouring in the physical features accurately on the blackboard map, but failed to notice they had traced the river from the mouth to the source. Miss Mason, who showed disapproval of poor work by *not* shaking hands with the class, declared that a 'living idea' had thereby been lost![41]

Challenging lunchtime talk hopefully prepared shy bairns to hold their own in society. Miss Mason recited Shelley's poems or fired off literary questions on Milton expecting total recall the following day. Afternoons were spent exploring the hills, skating in winter, learning about birdsong from Miss Kitching or studying native flora and fauna with Agnes Drury (1874–1958), a temperamental former student. One spring day, Miss Mason

Baking is tricky when you have never cracked an egg.

Ah! The old glue pot! Book binding on the terrace.

waved to the group from her carriage to say the bluebells 'were like a bit of heaven let down'. The flower monitress had to ensure fresh flowers adorned the rooms. Aghast at noticing flopped over bluebells, she swiftly replaced them with yellow dandelions and beech twigs. During lunch, Miss Mason rapped on the table and said, 'I thought yesterday that the flower monitress had taken too literally the quotation, "A thing of beauty is a joy for ever", but now I see she has redeemed her name with this delightful display.'[42]

At Tuesday drawing room evenings, based on Mrs Wynne's Bradford coterie, which Miss Mason rarely missed, the bairns read a cultured paper or played music. Miss Mason invited her prestigious friends, including, among others, Frances Arnold; the three sisters, Sophia Armitt (1847–1908), Mrs Annie Harris (1850–1933) and Mary Louisa (1851–1911); the founder of the Armitt Library (1909) Canon Rawnsley and his brother Willingham; Dr Hough; Gordon Wordsworth; and Herbert Bell, the photographer.[43]

The students' diary recorded a vast range of extra activities from 'At Homes' to picnics, games, sports, dances, children's parties, skits, plays and scout camps. Plays included Shakespeare's *Twelfth Night* and *The Merchant of Venice*, William Thackeray's *The Rose and the Ring* as well as Richard Sheridan's *The Rivals* and Oliver Goldsmith's *She Stoops to Conquer*. This was an invaluable training in responding imaginatively to unexpected requests for entertainment. Strenuous mountain walks made most students very fit; there was no time to be ill.

> So in spite of what would seem to the modern student impossible restrictions and lack of comfort, it was an incredibly happy and rewarding two years.[44]

The 1895 annual report confirmed the success of the training; forty students had posts in selected families. In July Miss Mason wrote happily to Netta:

> I am fearfully and wonderfully busy. I have let the house for seven weeks from the 1st and am off to Switzerland for all that time so I shall have a lovely holiday, shall I not?[45]

The PNEU gave Netta scope for her organisational abilities and offered a *via media* between the different faiths. Jewish people were taught to believe they were the chosen race. Opportunities for married gentlewomen to enter public life were also opening up. By 1892 Netta already had four children: Sydney, Marjorie, Geoffrey and Olive; Cyril was born in 1898. Michael, her last-born, best-beloved PNEU son arrived in 1903. Despite great wealth which enabled her to employ a veritable army of servants and a private secretary, Michael remembered his mother 'in bitter tears daily upon the sofa'; she was prone to violent headaches. As a mother she was not only warm, stimulating and devoted but also bad-tempered and managerial.

No easy chairs for the bairns.

Although she believed that children were the most important things in creation, she sought outlets for her energies.[46]

Believing children needed companions of their own age, Mrs Franklin promptly opened the first PRS class in a Bayswater studio for the 1894 autumn term. She employed Ambleside-trained governesses. Mrs Franklin's pioneering class of sixteen children, aged between six and ten, demonstrated that PRS methods could be adapted to school classes as well as to family groups. It paved the way for her eventual transformation of the PNEU from education for parenthood into an association of private schools. Winnie Kitching (CMT 1893), 'a woman of sound judgment and a great sense of humour', started a class in 1902 for Mrs Franklin's sister, Mrs Darcy Hart, and her friends. This continued until 1910, when she opened a PNEU day school, which she ran effectively for twenty-two years. Winnie moved to Rickmansworth in 1932, where she developed a PUS class into a leading PNEU school. She finally retired in 1943.[47]

A true Hebraist, as conceptualised by Matthew Arnold, Mrs Franklin worked by the light of others' ideas. To prove herself a good PNEU mother, she absorbed *Home Education* and registered for the MEC. She introduced her children to the delights of fresh air, open windows, nature rambles and picture study; she read aloud to them for twenty years. Actively developing the Hyde Park and Bayswater branch, she organised varied lectures, a natural history club, a girls' hockey group, classes in brush-drawing, Swedish drill and educational trips to museums and galleries. By 1907, it headed the branch league table with over 250 members, maintaining the lead until 1914 when the London branches were amalgamated. To keep her finger on the PNEU pulse, Miss Mason wrote regularly to her *chela*:

> I don't hear a word of what has happened at the Committee Meeting or when the Annual Meeting is to be or anything about the Report. Send me some news.[48]

In 1897 Mrs Franklin tested Miss Mason's methods by sending her ten-year-old daughter, Madge, to Ambleside to be 'habit-trained' out of an unspecified fault. Miss Mason had categorically asserted that if six to eight weeks were set aside for consistent behavioural habit-training, any child could be cured.[49]

> The child is lovely dearest & it is too touching for anything to see how fervently she loves Ambleside. . . . She is the more precious to me because everyone says – and I see it all the time – that she is so like her mother.[50]

Charlotte Mason's letters describing Madge's treatment, inevitably shared with the whole Scale How community, reveal that she was lovingly patient and flexible. The regime ended abruptly when Madge caught flu. Whether or not it worked, Madge returned in 1907 as the sole Jewish student, winning a first-class certificate in 1908. She subsequently trained as a doctor before joining the British Psycho-Analytical Society. When Mrs Franklin read Miss Mason's article on 'Docility and Authority', she was incandescent, suspecting that criticism of the parents of a little girl called Maude was based on Madge. A major row was only narrowly averted!

> I think, sweet friend – you will consider such an idea unworthy of both you and me. . . . Maude in the article is <u>not</u> Madge, but is hundreds of children who labour under such conditions.[51]

Mrs Franklin's second significant innovation, the first PNEU annual conference, replacing the 1897 AGM, was held at London House by kind permission of the Bishop of London. Lord Meath presided.

> How good of you to telegraph, dearest. I knew all was going well. I felt it in my bones. . . . Je vous embrasse, Ever Yours CM.[52]

Drawing together parents, teachers and educationists, the conference centred upon the author of *Home Education,* who spoke on ethical teaching, denying her Irish roots:

> We English, she said, were in the habit of taking morals for granted in bringing up our children. . . . Moral education must be definite, detailed and purposeful. A child's possession of a conscience, which prompted the choice of right rather than wrong, did not obviate the necessity of showing them [*sic*] which was right and which was wrong.

The principle of authority was as fundamental as gravity; habit formation provided the groundwork for all subsequent education.[53]

Mr Rooper reminded the audience how little had been done to extend PNEU membership to parents of all classes, as promised in the constitution. A British domestic training centre, comparable to the Pestalozzi-Froebel House in Berlin, would enable rich and poor females 'to study side by side, in the lecture room, or kindergarten or at the ironing board'. He returned to the same theme in 1898 because 'it is through the family that the character of the nation can be raised'. Rooper's democratic proposals failed to sway Mrs Franklin, who affirmed that the PNEU would be 'weakened by stretching out in too many directions'. Challenging Mrs Franklin's elitism, Mrs Anson forcefully called for artisan mothers to be invited to join local committees. Lienie Steinthal, who also produced Aunt Mai's children's section for the *Parents' Review*, added that lecture courses for all should be given in urban centres. Troubled by burgeoning controversy, Miss Mason changed the subject by declaring, 'Indeed, I think that Aunt Mai's work is at the very heart of the Union.' Lienie proposed a 'hearty clap' for all those members of the Committee who 'had organised the first conference'.[54]

To strengthen the PNEU organisationally, Mrs Franklin arranged conference sessions on the House of Education, the Mothers' Education Course and the PRS, discussed in Chapter 12. Inviting PNEU branch secretaries to the conferences fostered communication with the central office. Mrs Franklin also promoted PNEU reading circles to disseminate Miss Mason's teaching. There were question and answer sessions on the 'concrete difficulties experienced by educated-class parents and on training the proverbially ignorant children's nurses'. One of 'the right people' present recorded that the first conference had 'proved that the P.N.E.U. is a living power . . . and has grown to be what it is without push, without advertisement, through its own independent life', a compliment to Mrs Franklin's skilled management.[55]

Physically drained, Mrs Franklin wrote from her father's Hampshire estate to revitalise her special relationship with her guru:

> I have had two lovely rambles all alone in the woods . . . & I feel much refreshed and rested. It has been a lovely halting place to think out all one has heard, though I missed much through not having a mind at rest. I long to read it all. . . . I hope, dearest, that you are not too tired. I feel I have got nearer to you this time than ever. I miss you very much. I have to thank you for very very much, my girlie [Madge] & a better self, but above all I thank you for your love & friendship. It is only one who loves you as I do, & who knows the sacredness of friendship that knows what this means. Dearest! I thank you, I thank you. I cannot say more, but I can dedicate to you a life of loving, humble service in your work and a constant prayer that I may become worthier of you and it.
>
> Your loving Netta[56]

Here was the perfect disciple and clever interpreter of a changing world, working for the cause in distant London. Other friendships paled into insignificance beside the glowing testimony of this intelligent young mother's adoration. Yet Miss Mason needed to keep track of Netta's numerous activities.

> Thank you dearest, for your sweet letter. . . . I have been thinking much of my 'child' and wish to make you promise to run down to me once in a month or six weeks for the soothing calm of this sweet world and of your friend's love; yes – I feel rich in the possession of you dearest, but you will find me very exacting, not at all in the way of affection, that goes without saying, still less in the way of exclusive affection which thing is not lovely, but in the way of having you ever more and more God-fulfilled, ever more of your best, beautiful self. I could not let you be less than yourself. Happily you are like me a woman lover and you have lovely friends and one at least who holds you very close, but will probably not tell you so again, but will expect you always to trust her.
>
> The Conference was just lovely. I have just rested in the happiness of it ever since. How splendidly you managed everything and how you kept yourself a 'rush'. . . .
>
> Goodbye, darling,
>
> Always your CM[57]

The Mason-Franklin alliance was now centre stage. At Ambleside, Miss Mason was distanced from the harsh realities afflicting the poorer classes. The glamorous life led by the Franklin family and their political connections confirmed her need to be accepted by the higher echelons of society. Lienie's generous loving nature and commitment to service had ensured their friendship was affectionately relaxed. The Steinthal family did not welcome Mrs Franklin's driving forcefulness and modernising tendencies.[58] Acceptance as the mentor for Netta's ten-year-old daughter had permitted a flood of intense feeling to penetrate Miss Mason's strong emotional defences. The price of so demanding, yet elusive, a love could be dependency and jealousy, which had to be resolutely checked.

> My Dearest Netta
>
> I am wearying to hear from you; not a word all this time, and I am anxious to know about Madge. . . . I have repented that I had not courage to go and see the Girlie, but I have more pluck now. I had got badly out of tune and every little anxiety depressed me dreadfully. You know how, do you not? . . . Now tell me just all about yourself. I seemed to get so little of you as I passed through, but how good of you to come to me, dear. . . . How dear you were in Torquay. . . . I cherish happy pictures of our time there.[59]

Miss Mason's last class?

In the year of Queen Victoria's Diamond Jubilee on 22 June 1897, Miss Mason was said to be seriously ill. As in 1894, recovery was enhanced by a summer tour of the northern capitals of Europe with Sophia Armitt. On 22 July they travelled to The Hague, enjoying the picturesque buildings and delighting in picture study of Van Dyke's paintings at the art gallery. While visiting several magnificent cathedrals in France, Sophia Armitt made complex architectural sketches.

> Miss Armitt is a capital travelling companion and is very kind and helpful and most methodical about the exercises.

After attending the 1898 conference, Miss Mason withdrew from all missionary propaganda tours and public appearances at PNEU meetings outside Ambleside.

> Dr Oldham pledges me to invalidism – that is a comfortable position – least possible work – no people for two or three weeks or longer. . . . Given . . . a regimen of quietness and stillness, I may be quite well before May so I am going to be good and obedient.[60]

14.
The PNEU Educational Philosopher, 1898–1905

> We did not see very much of Miss Mason during the day, but her influence was felt in a most remarkable way throughout the house, whether she was actually in the room or not. That influence must have been entirely spiritual.[1]

As mistress of Scale How, Miss Mason quietly exercised unquestioned authority and remote leadership of the Union, powerfully backed by Netta Franklin in London. A relapse into chronic invalidism from 1898 enabled her lifestyle to be ordered around her health needs, giving time for writing and spiritual reflection, aided by her Ambleside disciples. Netta's family responsibilities, cultured social circle and liberal political connections rendered her less subservient. A skilled organiser, she had aspirations for the students, the Union and the PRS. Vigorous interchanges between guru and *chela* culminated in the acceptance of Miss Mason as the Union's original educational philosopher in 1904, obscuring her various theoretical inconsistencies.

Fanny Williams was summoned to Scale How from Dublin.[2] Appointed vice principal in January 1898, she took morning prayers, ran the House of Education and supervised the practising school, wearing her edelweiss apron. Apart from Crits and Meditations, Miss Mason relinquished lecturing but usually selected new applicants and their future governess posts. Secure in her position, she stated in the 1901 census that she was principal of a training college for women teachers in schools.

> Elsie Kitching appeared to be the busiest person I have ever known; but even in her 'busyness' there was a selfless, devoted quality – a kind of enjoyment. . . . Miss Williams was there, of course, guiding the stream of College life, but Miss Kitching was in and out to Charlotte Mason all day long and writing, writing.[3]

Barrow, the Head Man, awaits the Mistress.

Belief in the somatic aetiology of Miss Mason's chronic heart trouble is inseparable from the PNEU's reverential tradition. The style of her seclusion confirmed the mythic status, symbolically enfolding Miss Mason and her reputation. Cholmondeley's phraseology is suggestive: 'Lack of stable health frequently interrupted the course of daily life, though few of those who lived with Miss Mason realised her constant courage.'[4] Recalling Charlotte Mason's personal magnetism, Mrs Franklin remarked, 'She was quite small, rather frail, obliged eventually to plan her life as carefully as an invalid. But she burnt like a clear flame.'[5]

Miss Williams drove Miss Mason around in a pony cart. Unprotected from Lakeland downpours, this undignified mode of transport persuaded Mrs Franklin to provide a little Victoria carriage with an adjustable roof, two forward facing seats and a raised box for the driver. These elegant French carriages were popular with London ladies driving through Hyde Park. For the next twenty-four years, T.H. Barrow, Miss Mason's devoted coachman, reminiscent of Queen Victoria's John Brown, drove her out punctually every afternoon from 2:15pm until 4:00pm, unless there was a high wind or heavy rain, taking any one of twenty different picturesque routes. Known as 'the Head Man', Barrow, who wore a jaunty top hat decorated with a cockade, always referred to Miss Mason as 'the Mistress'. Kit Kit saw them off.[6]

> A quiet figure always near Miss Mason, at hand if needed, walking behind her to the front door where Barrow and the open coach stood waiting, putting a copper hot water bottle at her feet and tucking the rug around her; Miss Mason's gracious smile as the carriage bowled away down the drive was the signal to turn and go back to her work.[7]

She used to set out 'a little, frail old lady sitting alone, her head sunk in fur, but with blue, observant eyes'.[8] Returning home for tea, Miss Mason described the birds and flowers they had seen. Occasionally accompanied by a distinguished visitor, when passing the bairns out walking, 'she waved to us rather like the Queen', but rarely offered a lift. Never unnerved by icy roads or actual physical danger, when her horse fell down between the shafts or placed hooves on the bonnet of passing motor cars, she remained perfectly calm.[9]

As advised by Helen Webb, in July 1898 Netta arranged for Miss Mason to have six weeks of specialist heart treatment in London.[10] Not expecting her guru to live long, she sought a free hand. Pregnant with Cyril, Netta had no desire to be put out of action by her sentimental friend.

> I rejoice in the prospect of your 'retiring'. . . . I always think you dear mothers have such a lovely time of Holy Communion at those times; that alone ought to make you better than the rest of us.[11]

Every summer from 1898 until 1914, Miss Mason travelled with Kit Kit to the fashionable German spa, Bad Nauheim, near Frankfurt, to take the mineral baths treatment. They stayed at the Villa Langsdorf. Famed as it was for its salt springs used to treat heart and nervous diseases, many fashionable Victorians, such as the hypochondriacal Herbert Spencer, took Bad Nauheim cures, vividly described by Ford Madox Ford (1873–1939) in *The Good Soldier: A Tale of Passion* (1915), set before the Great War.

The trips to Germany began with a brief stay in the Franklin household, where Miss Mason was cosseted. To pre-empt clamour, the children were asked to visit her room in turn.[12] In Germany, Miss Mason's wide reading included Leo Tolstoy's new book, *Resurrection* (1899), and Ivan Turgenev's *King Lear of the Steppes* (1870) in German, as they were not available in French. She found Turgenev 'very charming' but thought Thomas Hardy's *Tess* 'very disappointing'; 'Hardy's contention of a pure woman disappears with one's enjoyment of his splendid writing.'[13] The Nach Kür, a short German holiday, was made comfortable and easy by Kit Kit's attentions, with the folding carrying chair and the 'dear tea-basket'. Miss Mason returned refreshed and invigorated. She told Netta in 1905,

> Dearest! We have been here for only six weeks and we have never before had so short a cure. The little autocrat is mighty pleased with his patient. I told him that instead of coming here for my 90th birthday, which he had always said I should, I should go to a ball.[14]

Nicknamed 'the Dragon', Kit Kit guarded her leader zealously. Miss Mason had virtually given up walking; her dressmaker remarked that she had grown stout.[15] Morning and evening, the senior monitress stood with her back to the stairway to deter prying eyes from observing the recumbent principal being carried up and down stairs, 'in a sort of red basket chair' called Phoebe, by Barrow and the odd job man. 'We soon learned to flatten ourselves and "Watch the wall my darling, while Miss Mason's carried by!"'[16] In the garden, Miss Mason was propelled in a wheelchair.

Elsie Kitching, a sketch by Fred Yates.

'Otherwise she lay on the blue sofa and would read to us from there.'[17] When breathless, the principal would pause. She wore loose homespun clothes in bright soft colours, mainly blue, which gave the impression of floating. In recalling Miss Mason's beautiful complexion, Dorothy Cooke (CMT 1913) could never remember seeing her feet! 'She was always remote.'[18] Miss Mason's creative malady gave her the space to develop her spiritual ministry.

Ah, Lord we are aweary!
And yet we think on Thee
On our beds remember Thee
But comfort fails to come.[19]

Years after her death in 1983, Lt Colonel Dr Courtney Walton MB FRCP, Geraldine Walton's husband, analysed the sparse medical evidence from Miss Mason's carefully preserved bath records and German and English prescriptions from 1899 onwards. He found no prescription for any heart condition, such as digitalis, although Dr Hough's sole prescription for 'Easton's Syrup', containing strychnine, might have been a heart tonic. Miss Mason's main complaints were indigestion, wind, diarrhoea, constipation, lack of appetite and an upset stomach, apart from dry skin, sore eyes, a sore mouth and a cough on single occasions. Medicines for indigestion or lack of appetite containing diluted strychnine, arsenic or spirit of chloroform could have made her feel worse. For someone so protective of her privacy, it is odd that Miss Mason left such an embarrassing record for posterity, unless the Latin prescriptions were neither translated nor explained.

Dr Walton explained that nineteenth-century psychiatric and cardiac diagnoses were fairly rudimentary. Any slight deviation, such as an insignificant heart murmur, was regarded as life-threatening. Advised against excessive exercise, people were confined to sofas and bath chairs. Dr Walton concluded that if Miss Mason's muscles had atrophied from disuse, she would have felt faint on rising to her feet. Restless nights may have been caused by lack of exercise. After studying her pulse tracings, the forerunner of the electrocardiogram, Dr Walton noted Miss Mason's good regular pulse was slightly faster after the bath, which suggested that she may have felt faint before the bath and better afterwards. The tracings revealed that the right and left ventricles were not beating exactly simultaneously. Although Dr Walton thought this insignificant, this finding may have been taken seriously at the time. He concluded that cerebral thrombosis (stroke) should have been the first cause of death, not *morbus cordis*.[20]

On 24 July 1914, Professor Dr Schott prescribed tincture of valerian for nervous indigestion in Bad Nauheim. Surely Miss Mason was reacting to escalating tension across Europe leading to Britain's declaration of war against Germany on 4 August 1914. Thanks to high-level interventions, the two travellers were brought back safely through Holland. From 1915 to 1921 Miss Mason took mineral baths in Wales at Llangammarch Wells and Builth Wells.[21] Whatever the baths effected, Miss Mason enjoyed them. They justified her holiday break.

> Supposedly she was taken to the Drawing-room and guided to her couch on which she lay hour after hour. But I was amazed at her ability to get 'shot' of all custodians and arrive in the kitchen where faithful maids were preparing her next meal.[22]

By receiving only one visitor at a time and retiring from view when she felt out of sorts, Miss Mason always appeared radiant. She postponed Netta's visit on 20 May 1901 because Mrs Dallas Yorke was expected:

> You know ever such a trifle throws me over the plank and I am anxious to keep going. Any two people . . . take lots more out of me than one does.[23]

Walking from the drawing room to the dining room, Miss Mason usually took Sunday lunch with the students and said her especial grace: 'The merciful and gracious Lord hath so done his marvellous works that they ought to be had in remembrance.'[24] On Wednesdays she shared *Punch* jokes delightedly.

> Miss Mason . . . radiated affection and gaiety and showed a quick interest in many things; such as nature, plants and flowers, people, books, household and school affairs and (I nearly said most of all!) in anything amusing. She had a splendid sense of fun and loved to hear or tell a good story. She often invented special names for her friends and liked to chaff the 'dear people' around her.[25]

Apparently Miss Mason no longer attended St Mary's Church with her bairns or listened to sermons; she received Holy Communion fortnightly at home. She sang the Sunday hymns with the students, perused theological

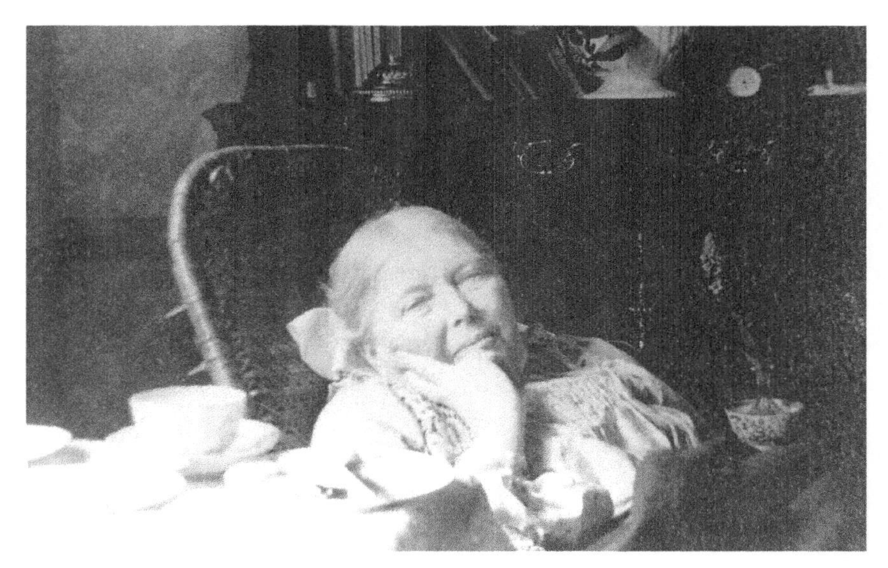

Miss Mason comfortably reclining in the basket chair.

works and sometimes talked with priests. The Revd Alexander Whyte DD, also born out of wedlock, whose preaching had inspired her in Edinburgh in 1875, brought his Bahai wife to Ambleside in 1895 and lectured on Dante's *Divine Comedy*. He gave Miss Mason a precious copy of his new book on the mystic, Jacob Behman (1575–1624), who, like George Fox and Dr Whyte, had been a shoe-maker's apprentice. The Revd Frank Lewis, first headmaster of Kelsick Co-educational Grammar School (founded in 1907) at Stock Ghyll, her one-time honorary chaplain, was a valued friend.[26] The Revd Alfred Thornley, a natural scientist and parish priest, annually assessed the seniors' nature studies from 1902 to 1937. Otherwise Miss Mason drew inspiration from many seventeenth-century divines, notably John Bunyan (1628–1688) and Benjamin Whichcote (1609–1683).

Like her Quaker forebears and contemporary women heads of educational institutions, Charlotte developed an independent personal ministry. She reflected on the Gospels with her students; they were never allowed to skip Sunday afternoon Meditations. 'She lay on her sofa and read and talked to us; she spoke very quietly – you had to listen with all your attention to hear what she was saying.'[27] 'Meds' were faithfully transcribed by Miss Kitching, and later by a student. From 1898 to 1899 printed copies were sent to weekly subscribers as outreach ministry; this lapsed due to low take-up. Some bairns were duly uplifted; others struggled to stay awake in the warm drawing room after a substantial tea. At Meditations, Miss Mason read verses from her six-volume poetic life of Christ, *The Saviour of the World*, published from 1908 to 1914, to explicate and draw inspiration from

Mrs Henrietta Franklin, an exceptional organiser.

passages in the Sunday Gospel. The theme of light runs through many verses; like her father she could repeat, 'I do but stand in the Light.' Essex Cholmondeley explained that Miss Mason was not trained in theology but arrived at her own ideas by herself.[28]

In 1898 Ernest Franklin commissioned the leading American portrait painter, John Singer Sargent (1856–1925), a friend of Henry James's (1843–1916), to paint Netta's soulful portrait. In 1900, Fred Yates (1854–1919), an English painter, with his wife Emily (1855–1941) and daughter Mary (1891–1974), met Helen Webb, their neighbour in Nottingham Place, London. After meeting Mr Yates at the Franklins' house, Miss Mason invited him to Ambleside to paint *her* portrait. Helen Webb said, 'My dear man, pawn your boots and go!' The Yates family arrived in 1901 and settled in the Lake District. Mary, also a notable artist, attended the practising school and stayed on in Rydal.[29]

Yates's portrayal of Miss Mason, comfortably clad in a richly glowing velvet jacket, subtly suggests deep reflection. Her enigmatic smile, reminiscent of Leonardo da Vinci's *Mona Lisa*, symbolises her mythic presence for all time. A student noted, 'He has managed to catch her brightest and happiest expression.' When Mrs Dallas Yorke arrived during the third sitting, she asked Mr Yates to stop painting as he had caught Miss Mason exactly. Yates lectured on J.F. Millet (1814–1875) at Scale How and sketched Millet's rural scenes in charcoal on the whitewashed walls of the handicrafts room.[30]

The impelling Mason-Franklin correspondence reveals behind-the-scenes struggles influencing the future direction of the Union, interspersed with family and Scale How news and gossip. Within a shared vision, their priorities diverged.[31] Mrs Franklin sought a clear PNEU manifesto for propaganda purposes, comparable to Lady Isabel's ill-fated pamphlet, to rebut the charge of 'absolute vagueness' and to facilitate tactical alliances with emergent feminist organisations, notably the International Council of Women (founded in 1888), affiliated with the National Union of Women Workers (founded in 1895).[32]

On 28 June 1899, Mrs Franklin invited Mrs Clement Parsons (1864–1934) to speak on the PNEU at a conversazione for ICW delegates in her home. Miss Mason was seriously displeased.

> We must not be swamped by 'women workers'. We are not women workers. Our Society is much more important because we have definite aims. They are a mere collection of units destined not to live.[33]

Like Mrs Humphry Ward, Miss Mason was neither feminist activist nor suffragist.[34] Not about to steal the limelight, Mrs Parsons' lucid pamphlet outlined PNEU principles based on 'Miss Charlotte Mason's . . . now almost famous book called *Home Education*', highlighting her stress on habit training.

> According to Miss Mason, the alpha and omega of education, thus understood, is habit, habit, habit. She takes with fervent literalness the famous sentence, 'Sow an Act, reap a Habit; sow a Habit, reap a Character; sow a Character, reap a destiny,' and applies it to the whole scheme of Education.

Adding that the PNEU aimed at harmonising home and school training by enabling parents to develop the child's powers of attention in co-operation with teachers, Mrs Parsons commended every PNEU project, especially the PRS.[34] Miss Mason's anxiety abated.

> You have sent me a feast of fair things, dearest. The Conference papers are simply splendid. We have never had anything like it, such power, such purpose, such unity of aim; such P.N.E.U.-ism throughout. We may just thank God and take courage, and then that amazing synopsis by Mrs Clement Parsons: you have put us on a rock by having that pamphlet printed, it contains everything and all put with such charming literary grace, all made entirely the speaker's own that it came forth well-arranged, easy, a symmetrical whole. I long to see Mrs Parsons. She is so truly us. You have made a brilliant disciple.[35]

From 1898, Mrs Franklin urged Miss Mason to explicate her educational philosophy by submitting annual conference papers to be read in her absence.[36] Mrs Franklin believed the PRS had much to offer boys' preparatory and public schools, whose representatives attended PNEU conferences. She was concerned about the isolation of the Ambleside students working as governesses in family settings and acutely aware that they needed further education to prepare for school teaching. They hardly saw a book or read the *Parents' Review*. To address these concerns, she arranged monthly meetings for London-based governesses at her house.

Far away in Ambleside, Miss Mason had been absorbed in writing an article on, 'School Books and How they Make for Education' (1900). Here, Miss Mason offered a liberal educational compromise between the extremes of 'faddism', an intense, short-lived idiosyncratic craze, and 'absolute vagueness'. Narration, as old as retelling Homeric tales, was described as a *new* method of assimilating *living ideas* and great thoughts, which owed much to Ruskin's emphasis on attentive reading line by line. Intellectual skills, acquired by mastering dry as dust 'disciplinary subjects' such as mathematics or grammar, were not transferable, offering no moral training. 'Remove the mathematician from his own field and he is not more exact . . . than other men.' Miss Mason also declared that the 'psychology of the hour', defining children as 'states of consciousness', failed to recognise how they developed a sense of duty towards those in authority.[37] She was resistant to her protected students joining classes at Mrs Franklin's house lest they were instructed by those with opposing views to her own.

'Mary Everest Boole.'
'Yes . . . and now psychology is going absolutely her way.'
'But I'll give you Mrs Boole. . . . She is the unprecedented.'[38]

Mrs Boole (1832-1916), a self-taught mathematician, used natural materials and physical activities to stimulate children's mathematical imagination. Interested in scientific investigation of the avant-garde psychology of unconscious learning, her paper at the 1899 PNEU conference had offered parents *implicit* ways of preparing their children's minds for scientific instruction. Mrs Boole's strange article on the Natural Priesthood of Parents (1899) had been unquestioningly published in *Parents' Review*. Although Dr Schofield's book, *The Unconscious Mind*, came out in 1898, as chair he warned the audience that Mrs Boole's views on children's unconscious motivation were antithetical to the rational PNEU physiology of habit training, rooted in religion and morality.[39] Around this time, G.K. Chesterton (1874–1936) used to sing, 'The Parents' National, highly rational Educational Union', when courting Frances Blogg (1869–1938), the PNEU secretary, at the London office in the mornings![40]

On learning that Mrs Franklin had invited Mrs Boole to a monthly meeting at her house for some Ambleside trained governesses, Miss Mason's fury manifested as illness. Expressing concern about her guru's relapse, Netta wrote,

Dear Friend,

. . . Apart from any question of personal loyalty, I always believed myself to be a clear-headed & knowing disciple. Was that all self-flattery? I thought I was supposed to know what PNEU meant even if I did not act up to it myself. Would I give up so much of my life to a cause, unless I valued it perhaps not as much as the inspirer & leader but only next to her & very nearly as much? Then, accepting the premise, that I know what I am about, would I lightly be able to

> accept any antagonistic teaching or even let it come near our borders? I always feel that it is because I believe less than you in 'parents' that I want to believe a very great deal in the possibilities of the students' work. . . . As regards PNEU lectures, is it not always your teaching that we ask no faddists but accept the best we can get from the real thinkers? Surely many articles in the *Review* are not PNEU teaching. . . . I wish so much that you would feel that what matters is that you should keep your strength, not so much for the students, or even for the parents, but to give forth the educational thought, which is in you, for those who can be inspired to take & work out.[41]

Dreading another 1894 contretemps, Miss Mason angrily compared Mrs Boole's 'negative influence' with the 'devitalised and spiritless work' she had observed in Netta's PRS school's exam papers. Suddenly, she realised how much she needed her *chela*.

> Never do I forget, dearest, your splendid intellectual fealty which is a much bigger thing than fealty of the heart alone and very much rarer. Indeed, the PNEU is a wonder to me. It is only by the Grace of God, working through this fealty that we have been able to keep a platform, devoted to steady leverage in a given place, instead of to the oscillations and vagaries of, let us say, the Sesame Club, which represents very faithfully the spirit of the day. . . . And then I went and doubted you. . . . That we should keep a broad platform is my fervent wish as much as yours. . . . No they [the students] are no fools and quite able to deal with opposition teaching . . . for they have not been reared in a hothouse. . . . You have all my eggs in your basket, dearest, and I have trusted you with what is more to me than my own soul, so you will forgive me a moment's mistrust, remembering that I have had to fight every inch of the way we have come and that, though I am resting in much ease and content, chiefly because of that intellectual fealty that I have spoken of, I sit like Botticelli's Fortitude, sword in hand, dreading unspeakably a possible affray. Help me dear, and pray for me: for you and for me and for all of us. The soil for P.N.E.U. is only more and more personal spirituality.[42]

Responding to Charlotte's cry from the heart, Mrs Franklin dropped Mrs Boole's mathematical instruction from the monthly meetings.

Pressure to reach parents of all classes threatened further conflict. As PNEU membership had only reached 2,464 by 1900, the question of affiliation with a larger body remained on the agenda. Concerned to help 'cottage mothers', the Mothers' Union had united with the National Union of Women Workers in 1897.[43] Lienie Steinthal and Mrs E.P. Arnold-Forster opened a loan-fund scheme to enable poorer people to save. After helping

Mrs Boyd Carpenter to launch the Ripon diocese branch of the Mothers' Union in 1901, Lienie left the PNEU for the MU in 1903, ill at ease with Mrs Franklin's elitist priorities. The loss of Lienie prompted Charlotte to back amalgamation with the MU. Mrs Franklin put her foot down. As a Jew, her PNEU standing would be radically weakened by affiliation with a leading Anglican Church organisation![44]

> I object to our Union & the M Union trying to cut each others' throats. You even suggest bringing the names more in accord. Which would make them still more competing parties. In this scheme no 'father' is mentioned & they do not seem to be considered. I very much dislike the M.U. way of having two kinds of prayers, pledges, for educated & non – it is snobbish in the extreme. . . . I hate 'pledges' & 'cards' & U & 'good resolutions'. I think they are weakening to the character & must be lightly made & easily broken. Surely you are very tired or you would say this is not P.N.E.U. . . . No let us frankly admit that we educate the so-called educated parents. The field is wide enough and they need it so much – our philosophy means some previous thought. Let us work indirectly among the poor. It is being done. . . . I shall fight it hard. . . .[45]

As Miss Mason again relapsed into protective illness, Lienie explained that she had taken up the MU to help poorer mothers:

> Mrs Carpenter and I are so anxious to get it on the lines of the P.N.E.U. This is all owing to you and your wonderful organisation. I began to realise the narrowness of breadth in the P.N.E.U. Committee and feel more satisfied to be able to work without distinction of creed, which must always injure good work. It is only right to give you this explanation. If we could have met, we would have had a nice talk. . . . You know I love the P.N.E.U . . . & believe me your loving Lienie.[46]

Miss Mason would also miss Thomas Rooper's wise counsels; he shared Lienie's and Mrs Anson's concern for poorer people. After moving to Southampton in 1897, where he helped to found the university, he died of spinal tuberculosis on 20 May 1903.

Meanwhile, instead of Miss Mason, Mrs Franklin was composing the PNEU contribution for the Board of Education's *Special Reports and Enquiries* (Volume VI, 1895–1903), requested by Michael Sadler, the Board's director. This opportunity marked a key stage in her assiduous cultivation of educationists occupying the corridors of power since launching the PNEU conferences in 1897. Sadler was a liberal educationist; up to 1912, he and his wife were members of the Weybridge PNEU branch, opened in 1896. The Balfour Education Act (1902), drafted by Robert Morant, had replaced

School Boards, established in 1870, with Local Education Authorities. The LEAs ran the elementary schools, developed secondary education *and* supported and regulated teacher training colleges. Through her family's liberal political contacts, Mrs Franklin met Robert Morant. A former tutor to the Crown Prince of Siam, Morant believed wholeheartedly in upper-class liberal education and was persuaded to employ Ambleside governesses for his children. In contrast, he thought lower-class elementary education should teach obedient followership.

In January 1901, Charlotte wrote to Netta:

> You are the very nicest person, dear! Not because you have written me a nice pretty letter . . . – but because – I have this morning received a paper entitled, 'The Home Training of Children'. I have purred over it a good deal and hugged the writer. It is good and very good that you know the true inwardness of us as you do. . . . It is most strong and convincing and goes straight to the mark in a way that will convince intelligent schoolmasters. . . . Of course this must be one of our pamphlets. It is just what we want to open the eyes of parents.[47]

Mrs Franklin's paper summarised the behavioural training and liberal education underpinning the PRS programmes, posted to home schoolrooms in Great Britain and overseas. Describing the PRS timetable for children from six to ten years, she stated that Miss Mason's balanced scheme of home education was a positive and progressive preparation for school. Her succinct presentation focused on narration methods, easily understood and applied:

> No lesson is valuable which does not promote self-activity by making the children think and do and work. . . . There are no better friends to the cause of the Parents' Union and the Parents' Union School than the public school masters who are more and more appreciating the work done and more and more asking for the intelligent co-operation of parents.

Not apparently published as a pamphlet, her landmark statement did not appear in *Parents' Review* until 1908. Why not? Was Netta's ease with government officials threatening to Miss Mason's position?[48] Instead, she praised her *chela*:

> You don't know how much I am making of you in my soul for the Conference is your baby or rather your five-year old, and is the most blessed, healthy, happy, holy child that Mother could desire.
>
> I just love Lady Campbell for backing you up so well and Lady Aberdeen for being so devoted and nice. . . . I have no doubt people liked to listen to her though her speech was long and slow. I have never

thought her very strong as a speaker. . . . It will be quite absurd of you not to come, so please do. I feel like drowning you under a perfect waterfall of love and blessings.

Ever Yours, C.M.[49]

But by June 1902, guru and *chela* were again at loggerheads over the vexed question of child study. Miss Mason had invited Mrs Ennis Richmond to Ambleside. A teacher and suffragette, she ran the West Heath Progressive School in Hampstead. As the author of *The Mind of a Child* (1889) and *Through Boyhood to Manhood* (1899), she backed scientific child study. Her conference lecture had upset Mrs Franklin, who found her 'hard and unimpressionable'; 'Mrs Richmond . . . spoke wanting in respect for children's truthfulness.' Although Miss Mason criticised Helen Webb for going over to child study, Mrs Franklin riposted that B.P. was 'the only member of the Committee who knows what we are at. This is not a judgment tinged by affection in the least. Mrs Glover & all are just amateurs, learning and not knowing, not grasping.' The vagueness of PNEU philosophy was again causing Committee tensions. Referring to Mrs Anson, Netta added, 'The whole spirit seems altered. She does not take the *Review*, as she dislikes it. She has no sympathy with our principles and teaching & she is . . . a dangerous spy & has really no right there.' In her next letter Netta added,

Dearest! You know I hate worrying you. It seems almost criminal to do so but all I can beg is that you must be worried. To begin with let me tell you that no explanation is necessary between us. You need not defend yourself to me nor answer me. . . . I feel . . . it due to your humility in never declaring what your colours are – I who go about so much know how vague even our best people are as to what we mean. . . .

That is to say, we live to spread principles and character training. If there is anything which the author of *Home Education* must believe it is 'Suggestion of Right' &'Belief in the children' – When Mrs Richmond spoke of them as 'liars & lying to gain their own end because they were selfish and greedy', I was terribly upset. . . . There was an audience of mostly new people who would say you ask us to hear this hard doctrine. . . . I spoke to what I know to be your doctrine 'affinities,' not predisposed truth or untruth – believe the best . . . belief in the power to help people by believing the best & not the worst of them. . . . Lady Campbell, a great friend, believes she is not P.N.E.U. You who never did justice to Mrs Boole, very likely wisely declared against her lecturing to us, but she with her abstract doctrine, which few could understand, could not do half the harm as this woman with her clear, decisive, hard phrases and belief in original sin.[50]

Miss Mason's equilibrium was restored by working on her definitive paper on 'Education as the Science of Relations', published in 1902.[51]

To launch the PRS into schools by 1903, Mrs Franklin needed the founder's definitive statement. Her preoccupation with Madge's infantile paralysis from February until just before Michael's birth on 11 April 1903 gave Miss Mason room for manoeuvre.

> I have been slaving with that paper – first revise – quite breathlessly. . . . You will soon have it. Lady Campbell will read it beautifully. . . . My dear, do you know where we are arriving at? A revolution in school children's education up to fourteen; and we must send round to the teachers broadcast. . . . Now just be sweet and good and believe with that big heart which I love. There will be plenty of fools to scoff but we want to carry a tremendous reform – and faith, our faith must be our lever.[52]

Although the seventh annual conference was postponed until October, 600 people attended the conversazione at Kensington Town Hall on 8 June 1903 to hear Lady Campbell read 'A PNEU Manifesto', written by Miss Mason. Alas, her copious treatise failed to please Mrs Franklin and Mrs Parsons. The introductory excerpt from the famous essay by Francis Bacon (1561-1626), 'Of Study', saying, 'Studies serve for delight, for ornament and for ability,' set the tone for a liberal discourse which took up forty pages of the *Review*. Unlike Mrs Franklin in her succinct statement for Sadler's *Special Reports*, Miss Mason had added endless passages from PRS children's examination answers to demonstrate the superiority of education based on *living* books over utilitarian instruction. Roundly criticised, but never discarded, the paper was adapted for her third book, *School Education* (1904).[53]

> Now I do think it most truly kind both of Mrs Parsons and you to have made this quite just criticism. The paper did lack clearness and adhesion; it was burdened with quotations and it most distinctly did lack form and style. I value Mrs Parsons' sincere and friendly protest sincerely. . . . As you know I have had a bad year. . . . I am not sure as to her verdict upon the children's answers. It is upon them that I depend to convince the world.[54]

In emphasising *knowledge* gained from books, the PNEU manifesto bypassed progressive, sensory-motor development through 'education by things'. Unappeased by Miss Mason's placatory tone, Mrs Franklin prevailed upon J.H. Badley (1865–1967), the progressive founder-headmaster of Bedales School from 1893 until 1935, to criticise the manifesto in open discussion at the October conference. Seriously perturbed, Miss Mason wrote from Paris to Mrs Franklin, highly relieved that none of her bairns, 'not a very brilliant set this year', could attend, as the Revd C.H. Parez HMI was holding his annual inspection that week.

> I hope dear Lady A is keeping well and will be quite brilliant. Please tell me what she is to wear on the great occasion. . . . The Conference is much in my thought and prayers, dear. The old prayer that we may be kept in the unity of the spirit, which is the bond of peace.[55]

As Badley opposed the public schools' competitive authoritarianism, Bedales was a liberal, non-denominational, co-educational secondary school. The liberal curriculum included English, modern languages, science, design, arts, crafts and drama. The boys took nature walks and kept gardens. The four Franklin sons were educated at Bedales between 1900 and 1919.[56]

Thanks to Mrs Franklin's skilful stage management, Miss Mason's prayers were answered; a face-saving compromise was agreed in her absence. Badley appreciated Miss Mason's plea for *real books* and disciplined individual study; both believed cramming and competition were antithetical to *true* education. In her written response, Miss Mason insisted that developing thinking and reasoning faculties was meaningless if separated from acquiring *knowledge*.

Criticising her excessive emphasis on books, Badley insisted that oral lessons were equally vital in arousing interest, as the German pedagogic philosopher, J.F. Herbart (1776–1841), had shown. Influenced by Dr Arnold's tradition of manly Christianity at Rugby, where the Steinthal sons were educated, Miss Mason affirmed the great public schools flourished because 'they live on books'. Badley, a first-class classical scholar, disagreed; in his view, traditional public school teaching was often 'mere information'.

Following the 'new education' tradition, earlier validated in *Home Education*, Badley recommended progressive learning through observation and experience; children's mental powers and manual skills developed from direct contact with 'things'. Still repudiating faculty training, Miss Mason restored the theoretical balance by re-naming her method 'education by books and things'. Satisfied with the outcome, Mrs Franklin again pressed for a distinctive PNEU manifesto.[57]

> I had hoped to have your communication re 'associates' and 'schools' by yesterday. . . . I am putting them on the agenda for Jan 20th. . . . I had a tussle yesterday against Mrs Anson who is nearly not one of us & who, though really powerless, is inclined to stray into a 'common platform'– it is difficult not to make (b) in our objects read as such. One gets told that we let Lady Isabel go because she wanted to stereotype & bind us all to a name & U. However, I think I won & Dr Schofield was A.1. and most emphatic in saying we had a 'Truth we must not sell'. If you have time in the next month to make a little statement for me to 'voice' it will be nice.[58]

Responding to Badley's critique, Miss Mason had been studying Herbartian pedagogy. A contemporary of Pestalozzi and Froebel and owing much to Locke, Herbart had been popularised by a new university professor of education, John Adams (1857–1934). Dr James Sully, founder of the British Psychological Society at University College, London, in 1901, and the redoubtable American philosopher and psychologist, Dr William James, were also Herbartian enthusiasts. Mrs Franklin's passing reference to 1894 provoked Miss Mason into declaring that her definitive PNEU philosophy did not contravene Object B:

> To create a better public opinion on the subject of the training of children, and, with this object in view, to collect and make known the best information and experience on the subject.

Mrs Franklin replied,

> I venture to stop your notice in the PR. It seems to me to be too bare to be in the least attractive & it might upset the Committee putting in anything before even the scheme has been in any way mentioned to them. I think myself, when the thing has matured, we ought to put the whole notice as you and I planned it in the *Review*. . . . It is quite formal bringing it up at the Committee, but until we have done it we must not . . . say that they are arranging it. If you can write to the list of schools you settled on & induce them to join I think three or four of them would & your Students' schools would.[59]

Ignoring this mundane task, Miss Mason was aglow. Her harbinger letter missed the Executive Committee meeting on 20 January 1904. She had sent it to Mrs Franklin who had untypically stayed at home, preoccupied with Cyril's dangerous attack of pneumonia.[60] In a stern tirade to the Committee, Miss Mason complained that the PNEU had been wasting its opportunities:

> It is practically a society for providing desultory lectures to parents. It might be, and was in my original intention a College of Parents existing to study a philosophy of education – I believe the only sufficient and efficient philosophy of education which exists. I take all the blame to myself that we have not lived up to our calling . . . because it is distasteful to have to proclaim one's own message on one's own that I have tried to take refuge in the unmeaning phrase – PNEU thought – a phrase which properly covers all the diverse thought of all the members and all the lectures.

Without claiming to have made 'this body of educational thought any more than Columbus made America', the time had come to attach her own name to it:

> To one man is given the idea of a new button . . . to one woman the perception of a new substance, to another woman – this woman – the perception of a beautiful, expansive, efficient and sufficient philosophy of education. The people who get the message are more than enough honoured by the message but it is necessary that it should bear their name or some equivalent name . . . to save the idea from corruption and disproportion. . . . It is the choice between a living organic whole and a composite whole with no quickening power. . . . I am getting old and am in feeble health and am no longer able to go about winning adherents by guile! Therefore will you think me bold if I say I must have disciples. . . . There is no other school of educational thought which even professes to have an adequate philosophy of education.[61]

Miss Mason forwarded *A Short Synopsis of Educational Theory* to each Executive Committee member, commenting to Mrs Franklin, 'Here is goodness and virtue! A long synopsis of our teaching. . . . That is what your last letter has produced.'[62]

Exhausted, Mrs Franklin was furious at being bypassed. Although Cyril had barely recovered he was despatched with his nurse to the seaside at Littlehampton.

> Dearest! You really are wonderful! All the time that we were corresponding re governesses, nurses & temperatures you were doing this. It is excellent and what we wanted. I fear I shall have a stiff job though . . . & people may say that this close defining is just what Lady Isabel M went off for with her faction.[63]

No longer fearing the faddist label, Miss Mason wrote again:

> The P.N.E.U. was formed in the first place to carry out the teaching in *Home Education* . . . and to carry out the intention of (b) in the Objects. . . . Lady Isabel Margesson and some other members left us in June 1894 because we could not receive their amendment pledging us to the 'New' Education as set forth by Pestalozzi, Herbert Spencer, and Froebel and other educational philosophers. . . . [T]he P.N.E.U. was designed as a tacit protest against the fundamental principles of the philosophers mentioned. . . . As people grow in earnest about education, they will either neglect us as amateurs or require to know what our platform is so it seems to me well to draw up, even an inadequate statement of what we teach; and it also seems necessary that this teaching is protected by the name of the originator or everyone has a right to say 'I think' and call it P.N.E.U. teaching. . . . But this statement is no new thing. The Society originated in the little manual called *Home Education* which contains the whole in the germ. . . .
>
> Truly yrs. C.M. Mason (E.K. Sec.)[64]

Mrs Franklin braced herself to mastermind the *Synopsis* through the Committee on 17 February 1904. Pointing out that dissenting members, notably Mrs Anson, might insist that the *Synopsis* clashed with Object B, Mrs Franklin asked Miss Mason to provide chapter and verse for each principle from the five-volume Home Education Series being prepared for publication, to enable her to devise branch reading and lecture courses. Miss Mason's revised *Suggestions for a Curriculum* would be sent to interested private schools.

Disturbed by another reference to Lady Isabel, which she had hoped to silence for ever with her *Synopsis*, Miss Mason refuted allegations of 'close defining', claiming that the eclecticism of the *Review*'s articles and branch lectures met the requirements of Object B. She retreated into a prophetic role to avoid the trouble of linking the points to her writings, thus avoiding scrutiny of her inconsistencies.

> Chapter and Verse – No, best of friends! – because it is all in the nature of line upon line, precept upon precept – every bit I think in Home Education but unfolded and unfolded until the last pamphlet – but what I am doing is to make a careful table of contents which shall guide people in their studies, that is – if anybody does study.[65]

On 17 February 1904, Mrs Franklin read Miss Mason's sheaf of explanatory letters and 'harangued the Executive Committee for half an hour' on the merits of the *Synopsis*. Proposing some alterations, Mrs Clement Parsons subsequently told a delighted Mrs Franklin that it supplied a long-felt need.

> This is really perfect. It is the whole educational philosophy one wants, it is the germ and heart of all her writings, except 'Books', 'Education the Science of Rel. & Ourselves'. What help are all Mrs Anson's friends' deep books to the mother compared with this?

Chaired by Dr Schofield, the Committee, apart from Mrs Anson, accepted the *Synopsis* after suggesting amendments. Kegan Paul agreed to publish the Home Education Series, provided the 875 remaining copies of *Home Education* were sold. The Committee agreed to purchase them. A reading course for parents wanting to become 'qualified members' was planned. Mrs Franklin's hard-hitting protestations had won the day.[66]

> You dear people are too sweet, and just make me cry. But truly I do not see all that in the little leaflet. I am very truly glad Mrs C P sees development. Of course P.N.E.U. is educating me but I thought I had gone back in style since *Home Education*. . . . Your (in the plural) acceptance of the 'confession' alters the footing of everything. The College, the School, my soul and body are identified with P.N.E.U.

> and there is no shadow of separation no holding back of college or anything else with a view to what some future committee that has no Lady A may decide.[67]

As the revised pamphlet, *Some Suggestions*, brought in many enquiries from schools, Miss Mason undertook to adapt the PRS programmes for their use. The Committee also approved this plan. Mrs Franklin's 'Hurrah!!!!' was not simply for their vote of confidence in Miss Mason's 'living philosophy and definite aims'. In backing the *Synopsis*, she had strengthened her alliance with the PNEU's founder and her matriarchal power over the Union in the year she was *finally* elected *sole* honorary organising secretary (1904).[68] Miss Mason was thrilled.

> I have been in a state of nervous overstrain (though very well) since that day, last February, was it not, when you took me out of the slough of despond & set the ideas in motion that have resulted in the School Register and the *Synopsis*. I want you to realise by way of a birthday gift to you how far the whole thing is due to your stimulating sympathy, even more than to your efforts. God bless you sweet friend, for all you have done for our great cause.[69]

Revered as her personal educational credo, the *Synopsis*'s eighteen points (see Appendix) opened with Miss Mason's definitive statement: 'Children are born *persons*.' In reflecting the age-old romantic view of the heaven-sent child, her individualist assertion directly challenged escalating post-Darwinian unbelief. Placing the child, rather than parent or teacher, at the heart of education was *not* an expression of the child-centred 'new-educational' progressivism, sternly repudiated in 1894. She maintained that the child's mind was no different from that of the adult but simply lacked knowledge and experience.

Secondly, Miss Mason sensibly refuted belief in original sin by stating that children are 'not born either good or bad but with possibilities for good or evil'. Thirdly, respect for the personality of children limited the 'natural, necessary and fundamental principles' of authority and obedience integral to all upbringing.

From points 5 to 8, her mantra 'Education is an atmosphere, a discipline, a life' explained that children should not be segregated in specially adapted environments but allowed to live freely in their natural home 'atmosphere' experiencing other people and 'things'. 'Discipline' referred to habit-training 'mind or body'. 'A life' explained that as the child's 'mind feeds on ideas', a generous curriculum was essential for intellectual, moral and physical sustenance.

At points 9 to 11, Herbart's views, extolled by Badley, were rebutted by protesting that 'the mind is not a receptacle' to be filled with 'enticing morsels' of knowledge, pre-selected by teachers, but 'a spiritual *organism* with an insatiable appetite for all knowledge'.

Point 12 explained that the child 'had powers of mind' to absorb all the knowledge presented, provided it was 'vital' and accompanied by 'informing ideas'. Linking this at point 13 to her new thesis that 'Education is the science of relations', Miss Mason adapted Wordsworthian romanticism to declare that children were *born* with 'affinities' or 'natural relations with a vast number of things and thoughts'. In practice, this meant training children 'upon physical exercises, nature, handicrafts, science and art and upon *many living books*' to enable them to understand the world around them.

Training the child to exercise appropriate will power by turning his thoughts in the right direction was explained at points 14 to 15. From points 16 to 17, Miss Mason suggested that children's reasoned judgement as to whether an 'initial idea was right or wrong' could be fallible, except where there was clear proof, as in mathematics. To combat error, children needed 'principles of conduct and a wide range of suitable knowledge' to enable them to judge whether to accept or reject 'initial ideas' for themselves – tricky.

The final point affirmed that there should be no separation between children's intellectual and spiritual life as the Divine Spirit had 'constant access to their spirits and is their continual helper in all the interests, duties and joys of life'.[70]

The 'definite aims' of the loosely constructed *Synopsis* have been open to varied interpretations. This guidance, best suited to training young children, was not designed to develop secular critical analysis, specialist knowledge or the clinical dissection of ideas. Instead Miss Mason sought to preserve the mystery and wonder infusing children's exploration of a magical world full of flowers, birds, music, stars, pictures and literature. A prototype for bringing up obedient Edwardian educated-class children with wide interests, knowledge of history and great literature, excessive freedom and well-developed imaginations could nevertheless lead children astray, as in an E. Nesbit novel.[71] However, the luminous open-endedness of the *Synopsis* enabled Mrs Franklin to adapt it for schools. Rooted as it was in Miss Mason's idiosyncratic philosophy, no one remarked that it did not comply with Object B.

The outcome was a surge of energy and unwavering trust in her message. Miss Mason wrote triumphantly after a Scale How gathering, 'I did more at our garden party than I have been up to for years.'[72]

> When there have not been a dozen original thinkers upon education in the world, when England has hardly had 3 or 4 – how can the P.N.E.U. believe that one of these has fallen to its share? Indeed, I can hardly believe it myself. . . . The answer always seems to be 'yes' but I am truly willing to leave the question to the 'modesty of time'.[73]

Having laboured with Kit Kit since 1900 to complete the landmark Home Education Series, Miss Mason declared, 'We want to do something that will really influence education.'[74] Although Charles Kegan Paul had retired in 1899, Miss Mason negotiated with his firm to sell the five books at 3s 6d a copy by 15 February 1904, just before the Committee accepted the *Synopsis*. Her tremulous introduction to the series, deploring 'the current misty and depressing educational outlook' while apologetically offering a *tentative* educational theory, masked underlying hubris. 'The treatment is not methodic, but incidental; here a little, there a little, as seemed most likely to meet the occasions of parents and teachers.' Taking 'the child as a person' as her core statement, Miss Mason claimed that her ideas were now embedded in 'general common sense', apart from the new insight that 'Education is the science of relations' guiding her wide curriculum.

> For between thirty and forty years I have laboured without pause to establish a working and philosophic theory of education; . . . each article of the educational faith I offer has been arrived at by inductive processes; and . . . verified by a long and wide series of experiments.[75]

The *Synopsis* was inserted into the introduction to each volume in the series, headed by a favourite quotation, attributed to Benjamin Whichcote, the well-known Cambridge divine and Platonist:

> The consequence of truth is great; therefore the judgment of it must not be negligent.

Revision was not Miss Mason's forte. However her indebtedness to Dr Carpenter was removed from *Home Education* and the curricula in Lecture V appropriately expanded. *Parents and Children* (1896), republished in May 1904, was tactfully dedicated to PNEU parents as 'An Expression of the Affection and Reverence with which Their Efforts Inspire Her'. The varied range of articles on parental responsibilities emphasised children's potential, drawing especial attention to 'The Great Recognition'. In Chapter XXI Miss Mason surprisingly upheld that the science of heredity confirmed the class-based prejudice that 'children of *lettered* and *unlettered* parents' needed different education. The former were 'born with an inheritance of self-developing faculties' that '*ignorant* or otherwise *deficient* children' apparently lacked.[76] This outmoded view would change in practice.

The third volume, *School Education* (October 1904), was effusively dedicated to Henrietta Franklin for spreading 'certain educational ideas' and for 'her singular apprehension of those ideas' – and for getting the *Synopsis* accepted! Miss Mason's conference papers from 1897 to 1904 were inserted, with three chapters on curricula and a critical review of Herbart and the new educationists. Narration, designed to instil the habit of attention by requiring the child to tell back the contents of a paragraph, page or chapter (according to age) after *one* reading was also elaborated.[77] Miss Mason boldly declared,

> If our educational creed is by no means conclusive, we think it is not narrow, because we have come across no problem of life or mind the solution of which is shut out from us by any dogma of ours.[78]

Thirty pages of children's selected answers to the non-competitive PRS exams were included, against advice, to demonstrate that her methods worked. Possibly derived from her precise training at the Ho and Co, exemplar lesson plans for oral teaching were appended.[79]

The title of the fourth volume, *Ourselves, Our Souls and Bodies* (May 1905), was taken from the first prayer of thanksgiving after Holy Communion in the Anglican Book of Common Prayer (1662): 'And here we offer and present unto thee, O Lord, ourselves, our souls and bodies, to be a reasonable, holy and lively sacrifice unto thee.' Back in 1901, Miss Mason had praised Mrs Franklin for 'reading "Ourselves"' in manuscript to her children.[80]

Ourselves, Our Souls and Bodies was Miss Mason's personal counsel of perfection, dedicated to her student disciples 'in the belief that they will make its teaching their own and disseminate it as they are able'.[15] Permeated with imagery from John Bunyan's allegorical novel, *The Holy War* (1682), *Ourselves* depicted the Christian journey and the battle between good and evil, also integral to Bunyan's most popular book, *The Pilgrim's Progress* (1678). Blithely assuming her twentieth-century disciples were drawn to seventeenth-century allegories to address modern moral questions, Miss Mason explained that everyone was a kingdom of Mansoul with the obligation to act morally in relation to the body, mind, heart and soul. Infused with puritanical ideals, the book's aim was to raise fallen human nature.[81] As the dictates of chastity demanded unnaturally cool detachment in personal relationships, by implication impulsive behaviours, sexual impropriety and idle gossip characterised the lower orders.

> The Instructed conscience learns to regard all excessive affection, undue fondness, as sullying the chastity of the self-controlled soul.[82]

Ourselves expressed Charlotte's lifelong striving for purity, only possible in controlled seclusion at Scale How. Holiness was not won through the bitter waters of experience perhaps clouding her problematic childhood, but by avoiding the first fall from grace. Bishop Tucker of Uganda wrote that in *Ourselves,* his lay workers 'would find much to keep them in their efforts to live nobly'.[83] The book's earnest aspirations were integral to Miss Mason's spiritual leadership of the Ambleside community and upheld her legendary influence.

The outdated last two *Home Education* lectures, VII and VIII, were transferred to Volume V, *Some Studies in the Formation of Character* (1906). The book was a quaint compendium of *Review* articles, chatty fictional pieces, studies drawn from books and discussions of the challenges of character formation in sulky pre-pubescent boys and girls at 'the difficult stage', and wives – never husbands – failing in their parental duties. In 'A Hundred Years After – 10 September 1990', Miss Mason imagined the PNEU centenary being celebrated at a small private dinner party in 1990. The discussion on educational progress was conducted by the *gentlemen* over their port *after* the ladies had withdrawn.[84] Belatedly in this final volume, Miss Mason acknowledged her 'indebtedness to Miss Elsie Kitching, for the constant interest she has thrown into the work, and her always intelligent co-operation as amanuensis'. Quintessentially Victorian, this compendium was not selected for PNEU reading courses.

Miss Mason asked Mrs Franklin to prepare lectures on each of the first six articles of the *Synopsis*, then on the next six, and then on the next. 'But it would be heavy work because it would mean close study of all the little books to see in how many ways every point applies – but the "*Child as Person*" will be the very crux for our crusade.'[85] Five years later only fifteen parents had qualified, after reading the first four volumes and answering the questions on each chapter. While recruitment of qualified members was intermittently pursued, the Mothers' Education Course declined during the First World War.

> The books frighten the dear people and I daresay they think I have an axe to grind. But truly I have not.[86]

Relaxing at Bad Nauheim in 1905, Miss Mason conversed happily with Dr Knittel, a German Jewish doctor who later organised a German translation of the Home Education Series. She told Netta that he considered Jewish people necessary to education because they stimulated thought and intellectual activity of every kind, adding, 'I think I must have Jewish blood, if I could trace it, or I should not be so bent on bringing up the world at large.'[87]

15.
A Liberal Education for All, 1905–1922

> Perhaps the greatest tribute to Miss Mason's work is that it has become in part absorbed into current thought. Every good teacher is a discoverer, and it is for the sake of loyalty to old truths that we try to be open to new ways of expressing them.[1]

The volte-face that propelled Miss Mason's upper-class liberal home education into lower-class elementary schools resonated with longstanding concerns about English teaching and the difficulties of teaching under the Code that had beset her Worthing years. Without government recognition of the Ambleside training, Mrs Franklin resolved to extend the private PNEU schools through parents' associations, alongside the home schoolrooms spread across the Empire. Lienie Steinthal's catalytic launch of liberal education in state schools would enhance her plans. Enlivened by the success of the movement, Miss Mason would emerge from seclusion in 1920 to meet with teachers; there is no record of her visiting their classrooms. At Ambleside children's parties, her enthusiasm for childhood was expressed in the peals of laughter she raised by asking riddles!

A vision of Charlotte Mason lying swathed in rugs on her blue sofa in the drawing room belies her keen-eyed interest in Scale How life, the Beehive practising school and all PNEU operations. She was kept in the picture by Miss Williams and the subservient Kit Kit. News from London and the wider PNEU was relayed by Netta, former bairns and disciples. If students brought problems or requests, Miss Mason, believed to deplore personal influence, would clarify the principles underlying a refusal, for example, to provide easy chairs, and send them away to think it over. Her view was invariably accepted! Following a complaint that teaching four classes simultaneously in the Beehive classroom was unduly distracting, Barrow stopped the Victoria carriage at the door. Dead silence greeted Miss Mason as she walked in. Where was the problem?[2]

Miss Mason lost Dr Schofield's gentlemanly support when he inexplicably resigned just before the May 1905 Executive Committee meeting. On 14 December, the young Earl of Lytton (1876–1947) replaced him as chair, a position he would retain until 1912. Active in the Duty and Discipline Movement, Lord Lytton shared Mrs Franklin's preference for school education and women's suffrage. His address on fatherhood at the 1906 Brighton conference doubtless kept the Mothers' Union at bay![3]

Miss Mason continued to encourage Netta Franklin's efforts to persuade more schools to use the PRS programmes. She wrote in April 1905,

> A word of birthday greeting to my Beloved Friend! May the coming year bring her much by-product of the kind she is seeking after so that her friend may be stimulated and helped to do (and think) better by more and more signs of growth.[4]

The promising establishment of the Schools' Register in 1904, which gained seventeen schools by 1905, strengthened Miss Mason's hopes of reaching state schools.[5] Robert Morant, permanent secretary to the Board of Education from 1903 to 1911, issued a new Code for Elementary Schools (1904), published with the *Handbook for Elementary School Teachers* (1905):

> The purpose of the public elementary school is to form and strengthen the character and to develop the intelligence of the children entrusted to it . . . assisting both boys and girls, according to their different needs, to fit themselves practically, as well as intellectually, for the work of life.[6]

The introduction of state-funded secondary-level schools in Morant's Education Act (1902) was also intended to improve elementary teacher-training. The day training colleges attached to universities, like Oscar Browning's Cambridge institution, were raising standards. On the issue of government recognition, Mrs Franklin urged caution:

> Dearest! Your scheme is wonderful but it is too sudden. . . . We must talk it over first. . . . Perhaps if you feel up to it I could get Mr Morant to come early and see you first. I believe & always have believed that you should try & see an occasional big gun. A few words from you do more than all our talking, but not socially, business.[7]

En route to Bad Nauheim in July 1905, Miss Mason met Morant at 50 Porchester Terrace, Mrs Franklin's house, to discuss recognition of the Ambleside training. Dashing off a subsequent response to Morant, she said, 'there would be difficulties in allowing *her* students to practise teaching in elementary schools.' To prove PRS methods worked, she enclosed a set of exam papers, 'hurried work by a girl of no particular intelligence or culture', suggesting another route to recognition. Six years of PRS courses

The Beehive classroom.

for elementary schoolgirls would give them 'the foundation of knowledge and culture a student should have on entering a training college'. As King's Scholars, she would train them, if the Board accepted the House of Education certificate. But, heir to the Queen's Scholarship system that had launched Charlotte's own teaching career, the King's Scholarship was abolished by 1907.[8]

Mr and Mrs Morant visited Ambleside in September. As in rival Germany, state-funded education, escaping universal Church control, was viewed as essential investment in Great Britain's economic future. Enlightened by Matthew Arnold's utopian vision, Miss Mason trusted in culture's ameliorating power. Morant concurred, but urged the need for technical and vocational training with legislation to improve the poorest children's physical health, fitness and nutrition following the dire findings of the Interdepartmental Commission on the Physical Deterioration of the Nation (1904).

Miss Mason told Morant she was planning an Ambleside conference with Mr Wynn Williams, the Westmorland HMI, for 'the best teachers in the district'. In December 1905 Mr Holmes from the Board attended the well-advertised Saturday meeting, chaired by Mr Williams, with nineteen elementary school heads, a preparatory school headmaster, two secondary school headmistresses and the Revd J. Hawksworth, vicar of Ambleside. After discussing ways of introducing the Ambleside 'common curriculum' into all classes of schools for children up to fourteen, three elementary schoolmasters joined the PRS.[9] Miss Mason sighed,

> The whole thing turns on how far we feel obliged to make 'instruction' in schools our business. If the powers that be [The Board] come to our aid in that matter, we may just go on in our own happy way, carrying

> forth our own work under our own name; but if it remains for us to reach teachers it may be at the cost of . . . sacrifices. . . . I have been feeling very sorrowful at the thought of losing our old P.N.E.U. name and changing our organisation.[10]

Early in 1906, W.B. Gordon, Miss Mason's solicitor, reviewed statutory recognition of the House of Education with L. Amherst Selby-Bigge (1860–1951) from the Board.[11] Although the college was annually inspected by HMIs, notably Mr Rooper from 1892 to 1901 and the Revd C.H. Parez, a parish priest, from 1902 to 1909, albeit unofficially, the scope and status of un-certificated teachers was declining. They were not accepted in state secondary schools. Without government certificates, the bairns were classed as unqualified supplementary teachers (ex-Article-68ers), only eligible for junior posts in infants' departments or small rural girls' schools.[12]

If Westmorland LEA had controlled the House of Education, as finally occurred in 1960, Miss Mason would have had to declare the college's total assets and relinquish control of the finances *and* her curriculum. The home-oriented practising school taking older girls and younger children would have had to adapt or close. Supervision of the students' teaching practice, at which Miss Mason excelled, would have been transferred to qualified local elementary school teachers. If government recognition demanded too great a sacrifice, the price of Miss Mason's independence was denial of the bairns' professional qualifications. Although their fees were £80 per annum by 1904–1905, Scale How was running at a loss, subsidised by £400 from PRS fees.[13] Hard-earned surplus funds paid for Miss Mason's travel, health costs, books, journals, hotel stays, coach and horse, coachman, maid, dressmaker, prizes (those pretty teapots to look up to), generous gifts to numerous godchildren and hospitality to friends. Mrs Annie Harris (née Armitt) recalled 'the generosity of her [Charlotte's] present dealings' and 'her readiness to take the heavier share of financial transactions'.[14]

An alternative was incorporation of the college, PRS and practising school. Although Mr Gordon drew up articles of association in 1911, a board of trustees would have legally controlled all Miss Mason's financial transactions. Fretting over the outcome with Netta, incorporation was deferred. Instead Miss Mason boldly took out a mortgage to purchase Scale How from W.L. Mason. Although the distinctive mansion was over-priced at £5,950 in 1911, she skilfully managed independently without guaranteed external backing.[15]

Mrs Franklin dominated Miss Mason's second landmark conference at Scale How in June 1906. The delegates, mainly from private schools, agreed to recommend the PRS curriculum or 'some similar scheme' to promote independent study in class. Nineteen teachers welcomed Miss Mason's method of encouraging children to form habits of concentration; wide reading improved English composition and spelling. Linking English subjects to history also extended children's range of knowledge.[16] At Mrs Franklin's conference for public schoolmasters, held at Porchester Terrace with Miss Mason in 1907, the non-competitive methods of the renamed Parents' Union School (PUS) were rejected by public school masters, hostage to classical studies, examination marks and specialisation.[17]

Miss Mason's reputation was growing apace due to prestigious PNEU connections. In April 1907, the conservative *Daily Mail* published her chatty articles on habit training, accompanied by cheeky cartoons depicting maternal inadequacies and degeneracy![18] Miss Mason's conservative paper on 'The Family and the State', surely reflecting Spencer's famous tract, *Man versus the State* (1884), was addressed to the anti-socialist British Constitutional Association at Oxford in July 1907. Masking her background, she argued against encroachment 'upon the duty of most persons however poor to support their own children. . . . [S]ustenance by the State implied State control.'[19]

Ellen Parish (1869–1947), a former senior monitress, was an attractive woman who 'even as a student at college . . . seemed . . . to have closer contact with Miss Mason than the rest of us'.[20] After teaching at the Spange PUS school in Ewhurst, Miss Parish was appointed as the PNEU's London organising secretary in 1907, under Mrs Franklin's direction. Her duties included launching new branches and offering guidance to parents, nurses and schools. Her diary (1907–1908), written for Miss Mason, illustrates the uphill nature of her task. She met with apathy or hostility unless an influential local enthusiast had worked up a meeting to launch a new branch.

> I want to know how <u>many</u> are necessary for a branch and what Mrs. Franklin means by getting the <u>right</u> people. It is the social side which baulks me.[21]

Miss Parish encountered complaints about membership expenses (10s for both heads of household), criticism of the embargo on kindergartens, the isolationist stance of the Union and a bland ignorance of Miss Mason's books. Some expressed sympathy but failed to join. A Mrs Schultz from Norwood thought the PNEU had had its day and was only suitable for younger mothers. Mrs Sieveking, from the Bexhill branch, was 'grossly insulting about the way the PNEU works for its own profit'. When Lingfield mothers regarded the Union with 'misgiving as a rival of the Mothers' Union, Lady Chichester from the Chair quickly put that right'. Mrs Scott of Kew declared that 'the ideals of the PNEU were so high as to be depressing'. A Mrs Wilson of Brondesbury said 'hard things' of Miss Parish's paper on 'Truthfulness'. Addressing mothers and nurses together was 'most difficult'.[22] Although Miss Parish's sterling efforts were sometimes rewarded, she recorded dismally, 'I would give anything to know why it is I don't make people join.'[23]

The Liberals gained power in 1906; Netta's MP father, Samuel Montagu, was elevated to the peerage as Baron Swaythling in 1907. The Hon. Mrs Franklin, an experienced mother of six, had little difficulty in generating enthusiasm. Invariably gorgeously attired, she wore her wealth and rank like royalty. She had a gift for committee work. 'Of course Netta was managerial . . . her mere voice, raised on some point of importance . . . carried across the room all the thunders of the wrath of Jehovah.'[24] Bypassing their father's and her husband's orthodox Judaism, Netta had enabled her sister, Lily Montagu (1873–1963), to launch Liberal Judaism with Claude Montefiore (1858–1938) from her drawing room in 1902. Their cousin Herbert, later Viscount Samuel (1870–1963), Asquith's home secretary, masterminded the enabling Children's Act (1908). Netta's brother, Edwin Montagu MP (1879–1924), served in Asquith's Cabinet, later achieving high office. On 3 March 1909, Netta's mother presented her at court.[25] Modest little Miss Parish could scarcely compete in the same league.

By 1914 the two propagandists had increased the PNEU branches from 32 in 1905 to 41, with about 3,000 members; one of the branches was in Victoria, Australia. Due to the overseas expansion of the PUS, the circulation of *Parents' Review*, renamed *A Journal for Parents and Teachers* in 1906, soared. The London Office mailed 15,783 copies to 123 population centres from Paris to Amritsar, from Shanghai to Waikaia and from Mafeking to Honolulu.[26] PNEU parental membership may have been affected, partly by women's improved education, but also by the Infant Welfare Movement, ideologically transforming parent education into instruction for the betterment of so-called 'feckless and ignorant' lower-class mothers, beleaguered by poverty and low wages.[27] Members of the Victoria Settlement group in Liverpool (1906–c. 1923), the only PNEU branch for artisan mothers, were excluded from leadership roles.[28]

During the ICW's Canada conference in 1909, Netta experienced pain in her right leg. Sarcoma was diagnosed and amputation at the thigh recommended. Against Ernest's wishes, Netta insisted that a woman surgeon, Louise (later Dame) Aldrich Blake, should perform the operation. Three weeks later the indomitable Netta joined the family holiday in Scotland. Missing country rambles and cycle rides, Netta refused to indulge in regrets and bravely kept up her 'royal progress' for the next fifty-seven years.[29] Miss Mason lovingly sympathised:

> I grieve about the pain, darling. . . . You little wretch to go and construe an innocent desire for a tray in your sitting room along with the sofa (which thing I love) into a luncheon party. . . . But seriously, Dearest, I must have you all to myself, except B.P. for a little while.[30]

Although Netta saw little of her masterful Jewish father during the eighteen months between the amputation and his death on 12 January 1911, because he disliked anything to do with illness, Jewish custom dictated the curtailment of social activities during the mourning year. Untypically deeply depressed in July, Netta's black-bordered letter reached Charlotte from Hull.

> My Dearest!
>
> I want, dear, to be one of your students again. . . . As time goes on, I become more and more imbued with the idea that life is only a preparation for something better & more & more long for that better. Every morning I am rather unpleasantly surprised there is another day before me. . . . I have a keen sense of duty . . . a desire to co-operate humbly in God's work. . . . But it affects me like this. I am positively glad when someone is ill and ready to die. It shocks me to hear of people mourning. . . . If I hear of someone making a failure of their life, I just think 'how nice if you could die'. . . . I wish I could talk to you. . . . I know you could help me to see straight.[31]

Charlotte replied within two days:

> My Beloved
>
> Thank you for opening to me the secret sacred Peace of your life. Your letter is very interesting and, I think, very important. . . . Like everybody else, I say with secret joy, 'How the weeks fly!!' . . . Like you I am not a bit sorry for people killed . . . not that I think death is a <u>relief</u> for everyone, but is just a going on, so to speak, a change of garments. But not like you, I take real pains to go on living. . . . I know you too receive Jesus as a 'teacher sent from God'. . . .
>
> But I want to tell you why I feel I <u>must</u> go on living as long as I am allowed. I do not look for anything . . . more than of the sort I get here – with the one vast exception of 'life more abundantly'. That is, I think, God-knowledge, God-consciousness. . . . I have a notion that we have to begin things in the flesh we shall go on with in the spirit. All the people we shall meet there, we ought to know, realise first. All the flowers in the world – all the stars in the universe. . . . I shouldn't wonder if this is the sort of Gospel our age is waiting for – and we are so sick of waiting that we play like children at a fair. Take, darling, this cup of healing and <u>pass it round</u>. I believe this is the one thing you and I have got to do; but I don't see how yet. . . .
>
> Dear, dear love CM[32]

Charlotte did not dismiss Netta's malady but offered future joy. Mr Dunning's letters confirmed her unshakeable belief in everlasting glory; Netta's despondency would pass.

Miss Mason's dutiful observance of her spiritual vocation, reaching back to her Quaker forebears, was sustained by the reverence with which her meditations and sacred poems were regarded at Scale How. Hoping *The Saviour* would be as well received as John Keble's *Christian Year* (1827), she despatched Volume I to the Episcopal secretary to the Pan-Anglican conference as an inspirational guide for training ordinands.[33] Seeking publication from 1908 onwards, she met resistance from Kegan Paul's successor:

> I must say that fully as I recognise the high intention which has been your motive, I am still disposed to think that this series is about sixty years too late to win real popularity. The tendency today . . . is to make these lessons as brief . . . and as 'real' as possible.[34]

Miss Mason never discarded any of her writings, believing her work was enlightened by the Holy Spirit. If she paid the publication costs, she expected PNEU members to purchase copies; the poems were placed on the PUS syllabus for twelve-year-olds. *The Saviour* won some positive press reviews. However, by 1927 Mrs Franklin told Mrs Foster that 'Miss Mason's friends are not particularly proud of [*The Saviour*] from the point of view of the verse rather than the sentiment.'[35] Today, across the Atlantic, her poems are read and treasured for their particular explication of the Gospels.[36] The bairns received Volume VI, *The Training of the Disciples*, on leaving Scale How.

Miss Mason's paper for the 1910 PNEU conference offered a rigorous critique of Rousseau's ban on book-learning before the age of twelve in *Émile*. She pleaded for *humane* education rooted in the humanities to inspire children to be good citizens in the service of their country.

In 1912, representing the Mothers' Union, Mrs Steinthal informed the Minority Report of the Royal Commission on Divorce in 1912 that 278,500 mothers, mainly from the English and Welsh working-classes, were MU members. Marriage failure could be addressed, not only by improving the social environment, but by equipping young adults for family life with 'a more permanently effective system of elementary education'.[37]

That year, Miss Mason fired off six rhetorical letters to *The Times*, published as *The Basis of National Strength*, the harbinger of liberal education for all children.

> It is for their own sakes that children should get knowledge to acquire the power to take a generous view of men and their motives, to see where the greatness of a given character lies, to have one's judgment of present events illustrated and corrected by historic and literary parallels, to have, indeed, the power of comprehensive judgment. . . . Knowledge is not instruction, information, scholarship, a well-stored memory. It

> is passed like the light of a torch, from mind to mind, and the flame can be kindled at original minds only. . . . It is as vital thought touches our minds that our ideas are vitalized and out of our ideas comes our conduct of life. . . .
>
> If we let people sink into the mire of a material education our doom is sealed; eyes now living will see us take even a third-rate place among the nations.

With this powerful polemic against materialist education, our Hellenistic prophet proclaimed that books lay at the heart of education; 'letters are the accessible vehicle of knowledge'. Narrowing her previously broad curriculum, she unthinkingly asserted that other subjects, from maths to languages, crafts, activities, nature studies and science required no reform; they were adequately taught.[38] Without wide knowledge, reason could lead children astray, encouraging rebellion. The letters appealed to conservative religionists fearing further secularisation of education, social unrest and the decline of a great imperial nation.

Fresh from arguments with 'the great O.B.' during his annual inspection of the House of Education in 1912 over the merits of Montessori education, Miss Mason wrote to *The Times Educational Supplement* criticising the Dottoressa's neglect of books and her utilitarian, scientific pedagogy, which segregated children in simplified environments while denying their personalities.

> The Montessori child . . . sharpens a single sense to be sure at the expense of a higher sense but there is no gradual painting in of the background to his life; no fairies play about him, no heroes stir his soul. God and good angels form no part of his thought; the child and the person he will become are a scientific product.[39]

While child study, research psychology and new educational theories were making an impact on the teaching profession, Miss Mason pressed the case for liberal education. In 1914, the pressure to work caused half the children aged between twelve and fourteen to leave school. Children living over two miles from rural schools were excused attendance. Although Fisher's Education Act (1918) made schooling compulsory for all children up to fourteen, many still failed to attend.[40]

Anxieties about English teaching dated from the 1875 Code, when English was made an optional subject, although it was later upgraded to a class subject in 1882. The Revised Code was not finally abolished until 1897. As reading literature was shown to improve children's command of grammar, English replaced some grammar lessons. Two London County Council (LCC) conferences in 1906 and 1908 on English teaching led to a book exchange between schools, which extended their libraries without extra cost. Selected books included PUS favourites such as *Aesop's Fables, Robinson Crusoe* and *Tales from Shakespeare*, and contemporary children's stories. By 1920 the scheme covered the whole LCC area.[41] Charlotte's half-great-niece, Gertrude Mary Anderson (c. 1875–post-1924), Joshua Mason junior's granddaughter, was headmistress of Ben Jonson LCC School in Stepney. Assuredly her school would have participated.[42]

Despite the splendid pageantry of the well-organised week-long Winchester children's gathering in May 1912 for 250 children and 350 parents, governesses and well-wishers, organised by Mrs Franklin to mark the 21st birthday of the PRS/PUS, the Schools' Register had only added 8 more private schools to the 19 girls' schools, 5 boys' schools and 7 mixed schools that had joined by 1908.[43] The absent Miss Mason's welcoming letter was read to the children.

In 1913 Mrs Steinthal relinquished her MU responsibilities and presidency of the Anglican Girls' Friendly Society (founded in 1875) to re-launch Charlotte's mission. Artistic and creative, she was a born teacher who cared passionately about poorer people's lack of education. The young Lienie had held meetings to encourage aimless street boys to improve their lives. Unfailingly generous with her time, she had supported Miss Mason in all her endeavours. After guiding her children through the PRS, teaching Ambleside students 'blobs' watercolour painting and metal work, and holding painting and sculpture classes with Bradford teachers from 1900, she knew the Yorkshire teachers and understood liberal education. Mrs Steinthal had probably previously met Miss Ambler, headmistress of Drighlington Girls' Elementary School in a drab West Riding Yorkshire village, and knew of the shortage of resources at her school.

> The outside environment, a mining village . . . consists of a black-gray expressionless street of bare cottages in barren gardens, the only colour enamel advertisements of blackleads and soaps nailed to the walls. Nothing else visible but slate shingles, gray stone, and, near the school, where the village ends, the road, between black hedges, murkily sloping to the moor. . . . A few women with shawls over their heads move about raucous-voiced. Some . . . mothers are temporary workers and where there can be no home midday meal the children bring their bread and butter to school and get their cocoa heated on the school stove.[44]

In the spring of 1914, Mrs Steinthal donated £20 for a year's supply of selected PUS books for 160 Drighlington children to begin their liberal education. Miss Ambler agreed to try the PUS programmes because her deprived children lacked 'living interest'; 'their powers of expression were weak, their vocabularies poor and their mental development arrested.' Too

Mrs Steinthal leaves the Mothers' Union to start the PNEU liberal education mission.

much effort was made by the teacher and 'too little by the child'.[45] Mrs Steinthal stayed at hand to advise on upholding interest with short lessons, picture study and heroic tales and to explain narration technique to secure the attention of hungry children.

Agnes Drury (CMT 1902), Miss Parish's gifted, sometimes explosive, contemporary, had been recalled to Scale How in 1907 to teach nature study and science. In 1914 Miss Mason despatched her to the West Riding to assist Mrs Steinthal in setting up a 'memorable meeting of elementary school teachers' to familiarise them with PUS principles, as they translated methods devised for home schoolrooms into large, noisy classrooms. Mrs Steinthal exclaimed,

> Think of the meaning of this in the lives of the children, – disciplined lives, and no lawless strikes, justice, an end to class warfare, developed intellects, and no market for trashy and corrupt literature! We shall, or rather they will, live in a redeemed world.[46]

The Steinthal family fortunes crashed after the First World War blocked co-operative business enterprises with Germany. From 1915 to 1921 the Steinthals let their mansion, St John's, a northern centre of hospitality where G.K. and Frances Chesterton were welcome visitors. They settled at Mount Stead, Ben Rhydding, Ilkley.[47] Miss Mason was thrilled by Lienie's new initiative:

> My Dearest Lienie, It's just breathlessly wonderful that you should have this great opportunity . . . for this is what we are doing, offering the best we know or could conceive of, for 'the education of the people.'

Hoping that Mr A.C. Coffin, the West Riding Director of Education, would cover the cost of the books and fearing that Lienie would be overworked, Miss Mason suggested starting with only four to six schools. It was 'pioneer work that will have to be carefully watched because a good thing debased is worse than a bad thing is it not?'[48] Her insistence on one book for each child who could read was costly. Much more had to be done to convert the 'antis' and the overworked, war-weary teachers. Her next letter enthused,

> I have thought and dreamed wonderful things since your letter came . . . visions in the night of quite wonderful books. . . . I can hardly tell you how impressed I am with your great work. Yes, dear, the whole of this wonderful movement is your 'fault'! From the first notion until the last meeting you have done it all. . . . It seems to both of us, does it not? that all this comes from a higher source. . . . Indeed, yes I feel like tears whenever I think of it. I don't know of anything more hopeful for the country than the excess of enthusiasm you have excited in the teaching profession. It shows what stuff they are made of.[49]

The timing was right. A manageable method of self-education by children compensated for the wartime shortage of teachers and funding. As the PUS had been centrally organised from Ambleside for twenty-five years, with Kit

Kit's team marking the termly examination papers, Miss Mason could judge for herself the work undertaken, while guiding the choice of books and exam questions. From 1914 onwards, they responded to a rising number of state schools, PNEU schools and home-school children in Britain and overseas.

After a 'bad year' in 1914, Miss Mason announced that she would take *two* courses of baths at Bad Nauheim 'with a Nach Kür in between'.[50] Ignoring threatened conflict, Miss Mason and Miss Kitching left for Germany. By September 1914 they were trapped in the war zone and interned; their passports were confiscated. Trainloads of German troops passed, bound for the front. Mrs Franklin wrote to Lady Aberdeen; his Excellency contacted the US ambassador in Berlin who arranged travel permits for Holland. Mrs Steinthal communicated through cousins at The Hague; Miss Parish contacted a Mrs Sandberg who offered hospitality. Sydney Franklin persuaded an Amsterdam bank to honour Miss Mason's cheques; Miss Williams telephoned from Switzerland; Helen Webb's friend offered assistance. Safely returned home, there were Belgian evacuees to be accommodated, financial strictures, rationing and shortages of staff and students. As the war progressed, in 1917, Charlotte remarked in a letter to Netta, 'the war is straining people's nerves isn't it? Three housemaids gave notice this morning.' Then they had to face the 1918 flu epidemic at Scale How. Unquestioningly loyal to the British Empire, Miss Mason insisted that 'the abysmal ignorance shown in the wrong thinking of many of the men who stayed at home' and their lack of 'generous impulse, of reasoned patriotism' were due to 'errors in education'. Yet she grieved with a student over the death of her brother.[51].

Professor Campagnac, from Liverpool University's Education department, arrived for the annual inspection in November 1914; he longed to introduce liberal education into Liverpool schools. Miss Mason asked Lienie to explain the scheme. Would it work in two classes, if someone spent £50 on books? Charlotte later wrote to Lienie, 'I should not have had a word to say if I had not had you to fall back upon.'[52]

Delighted by the Drighlington children's exam papers, Miss Mason congratulated Miss Ambler in 1915:

> The children have done extremely well in every subject and the best is more remarkable seeing that they took the examination after a six week absence but that is what we find. Children taught in this way do not forget. I am much struck by the able way in which your teachers have taken up the method and your way of conducting the examination answers perfectly.[53]

In 1916, Mrs Steinthal reported that the Drighlington children were far more 'alert and keen' than before. They narrated 'clearly and intelligently; delight was shown in all their studies. There is no need to shout in this school for order and quietness, the children are too much interested.'[54] Given the lead, the teachers did not cram the children with facts but let them discover what they needed to know for themselves. That year, Mrs Clement Parsons also observed 'the self-activity of the children, the absence of wandering glances, listless faces and sleepy minds'.[55]

Complementary papers by Miss Mason and Miss Drury on 'The Theory and Practice of a Liberal Education in Schools' were presented to a council teachers' conference, organised by Mr Coffin, at the Bingley Training College in 1916, with Mr Wood HMI. Published as sixpenny pamphlets, 7,000 copies were posted to LEAs, HMIs and elementary school heads. The covering letter affirmed that the Yorkshire experiment had proved 'that it is possible to give children of the working-classes such an education in English, as should make them patriotic and large-minded citizens with resources for their own leisure and pleasure'.[56]

In September 1917, Miss Mason and Mrs Steinthal hosted a teachers' conference in Ilkley, led by Miss Ambler and her staff. Miss S.E. Bargh from Skipton wrote to a colleague, 'We all came home as keen as mustard to do our best with the new system and since then we have improved wonderfully.' By now Mrs Franklin was visiting schools and told Miss Bargh that her school was doing better than Drighlington! The latter found Mrs Franklin an exceedingly thorough visitor, 'whose eyes took in every single thing on the walls and in the rooms and her ears missed nothing either!' Delighted with the way the children had taken to narration and to *almost* all the books, apart from Arabella Buckley's *Life and Her Children* (1881), Miss Bargh confessed that they discussed points at the end of the lesson to leave the correct impression, although she knew Miss Mason opposed this.[57]

Canon Rawnsley and his brother, Willingham, visited Yorkshire schools with Mrs Steinthal and gave talks. Charlotte was excited by Lienie's assurance of more classes joining. She hoped 'the Board (or someone else) . . . will have the papers printed and distributed and seeing that children need not be denied education on the grounds of "no vocabulary" people will begin to take things seriously'.[58] Lienie reminded Charlotte of how they had started the PEU at that 'gilt-edged meeting'. Did mixed feelings aroused by this reminiscence impel her to write to Netta about naming the movement?

> P.N.E.U. Method does not do. . . . I hate the vulgarity of it, but I suppose it must be the 'Mason Method', which is short, neat and true – as it involves a whole new scheme of educational thought.[59]

On Mrs Franklin's watch, the PNEU name would be retained. Because of this, perhaps not surprisingly, many twentieth-century PNEU pupils have never heard of Charlotte Mason, who had helped to launch Netta's educational career. The term 'Mason method' has, however, been adopted across the USA and in Canada.

Horace West Household,
Director of Education for Gloucestershire.

Fisher's Education Act (1918) allocated study hours for young workers at continuation schools. As the PUS was adapted to secondary level, Miss Mason hastily wrote another pamphlet, *The Scope of Continuation Schools,* which offered an education in the humanities to counteract the effects of utilitarian teaching, with the added 'inspiration and delight of entering into an intellectual world full of associations . . . a well of healing and fountain of delight'. Miss Mason became obsessed by children's mastery of enormous lists of names! H.A.L. Fisher (1865–1940), a distinguished Oxford historian, visited Drighlington School. He praised Miss Mason for showing 'how readily English children respond to the appeal of the masterpieces of English literature'.[60]

However, teaching by *one* specific method went against the grain. The Board of Education's *Suggestions for Teachers in Public Elementary Schools* (1918) stated, 'Each teacher shall think for himself and work out for himself such methods of teaching as may use his powers to the best advantage and be best suited to the particular needs and conditions of the school. Uniformity in details of practice . . . is not desirable even if it were obtainable.'[61]

The catalyst was waiting in Gloucestershire. Horace West Household MA Oxon (1870–1954) had taken teacher-training. In 1903 he was appointed secretary of Gloucestershire LEA and later became its director until 1936. A committed liberal educationist, Household visited his elementary schools very regularly.[62] In November 1916, the PUS propaganda pamphlets arrived. Instead of dropping them in the wastepaper basket, he read them and was instantly converted. Securing permission from the Education Committee chairman, he resolved to test the Drighlington scheme in schools that usually achieved good results. At Christmas he wrote to Miss Mason, echoing Thomas Rooper's 1880s lament about books:

> I have no doubt whatever about the success of this scheme in the hands of a good teacher who has some education and is gifted with imagination. . . . The great want of the Elementary Schools has been

> good books. That the scheme supplies. The one hopeful method seldom or never tried in the Elementary School is reading aloud and that the scheme suggests. . . . I am sure you are right in saying there is practically no difference between the work of children of educated and illiterate parents, given the opportunity . . . where there has been access to good books and sympathetic imagination has inspired the methods.[63]

Not prepared to risk the method in the hands of unqualified teachers, he provided five selected schools with the PUS 'living books', such as Louise Creighton's *First History of France* (1901), H.O. Arnold-Forster's *History of England* (1913), Arabella Buckley's *Life and Her Children,* Annie and E. Keary's *The Heroes of Asgard* (1908), H.E. Marshall's *Our Island Story* (1905), Shakespeare, Scott and Charlotte's geographical readers, re-issued as the *Ambleside Geography Books,* among others. Class teachers received single copies of difficult books, notably North's translation of Plutarch's *Lives*, on citizenship, to read aloud to older children before they narrated, either verbally or in writing. Difficult words were written on the blackboard to be learnt and reproduced correctly. Miss Parish was appointed adviser to Gloucestershire schools under Mr Household's direction. Although she had not taught for years, she had gained a wealth of experience at the PNEU London office and would succeed Miss Mason as the House of Education principal. At the former students' Ambleside Conference in 1917, Miss Mason urged her bairns to trumpet the news of this great national work.[64]

Mr Household had to convince the qualified teachers of the value of the PUS programmes, devised by unqualified staff at Ambleside, who set the termly examination papers and marked selections as numbers grew, albeit under Miss Mason's oversight. As most teachers also assessed their pupils, little time was saved. Household always listened sympathetically to the teachers' issues concerning the choice of books, how much explanation to give and how to manage different levels of ability, maintain attention and give enough time to the so-called utilitarian subjects such as maths, crafts and games. In reality the pneumatic method, as it came to be known, was never uniformly applied in Gloucestershire but, as its adoption became the hallmark of an effective school, it spread like a beneficent infection! Geoffrey Household (1900–1988), author of the suspense novel *Rogue Male* (1939), said of his father, 'the methods of Charlotte Mason were the most satisfying discovery of his life and deserve more general recognition.'[65]

The exuberant flowering of the Liberal Education for All Movement had strengthened Miss Mason's health and determination to protect her educational legacy. Indebted to Netta for enhancing her public standing, but wary of modernisation, she set the scene for perpetuating her mythic influence:

> You will understand what it means when I say that the spiritual influence of the PUS is rather a thing by itself. I hardly know how it comes about but I am very anxious to safeguard it and believing that we are allowed in the Afterwards to go on helping in the work we care for, I have a mystical notion that if we can keep that atmosphere while I am here it will go on always.[66]

The PNEU's acknowledged founder carefully arranged her succession. On 10 April 1919 she signed her last will, bequeathing the House of Education, its educational work, premises and land to a private trust. Chosen trustees would be empowered to arrange the conduct of 'the said business . . . as carried on by me in accordance with the views expressed in my "Short Synopsis" and more fully set forth in the five volumes of "The Home Education Series"' unless it became 'for any reason . . . impossible or impracticable to do so'. The tenth clause named Ellen A. Parish as the first principal of the House of Education with an annual salary of £250 and powers to select the staff. Rewarded for running the PUS, Miss Kitching was designated its first director on £200 per annum. Both posts were tenable for life with free board and lodging. Having assisted Miss Mason with most of the editing, Miss Kitching was appointed editor of the *Parents' Review*, owned by the PNEU since 1902. The task of writing volumes VII and VIII of *The Saviour*, along with £200, was allocated to Canon Rawnsley or 'some other fit person' who could complete the poems in her lifetime. The final volumes were never written, as Canon Rawnsley, a popular Lakeland poet, died in 1920.[67]

That summer, Mr Household paid his first visit to Ambleside. Expecting a weary invalid, he was instantly captivated by Charlotte's brilliance:

> She had quietly (for she was always quiet) put pain and weakness and age away from her, and you were conscious only . . . of her surpassing gifts; it did not seem to you that she lacked anything. Her face was full of light, of wide sympathy and understanding, of delicate humour and gentleness and love. She always knew. From the first moment, the first word, the first letter, you had no doubt. She knew.

He added: 'Her gift for inspiring deep personal affection in the hearts of many who never saw her was rare, if not unique.'[68] Although Miss Mason reputedly deplored the pervasive cult of personality, she embraced validation of her mission and commented drily,

> His little visit was very pleasant. He is enthusiastic. . . . His Gloucestershire work is a dear child to him. . . . I do not think you will find any prejudice on his part any more.[69]

As Mr Household launched the programmes into junior forms of secondary schools, other LEAs, including the LCC, tested the method. In Leicestershire, W.A. Brockington, another distinguished liberal Director of Education (1903–1947), gave guarded approval to introducing the PUS in 16 schools, fearing his teachers' style would be cramped by sticking to one approach, however respectable in origin. As in Gloucestershire, he limited the experiment to flourishing schools with keen headmasters. Helen Wix (CMT 1903), another torch-bearing former student, had been visiting schools with Miss Parish; she was appointed HMI for Leicestershire (1921–1929), finding it a tough assignment. At Ambleside in May 1920, Mr Household planted a young oak tree to celebrate fifty schools joining the PUS and enthused to the students about his Gloucestershire experiments.[70]

Mrs Franklin invited five 'token' girls from a Durham county elementary school to the second highly successful children's gathering at Whitby in May 1920. They proved to the delegates' satisfaction 'the cheering discovery that elementary school children were capable of taking their place side by side . . . with . . . children from far superior environments'.[71]

Despatched with 'flying colours' by her Llangammarch Wells doctor, Miss Mason emerged from invalid seclusion in September 1920. Mrs Franklin was safely out of England meeting the King and Queen of Norway for the International Council of Women.[72] Not ideal timing for Mr Household, who emerged from a nursing home to meet Miss Mason and Miss Kitching at the Bell Hotel in Gloucester. Miss Mason took tea with the Education Committee. She spoke magnificently to sixty teachers at the Shire Hall, known to her from their correspondence and their children's exam papers. After resting on Sunday, the two ladies travelled north to stay at Highfield House to carry out a similar programme with Mrs Steinthal in Bradford.[73]

To bring Miss Mason's future plans for the College to fruition, Fanny Williams was sacrificed. Persuaded to retire as V. P. at Christmas 1920 in Miss Parish's favour, her loyalty was assumed. Amy Pennethorne (CMT 1898), whose mastery of quadratic equations showed her 'intellect had power', succeeded Miss Parish as the PNEU's London organising secretary, becoming a leading twentieth-century interpreter of Miss Mason's teaching.[74] Furious that she had not been consulted, Mrs Franklin secured Miss Parish's co-option as an ex officio member of the Executive Committee, currently chaired by the Revd Harold Costley-White (1878–1966), headmaster of Westminster School from 1919 to 1937 and DD in 1924.

> We have, as you know, lost the dear V.P. and after 23 years you will guess there is a bad sore place in my heart – but fine teacher as she was, she herself felt that it was time to retire. I shall miss her companionship. . . . I can't tell you how sweet Miss Parish is & how able but you know & I hope that will go very well indeed. . . .

> Have just walked downstairs – took my own bath this morning with just a little help from the District Nurse who comes in for an hour every day. Now I mustn't write any more as Kit Kit is keeping watch. How good she has been to me.[75]

Unremitting concerns about English teaching found expression in the Newbolt Commission's Report (1919–1921). The Commission was chaired by Sir Henry Newbolt (1862–1938), a champion of chivalry who was famous for resounding poems such as 'Drake's Drum' and the phrase 'Play up, play up and play the game' from his poem 'Clifton Close' (1892). To Mrs Franklin's dismay, Miss Mason declined to give evidence. The sole PNEU representative, Miss Parish, spoke on 'The Use and Enjoyment of Books'. The commissioners learnt that more than one hundred schools had adopted the widely known PNEU experiments. 'Manuals and textbooks are superseded by books of literary value and the pupils are encouraged to get knowledge for themselves.' One headmaster told the Commission of his satisfaction with the results. The Commission agreed that children should discover delight in books but held that the crux was the personality of the teacher.

Newbolt members concluded that English was still unduly neglected in many schools, insisting that it should be embedded in all educational experience from elementary schooling to university level. Understanding literature should take centre stage; pupils should be taught how to form well-constructed arguments. Household was convinced that Miss Mason had influenced the Commission's view that

> The real teachers of literature are the great writers themselves – the greater the work the more it speaks for itself; but this only leads to the conclusion that for teachers we must have those who will not come between the pupils and the authors they are reading.[76]

This emphasis on 'great' literature accorded with post-war nostalgia for Victorian chivalric imperialism in a rapidly changing world. However, the Newbolt commissioners asserted that teachers should be given a free hand; their professional competence, cultural knowledge and personality were essential to rightly developing children's understanding of English, more challenging in large classes with fewer books than in home schoolrooms.

By 1921, post-war spending cuts obliged Mr Household to devise the group method. From infant classes upwards, groups of children narrated from one shared book. He justified it on progressive grounds as brighter children could move on at a faster pace, contrary to Miss Mason's principles. He asserted that the results from the group method were astounding; the children co-operated effectively with their group leader.[77] He took pains to point out that every child enjoyed a full curriculum, with plenty of 'things', including gardening and pig-farming in rural schools. His irrepressible enthusiasm at the Cirencester PNEU conference in 1927 inspired *Punch* to extol Miss Mason's fame in five verses:

O happy county, foremost in the van
Of culture, where two-thirds of all its schools
Are now conducted by the kindly plan
Laid down by Charlotte Mason in her rules
And no pedantic or repressive ban
The infant's self-expression checks or cools
But the long-needed change has come to pass
Which makes the child the unit not the class.

Where teachers, though originally taught
Wrongly in schools or colleges to aim
At suffocating independent thought
In pupils, treating them as all the same,
Have now at last been gradually brought
To recognise the individual's claim.
Abandon arid text-books, black-board chalking
And cease as far as possible from talking!

Marshall Jackman HMI studied Gloucestershire schools in 1927. He saw much to value in narration and picture study, if used creatively with the teacher's guidance. However, the single reading rarely worked; revision was required. Only selected exam papers were sent to Ambleside for marking. He noted inaccuracies arising from the shared book group method and raised concerns about the Ambleside team's uniform choice of old-fashioned books and the monochrome picture study cards. He stressed the need for specialist teaching in subjects such as history and geography. While the state school liberal education movement gradually declined after Mr Household's retirement in 1936, in that year 40,000 children were learning from the PUS programmes across the world and in Mrs Franklin's PNEU schools.[78]

The PNEU annual report of 1920–1921 revealed promising post-war expansion. Professional educationists' approval of the pneumatic method gave credence to Mrs Franklin's plans to extend the network of private PNEU schools. In February 1921, nearly 70 schools with a combined total of 10,500 children had joined the Register; of these, 22 were run by or employed former students. Surprisingly, in her *L'Umile Pianta* letter of 1918 Miss Mason commended the benefits of teaching few children in families to help the war effort, rather than in large school classes. Furthermore, in 1919, Miss Mason thwarted Essex Cholmondeley's plea 'to be given' an elementary school 'because her sympathies were with the poor and needy', by asserting that every child in every circumstance is poor and needy![79]

On 21 June 1921, the PNEU Council finally passed the incorporation measure giving the Union the 'power to hold property with continuity independently of the individual members'.[80] Strengthening the powers of the Executive Committee, composed of Mrs Franklin's allies, incorporation marked a significant stage in the honorary organising secretary's long-term aim to bring all PNEU operations under her metropolitan control. Mrs Franklin pushed through her grand scheme to close the smaller branches of fewer than fifty members. Residual floating members would be encouraged to join Area Associations, supporting or developing private PNEU schools. As the powerful Birmingham branch led by Mrs George (later Dame Elizabeth) Cadbury (1858–1951), a leading Quaker, unanimously agreed to the changes, incorporation sounded the death-knell of the weak branches.[81]

Having secured her Ambleside succession, Miss Mason resolved to finish her magnum opus. At Llangammarch Wells with Kit Kit in July 1921, drought delayed the mineral baths for a month. Armed with sheaves of papers describing liberal educational successes, Miss Mason told Mrs Franklin, 'I am writing a book summing up the PUS teaching so I dictate in the morning and E.K. types.' To make amends, she invited Fanny Williams to Llangammarch Wells for three weeks in August, telling Netta that although her twin brother 'had rather played havoc with her' she 'went away mended'![82]

On Sunday 7 August 1921, Lienie Steinthal died suddenly from a coronary heart attack at Mount Stead. Writing from Llangammarch Wells, Charlotte told Dorothea how much she had treasured her mother's friendship:

> I never loved her so tenderly & so reverently as last summer. I felt a change in her which I could only think of as the beauty of holiness. My heart goes out to you dear ones in your immeasurable loss . . . but the sore ache of her visible presence – how you will all feel it. . . . It seems so sad that I a lonely old woman should go on living, while she – the very source & centre of a beautiful family life . . . should be taken from us. My heart is very full of all her goodness, to me all her staunch support . . . & her true and tender love. . . . The PNEU cause has had a heavy loss, but I think she will still be allowed to help.

Affectionately describing Lienie as the 'Angel in the House' imbued with the old domestic graces, she told Francis Steinthal how many would miss her 'radiant personality'; '[Although] there is so little that can die of all we loved in her . . . I grieve to think of the aching, aching hours & days before you.' Mr Steinthal replied how he had longed hear from her: 'You were so very dear to her. You knew her so intimately that you can realise what we, what I have lost . . . as we begin to long for the sound of her voice and the touch of her hand.'[83] In view of these tender memories and Kit Kit's observation to Mrs Harris that 'Mrs Steinthal's sudden death last week was a great shock to Miss Mason', it seems inexplicable that two months later she complained to Francis Steinthal about the way the founding of the PNEU had been reported in Lienie's obituary notices.[84] His startled response was upset, but courteous:

> I am so sorry to read that you have been pained by some silly newspaper reports. When I think of Lienie I don't know what she would say. She would be quite upset. . . . I stated the facts as I remembered them. Of course I never dreamed of claiming for Lienie the sole foundership of the P.N.E.U. If some stupid papers have made such a statement it is entirely their doing and I hope you will believe me that neither I nor any of us have any knowledge of it. . . . Your position is so secure that you should not give the matter any further thought. I do hope that you will never doubt our entire loyalty to yourself and the great cause for which you stand.[85]

Since 1904 Mrs Franklin had won her leading position in the PNEU by backing Miss Mason as the *sole* founder and philosopher. Did she object to references to the *joint* founding of the Union? Miss Mason prudently decided not 'to trouble a man in his sorrow' by asking him to send 'a denial to those papers', and kept in touch with Dorothea.[86] The negative advantage of Lienie's death was cessation of the veiled conflict between her two beloved leading PNEU ladies. Miss Mason sought peace of mind by writing a warm appreciation of Mrs Steinthal as the instigator of the movement that had awakened a 'general soul at the touch of knowledge' in the Preface to her final opus.[87]

'After the wonderful baths,' Miss Mason wrote, 'I am dreadfully busy trying to get my book off the stocks & of course greatly helped by E.K.'[88] Hurriedly dictated, mainly in Wales, *An Essay towards a Philosophy of Education* celebrated the Liberal Education for All Movement. Full of creative suggestions and highly valued by transatlantic twenty-first century followers, it is a detailed, discursive exposition of her well-established, imaginative ideas.

In offering a 'few salient principles', her preface charted the blending of home and school education. Narration, the new intellectual habit training, was belatedly inserted between points 13 and 14 of the otherwise unchanged *Synopsis*, as the most effective method of acquiring knowledge from literary works. In the Author's Preface, Charlotte Mason judiciously warmly acknowledged Mrs Steinthal's contribution *and* Mrs Franklin's launch of a LCC school parents' association. She added, 'The Parents' National Educational Union has fulfilled its mission, as declared in its first prospectus, nobly and for the benefit of all classes'. Across the world, children in each class, in school or at home, were reading the same recommended book simultaneously![89]

Emphasising the mind's hunger for knowledge and the sacredness of personality, Miss Mason revealed for the *first* time her life-changing engagement with the home education of Miss Brandreth's insatiably curious young Anglo-Indian niece and nephews, while deviously enhancing her Worthing teaching experience.[90]

In Book I, she finally linked the *Synopsis* points to her familiar educational themes, a considerable achievement. Now at last, she questioned whether habit training irrevocably marked the physical brain! Much of the book was taken up with the detailed curriculum, graphically illustrated by selected children's answers. She placed self-education in the humanities at the heart of her method, repeating, without evidence, that mathematics, physical activities and Badley's 'things' were adequately taught. Utilitarian education had lost Germany the war. 'Mathematics, for all its usefulness in the war effort, did not make for general intelligence' or prepare children to apply sound reasoning powers, only achieved through wide reading and mastering the lessons of history. Yet her economic survival had depended upon meticulous account-keeping!

Charlotte Mason with Miss Parish and Lady Olave Baden-Powell.

Still fearful of encouraging unbridled reasoning, she again averred that it should be limited to exposing fallacies such as Marxian theory; critical analysis was not part of her educational plan. To acquire knowledge of God, she suggested that verse would inspire more reverent handling than prose. Her protected lifestyle, reliant on servants and friends for every service, may explain her somewhat arbitrary dismissal of practical skills, mathematical prowess and the value of sensory experiences. Still rejecting faculty training, psychological pedagogy, specialisation and technical education, she claimed that the study of feelings and unconscious motivation had *no* educational relevance.[91] The applied theory in Part II of *An Essay* included the three pamphlets and *The Basis of National Strength*. Addressing new educational theories was not her priority.

> The truth she saw was simply this, that all that is great and beautiful in Literature, art, music and nature can make an appeal not to the well-to-do but to the very poorest of our people.[92]

The work finished, she wrote to Netta after returning to Scale How:

> Elsie is away for her holiday and dear Miss Parish is doing beautiful work and being very dear. I think she is almost normal again but it

> took her one or two terms to get rested again after a good many years of very delightful work. It is such a comfort that she was so long at the office. She knows about everybody and everything. I am very well, partly because of the baths, and partly because I have got rid of that book which has been an incubus this long time – think of it, dear, to have to make a big book which is destined to convert the world (in a hundred years) when you are eighty in a month.[93]

Mrs Franklin visited some Gloucestershire schools in November 1921. She persuaded Mr Household to join the Executive Committee, a masterly stroke connecting the state schools' exciting progress with the developing PNEU higher-class private schools.[94]

Miss Mason's numerous handwritten letters suggest excellent sight and the energy of good health at this time. In December she and Barrow observed two waxwings with uplifted crests, matching her raised spirits during her happiest year. The magnum opus completed, Miss Mason joyfully anticipated the 1922 spring conferences at Scale How. For the children, she remained a faraway figurehead.

> I want to meet our friends & I hope we may all burn with the same great purpose & go forth conquering. . . . We shall not waste time in futile discussion but should really go on & drive forward what is of saving grace for the world. You know, Dearest, I shall be eighty when the year comes in and I want to leave a body of enthusiasts when I go who know that we have found practically all we want in education.[95]

In May 1922 Miss Mason dominated her final old students' gathering attended by ninety-nine former bairns, now private governesses and PNEU school teachers. With unprecedented energy, she attended every meeting and demonstration, leading every discussion. None of those present would forget her magnetic presence and crystal clear liberal educational vision.

> It was indeed very 'happy making' to see all those dear people and to hear . . . of the good work they are doing and all so simply and happily with such a great love for the children. I felt it a great uplift of heart to know that we are supported in our P.N.E.U. work by such a band of thoughtful women.[96]

On 26 May 1922, Miss Mason graciously received Lady Olave Baden-Powell. As dictated by the great B.P., she capitulated over transforming the PUS girl scouts, launched by Jessie Tasker (CMT 1909) in 1910, into guides. From the terrace, they enthusiastically watched the cadets and guides march past.

At the twenty-fourth PNEU Whitsuntide conference at Ambleside, Miss Mason addressed the Committee, members and delegates representing the whole United Kingdom from hand-written notes.

Miss Mason expounds her principles.

Excellent addresses were given, but the whole reality of the Conference was centred on the actual presence of Miss Mason. She called the members of the Union round her, and as children who only want to learn; they paid their homage and sat at her feet. Twice she outlined the history and policy of the Union, and her second address – P.N.E.U., A Service to the State – gives just that inspiration which is needed for the carrying on of her great work.[97]

A mystical sketch of Charlotte Mason by Fred Yates.

16.
The Unseen Presence, 1923

During the autumn of 1922, quietly enjoying her ordered lifestyle at Scale How under Kit Kit's watchful eye, Charlotte reflected on the vital educational commission to be taken forward after her death. In the light of Quaker tradition, she believed each person is unique, precious, a child of God. Her 'great recognition' at Santa Maria Novella in Florence had revealed the influence of 'the teaching power of the Holy Spirit: the 'wind of God' or 'the breath of life', her Ἅγιον *Πνεῦμα*.[1] Was she hoping her unseen influence would flow out from 'the afterwards'? A remarkable personality in her own right, the lonely orphan had won first place in the Union, thankful for her disciples' constant service. Restored health and peace of mind uplifted her last years, crowned by the late surge of liberal educational fame. 'An Old Pupil' observed,

> In spite of her frail body – which, indeed, had grown a little stronger of late years – she seemed to have perennial youth and the keenness and vigour of her mind were unimpaired.[2]
>
> She had snow-white hair, a parchment, but soft skin, and those searching blue eyes.[3]

Michael Franklin recalled,

> She seemed to me to be always smiling – her smile was indeed infectious. . . . I always felt that Miss Mason had something of the fairy, of the Robin Goodfellow, of 'Lob' in 'Dear Brutus'. She was so young and so whimsical.[4]

Miss Mason attended Thursday morning Crits and Scale How Tuesday evenings, taking Sunday Meditations as usual, reclining on her beloved sofa. She was present throughout Professor William de Burgh's three-day annual inspection in November. Impressed with their 'liberty of individual development', arising from the varied curriculum, he found the students 'taught *naturally*' without either 'stereotyped imitation' or 'superficiality'. Their teaching would develop 'from a flowing stream not from a stagnant pool'.[5]

> It might have been a sleepless night, or a night of pain, but always after her morning preparation for the day there was a radiance of countenance, that grew as the years passed, that made one hesitate in awe, a radiance that only 'gospel books' could bring.[6]

Miss Mason was present at the seniors' final talk. A student recalled,

> My last memory of her is at the Christmas Party in December 1922. We had all dressed up that year as characters from children's story books. I believe I was Peter Rabbit. Miss Mason was wheeled in, in her chair, and we stood round in a circle. She had a black dress and a red shawl round her shoulders and she smiled at us as she was wheeled round.[7]

With Barrow, she drove out on 16 December 1922, wrapped in furs. Influenza at Christmas weakened her physical reserves, although she discussed letters and articles and enjoyed being read to up to a few days before her death. Lizzie Groveham, her devoted friend for sixty-four years, replied affectionately to her card saying that she was unwell:

> I more than guessed you were ill, for the old kinship spirit told me, and I knew. For weeks past you have been constantly in my mind, and in my prayers. And now that you are recovering I may gladly offer my birthday greetings. God bless you now and ever.

By 1911 Mrs Groveham had moved to 6 Riverview Terrace, Woodbridge, in Essex, near her widowed youngest daughter, Mabel Curjel, aged forty-seven. She was very proud of her three grandsons: Alfred, aged twenty-one, entering the legal profession; Bill, aged nineteen, reading chemistry at Oxford; and Harald, aged fifteen, at school. She humbly added that 'her dear friend . . . was always so good to be interested in the boys'. Although she undoubtedly wrote regularly, her letters were not preserved. Lottie bequeathed £25 to the great-hearted Lizzie, who survived her by seven years, dying at eighty-nine in Alfred's presence.[8] Apparently, Charlotte never mentioned the magnitude of her faithful friend's longstanding support.

Dictated to Mr Household, Charlotte Mason's last letter passed the blazing torch to her ardent disciple:

> The thing we have to handle is a big thing. Its fire almost takes my breath away for we hardly know where it will go to. . . .
>
> Ever Yours C.M. Mason[9]

On Miss Mason's birthday, her bed was brought down to the drawing room, where, surrounded by her books and favourite pictures, she could lift up her eyes to the Lakeland hills through the French windows. On Friday 12 January 1923, she reviewed answers to some letters. Early the next morning, 'after speaking of the beauty of the starlit sky, with a jesting word to the nurse, she fell into a quiet sleep which lasted until she died, very peacefully' on Tuesday.[10] Miss Williams and Mrs Franklin were summoned to her bedside, as Netta recorded in her diary:

> January 15th was telegraphed for to go to Charlotte Mason who was dying. She was unconscious when I arrived. Sat up all night. She passed away at 12.15 on January 16th in the presence of Miss Kitching, Miss Williams and myself.[11]

The new students were writing examinations when Miss Williams, Miss Parish and Miss Kitching solemnly entered the classroom with their hands folded together as in prayer. Lisping, Miss Williams told the forsaken students of the quiet passing of 'one of the great ones of the earth'; they 'stood for five minutes for prayers'.[12] Dr Hough, Miss Mason's medical adviser, celebrated her 'powerful personality' at a solemn evening service in the drawing room:

> Miss Mason . . . was beloved far beyond the limited precincts of the House of Education, and as years went on with a stronger and deeper love throughout an ever widening circle that continued to be impressed by her magical influence and irresistible charm. . . . She had well and truly laid the foundations of a priceless tradition in and around that place and she had built upon that sure foundation a structure that no storm of controversy could ever destroy or time efface.[13]

Surrounded by flowers, Miss Mason's body was ceremonially laid out on the blue sofa in the drawing room. The bairns and new entrants were invited to see her; not all could face this. One student recalled, 'She looked perfectly beautiful and much younger. Her face was so restful and the lines were gone.'[14] So had the young ladies of Cheltenham College filed solemnly past the mortal remains of the great Dorothea Beale in 1906.[15] Treasured for years until it mysteriously vanished, the sofa was revered as a taboo object; touching this cultic symbol of Miss Mason's unseen presence was forbidden. Once, a hapless student sat on it. As she leapt up horror-struck, Miss Parish raised her pince-nez and adjured her, 'remain there, it may do you good'![16]

Miss Mason's will was read on 18 January 1923. The executors were Mr Gordon, Mr Lewis and Mrs Franklin. Mr Lewis and all the House of Education and practising school staff were left £5 apiece to buy memorial rings; the servants were similarly left £3 each, apart from Barrow who inherited a five per cent war loan for £100. 'My friend' Miss Williams and

St Mary's Church, Ambleside, where Charlotte Mason rests.

'the said' Miss Kitching were also left legacies to purchase memorial rings (£30 and £20 respectively), alongside Mrs Groveham's bequest. As the owner of Scale How mansion and Fairfield, still mortgaged, with the lands and adjacent properties, valued at £10,057 0s 5d, Miss Mason had bequeathed her substantial estate to *continue* her educational work.[17] On the morning of the funeral the newly appointed Ambleside Council of Trustees, chaired by Mr Household, confronted Miss Mason's irreversible resolve to keep the mystical Ambleside atmosphere intact.

On Friday afternoon, 19 January 1923, wind and rain blew coldly up from Lake Windermere. Under a leaden sky the coffin, covered in the school children's wreaths of brown wintry beech leaves and berries, was propelled by Barrow and the gardener on a wheeled bier. Umbrellas shielded the long procession, headed by the slowly limping Mrs Franklin with Miss Parish, Miss Kitching and Miss Williams, followed by past and present students, local friends, Scale How staff and servants and the practising school children carrying nosegays. As the cortège passed, Ambleside villagers stood in their doorways; the men raised their hats. Myriad bouquets and wreaths had arrived. At the churchyard, 'We laid the flowers beside the grave and passed, one by one. It looked so small to be the resting place of that great spirit.'[18]

The funeral service at St Mary's Church was read by the Revd Harold Costley-White, the executive chairman, assisted by the Revd Frank Lewis and the Revd J. Bolland, vicar of Ambleside. The hymn 'Rock of Ages' was sung and the 'Nunc dimittis' chanted. The organist played Handel's 'I know that my Redeemer liveth' and 'Lament' by Gladstone as the procession entered the Church and 'O Rest in the Lord' by Mendelssohn as the congregation left for the graveside committal conducted by Mr Costley-White. A central plot had been secured. Charlotte Mason was interred between the obelisk raised in memory of W.E. Forster (1818–1886), her former Bradford MP, and the Arnold family's graves.[19] Her final resting place symbolised the bridge she had raised between Ruskin's and Arnold's liberal culture and state elementary education extended under Forster's

Education Act (1870). In death as in life, Charlotte Mason was placed with the great and the good. An ornate granite Celtic cross marks the grave of the Irish orphan, adorned with her aphorisms:

In loving memory of
Charlotte Maria Shaw Mason
Born January 1 1842, died January 16 1923
Thine eyes shall see the King in his beauty
Founder of the Parents' National Educational Union
The Parents' Union School and the House of Education
She devoted her life to the work of education
Believing that children are dear to our heavenly Father
And that they are a precious national possession
'Education is an atmosphere, a discipline, a life.'
'I am, I can, I ought, I will.'
'For the children's sake.'

In 1947, Ellen Parish's ashes were buried nearby, and in 1955 Elsie Kitching's remains were interred under the plain stone slab at the foot of the grave, marked with a 'K' at each corner. Agnes Drury 'rejoiced' in Kit Kit's 'exaltation'; when she died in 1958, her ashes were placed close at hand.[20]

Mr Household asked the Gloucestershire teachers if, when the 'Spring flowers begin to appear, the children of any school cared to bring them – wild flowers gathered by their own hands – and send them to be laid with their grateful and loving devotion upon her grave, I can imagine nothing that would have been more dear to her heart.' The teachers were to carry on her programmes 'for the children's sake'. The children's flowers duly arrived and were placed in pots around the grave. Every year on 16 January, the practising school children, whose predecessors had enjoyed many parties, games, scouting activities and sports days watched with delight by Miss Mason, were led on their annual pilgrimage to the graveside.[21]

A reverential conference was held at Mortimer Hall in London on 26 March 1923:

> It was a happy idea to have her portrait on the platform, smiling down at us from a host of golden daffodils and at the end of three days her features had become so familiar that she seemed to us, who had not known her, no longer a stranger but a friend. Her spirit seemed to fill the room and there was a consciousness that she 'being dead, yet speaketh'.

The conference closed with a solemn memorial service at St Martin's-in-the-Fields on 29 March 1923. Leading the service, the Revd Harold Costley-White extolled Miss Mason's wonderful powers, which she had fully used in the service of others. As they departed to Basil Harwood's 'Requiem Aeternam', the congregation experienced an overwhelming sense of Miss

Mason's unseen but living presence; as in life her charismatic influence emanated from distant Ambleside. Her mystical reputation was upheld by the reverential flow of admiring letters and adulatory recollections, recorded for *In Memoriam: Charlotte M. Mason* (1923).[22]

Charlotte Mason was blessed with the good fortune to end her life as her unifying liberal cultural mission for *all* children reached its zenith. Charles Chase, vicar of Ambleside from 1882 to 1891, who knew Miss Mason before her 'great work began', had sensed her driving force. 'The one outstanding lesson of her life . . . seems to be that difficulties are made to be fought and overcome.'[23] She had inspired awe; scant regard was paid to those who had enabled her rise. Olive Marchington recalled, 'When I first came to the practising school and saw Miss Mason, I had it carefully explained to me by the other girls that she was a very great and wonderful person . . . and I was very surprised to find that she was the sweetest, kindest-looking old lady instead of the learned person I had expected to see.'[24] Miss Bicknell (CMT 1922) retained a 'vivid memory' of visiting Scale How with her parents. Miss Mason showed no interest in her past school achievements and quietly explained that *she* would choose whether Miss Bicknell was accepted for the training or not after the week's trial. 'I doubt if we were in the drawing-room for half an hour, but I came out knowing I had met a really great person and that, although she had made me feel very small, I was determined to get to the College and try to work for the PNEU.'[25]

By 1923 Miss Mason was venerated as the distant friend of every child studying her liberal education in 113 secondary and 211 elementary schools, 33 private PNEU schools, 70 schools on the PUS Register, in about 4,000 world-wide home schoolrooms and known to almost 4,000 PNEU members, 434 former students and 30,000 *Parents' Review* readers.[26]

> Dear Miss Mason was so full of spiritual light that few could ever have met her without having lasting help given them. . . .
>
> One feels with such a personality as hers death is merely . . . an episode in life: and there is so much of her still left in this world.[27]

The obituaries praised Miss Mason's educational contribution as the Union's founder; the great-hearted Lienie Steinthal's sterling contribution was overlooked. The former had filled a gap by conducting 'what was in effect a training college for governesses . . . sought all over the English-speaking world'; her education offered a 'balanced union of religious belief, literary and scientific thoroughness'. She was commended in *The Times* as 'a pioneer of sane education', because 'with other educational reformers of today she saw children not as unwilling receptacles for information but as growing creatures struggling towards the light, eager to learn, eager to work, and too often starved of the means of doing so'. However, her percipient obituarist added,

The graves of Charlotte Mason and Elsie Kitching.

Her personal influence was probably more widespread than any educationist of her time. The loyalty which she inspired was more than could be accounted for by the mere weight and force of her educational philosophy.

References to Locke and habit training were excised from the *In Memoriam* reprint. Instead, the influence of Ruskin, Arnold of Rugby and Wordsworth emphasised by Sadler confirmed Miss Mason's acclaimed literary liberal educational orientation.[28]

Other obituarists questioned her methods. The *East Anglian Daily Times*, found it 'a little difficult, without considerable tests, to estimate with certainty the advantage or otherwise of Miss Mason's system' but noted, 'it is certainly an interesting one.' Favourably comparing her to her opponent, Dr Montessori, for advocating 'individual methods of teaching', *The School Guardian* said 'the textbooks associated with Miss Mason's schemes' left 'something to be desired in the way of vivacity, variety and interest' for the modern teacher![29]

Sensitive to the limitations of *An Essay,* hurriedly put together when she was almost eighty, Miss Mason had told Netta, 'besides dear, the work that has been done has been done by pamphlets – not books.'[30] The Revd Hon. Dr Edward Lyttelton DD DCL (1855–1942), former headmaster of Eton from 1905 to 1916, educational writer and PNEU vice president for twenty years, was the dean of Whitelands Training College at this time (1920–1929). The trustees asked him to write the introduction for *An Essay*. He said that the book had 'a grip on fundamental principles', but that it was 'not one you could read fast'. To address the repetitions, he recommended cutting it to 300 pages. Mrs Franklin agreed, hoping Mrs Clement Parsons' revisions would be accepted; seemingly, few were undertaken. Letters flew back and forth. Offered £100 by the trustees in 1923, Macmillan insisted on their shouldering the whole risk because 'such books just now are most difficult to sell'. Although Lyttelton was 'paid . . . for his name' and his 'fathering of the work', Mrs Franklin and Miss Kitching joined forces in condemning his 6,000-word critical introduction which confirmed Charlotte's dependence on earlier educational thinkers. Mrs Franklin took particular exception to his 'stilted and ugly' reference to 'this late-lamented early Victorian'. As his introduction threatened all hope of presenting Miss Mason's method as pioneering and original, the two disciples persuaded the wryly amused Dr Lyttelton to withdraw it. They approached Kegan Paul and Co., who asked for £100, regretting the dismissal of Lyttelton's introduction because 'it will assist in selling the book'. They hoped for an American publisher. Lyttelton courteously substituted a one-page foreword commending Miss Mason's 'rare combination of intuitive insight and practical sagacity' and her recognition that education should be led by 'the child's desire for knowledge', adding that the 'experiments' in the elementary schools should be continued. The trustees met the publication costs.[31] To compensate for *An Essay*'s long-windedness, a usefully succinct booklet explained the PUS programmes for state and PNEU schools as well as home schoolrooms, affirming that they equipped older pupils to pass public examinations.[32]

Alert to Miss Mason's limitations, Mrs Franklin focused her campaign on her best writings. Although the trustees funded the re-issue of *Some Studies in the Formation of Character* in 1923, Netta told Kit Kit in 1935, 'It is not to the glory of Miss Mason that we should once again emphasise this volume . . . written at odd moments. She was never very proud of it and, with the exception of "He has a Temper" all of it should be buried – in my opinion – in oblivion.'[33]

An Essay came out in 1925. The *London Mercury* saw it as 'a breeze from the hills' through the elementary sector; the *Southampton Times* felt it answered the religious problem in schools. Amongst the positive reviews celebrating the Liberal Education For All Movement, criticisms surfaced. The *Manchester Guardian* was not convinced 'that book-learning is suitable for all types of character, all grades of mentality or in all social circumstances'.[34] In commending the universality of her educational method, the Anglo-Catholic *Church Times* reviewer deplored

> the atmosphere of incurable 'faddiness' which Miss Mason introduces into the whole discussion. Through her failure to recognize that children are born young . . . she postulates an impossible independence for the pupil and only makes any education possible at all by smuggling back an influence of the teacher, camouflaged by such phrases as the atmosphere of environment, the discipline of habit and the presentation of living ideas, which on her own principles ought not to be allowed. Because children *are* children, they have to be taught.

The pejorative label of 'faddist' had finally caught up with her; this broadside from the *Church Times* would have hurt. The reviewer found Miss Mason's ideas 'protestant and vague'; they bypassed Church teaching in asserting that 'the Bible is the oracle of God and our sole original source of knowledge concerning the nature of Almighty God'. Asserting that she was a lifelong Anglican churchwoman, Miss Mason's followers sent forceful rebuttals to the *Church Times* challenging the reviewer's accusation that she had ignored the established Church's doctrinal teaching through an independent Bible-based ministry.[35]

In conservatively creating the all-embracing Scale How atmosphere, Miss Mason had not anticipated the radical opening up of the rigid Victorian social class structures or the development of wide-ranging specialist expertise and diversity in teaching practice. The terms of her will stalled modernisation at Ambleside. Mrs Franklin's precipitate campaign to bring every PNEU operation under her metropolitan control antagonised the prickly Miss Parish and upset the gentle Miss Kitching.[36] Notwithstanding deep affection for her guru, Netta had waited twenty-nine years to take the lead. Like Miss Mason she had a paramount need to be first. There was no gainsaying the strength of the resistance to interference at Ambleside, infused with Miss Mason's unseen presence. Mr Household consoled Miss Parish by saying, 'Mrs Franklin is in a quite unnecessary hurry and she must be content to go slowly.'[37] Miss Parish, loyally adhering to the status quo, even lying on a sofa and dressing like her gracious predecessor, was 'determined to maintain the letter of the law and anxious to preserve the spirit of the house . . . to keep everything as it had been in the days of the great founder'.[38]

The unresolved question of the students' qualifications depended upon adapting Miss Mason's wide non-specialist curriculum to the Board of Education's requirements. Following the Board's disastrously critical report on the House of Education in 1927, Mr Household, as enthusiastic about pneumatic education as ever, communicated the unthinkable to Mrs Franklin:

> If we are to train young men and women in Miss Mason's methods for service in the schools of the country at large, it will have to be elsewhere than at the House of Education.[39]

Mrs Franklin had upheld Miss Mason's originality and 'magical influence' to maintain unity of purpose and safeguard her position in the face of the Union's uncertain future. In 1927 she sent Mr Household copies of her intimate correspondence with Miss Mason, which she subsequently presented to Mrs Walton in 1958 for PNEU records. Household immediately grasped her contribution

> in the long and difficult task of bringing the world to a knowledge of Miss Mason's teaching & principles . . . always keeping the movement before the world in the best and wisest way. You have been the great organiser throughout. You knew Miss Mason's mind as no other living being knew it . . . and had an influence with her (as well as with the world) without which her own generation would never have been won to the knowledge of her.[40]

Rewarded with a CBE for her services to education in 1950, the year Ernest died, Mrs Franklin's crowning achievement lay in developing the network of highly-regarded private PNEU schools. Sometimes weak on mathematics, PUS self-education in the humanities was well-suited to non-competitive children seeking an English education in small school classes or far-flung home schoolrooms. They delighted in Shakespeare plays, nature walks and picture study. Mrs Franklin founded Overstone PNEU Girls' School (1929–1979) in Charlotte Mason's memory and later Desmoor Boys' Preparatory School (1947–1968). She loyally declared that Charlotte Mason's main contribution to the educational thought of the nineteenth century was 'respect for the individual child. In her relations with children – there was a really beautiful reverence and courtesy. She had a great sense of humour, too, and that helped her to understand children.'[41]

Mrs Franklin tirelessly developed the PNEU schools.

For thirty years, Miss Kitching had unobtrusively served Miss Mason as attentive companion and devoted scribe. As director of the PUS and editor of *Parents' Review*, she was admired for her breadth of vision and humour as the most knowledgeable interpreter of Miss Mason's thought. Symbolically placed at the gateway to Scale How, Kit Kit remained at Low Nook, a loyal churchwoman, immersed in Miss Mason's ideas. Her leader's self-confidence had been truly remarkable.

> She never hesitated as to the value of this philosophy. It had come to her, much of it at 25, or even earlier, and she often said how strange it was that she *could* only repeat what she had said so often.[42]

Loved by generations of students and their families, Miss Kitching never betrayed her leader's trust, despite struggling with buried biographical discoveries.

PUS liberal education in state schools declined after Mr Household's retirement in 1936. Outside the private PNEU sector, the uniform programmes sent out from Ambleside conflicted with professional teachers' preference for more varied, modern methods. Visiting Gloucestershire schools, Robin Tanner HMI noticed that while the children's practised capacity to narrate in sing-song voices was remarkably accurate, they had no chatter about their ordinary doings. He concluded, 'narration seemed singularly un-English and feudal to me; it stifled initiative, it bored and it drained the colour out of life.' L.C. Taylor, who appreciatively related

Charlotte Mason's person-centred, literary self-education to modern resource-based learning, heard that during the 1940s a young teacher in a Gloucestershire school had found

> a cupboard crammed with books – strange books he thought for children. There in bewitched piles slept copies of North's translation of Plutarch's *Lives*, the *Life of the Ichneumon Fly*, *Twelfth Night* and the rest of those 'living books' of the PNEU, preserved by the reverence of schoolmasters for the printed word.[43]

More recently, others have delighted in Charlotte Mason's principles, asserting their lasting educational and moral value. Susan Schaeffer Macaulay, the evangelical daughter of Presbyterian Christian parents, writers and thinkers, distilled her personal understanding of Charlotte Mason's philosophy into her first book, *For the Children's Sake: Foundations of Education for Home and School* (1984). Mrs Macaulay found that her own ideas and practical experience of raising and educating a family, in the light of Charlotte Mason's writings, could be applied, as in the past, to any educational setting, especially the family home. She opened a school in England and wrote other books. Her widely-read treatise guided the strong home-schooling movement in the United States.[44] Rooted in biblical Christianity and modern interpretations of Charlotte Mason's writings, a movement called Child Life ('A Christian organisation devoted to assisting all those who serve children') was backed by Susan and her husband, Ranald Macaulay. A new edition of the Home Education Series was brought out in America in 1989 by Karen Andreola, with the aim of making Charlotte Mason's teaching accessible to all. *Ambleside Online* for homeschooling 'moms' offers transcriptions of *Parents' Review* which, with other modernised texts, have edged Miss Mason's writings into a timeless zone.

The charity Child Light USA, founded by transatlantic academic educationists in 2005, was renamed the Charlotte Mason Institute in 2013. The aim is 'to support a world-wide community of learners in an authentic practice of Charlotte Mason's paradigm of education', to be raised to a greater humanity, 'while recovering the organizational structure which spread her teaching across many countries'. Annual Charlotte Mason conferences and meetings are held across the USA and Canada. There is Heritage School in Cambridge, UK. In Australia, alongside the home schoolrooms, philanthropic Mason educators have been running a PNEU school for disengaged, troubled young people, reflecting Mrs Steinthal's emphasis on the educational needs of poorer children.

Since 2000, theses, dissertations and blogs have been explicating Charlotte's 'living' educational ideas in varying ways. In updating Mason principles for present times, many new followers select their own modern 'living books'.[45] Hopefully with fewer dated Victorian strictures, her liberal

Miss Kitching upheld Miss Mason's philosophy.

methods are being creatively adapted to upbringing and the teaching of all subjects in privately and publicly funded Mason schools and home schoolrooms. Gladys Shaefer encapsulated what Charlotte Mason's educational ideas had meant to her:

> Charlotte Mason has become a sweet presence in my life. Her wisdom has nourished me and has influenced how I have raised my children and taught my students. Her desire to follow God and learn from him is so evident from her writings.[46]

Overjoyed by this fast growing discipleship, the splendidly serene Miss Mason would have said, 'You dear people are too sweet, and just make me cry,' happy to be influencing education from 'the afterwards'. While for many the Mason method was not the complete, unifying philosophy of education she had dreamed of in 1904, to her transatlantic followers today it is an inspiration. Their wealth of respectful reflections and interpretations have influenced a vibrant twenty-first-century evangelical Christian educational movement, hopefully taking account of the vast growth in knowledge, mathematics, science and technological expertise of the past century.

Lifting Charlotte Mason's educational ideas *out* of the British imperialist, Victorian, class-dominated historical context that brought them to birth gives credence to the mistaken notion that Charlotte Mason's philosophy was both entirely original and progressive. The need to collude with her post-1894 denial of dependence upon the so-called 'new educational' thinkers from Locke to Rousseau and Pestalozzi for many of her creative ideas has surely passed. Aside from these key influences, she held that education should be firmly rooted in the 'great literature' of the past and the Bible, fearing the consequences of allowing docile children to acquire habits of unrestrained criticism. Significant new educational theorists have emerged during the twentieth and twenty-first centuries; relating their valued contributions to Charlotte Mason's inimitable philosophy is a task for others.

Charlotte Mason's genius lay in a certain magical quality of personality which lit up her audiences. Her clarity of exposition and brilliant talk were belied by her more diffuse old-fashioned writings, borne of the Victorian age. Beneath her outward mantle of calm humility was an imaginative, rigorously disciplined, controlling woman who, step by step, anxiously triumphed over innumerable obstacles to fulfil her educational mission. Day by day, she lay on her sofa after the manner of her gently-born heroine, Florence Nightingale, burning like a clear flame with the missionary zeal of her Quaker ancestors. Rousseau's *Émile*'s early exploration of the natural world and Pestalozzian respect for children's personalities taught her that education depended upon engaging their imagination, curiosity and interest in 'things'. Wordsworth, Arnold and Ruskin inspired her to pass on her love of literature, pictures, poetry and drama to avert the failure of many children to enjoy their studies or conquer the basics of reading and writing. Notwithstanding its seventeenth-century puritan moral compass, Locke's habit training advice speaks to present day anxieties about discipline and citizenship.

For Charlotte, the consequence of truth was too great. Success depended upon secrecy. To win recognition within superior Victorian upper-class society, our unprotected spinster had to face down her Irish background, her birth before wedlock, her parents' delayed marriage, her father's dissent and her mother's Roman Catholicism, still unacceptable due to the resurgence of Irish republicanism. Conferring standing on his unmarried daughter, Charlotte's gentleman father could be identified as a Liverpool merchant, but not as an Irish Friend or dissenter. During the 1840s her fortitude may have grown from *feeling* she was the special only child of only children, living with isolated parents in Dublin or on the Isle of Man. Loved by her wayward mother as a precious only daughter, she rejected her hidden Roman Catholic influence as she embraced Anglicanism.

The investment of the last hopes of her disillusioned, ageing father in the education of his bright thirteenth child may have powered the shy pupil-teacher's aspirations. His interest may have aroused jealousy in his older daughters, notably Hannah, contributing to Charlotte's unexplained breach with her father's family. Early conflicts and the clash of religious differences probably engendered a lifelong terror of controversy and confrontation. Learning how to protect herself through the devoted service of generous friends, notably Lizzie Groveham, Selina Fleming, Fanny Williams, Lienie Steinthal, Elsie Kitching and Netta Franklin, enabled her to fulfil her educational mission.

Did Joshua Mason tell Charlotte stories about their dynamic Quaker ancestors, committed to education and ministry, or that four of her half-sisters were teachers? Charlotte's Westmorland Irish Quaker heritage assuredly permeated her passion for education and ministry. We know that she read the Bible and Bunyan assiduously, seeking inner light and the Holy Spirit's guidance as she undoubtedly puzzled over her parents' religious conflicts. Mr Dunning had demanded holiness. Charlotte's lifelong devotion to the evangelical wing of the Anglican Church, begun in Birkenhead, seems threaded through with the Friends' recognition of 'that of God in everyone', exemplified by her ability to bring out the best in others. While insisting on her students' Anglican practice, Charlotte was tolerant of other faiths, notably Netta's Jewish beliefs. Her preserved piece of unbleached linen and delight in Netta's simple Holland frock tentatively hint at stories told by her father about her flax-growing grandfather, the Moyallon meetings and his childhood by the River Bann. Both Lisburn Friends' School, launched by Charlotte's great-grandfather, and Newtown School, which educated her five half-brothers, with her father's support, were flourishing in her time, as they are today.

While teaching in the tumultuous Davison schoolroom under the restrictive Code, the proverbial cry, 'Oh that children were born without parents' took hold. As a visiting 'Tante', Miss Brandreth's home education opened Charlotte's eyes to the delights of teaching intelligent children in a gracious, well-ordered home, supported by nursemaids and servants. As the 'onlooker who sees most of the game', Charlotte observed the relative inadequacies of their returning Anglo-Indian parents. In discovering her academic potential at Chichester, Carpenter offered the touchstone. If parents conscientiously trained their children in good habits, discipline problems would vanish. Habit training cut a shining path through the mists of 'absolute vagueness'. She absorbed Miss Trevor's method of running a gentlewomen's college, remotely, yet lovingly, caring for her family of students as surrogate daughters and missionaries.

Studying the manners and morals of upper-class family life in the Victorian novels of Scott, Yonge, Trollope and Thackeray, Charlotte steadily educated herself into a great lady of culture. Her immaculate image was formed by leaping over the Victorian social class barriers excluding state-funded professional teachers from the best circles. Mr Read had demanded perfection. Self-education was the key. Unsuited to be Miss Brandreth's long-term docile companion, the protected years at Lizzie Groveham's private school enhanced her status, launching her as published writer and educational innovator. As always, illness relieved nervous stress and anxiety, bringing the comforts of loving care. Like Rousseau, who despatched his five illegitimate children to the orphanage, to fulfil her aim of inspiring parents and teachers, Charlotte needed freedom from distraction.

To exert due influence, Charlotte Mason *had* to join the upper classes. In knowledgeably addressing the contemporary educational deficiencies besetting disempowered Victorian higher-class mothers and daughters, she was accepted as a person of consequence. When the PNEU and imaginative Lakeland educational projects were established, with Lienie Steinthal's unstinting support, she became the Madame de Genlis of Scale How, with obedient bairns at her beck and call. After the realist Mrs Franklin had tested her idealist theories by sending Madge to Scale How for habit training in 1897, creative malady released Charlotte from uncontrolled meetings with children or challenging grown-ups. She coolly discarded those whom she no longer needed; blessed seclusion at Scale How kept anxiety and conflict at bay. Always appearing at her best, her gracious manner imperceptibly strengthened her benign, yet impelling influence. Even Lady Isabel gave way.

Little has been said about Sapphic tendencies. Although Charlotte intensely loved her close women friends, notably Netta, delighting in her pretty maid or settling with Ellen Parish in a nest of heather by Highfield House, the ideals in *Ourselves* demanded rigorous self-control.[47] With steely determination, drawing spiritual strength from Gospel meditation, she surely rarely fell below her own high standards. Her tightly organised lifestyle of reading and being read to in spare moments protected her from straying thoughts.

The PNEU movement took off, guided by Charlotte's intense, challenging friendship with Netta, a dynamic organiser, who developed her thinking and ratified her standing as a leading liberal educationist. Moving away from proclaiming idealised methods of home training, Charlotte Mason's acceptance as the Union's original educational philosopher in 1904 confirmed her self-belief and the authenticity of her teaching mission. Only Netta could question her ideas; Kit Kit had to applaud and agree.

Mrs Steinthal's wartime liberal educational movement was timely and enjoyed by many state school children. The remarkable quality of the selected children's exam papers suggested that by reading great literature, line by line, every child could join the educated classes, if they so wished. The emphasis on the humanities had transformed the original notion of educating for parenthood into a school-based unifying educational philosophy for all classes. Although the pneumatic method bypassed their role, dedicated teachers made it work for years. The movement survived the lean post-war period of 1914 to 1918, giving ground to new educational guidance for state schools as the century progressed. Meanwhile, on Mrs Franklin's Hebraistic watch, private PNEU schools returned Miss Mason's literary liberal education as a gift to children of the middle and upper-classes.

Modelled on Victorian upper-class evenings at home, Charlotte Mason's Hellenistic principles of education for life through books *and* things gave her former bairns' wide interests and adventurous spirits. She understood the delight of all young children in exploration and discovery, within and outside the home. Adapted to schools with varying degrees of success and with mixed reactions from the teaching profession, she sensibly centred the child at the heart of the learning process. Her non-competitive, humane literary educational ideas have contemporary relevance, if appropriately developed in response to a changing, increasingly complex, technologically-oriented, post-imperial world. While excessive cramming and dull textbooks still deaden the interest essential to satisfactory learning, older children also need to develop untrammelled critical reasoning powers to specialise and undertake advanced research. Children require a humane moral compass to be able to respond with understanding to the wide varieties of religious practice and beliefs in our multi-cultural world. Diverse post-Darwinian scientific discoveries about the nature of the universe and human existence, which Charlotte Mason could not have apprehended, also challenge traditional beliefs.

With her *Mona Lisa* smile and leprechaun playfulness, 'she always knew'. Who could gainsay her? Having inspired leaders of thought and aristocrats, Miss Mason had no desire to challenge conservative Victorian social class structures or the patriarchal status quo. Framed by Arnold's 'sweetness and light', she and her disciples believed the purified Ambleside atmosphere would last as she took her secrets to the grave. Residual shame had been cleansed by giving back 'the best that has been known and thought in the world' to the descendants of her former pupils whose circumscribed education had been cast in narrower lines.

Farewell to Scale How.

Appendix: *A Short Synopsis of Educational Theory* (1904)

updated for *An Essay Towards a Philosophy of Education* (1925)

'The Consequence of truth is great;
therefore the judgment of it must not be negligent.'

1. Children are born persons.
2. They are not born either good or bad but with possibilities for good and for evil.
3. The principles of authority on the one hand, and of obedience on the other are natural, necessary and fundamental; but
4. These principles are limited by respect due to the personality of children, which must not be encroached upon, whether by direct use of fear or love, suggestion or influence, or by undue play on any one natural desire.
5. Therefore, we are limited to three educational instruments — the atmosphere of environment, the discipline of habit, and the presentation of living ideas. The P.N.E.U. Motto is: 'Education is an atmosphere, a discipline and a life.'
6. When we say that 'education is an atmosphere,' we do not mean that a child should be isolated in what may be called a 'child-environment' especially adapted and prepared, but that we should take into account the educational value of his natural home atmosphere, both as regards persons and things, and should let him live freely among his proper conditions. It stultifies a child to bring down his world to the 'child's' level.
7. By 'education is a discipline,' we mean the discipline of habits, formed definitely and thoughtfully, whether habits of mind or body. Physiologists tell us of the adaptation of brain structures to habitual lines of thought, i.e. to our habits.
8. In saying that 'education is a life,' the need of intellectual and moral as well as of physical sustenance is implied. The mind feeds on ideas, and therefore children should have a generous curriculum.
9. We hold that the child's mind is no mere sac to hold ideas; but is rather, if the figure may be allowed, a spiritual organism, with an appetite for all knowledge. This is its proper diet, with which it is prepared to deal; and which it can digest and assimilate as the body does foodstuffs.

10. Such a doctrine as e.g. the Herbartian, that the mind is a receptacle, lays the stress of Education (the preparation of knowledge in enticing morsels duly ordered) upon the teacher. Children taught on this principle are in danger of receiving much teaching with little knowledge; and the teacher's axiom is 'what a child learns matters less than how he learns it.'
11. But we, believing that the normal child has powers of mind which fit him to deal with all knowledge proper to him, give him a full and generous curriculum; taking care only that all knowledge offered to him is vital, that is, the facts are not presented without their informing ideas. Out of this conception comes our principle that, —
12. 'Education is the Science of Relations'; that is, that a child has natural relations with a vast number of things and thoughts: so we train him upon physical exercises, nature lore, handicrafts, science and art, and upon many living books, for we know that our business is not to teach him all about anything but to help him make valid as many as may be of —

'Those first-born affinities
That fit our new existence to existing things.'

Paragraphs 13-15 were added by 1920:

13. In devising as SYLLABUS for a normal child, of whatever social class, three points must be considered:-

    (a) He requires much knowledge, for the mind needs sufficient food as much as does the body.
    (b) The knowledge should be various for sameness in mental diet does not create appetite (*i.e.* curiosity).
    (c) Knowledge should be communicated in well-chosen language, because his attention responds naturally to what is conveyed in literary form,

14. As knowledge is not assimilated until it is reproduced, children should 'tell back' after a single reading or hearing: or should write on some part of what they have read.
15. A *single reading* is insisted on, because children have naturally a great power of attention; but this force is dissipated by the re-reading of passages, and also by questioning, summarising and the like.

    Acting upon these and some other points in the behaviour of mind, we find that *the educability of children is enormously greater than has been supposed,* and is but little dependent upon such circumstances as heredity and environment.

    Nor is the accuracy of this statement limited to clever children or to children of the educated classes: thousands of children in Elementary Schools respond freely to this method, which is based on the *behaviour of mind.*
16. There are two guides to moral and intellectual self-management to offer to children, which we may call 'the way of the will' and the 'way of the reason.'

17. *The Way of the Will:* Children should be taught, (a) to distinguish between 'I want' and 'I will.' (b) That the way to will effectively is to turn our thoughts from that which we desire but do not will. (c) That the best way to turn our thoughts is to think of or do some quite different thing, entertaining or interesting. (d) That after a little rest in this way, the will returns to its work with new vigour. (This adjunct of the will is familiar to us as *diversion,* whose office it is to ease us from will effort that we may 'will' again with added power. The use of *suggestion* as an aid to the will is to be deprecated, as tending to stultify and stereotype character. It would seem that spontaneity is a condition of development, and that human nature needs the discipline of failure as well as of success).
18. *The way of reason:* We teach children too not to 'lean (too confidently) to their own understanding'; because the function of reason is to give logical demonstration (a) of mathematical truth, (b) of an initial idea, accepted by the will. In the former case, reason is, practically, an infallible guide, but in the latter, it is not always a safe one; for, whether the idea be right or wrong reason will confirm it by irrefragable proofs.
19. Therefore, children should be taught, as they become mature enough to understand such teaching, that the chief responsibility which rests on them as *persons* is the acceptance or rejection of ideas. To help them in this choice we give them principles of conduct, and a wide range of knowledge fitted to them. These principles should save children from some of the loose thinking and heedless action which cause most of us to live at a lower level than we need.
20. We allow no separation to grow up between the intellectual and 'spiritual' life of children, but teach them that the Divine Spirit has constant access to their spirits, and is their continual Helper in all the interests, duties and joys of life.

— C.M. Mason, *An Essay Towards a Philosophy of Education* (London: J.M. Dent and Sons Ltd, 3rd edn 1954), xxix-xxxi.

Notes

1. Introduction: Who Was Charlotte Mason? (pp. 1-15)

1. Sir Michael Sadler, 'Official Tributes', Part II, in PNEU (ed.), *In Memoriam: Charlotte M. Mason* (London: PNEU, 1923), 17. Sadler was a classical scholar and academic educational adviser to the Board of Education in 1901; Stephanie, Comtesse de Genlis (1746–1830), was a French writer, ingenious educational theorist and vivacious wit.
2. Morant drafted the Education Act (1902); General Sir Robert Baden-Powell, 'A Field Marshall's Governess', *In Memoriam*, 22; Rose Kerr, *The Story of the Girl Guides* (London: The Girl Guides' Association, 1932); Essex Cholmondeley, *The Story of Charlotte Mason 1842–1923* (London: J.M. Dent and Sons Ltd, 1960), 100.
3. Stephen Gill, *William Wordsworth: A Life* (Oxford University Press, 1990), 117, 493; J.M. Carnie, *At Lakeland's Heart: Eighteen Journeys into the Past of Ambleside and its Locality from Rydal to Clappersgate until AD 1900* (Windermere: Parrock Press, 2002), 39 and 225-226.
4. Charlotte Mason, *A Short Synopsis of Educational Theory* (see Appendix).
5. John Ruskin, 'Of Queen's Gardens', *Sesame and Lilies* (London: George Allen, 1865; 1906), 136.
6. Coventry Patmore (1823–1896) composed 'The Angel in the House' in 1854 about his wife, Emily, who was painted by Millais; Ian Anstruther, *Coventry Patmore's Angel* (London: Haggerston Press, 1992); J.H. Newman, *The Idea of a University* (London: Longmans Green, 1912).
7. Mid-century debate on women's education in Barbara Caine, *English Feminism 1780–1980* (Oxford University Press, 1997); Sir James Crichton-Browne MD LLD FRS (1840–1938), 'An Oration on Sex Education', *Parents' Review*, vol. 3, 1892–93; ditty attributed among others to J.C. Tarver, Clifton College, c. 1880s, said to have been composed at a garden party attended by the two headmistresses; Josephine Kamm, *How Different From Us: A Biography of Miss Buss and Miss Beale* (London: Bodley Head, 1959).
8. C.M. Mason, Lecture VII: 'The Training of Young Maidens at Home', *Home Education: A Course of Lectures to Ladies* (London: Kegan Paul, Trench, Trübner and Co. Ltd, 1886; 3rd edn 1899), 269-303; Kathryn Hughes, *The Victorian Governess* (London, New York: Hambledon Continuum, 2001), 33-53.
9. Dr C.H. Hough, 'Charlotte Mason', *Parents' Review*, vol. 34, no. 3, March 1923.

10. Ex-Students of the College, 'Letters to Scale How' 3, *Parents' Review*, vol. 34, no. 8, 1923.
11. Frances Bailey (CMT 1924), conversation with author, 5 December 1981. For convenience, CMT with the year of qualification refers to all House-of-Education-trained students, although the term CMT was not used in Charlotte Mason's time.
12. G.M. Young, *Portrait of an Age: Victorian England* (Oxford University Press, 1936; 2nd edn 1964), title page.
13. Sister Sheila Mary (CMT 1922), Society of the Sacred Cross, conversation with author, Ty Mawr Convent, 17 April 1982; Dorothy Cooke (CMT 1913), conversation with author, 11 October 1985.
14. Elsie Kitching, 'The Beginning of Things', *In Memoriam*, 118.
15. Ibidem, 119; John 5:31 (Authorised Version).
16. Old Students of the House of Education, 'Miss F.C.A. Williams ("V.P."): Some Memories', *Parents' Review*, vol. 36, nos 7 and 11, 1925.
17. F.C.A. Williams, 'Some Reminiscences', *In Memoriam*, 56.
18. House of Education Visitors' Book (1898–1966), CM22cmc145.
19. Elizabeth Groveham, letter to Elsie Kitching, 10 June 1923, PNEU2Bpneu31.
20. Kitching, notes from meeting Groveham at Woodbridge, 1923, PNEU2Bpneu31.
21. Groveham, letters to Kitching, 28 May 1923, 9 July 1927 and 28 May 1923.
22. Groveham to Kitching, two postcards sent 23 June 1924 and 9 July 1927, PNEU2Bpneu31.
23. Groveham, last letter to Charlotte Mason, 29 December 1922, PNEU2Bpneu31.
24. Old Students of the House of Education, 'Miss F.C.A Williams'.
25. 'Charlotte Mason: a Pioneer of Sane Education', *The Times*, 17 January 1923, reprinted in *In Memoriam*, 24-26; death certificate for Joshua Mason, 1859, Liverpool Register Office.
26. Mary Yates in PNEU (ed.), *Elsie Kitching 1870–1955: Recollections* [pamphlet] (London: PNEU, 1956), CM48cmc363, 18.
27. William Shakespeare, *Henry IV*, Part 2.
28. Elsie Kitching's last will, 31 July 1953, CM11cmc72.
29. Mrs H.C.M. (Geraldine) Walton, 'A Tribute to Essex Cholmondeley', *Journal of the World-wide Education Service of the PNEU*, vol. 20, no. 3, October 1985, 34.
30. Bishop Heber wrote 'Holy, Holy, Holy' and 'From Greenland's Icy Mountain' (1819), condemned by Gandhi for its racism.
31. Census, Westminster, 1911; Walton, 'A Tribute to Essex Cholmondeley', 34-36; student enrolment registers 1891–1948, CM10cmc62.
32. Essex Cholmondeley, 'Elsie Kitching', *Parents' Review*, vol. 67, no. 2, February 1955.
33. Mary Cholmondeley, *Red Pottage* (London: Virago Press, 1899; 1985); Cholmondeley family tree, courtesy of Jeremy Hills: Mary, the third of ten children, was Essex's aunt.
34. Walton, 'A Tribute to Essex Cholmondeley', 34-39.
35. Monk Gibbon, *Netta* (London: Routledge and Kegan Paul, 1960).
36. Eve E. Anderson, Chairman of the Charlotte Mason College Association, 'Preface' in Essex Cholmondeley, *The Story of Charlotte Mason 1842–1923* (reprinted, Petersfield: Child Light Ltd, 2000), i.
37. Caroline Kidson, British Museum Central Archives, telephone conversation with author, 25 October 1982.
38. M.A. Coombs, *Some Obstacles to the Establishment of a Universal Method of Education for Parenthood by the PNEU* (unpublished MPhil thesis, Aston University, 1984).
39. Geraldine Walton, letters to author, 14 July 1981–3 June 1983, author's copies for Armitt.
40. Essex Cholmondeley, conversation with author, Nynehead Court, 5 April 1982.

41. Cholmondeley, *Story*, 1-5; a careful search of *Parents' Review* vols 1-36 revealed no 'Memories'; no manuscript entitled 'Recollections' was found in the PNEU archives.
42. Mrs Esther Card (CMT 1943), conversation with author, 25 November 1982, in which she said Charlotte Mason told her mother, a favoured student, that her white dresses were made from her mother's trousseau petticoats; Jack Cassin-Scott, *Costume and Fashion in Colour (1760–1920)* (Dorset: Blandford Press, 1971), 44, 66: a 'bertha' (1842) was a collar of lace frills surrounding the décolletage; 'pelisses', fashionable in the 1830s and 1840s, were over-garments trimmed to match the dress beneath.
43. Maria Edgeworth, *The Good Governess and Other Stories* (London, Glasgow: Blackie and Son Ltd, n.d.), 223; Liverpool and Birkenhead directories for 1850–1860 yielded *no* entry for Joshua Mason as drysalter; see Chapter 4 for his links with Liverpool freemen.
44. Robert Drake, a PNEU pupil's father, sent Worthing (Broadwater district) censuses for 1861 and 1871.
45. Typed copy of letter attributed to Elizabeth Groveham, 7 May 1924, PNEU2Bpneu31.
46. Blanche Clough, *Memoir of Anne J. Clough by her Niece* (London: Edward Arnold, 1897), 20; Groveham, letter to Kitching, 18 May 1924, PNEU2Bpneu31; Cholmondeley, *Story*, 3.
47. W.G. Collingwood, *The Life of John Ruskin* (London: Methuen and Co., 1900); John Ruskin, *The Ethics of the Dust* (London: J.M. Dent and Co., 1865); Joan Burstyn, *Victorian Education and the Ideal of Womanhood* (London: Croom Helm, 1980).
48. W. Lyon Blease, *The Emancipation of English Women* (London: Constable, 1910), 55-56, 96-107; Duncan Crow, *The Victorian Woman* (London: Allen and Unwin, 1971) 45-49; Newman, *The Idea of a University*.
49. Essex Cholmondeley, letters to author, 8 July 1982 and 14 May 1983, author's copies; Walton, 'A Tribute to Essex Cholmondeley', 34; E.F.B. in *The Story*, iii-iv; Kitching, 'The Beginning of Things', *In Memoriam*, 118.
50. Cholmondeley, *Story*, 179.
51. M.A. Coombs, 'A Journey of Discovery: Charlotte Mason's Secret Past and Hidden Quaker Heritage' in J. Carroll Smith (ed.), *Essays on the Life and Work of Charlotte Mason*, published by the Charlotte Mason Institute (Pennsylvania: Riverbend Press, 2014); Ex-Students of the College, 'Letters to Scale How', 3.

2. A Westmorland Quaker Heritage (pp. 16-27)

1. Alfred Neave Brayshaw, *The Quakers: Their Story and Message* (York: William Sessions Book Trust, Ebor Press, 1982), 33-55; Kendal Record Office Friends' Record Book 1216 gave 1720 as John's birth year (with permission from Cumbria Archives Central, Kendal (CACK)). However, his restored gravestone, behind the former meeting house on Railway Street, Lisburn, gives his date of birth as 1721.
2. James Gough, *Memoirs of the Life, Religious Experience and Labours in the Gospel of James Gough, late of the City of Dublin, deceased compiled from his original memoirs by his brother John Gough*, ed. John Gough (Dublin: Robert Jackson, 1781).
3. Brayshaw, *Quakers*, 42-43; nowadays the phrase is 'that of God in *everyone*'.
4. Ibidem, 83; Christopher Moriarty, 'All bloody principles and practices we do utterly deny', *Teaching Religious Education*, Issue 3, December 2008.
5. A.G. Chapman, *History of the Religious Society of Friends in Lurgan* (Lurgan Friends' Meeting, 1997), 1, 5-9, 30-33; A.G. Chapman, *Quakers in Lisburn: Four Centuries of Work and Witness* (Ulster Friends' Home Mission, 2009); George R. Chapman, 'Quaker Meeting Places in the Lurgan Area in the 17th Century', *Review-Journal of*

the Craigavon Historical Society (c. 1963), vol. 2, no. 1, n.d.; Ross Chapman, *Notes from Lisburn Monthly Meeting for Joan Johnson*, 29 October 2009, forwarded to author.

6. Brayshaw, *Quakers*, 44-82, 151-165; Rex Ambler, *What Happened to the Light Within?* [talk], Quaker History Group, London, 25 February 2014, 1-6, copies held at Friends' House Library, London.
7. Richard S. Harrison, *A Biographical Dictionary of Irish Quakers* (Dublin: Four Courts Press, 1997; 2nd edn 2008), 1-14; Brayshaw, *Quakers*, 140, 252, 166-174; the Quaker Act of 1662, which was repealed in 1812, suppressed Friends' meetings and made refusals to take the Oath of Allegiance illegal; Harrison, *Irish Quakers*, 19.
8. Brayshaw, *Quakers*, 210; A.G. Chapman, *Friends in Lurgan*, 22.
9. Neville H. Newhouse, *A History of Friends' School, Lisburn* (Lisburn Friends' School, 1974).
10. Brayshaw, *Quakers*, 167-174.
11. Ibidem, 32, 71-82.
12. John Gough's 1711 marriage to Mary Mansergh was among the earliest recorded by Westmorland Friends, in the Quaker Digest of Marriages (1643–1836), Westmorland Book 1216, CACK, www.cumbria.gov.uk/archives.
13. Harrison, *Irish Quakers*, 19; notes by David Butler, Kendal Meeting, n.d., CACK.
14. Birth records, ref. JAC, 1781, CACK; Mary's birth on 24 August 1714 and Alice's on 14 June 1716 are their sole record found.
15. 'Two Centuries of the Friends' School: an active and conspicuous part to play in the educational History of Westmorland', *Kendal Mercury and Times*, 14 July 1899, reprint in File WDFC/F/1, CACK.
16. Isaac and Rachel Wilson, 'Letter' in Brayshaw, *Quakers*, 179, 217.
17. Gough, *Memoirs*, 5; George Fox, 'A Journal or Historical Account of the Life, Travels, Sufferings, Christian Experiences and Labour of Love in the works of the Ancient, Eminent and Faithful Servant of Jesus Christ, George Fox (1624–1691)' in Thomas Ellwood (ed.), *The Works of George Fox* (1831), chapter 3.
18. Gough, *Memoirs*, 1-2.
19. Mason, Lecture VI: 'The Will', *Home Education*, 182-193.
20. Gough, *Memoirs*, 5.
21. Ibidem; Mary Leadbeater, *Biographical Notes of Members of the Society of Friends who were Resident in Ireland* (London: Harvey and Darton, 1821/3), 267.
22. Gough, *Memoirs*, 5-6.
23. Leadbeater, *Biographical Notes*, 289.
24. James Gough, *A Practical Grammar of the English Language Tongue Containing the Most Material Rules and Observations for Understanding the English Language well and Writing it with Propriety* (1764), ed. John Gough (1771) (Dublin: Robert Jackson), Friends' Library, London (FLL).
25. Gough, *Memoirs*, 2.
26. Mason, Lecture I, *Home Education*.
27. Gough, *Memoirs*, 6.
28. Leadbeater, *Biographical Notes*, 289.
29. Gough, *Memoirs*, 17-20.
30. Bill Samuel, 'William Penn', 1 October 2000, http://www.quakerinfo.com; Brayshaw, *Quakers*, 74-75, 83-87. John Gough's Introduction to James's *Memoirs* shows familiarity with Penn's book *No Cross, No Crown* (1682).
31. Quoted in Newhouse, *Friends' School*, 6.
32. Gough, *Memoirs*, 20 ff; Bob Russell, *Mason, Birchall, Pim, Leckey and Morris Genealogical Records*, researched for author, deposited at the Armitt Trust and Friends' Historical Library, Dublin (FHLD).

33. Newhouse, *Friends' School,* 6; Augustus C. Bickley, 'John Gough' in *Dictionary of National Biography*, vol. 22, 1890.
34. Leadbeater, *Biographical Notes,* 172; Gough, *Memoirs*, 102.
35. Ibidem; Newhouse, *Friends' School*, 6.
36. Leadbeater, *Biographical Notes,* 172, 289.
37. Newhouse, *Friends' School,* 6-7; 'Preface' in John Gough, *Treatise of Arithmetic in Theory and Practice* (Dublin: Robert Jackson, 1767), aka 'The Gough', iv-v, FLL and FHLD; Harrison, 'John Gough', *Irish Quakers*, 18.
38. Taken from 'The Gough', pages not noted.
39. 'Preface' in Gough, *English Language*, vii.
40. Ibidem, iv-xi.
41. Ibidem, xi-xii.
42. Gough, *Memoirs*, 113.
43. Leadbeater, *Biographical Notes,* 279.
44. Newhouse, *Friends' School,* 8; Harrison, 'James Gough', *Irish Quakers,* 19.
45. Newhouse, *Friends' School,* 2; John Gough junior, *A Tour of Ireland 1813-14* (Dublin, 1817), which Newhouse reported was difficult to obtain in 1974; Harrison, 'James Gough', 2.
46. 'History of Lisburn', *Lisburn.com*, www.lisburn.com/history.html; A.G. Chapman, *Quakers in Lisburn,* 20, 26-7, 73, and letters to author, 26 February 2013 and 11 September 2013; Chapman, *Friends in Lurgan*; David M. Butler, *The Quaker Meeting Houses of Ireland* (Historical Committee of the Religious Society of Friends in Ireland, 2004).
47. Newhouse, *Friends' School*, 1-10.
48. Ibidem, 8.
49. Quoted in ibidem, 9.
50. John Gough, *Tracts on Tithes: Brief and Serious Reasons why the People Called Quakers do not Pay Tithes* (Dublin: Robert Jackson, 1786); John Gough, *An Epistle from the National Half-Year's Meeting held in Dublin 3 May 1778 to the Monthly and Quarterly Meeting of Friends in Ireland*, Dublin, FHLD.
51. Newhouse, *Friends' School,* 10-12; Lisburn Monthly Meeting minutes (LBMMM), 17 March 1785 and 25 July 1790, Lisburn Friends' Archives (LFA), Meeting House, Prospect Hill, Lisburn.
52. Gough, *Memoirs,* 161; on p. 9 of *Friends' School*, Newhouse cites W.C. Braithwaite's view that John Gough's *History* drew more upon William Sewel's *History of the Quakers* than upon original research; 'John Gough', *Dictionary of National Biography*, vol. 22.
53. Leadbeater, *Biographical Notes,* 290.
54. Newhouse, *Friends' School*, 15.
55. Ibidem, 12.

3. Charlotte Mason's Grandparents: Arthur Mason and Mary Gough, 1744–1795 (pp. 28-33)

1. Newhouse, *Friends' School,* 8
2. The FHLD database confirmed Luke's marriage to Eleanor Fayle of Killowen in 1747; Joshua's father was Arthur N. Mason of Levaghery; Russell, *Mason Genealogy.*
3. Newhouse, *Friends' School,* 8.
4. A.G. Chapman, email to author, 29 October 2009; A.G. Chapman, *Quakers in Lisburn*, 28-30; George R. Chapman, *Historical Sketch of Moyallon Meeting* (Lisburn: Moyallon Friends, n.d.); the late Hugh Richardson's 'Moyallon Notes' (typescript).

5. FHLD database; LBMMM, 9 February 1777, 23 November 1777 and 5 July 1778; LBMM Family Record Book, ref. LGM 5/2 7953; Ross Chapman, email to Joan Johnson, 29 October 2009 and 7 August 2010; Muriel Cameron, email to author, 10 December 2009, stated that she could find no burial record for Arthur Mason.
6. FHLD database; Samuel and Thomas Mason were probably not Joshua's younger brothers, as they did not attend his wedding; LGMM records, 115 (1805), 149 (1808) and 164 (1809) for S. and T. Mason's removals to Waterford; FHLD database.
7. Richard Jones, Hall's Mill Deed, 1761, © Dublin Registry of Deeds (253/285/16475); Hall's Mill by Laurencetown, on the south-east side of Knocknagore, Co. Down, belonged to the late Sir Frances Hall; his daughter Rebecca Hall transferred the leasehold in 1761; Marilyn Cohen, *Linen, Family Tullyish, County Down* (Dublin: Four Courts Press, 1997), 176.
8. FHLD database; Chapman, *Moyallon Meeting*; Butler, *Quaker Meeting Houses*, 181-184; Arthur Chapman, email to author, 29 October 2009; Richardson, 'Moyallon Notes'.
9. See Cholmondeley, *Story*, 2 for Charlotte's alleged memory of her father.
10. *The Flax Growers List* (Spinning Wheel List) (Ireland, 1796) from Bob Russell. Those cultivating one acre earned four spinning wheels; five acres earned them a loom.
11. Walter Harris, *The Ancient and Present State of the County of Down* (Dublin, 1744), 106, cited in W.H. Crawford, 'Drapers and Bleachers in the Early Ulster Linen Industry' in L.M. Cullen and P. Butel, *Négoce et industrie en France et en Irlande aux XVIIIe et XIXe siècles* (Paris, 1980); 'The Religious Society of Friends and the Manufacture of Linen', 1-3, Craigavon Research article, Lurgan Local History, date not noted; Kathleen Rankin, *The Linen Houses of the Bann Valley: The Story of Their Families* (Ulster Historical Society, 2007); Peter Collins, *The Making of Irish Linen: Historic Photographs of an Ulster Industry* (Belfast: Friar's Bush Press, 1994).
12. Arthur N. Mason's Friends' membership confirmed by removal notice he signed for Joseph Linton on 11 December 1793, Lurgan Monthly Meeting Minutes (LGMMM), ref. 1/3, 306. No record was found of Arthur's disownment.
13. Newhouse, *Friends' School*, 14-15.
14. Ibidem, 15; LBMM Removals Records and LGMMM, vol. 1/3, 306; FHLD database; BRGR.
15. LGMM, K3 records (1798) for Margaret Gough's death on 19 January 1814; FHLD database for LGMM death records; Ross Chapman's note from LGMM records.
16. Richard Lucas's Directory (1788), listed 'Richard Jacob, soap and candle-maker, King Street, Waterford'; FHLD database.

4. Joshua Mason's Forty Years in Waterford, 1795–1835 (pp. 34-44)

1. Joshua Mason's Removal Record, June 1795, LGMMM, 11, K3, 129; see his application for freeman status by Royal Charter of King Charles I, Waterford City Archives (WCA), http://www.waterfordcity.ie/departments/archives/; Brayshaw, *Quakers*, 128-129.
2. Richard Lucas's Directory (1778), south-east Ireland; Waterford Monthly Meeting minutes (WMMM); Ross Chapman, email to Joan Johnson, 29 October 2009; Greer, Lowry and Alexander papers, PRONI Belfast, D1044/815.
3. *The Flax Growers List* (1796) listed only *one* flax grower for Co. Waterford.
4. The City Corporation had immense power under the Royal Charter; Samuel Lewis, 'Waterford City', *Lewis's Topographical Dictionary* (London: S. Lewis, 1848); T.P. Power, 'Electoral Politics in Waterford City 1692–1832' in William Nolan and Thomas

P. Power (eds), *Waterford History and Society* (Dublin: Geographical Publications, 1992), 227, 231-235; Waterford's Irish names were Cuan-na-Groith and Glean-na-Gleodh; Eamonn McEneaney, 'A History of Waterford and Its Mayors from the 12th to 20th Century' in Nolan and Power (eds), *Waterford History*, pages not noted.

5. Joe Falvey, 'The Quakers and Waterford', *Munster Express Online*, 2008; Joan Johnson, conversation with author, 10 September 2009; Donal Moore (WCA), conversation with author, 10 September 2009.
6. Des Cowman, 'Trade and Society in Waterford City, 1800–1840' in Nolan and Power (eds), *Waterford History*, 427-492; Pigot and Co. Directory (1824).
7. Richard Lucas's Directory (1778).
8. Donal Moore explained tallow to author in 2012 by email; Cowman, 'Trade and Society' in Nolan and Power (eds), *Waterford History*, 427-492; Marjorie Dorfman, 'Candles in the Wind', *Home is Where the Dirt is*, 2006, www.housenotsobeautiful.com/Articles/candle_p.html.
9. Marietta and Arthur Ellis, booklet prepared for the soap factory, New England, USA, n.d.
10. Daire Keogh, 'Thomas Hussey, Bishop of Waterford and Lismore 1797–1803 and the Rebellion of 1798' in Nolan and Power (eds), *Waterford History*, chapter 16.
11. Maurice J. Wigham, *Newtown School, Waterford: A History (1798–1998)* (Waterford: Newtown School, 1998), 13.
12. Wigham, *Newtown School*, 6-9; Munster province consists of Cork City, Co. Cork, Co. Clare, Co. Kerry, Co. Limerick, Limerick City, Co. Tipperary, Co. Waterford and Waterford City.
13. Marriage records, Waterford Newtown Friends' Archives (WNFA); see Newhouse, *Friends' School*, 5 for information on marriage rules.
14. Waterford Friends' Burial Register, Newtown; WMM family records, WNFA.
15. 1834 map supplied by WCA, 21 March 2011; indented deed between Joshua Mason junior and Robert Adcock, 19 February 1835 (vol. 3, no. 270, 1835), © Dublin Registry of Deeds (DRD).
16. WMM family records: Jacob Family; WMMM, 27 November 1803, WNFA.
17. WNFA birth records and FHLD database; from 1812, WMM recorded children's birthplaces.
18. Issue 943 of the *Waterford Mirror* listed all voters for each candidate and those denied a vote (Issue 943 at Cara/Links Irish Search Engine).
19. Wigham, *Newtown School*, 20-25
20. Pupils' Register (1798–1882), Newtown School Archives (NSA), nos 206 and 237; FHLD database; Joan Johnson, email to author, 8 October 2009; Tabitha Driver (FLL), email to author, 1 September 2011.
21. Minutes of Munster Provincial School proceedings 1813–1820, NSA.
22. Wigham, *Newtown School*, 7-10.
23. Stirabout was porridge; pattens were shoes or clogs, with a raised sole or set on an iron ring.
24. Wigham, *Newtown School*, 22-30; Lindley Murray (1745–1826) was an American born Quaker grammarian, author of *English Grammar Adapted to the Different Classes of Learners* (1795).
25. Minutes of the Library Committee of Six 1811–1817, NSA.
26. Waterford Friends Burial Register, no. 17, WNFA.
27. List of Freemen 1700–2008; copy of Joshua Mason's handwritten appeal, TWC1/1/1408, WCA; see Nolan and Power (eds), *Waterford History*, 227-264 for information on freemen's status.

28. Slater's Directory (1846, 1856); Waterford Directory (1856); T. Shearman, Commercial Directory (1839), 51, 73; Pigot's Provincial Directory of Ireland (Munster) (1824).
29. Pigot's Surname Index for Waterford City and County, Youghal, New Ross, Carrick-on-Suir (1824); Joshua Mason was listed as a corn merchant on Summerhill in one version of Pigot's Directory; Des Cowman, 'Trade and Society in Waterford 1800-1840', 457 and 'General Tables of Occupation'; Appendix 2, 'Manufacturing Industry in Waterford City 1820–1840', both in Nolan and Power (eds), *Waterford History*.
30. Joan Johnson citing Newtown records by email to author, 30 March 2011.
31. Russell, *Leckey Genealogy* (from Roots Web); FHLD database; selected records from WMM.
32. Jimmy O'Toole, *The Carlow Gentry: What Will the Neighbours Say?* (Carlow, Ireland, 1993), 149-52; Ordnance Survey Field Name Books of County Carlow vol. 1, A-C typescript, Carlow Local Studies (CLS), Carlow Library, 36
33. Deed 56, Mason Yaur Jeffares, finalised 24 November 1840, © DRD; Donal Moore, email to author on tithes, 22 March 2011; on tithes, see Anthony Wood, *Nineteenth Century Britain 1815–1914* (London: Longman, 1982), 22, 107.
34. *Waterford Chronicle*, 15 April 1819, Waterford Library; Russell, *Leckey Genealogy*.
35. Waterford Friends' Birth Register from 1812, WNFA; FHLD database; M.A. Coombs, 'Joshua Mason Junior', *L'Umile Pianta*, Spring 2010.
36. Newtown School Pupils' Register (1798–1882), no. 303, and Joseph Mason's apprenticeship, Newtown School Register, no. 257, NSA; Removals List, Richard J. Mason, WMMM, WNFA.
37. E.H. Bennis, 'Reminiscences of Old Limerick', *Limerick Chronicle*, 1936, gives information on the Baylee family.
38. Cholmondeley, *Story*, 4; Russell, *Leckey Genealogy*; Russell, email to author, 5 December 2009.
39. Liverpool Record of Waterford Freemen: Mason (father and son) certificates, Box ACC1354, LRO.
40. Cholmondeley, *Story*, 1; Daniel Defoe, *The Complete English Tradesman* (London, 1728), chapter IV.
41. Russell, email to author, 7 December 2009, citing will of Joseph Woodward of Deptford, Kent, 3 May 1810; *The Times* deaths, 1 June 1820, reporting Mrs Mary Adcock's death.
42. Junior's Deed, 19 February 1835, DRD.
43. Russell, *Mason Genealogy*; WNFA Family Records.
44. Shearman's Directory (1839).
45. From 1812, Waterford Friends' Birth Register noted birthplaces, which showed where the family lived; FHLD database; WMMM, 28 May 1935, 180-181, WNFA, confirmed by Carlow Monthly Meeting Minutes (CMMM) for 12 June 1835.

5. Trouble at Staplestown Mills, 1835–1841 (pp. 45-54)

1. T.P. Walsh, 'Staplestown', *Old Carloviana*, the journal of the Old Carlow Society, 1948, 1-4, published annually by County Carlow Historical and Archaeological Society, Carlow Local Studies (CLS); author telephoned Sean Swan, present owner, March 2015.
2. Lewis, 'Carlow County' in *Lewis's Topographical Dictionary* (1837), 1 of 3 vols; 'Parish of Ballinacarrig', *Ordnance Survey Field Name Books of County Carlow*, vol. 1 A-C (1839), 36, typed copy, at CLS.

3. Carlow County Ireland Genealogical Projects (IGP) took list of MPs for Co. Carlow from Walsh's *Staplestown* (no page given); the Rt Revd James Doyle, Bishop of Carlow, said in 1819, 'Bruen ministered to his own pleasures'; Henry Roberts and Robert Power, *Oak Park Demesne and Forest Walk* (Co. Carlow, Ireland: Knockbeg College, 2008); O'Toole, *The Neighbours*, 53, Carlow Library.
4. CMMM, June 1835; Olive C. Goodbody, *Guide to Irish Quaker Records 1654–1860* (Irish Manuscripts Commission, 1967); Butler, *Quaker Meeting Houses of Ireland*; Irish Friends Historical Committee recorded that the land was sold in 1927 and Carlow Meeting House moved (MS box 9/35, FHLD).
5. CMMM, 22 January 1836, FHLD; Russell, *Leckey Genealogy*.
6. CMMM, 6 May 1836, FHLD.
7. Lewis, 'Ballinacarrig and Staplestown, Civil Parish', *Lewis's Topographical Dictionary of Ireland* (1837). The two townlands were merged as they are today; four steam-powered grain mills were constructed in Carlow during the 1840s; in 1852, Griffiths' Primary Valuation of Tenements (1848–1865) showed that old-fashioned water-powered mills were rare.
8. In 1844, Griffiths' Primary Valuation (1848–1878) assessed the townland valuation; Joshua Mason's lands at Co. Waterford and Staplestown may have been liable for tithes as part of the rent to the established Church of Ireland (before disestablishment in 1869). Following the tithe wars in Ireland (1831–1836), tithes were reduced and added to rents under the Tithe Commutation Act of 1836. Although tithes were technically abolished by the Tithe Commutation Act of 1838, they were still extorted for agricultural land. Local church wardens were legally entitled to obtain an order to requisition goods to the required amount plus their costs. As Friends were expected to abide by state laws, after a refusal gesture, distrainment of money or goods to the value of the tithe was unavoidable. In 1833, Church of Ireland membership was a ninth of the total Irish population. Carlow Friends' Monthly Meeting minutes recorded Quaker 'sufferings' through injustices, including payment of fines for tithe distraint; Donal Moore, email to author, 11 April 2011.
9. Charles S. Ottley, *Burrin Drainage: Report and Final Award 1847* (Dublin: Alexander Thom, 1847), especially p. 16, CLS.
10. Ordnance Survey (1839); Lewis, *Ireland* (1837), vol. 1 of 3.
11. Ibidem.
12. CMMM, 10 November 1837, FHLD.
13. New Commercial Directory for Carlow (Kinder and Son, 1839), CLS.
14. Lewis, *Ireland* (1837), vol. 3, 'Waterford City Subscribers' list'.
15. WMMM, 27 July 1837, WNFA.
16. Wigham, *Newtown*, pupil list; Henry Thompson, *A History of Ackworth School during its First Hundred Years* (Pontefract: Ackworth School, 1879), with list of scholars (1779–1879); Gough, *Memoirs*, 14.
17. WMMM, 22 March 1838, WNFA; although Slater's Directory listed Richard Mason in 1839, he may have left earlier for Liverpool; death certificate for Richard Jacob, 5 August 1846, Liverpool Register Office.
18. Disownments database, FHLD.
19. CMMM, 10 August 1838, FHLD.
20. *Carlow Sentinel*, 30 November 1838.
21. The school was under the oversight of Hardshaw West (Liverpool and Birkenhead) and Hardshaw East (Manchester) Friends; J. Spence Hodgson, *History of Penketh School 1834–1907* (1907), FLL 044.06 PEN.

22. Ibidem; only deaths that took place *at* Penketh Friends' School were recorded; Penketh School scholars' list, 19-30.
23. CMMM, 6 December 1839, FHLD; David H. Milligan, *Quaker Marriage* (Kendal: Quaker Tapestry Books, 1994), 26, 1-5, 10-22.
24. *Carlow Sentinel*, 10 February 1840, CLS.
25. CMMM, 6 March 1840, FHLD.
26. Census, Garth Village, Bangor, Caernarvon, 1841.
27. *Carlow Sentinel*, 4 April 1840, CLS.
28. CMMM, 11 September 1840, FHLD
29. WMMM, 8 October 1840, WNFA.
30. Memorial Deed, Mason Yaur Jeffares, 11 May 1840/24 November 1840, no. 56, 25 November 1840, © DRD; advertisement to let or sell interest on Bridge St. premises, *Waterford Mail*, 25 July 1840 from www.findmypast.co.uk, sent in Russell, email to author, March 2015.
31. *Carlow Sentinel*, 3 October 1840; Poor Relief (Ireland) Act (1838).
32. Death certificate for Margaret Mason, aged forty, wife of Joshua Mason, retired merchant, 16 September 1858, Birkenhead Register Office.
33. Joshua Mason, letter to Waterford Friends, 27 May 1841; Hannah Mason's marriage record for 1 July 1840, WMMM, WNFA, emailed to author by Joan Johnson, 3 March 2011; 'Leeds: Merchants' Listings' in Slater's Directory of Ireland.
34. CMMM, 12 August 1842, FHLD; Joshua Mason, gentleman, *not* listed in the 1842 Carlow Directory.
35. *Carlow Sentinel*, 5 April 1840, CLS.
36. 'Migration to Australia 1832–1850', *Skwirk*, Year 9, SOSE: History, SA, http://www.skwirk.com/p-c_s-56_u-426_t-1075_c-4146/SA/9/Migration-to-Australia-1832–1850/Mass-migration/Becoming-Australian/SOSE-History/.
37. George Washington Baker (1800–1859) and James Backhouse (1794–1869) were Quaker missionaries (Australian *Dictionary of National Biography*).
38. T.H. Webb (a Quaker genealogist for nineteenth-century Friends), *Mason Genealogy*, FHLD.
39. Ottley Report (1847), 16-18.

6. Charlotte Mason's Mysterious Childhood, 1842–1852 (pp. 55-67)

1. Census, Bangor Borough and Parish, Garth Village, 1841; the 1851 census stated that Peter was thirty-seven and Huldah Jane was thirty-six – not thirty-eight, her true age!
2. No passenger lists could be found for Joshua's voyages to and from Sydney; Department of Justice and Equality, *Report of Interdepartmental Committee to Establish the Facts of State Involvement with Magdalen Laundries* (2013), chapter 3.
3. Fruitless searches: searching at the National Register, Birmingham Reference Library and National Archives yielded nothing; the Assistant Chief Registrar, Douglas IOM, searched all IOM parishes from 1841 to 1858 and sent a letter to the author on 14 July 1982; Mrs Sidebotham (CMT 1932) searched Welsh records extensively and sent a letter to the author on 3 April 1993; Carmel Flahavan (CLS) searched all Roman Catholic and Church of Ireland parishes in Leinster diocese for Co. Carlow and emailed author on 24 May 2011; Father Morrin of St James and Our Lady Church (founded in 1866), Bangor, communicated on 7 October 2009 by letter and telephone that he had found *no* early Roman Catholic records of registration of births at Bangor/Bethesda area; Dep. Sup. Registrar Dewi Williams

and A. Jones Swyddoc Archifau wrote letters and emails between 7 October 2008 and 16 June 2009 to say they had found no records after searching all Caernarfon (previously Caernarvon) church records.

4. M.A. Coombs, 'Puzzling over Charlotte Mason's Date of Birth', *L'Umile Pianta*, Winter 2010; see census records, Worthing (Broadwater), 1861 and 1871; Sarah Harriett Doyle was also born in Bangor c. 1843.
5. Elen Wyn, Archivist, Bangor University, sent a letter to the author on 25 August 2011 with two undated news reports by R. Idloes Owen, 'A History of Our Lady Immaculate: Fever and Plague, Colour and Charm' (n.d.) and 'Historical Notebook' (n.d.), Bangor Library MS 34582, referring to Bishop Collingridge's Bangor mission.
6. P. Gutridge for Father Adrian Morrin, letter to author, 1 October 2009; Mrs Fyfe-Shaw of the National Catholic Library, Farnborough, explained in a telephone conversation with the author (13 June 2011) that *The Book of Sources*, held at the library, confirmed the destruction of all Bangor RC records in 1856; B. and M. Pawley, *Rome and Canterbury Through Four Centuries: A Study of the Relations between the Church of Rome and the Anglican Churches 1530–1981* (London and Oxford: Mowbray, 1974; 2nd edn 1981), 105; Russell emailed the author on 2 July 2015 to confirm that Peter Doyle's parents were Roman Catholics.
7. Alan Bond and staff at National Catholic Library, Farnborough, confirmed on 13 June 2011 the validity of a baptism performed by a lay person who followed established ritual; John Benson, Chester Record Office, emailed the author on 22 October 2009 to confirm that he had found *no* Roman Catholic baptism record for C.M. Mason or C.M. Shaw at St Werburgh's Church, Birkenhead (ERC30/6535/1); Bob Russell emailed author to confirm that Peter Doyle's parents were Roman Catholics on 2 July 2015.
8. Cholmondeley, *Story*, 2; Elsie Kitching's notes from meeting Groveham in 1923, PNEU2Bpneu31; Kegan Paul's annotations to *Home Education* proofs, CM51cmc416.
9. Census, Birkenhead, Holy Trinity, 1851: Sarah H. Doyle, aged eight, born c. 1843 at Bangor, Caernarvon; Russell, *Mason and Doyle Genealogy*.
10. Marriage record from Representative Church Body (RCB), Dublin, P277/3/5, see www.irishgenealogy.ie; Index of Marriages, National Archives of Ireland: Joshua Mason and Margaret Shaw 1844, ML 540; in 1843 Gore's Directory noted that a Margaret Shaw ran a 'beer house' in Birkenhead market area, near other Shaws and St Werburgh's Catholic Church in Grange Road; no further suggestive clues found.
11. Joshua's address in the Mason marriage record; King George IV changed Dublin port's name from Dun Laoghaire to Kingstown to celebrate his Dublin visit in 1821.
12. Harrison, *Irish Quakers*, 65, and conversation with author, 3 September 2009.
13. Marriage record (1844); Dr Raymond Refaussé, RCB Library Dublin, email to author, 2 November 2013: a marriage licence (ML) gave permission for a prompt marriage; a marriage licence bond (MLB) indemnified a clergyman from inadvertently conducting an illegal marriage.
14. *The Church i.e. – a Brief History* typescript from The Church, Dublin (formerly St Mary's Church); no record found of the Masons' marriage in *Dublin Gazette* or *Dublin Monitor* in 1844. No connection found with Masons and Shaws listed in Dublin Directories (1840–1850).
15. Clergy and Parishes, Dublin Directory (1840), National Library, Dublin.
16. Russell, *Mason Genealogy*; Cambridgeshire marriages (parish records' collections) transcription from Cambridge Family History Society from Russell by email; M.A. Coombs, 'Joshua Mason Junior (1805–1846)', *L'Umile Pianta*, Spring 2010, 12-17.

17. Russell emailed Griffith's Valuation (1847–1856) to author; Slater's Directory (1846, 1856) and Waterford Directories viewed online via Waterford County Library (1851).
18. WMMM, 27 August 1846, MMXI, 116, WNFA.
19. Death certificate for Richard Mason, 24 July 1846, Liverpool Register Office.
20. Death notices index: Joshua Mason junior, WAT IRL, *Cork Examiner* (COR, IRL), 21 August 1846.
21. WMMM, 25 February 1847, 521, 526, WNFA: Eliza Mason's removal to Croydon.
22. Russell's emailed notes to author: Robert Adcock (1783–1854), including will, dated 9 November 1854, proved in London 15 February 1855, transcribed by Geoffrey Woollard on 21 October 2009: Adcock left a token £19 to Mary as Arthur Mason provided for her and Eliza received a £20 annuity; Annual Monitor of Obituaries of Members of the Society of Friends in Great Britain and Ireland 1862 and 1871, 143; Arthur Mason died on 31 August 1861 (WNFA, 344); Mary, 'relict of Arthur', died at Suir View, Tipperary (TIPP, IRL), *Cork Examiner* (COR, IRL), on 24 June 1862; 'List of Pupils' in Wigham, *Newtown*; Friends' Apprenticeship Records, NSA.
23. Census, Croydon, 1851; *The British Friend*, November 1852, 297, emailed to author by Russell.
24. FHLD deaths database.
25. Slater's Royal National Commercial Directory of Ireland; SLAT, 1846, 333; SLAT, 1856, 373.
26. Russell, *Pim Genealogy*, emailed to author on 7 November 2009 and 5 December 2009; Pigot and Co. City of Dublin and Hibernian Provincial Directory (1824), 321, 323; *The Times*, 16 December 1848; ref. *London Gazette*, Issue 21126, pub. 22 November 1850, p. 3153; cf. Cholmondeley, *Story*, 4.
27. Hardshaw West Quaker membership records 1837–1860, 289 QUA 6/7 from Roger Hull, LRO; no Quaker records for Joshua Mason, the Birchalls or the Doyle were found; Tracey O'Hare, ref. E/2009/199 Wirral, confirmed by email that Friends met in Birkenhead from 1836.
28. Russell sent Birkenhead census household transcription, Wirral: Birkenhead, Bidston, 1841 and 1851.
29. Census, Birkenhead, Holy Trinity parish, 1851, for Doyles; 'Oliver's Alphabetical Index' in Hodgson, *Penketh Scholars.*
30. C.M. Mason, *Some Studies in the Formation of Character* (London: Kegan Paul, Trench, Trübner and Co. Ltd, 1906; 2nd edn 1914), chapter 9, 114-115.
31. A.H. Layard, *Illustrations of the Monuments of Nineveh* (London: John Murray, 1849); Daniel Defoe, *Robinson Crusoe* (London: Illustrated Classics, 1719), *Aesop's Fables* (London: Illustrated Classics, 1947); Henry Butters, *The Etymological Spelling Book and Expositor Being an Introduction to the Spelling, Pronunciation and Derivation of the English Language adapted to the use of Classical and Ladies' schools and also for Adults and Foreigners* (London, 1830) which included *Aesop's Fables*; Jean-Jacques Rousseau, *Émile,* trans. Barbara Foxley (London: Dent Everyman, 1974), 147; Cholmondeley, *Story*, 4.
32. Russell, *Birchall Genealogy*: Edwin Birchall Senior; Slater's (Ireland) Directory (1846) for Leeds: Merchants and Stuff Manufacturers; Cholmondeley, *Story*, 4.
33. Picture no. 40 of Holy Trinity Church in Ian Boumphrey, *Birkenhead: A Pictorial History* (West Sussex: Phillimore Press, 1995).
34. John Green, *Brief History of Oxton* [pamphlet] (Oxton Society, n.d.).
35. Birkenhead Directories, Birkenhead Reference Library (BRL).
36. Birkenhead Churches Register, Chester Record Office (CRO).

37. History Gazetteer Directory, Cheshire, 1850; Philip Sulley, *History of Ancient and Modern Birkenhead* (Liverpool, 1907); W.M. Murphy, *Liverpool,* 318-325, Wirral Archives.
38. H. Gamlin, *Memories of Birkenhead* (1892), Wirral Archives; Gore's Birkenhead Directory (1851) for Sunday services timetable, BRL.
39. Crockford's Clerical Directory (1858) for Baylee's qualifications; F.B. Heiser, *The Story of St Aidan's College, Birkenhead 1847–1947* (Chester: Phillipson and Golder, 1947), 1-10; David Dowland, *Development of Nineteenth Century Anglican Non-Graduate Theological Colleges with Especial Reference to Episcopal Attitudes* (unpublished DPhil thesis, University of Oxford, 1993), 77.
40. Heiser, *St Aidan's,* 10.
41. Dr H.J. Burgess and Dr Paul Welsby, *A Short History of the National Society 1811–1961* (London, 1961); 12,000 schools opened by 1851.
42. Accounts and Papers (A and P), Committee of Council on Education, vol. XLVII, 1855–1856, Bodleian Law Library (BLL), recorded grants to the Holy Trinity Schools; see also *Schools Aided by Parliamentary Grants* (CRO) listing Holy Trinity School grants in Mason's time for certificated teachers, and retirement pensions of £196 13s 4d on 26 September 1855 and £393 16 8d on 6 August 1856 for pupil-teachers under the heading 'Birkenhead entries'.
43. Baylee, letter to Revd Wm Harrison, 2 September 1845, Lambeth Palace Library, Baylee Collection.
44. Law's Directory, Birkenhead and Environs (1845), BRL, Birkenhead entries; Holy Trinity School log book, 27 July 27 and 31 August 1863, Wirral Archives, https://www.wirral.gov.uk/my-services/leisure-and-culture/wirral-archives-service.
45. Groveham, letter to Kitching, 9 July 1927, PNEU2Bpneu31.
46. The first St Aidan's Church, off Victoria Road, Liverpool, was not consecrated until 17 February 1860, after Charlotte had left Birkenhead.
47. Philip Gale, Records Manager, Church of England Records Centre, London, wrote a letter to author, 18 August 2008; Crockford's Clerical Directory (1865); advertisement in Ward's Directory of Birkenhead (1857) recording St Aidan's aims; Heiser, *St Aidan's,* 11-30; Dowland, *Non-Graduate Theological Colleges,* 81-5, 199-213; Gore's Directory (1853); Osborne's Directory (1854); Mortimer and Harwood, Directory of Birkenhead (1843), BRL.
48. H.G. Wells, *Ann Veronica,* (London: Virago Press, 1909; 1980), 204.
49. Kitching, Groveham notes, PNEU2Bpneu31.
50. Francesca Anyon, Wirral Archives, confirmed on 6 November 2009 that St Werburgh's School only opened in 1857; no female pupil-teachers were listed in Roman Catholic schools by 1859.
51. Cholmondeley, *Story,* 4-5.
52. Holy Trinity school staff listed in Osborne's Directory (1851); 'Tabulated Reports on Schools for Chester, Salop and Stafford region' (1840–1858), Holy Trinity girls' class July 1852 and August 1853, inspected by Revd J.P. Norris HMI, *Inspectors' Reports, Great Britain Committee of Council on Education,* London, HMSO, 100, Newsam Library and Archives, University College London, Institute of Education.
53. Census, Everton, Liverpool, 1861, placed the Doyle family at 39 Woodville Terrace, Everton, Liverpool; Hodgson, *Penketh Scholars.*
54. Conservative in tone, the weekly *Spectator* (founded in 1828) gave Mason 'a metaphysical and a literary turn' (C.M. Mason, *Parents and Children* (London: Kegan Paul, Trench and Trübner, 1896; 5th edn., n.d.)), 71.
55. Kitching, 'The Beginning of Things', 119-120; Mason, *Some Studies,* 215.

56. Kitching, 'Day's Work', *In Memoriam*, 70.
57. Gore's Directory (1855); Ward's Directory (1857), BRL.
58. Cholmondeley, *Story*, 5.

7. Pupil-Teaching at Holy Trinity School, Birkenhead, 1854–1859 (pp. 68-80)

1. Fly leaves, 1 January 1857 and 26 August 1859, both 'with E.A.B.'s love', PNEU2Apneu7; William Paley, *Natural Theology or Evidence of the Existence or Attributes of the Deity, Collected from the Appearances of Nature*, ed. M.D. Eddy and David Knight (Oxford University Press, 1802; 2008); C. Girtin, *Physiology* (London: John W. Parker, 7th edn 1852).
2. Committee of Council on Education (C of C) Minutes 1854–1855, nos 6 and 100, A and P, Bodleian Law Library (BLL); *Christmas Examinations 1859-61-62-63-64-65-66 Questions and Class Lists*, Newsam Library and Archives, University College London, Institute of Education; Charles Birchenough, *A History of Elementary Education in England and Wales from 1800 to the Present Day* (London: University Tutorial Press, 1938), chapters 2 and 11 on the monitorial system; Asher Tropp, *The School Teachers: The Growth of the Teaching Profession in England and Wales from 1800 to the Present Day* (London: Heinemann, 1956), 3, 18-24; S.J. Curtis and M.E.A. Boultwood, *An Introductory History of English Education since 1800* (London: University Tutorial Press, 2nd edn 1962), 54-68.
3. James Gribble (ed.), *Matthew Arnold*, Educational Thinkers Series (London: Collier-Macmillan Ltd, 1967), 9-31, 61-5; Holy Trinity School log book (1863), Wirral Archives.
4. C of C Minutes 1854–1855, no. 6, BLL.
5. Bruce Jackson, County Archivist, Lancashire (ACS) Record Office, ref. 2011/2434, informed author by telephone and letter, 30 September 2011; Mason's pupil-teacher indenture has not survived; no pupil-teacher indentures could be found before the 1880s.
6. I noticed how frequently Baylee took baptisms when searching vainly for Charlotte's baptism record in Holy Trinity records, CRO.
7. *The Infallibility of the Church of Rome: A Correspondence between the Right Reverend Bishop Brown of Chepstow and the Reverend Joseph Baylee* (London: Longman, 1851); *Protestantism v. Roman Catholicism, Report of the Discussion between J. Baylee and M. Bridges, Held at Stroud* (London: F.W. Harmer, 1856).
8. C.M. Mason, *Ourselves, Our Souls and Bodies* (London: Kegan Paul, Trench, Trübner and Co., 1905; 2nd edn. 1921), 197.
9. No Holy Trinity confirmation record for Charlotte found at CRO; none available before 1928.
10. Article 143 inserted into Minutes and Regulations of C of C Articles 17, 118, 124-5, 143 etc.; A and P, vol. LIII, 1860, reduced to Code form; C of C Minutes and Regulations regularly updated; this letter updated C of C Minutes (1850–1851), A and P, vol. XCII and XCIV, BLL.
11. Tropp, *School Teachers*, 22; R.W. Rich, *The Training of Teachers in England and Wales during the Nineteenth Century* (Cambridge University Press, 1933), 120.
12. Census, Birkenhead, Holy Trinity parish, 1851; Hardshaw West Members List, Wirral Archives and Liverpool Record Office (LRO), 289QUA6/7.
13. Revd J.P. Norris, 'Holy Trinity NS, Birkenhead' (10 August 1854) in *Tabulated Reports on Schools Inspected in Cheshire, Shropshire and Staffordshire* (1853–1854), Newsam

Archives, call no. 100 (1840–1858); F.H. Spencer (pupil-teacher 1886–1891), *An Inspector's Testament* (London: English Universities Press Ltd, 1938), 80-81.

14. Pupil-Teacher Broadsheet in *Christmas Exams*, also in *Journal of National Society,* monthly paper, no. 158, April 1960, London, Newsam Archives.
15. Ibidem; scrofula, formerly called King's Evil, is a disease with glandular swellings, associated with tuberculosis.
16. A and P, Table LIV, 1860; numbers recorded, 31 December 1855, and C of C Annual Report 1859; C of C Report for HM Queen, A and P, vol. LVI, 1860, BLL.
17. Pupil-Teacher Broadsheet.
18. *The Pupil Teacher: A Monthly Journal of Practical Education* (1857–1859), London, G.L. Stevenson, 54 Paternoster Row, listed school holidays: twenty-one days at Midsummer, fourteen days at Xmas, seven days at Easter, two days at Whitsun and every Saturday; Professor Wendy Robinson, *Pupil-Teachers and their Professional Training in Pupil-Teacher Centres in England and Wales 1870-1914* (Exeter: E. Mellen Press, 2003) and Robinson, email to author, 31 August 2010.
19. Rich, *Training Teachers*, 142-145; Tropp, *School Teachers*, note to p. 22.
20. Mason, *Parents and Children*, 47-58.
21. R.R.W. Lingen, circular letter to HMIs outlining new rules for pupil-teachers, 15 June 1855, A and P, vol. XLVII, 1855–1856; minutes for 1850–1851, vol. LI, 93-4.
22. Norris, HMI Reports, 1854, 1858–1859 and 1859–1860, Newsam Archives.
23. C of C, Special Minute 24 April 1857 in 1856–1857 Minutes, 28; C of C (1859) Annual Report, to HM the Queen in Council, A and P, vol. LVI, 1860, 20 ff, BLL.
24. Norris, HMI Reports 1853–1854, 1857–1858 and 1859–1860, archive call nos 100/1858/59-1898/99, and *Christmas Exams* listed teachers' certification with dates; Gore's Liverpool Directory 1857 listed Holy Trinity school staff.
25. Gore's Directories 1855 and 1857, BRL; *Christmas Exams* listed class and type of teaching certificate gained.
26. One particular bound volume of Gore's Birkenhead Directory 1855 at BRL; census, Birkenhead, Holy Trinity parish, 30 March 1851: Mrs M.A. Watson, annuitant with son and wife, listed as landholders at 6 The Meadows, Watson Street.
27. Hardship West Membership Records, 289QUA6/7, LRO, for the Pim family and Mary Pim's removals; Russell, *Leckey Genealogy*: death certificates for William R. Leckey (12 February 1867), Jane Leckey (24 February 1880), Emily Mason (24 May 1888) attended by Anna Jacob (née Pym), and Isabella Clark (née Mason) (30 July 1883); Slater's Directory (1881).
28. Gore's Directories 1856–1858 listed Baylee on the New Brighton House Committee, run by Matron, Mrs Clifford and Dr A. Parr.
29. Mason, *Some Studies,* 115, 117.
30. Russell, *Birchall Genealogy*; census, Birkenhead, Holy Trinity parish, 1861; the Birchalls were *not* listed by HW Friends for the period 1837–1860; Russell found E. Birchall in *The Entomologist's Monthly Magazine*, vol. XIII, 1876, and obituary in vol. XXI, 1884–1885; FHLD database; Ackworth Scholars' List; vol. B for Birchall, Red Index of Friends, FLL; 'Mrs Gaskell informed Florence's sister [Parthenope that] babies ad libitum are being christened Florence', quoted in Mark Bostridge, *Florence Nightingale: The Woman and her Legend* (London: Viking, 2008), 262.
31. Gore's Directories 1857–1859; directory listings are often a year late.
32. Essex Cholmondeley, conversation with author, 1983.
33. Ruth Brown MacArthur, *The Little Mother* (London: G. Harrap and Co., 1918).
34. The Birkenhead census of 1861 showed Eliza Mason's daughter, Eliza (1841–c.

1931), visiting the Birchalls; the London St Pancras census for the same year showed Eliza Mason with family at 203 Euston Road.
35. Death certificate for Margaret Mason, Birkenhead Register Office.
36. The Birkenhead censuses for 1851 and 1861 varied the spelling between Hughway (1851) and Highway (1861), while Heighisway appeared on Margaret's death certificate. 15 Whetstone Lane was rebuilt in 1908 and was a pram shop in 2009.
37. Funeral note, trans. Professor John Thorley, St Werburgh's, Birkenhead Collection, ERC 30/6535/8, CRO.
38. Death certificate for Joshua Mason, Liverpool Register Office.
39. M. Muriel Shearer, *Quakers in Liverpool* (Liverpool: Preparative Meeting of the Religious Society of Friends, 1982); Joshua Mason was interred at Hunter Street Quaker Burial Ground on 19 March 1859 by Paul Smith, grave-maker (Burial Note, 289 QUA, LRO); the Register and Index to the Friends' burial ground, compiled when Hunter Street ground was demolished, shows Joshua's bones were re-interred in Allerton Cemetery, Liverpool, on 16 August 1948.
40. Kitching's Groveham notes, PNEU2Bpneu31
41. The Revd S.J.G. Fraser and Norris, HMI Reports 1858–1859 and 1859–1860.

8. 'A Bud to be Unfolded': At the Home and Colonial Training Institution, 1860–1861 (pp. 81-96)

1. 'A Wilson with love', no title, book plate, PNEU2Apneu7.
2. Cholmondeley, *Story*, 5.
3. C of C Minutes, A and P, vol. XVI, 1857–1858; Appendix II, C of C: Tabular HMI Reports with Tables of Training Colleges 1857–1858 and 1859–1860, 319-21, BLL (or Newsam Archives, call no. 100/1857–1860); Birchenough, *Elementary Education*, 486.
4. Revd F.C. Cook, *Special Report on C of E Training Colleges for Women School Mistresses* (1861), commissioned by C of C, A and P, vol. XVII, 1860, 358.
5. Robert Owen (1771–1858) opened New Lanark infant schools in 1816 and 1818, visited Pestalozzi at Yverdun and persuaded Samuel Wilderspin (1792–1866), who opened Spitalfields' infant school in 1820, to read Pestalozzi; Curtis and Boultwood, *English Education*, 121.
6. J.H. Pestalozzi, *How Gertrude Teaches her Children: An Attempt to help Mothers Teach Their Own Children and an Account of the Method* (1801), trans. Lucy E. Holland and Francis C. Turner (London: Swann Sonnenschein, 1894); J.J. Rousseau, *Julia or the New Éloise* (1761; London, 1803), trans. anon.; Rousseau, *Émile*; Pestalozzi, *Letters on Early Education to J.P. Greaves Esq.*, trans. C.W. Barden (London, 1898); William Wordsworth, 'Ode: Intimations of Immortality from Recollections of Early Childhood' (1807), Stanza VII; John Locke, 'Some Thoughts Concerning Education' in James L. Axtell (ed.), *The Educational Writings of John Locke* (Cambridge University Press, 1968), 114-325.
7. Margaret E.M. Jones, A *Brief Account of the Home and Colonial Training Institution and of the Pestalozzian System as Taught and Practised in Its Schools* (London: Groombridge and Sons, 1860), 3-4.
8. *The Times*, 21 February 1837 and 19 August 1837.
9. Jones, *Home and Colonial*, 3-4.
10. Newcastle Commission's discussions: *The Report into the State of Popular Education in England: Part 1: Education of the Independent Poor*, 28 ff; 'Infant Schools' in A and P, vol. XXI, Part I, 1861, BLL.
11. Jones, *Home and Colonial*, 4-7; Cook, *Special Report*, 345-346.

12. Birchenough, *Elementary Education*, 300-311; S.J. Curtis, *History of Education in Great Britain* (London: University Tutorial Press, 1953), 209-213.
13. Kate Silber, *Pestalozzi: The Man and His Work* (London: Routledge and Kegan Paul, 1960).
14. Robert Rusk, *The Doctrines of the Great Educators* (London: Macmillan, 1918; 1957), 193-202, 202-208; Oscar Browning, *An Introduction to the History of Educational Theories* (London: Kegan Paul, Trench, Trübner and Co. Ltd, 1881), 152-153, 156-157; L.E. Roberts, *Parents' Review*, vol. 9, no. 6, 1898; Jones, *Home and Colonial*, 3.
15. Groveham, letter to Kitching, n.d., PNEU2Bpneu31.
16. C of C, 'Education Examination of Candidates for Infant School Certificates', Michaelmas 1860, *National Society Monthly Paper*, no. 172, March 1861; also Article 84 in Minutes and Regulations, C of C, A and P, vol. XVII, 1860, 53, BLL; see also C of C Minute, 24 April 1857 (Minutes 1856–1857), 28-29; Report of C of C (1859–1860), *National Society Monthly Paper*, no. 158, October 1860, Newsam Archives: 'My Lords approved a specified maximum number of teachers to train for infant teaching.'
17. *National Society Monthly Paper*, October 1860; Jones, *Home and Colonial*, 7
18. Selina Healey's birth certificate; *Christmas Exams*, 1859; Elizabeth Bateson, *Charlotte Mason, the PNEU and the House of Education: Perspectives on Female Education in the Late Nineteenth and Early Twentieth Centuries* (unpublished Master's thesis, St Martin's College Lancaster, 2004); *Home and Colonial Educational Paper*, April 1861, iv, Brunel University Archive, Home and Colonial, ref. BFSS, file 314.
19. Clough, *Memoir of Anne J. Clough by her Niece*, 72-73.
20. Letter to Miss G. Bell, n.d., CM44cmc293.
21. Jones, *Home and Colonial*, 4.
22. 'General Examination of Training Schools' (1859) (for candidates for Queen's Scholarships), *Christmas Exams 1859 with Questions*, 3-12 – some 1859 papers are missing; *National Society Monthly Paper*, 1860–1861, 105-7, Newsam Archives.
23. Cook's HMI Report on Female Training Colleges, A and P, vol. LIV, 1859, 373, BLL.
24. Cook, *Special Report on C of E Schoolmistresses' Training Colleges*, A and P, vol. XVI, 1859, 319, BLL.
25. Jones, *Home and Colonial*, 7.
26. *Christmas Exams* (1959), 26; Table 2, Ho and Co listing for 1859; A and P, vol. XVI, 1861, BLL; *The Pupil Teacher: A Monthly Journal of Practical Literature*, 1859, 50-53.
27. Cook, *Special Report on Home and Colonial*, commissioned by C of C, A and P, vol. XVI, 1860, 358, BLL; Jones, *Home and Colonial*, 7.
28. Spencer, *An Inspector's Testament*, 121-125; his 1890s training college life was equally Spartan.
29. Cook, *Special Report* (1860).
30. Census, St Paul's, Preston, 1851, recorded the Pendlebury family at 24 Park Row.
31. Jones, *Home and Colonial*, 7; H.C. Dent, *The Training of Teachers in England and Wales* (London: Hodder and Stoughton, 1977), 35.
32. Frances Widdowson, *Going up into the Next Class: Women and Elementary Teacher Training 1840–1914* (London: Hutchinson, 1983), 47 ff; Spencer, *An Inspector's Testament*, 123-124.
33. Census, St Jude in St Pancras, Gray's Inn Road Ward, Borough of Marylebone, 1861; the present-day block of Georgian terraced houses in St Chad's Street are probably former Home and Colonial Training College hostels.
34. Cook, *Special Report* (1860); Cook HMI College Reports, 1859 and 1860.

35. London Metropolitan Archives, ref. GB 0074 P90/BAT.
36. Kitching's Groveham notes, PNEU2Bpneu31; John Thorley, 'Charlotte Mason's Early Correspondence 1860-1879: the life and times of a Victorian teacher and teacher-trainer 1860-1890' Part 2 in J. Carroll Smith (ed.), *Essays on the Life and Work of Charlotte Mason*, 37-40.
37. Cook's HMI Report *Ho and Co Inspection* (1858) noted that average consumption of *each* student for *each* quarter year was 30lbs meat, 72lbs bread, 4.5lbs butter, 15 pints milk, 6lbs sugar, 15oz rice and 24lbs potatoes, but no fresh fruit or vegetables.
38. J. Pidduck MD, 'Medical Officer's Report', February 1860 in Cook, *Special Report*, A and P, vol. LIV, 375-376, BLL. Some Victorian medical diagnoses seem very strange; for example, William R. Leckey died of 'gout to the heart in half an hour' in Tramore in 1867. Erethism was excessive sensitivity in part of the body. 'Gastro-blurred vision' may have been related to indigestion or nervous tension. The Ho and Co course was extremely taxing.
39. Cook's HMI Report on Fussell's inspection (1859–1860), 373, BLL.
40. Drake, letter to author, 31 October 1984, regarding Dunning's career.
41. Jones, *Home and Colonial*, 5-6; children up to eight studied lessons on religious and moral subjects and on colour, form, size, weight, place, number, the human body, animals, plants, common objects, pictures, inventive drawing, kindergarten occupations, reading and writing.
42. Fussell in Cook's Report; census, St Jude in St Pancras.
43. Cook, *Special Report*, 321, 330. All passes: 159 first class, 194 second class, 65 third class with 5 'schedules' and 3 failures.
44. Kitching, Groveham notes, PNEU2Bpneu31.
45. Groveham, letter to Kitching, 7 May 1924, disputed typed copy, PNEU2Bpneu13.
46. Fussell in Cook's Report.
47. Dunning, letter to Mason, Friday afternoon, 1861, PNEU2Apneu10.
48. R.R. Lingen, letter to HMIs, 2 June 1956, A and P, vol. LI.

9. Mistress of the Davison Memorial Infantine School in Worthing, 1861–1873 (pp. 97-118)

1. Mason, letter to Groveham, c. late March 1861, Groveham's transcript, PNEU2Bpneu31; a framed record on the classroom wall declared, 'Worthing and Broadwater Infantine Schools were Established in May 1817 and were the first established in England'; other sources suggest Davison founded two infant schools in 1815; Valerie Hetzel, *A History of The William Davison Church of England High School for Girls, Worthing* (unpublished undergraduate dissertation, Brighton College of Education, 1975), CM47cmc336; R.F. Drake, *The Infant Schools of Broadwater Parish* (Sussex Archaeological Collections, 1990), 128, Worthing Reference Library (WRL).
2. Census record, Broadwater district, 7 April 1861; salary figures sent to author by Drake from *Annual Accounts* (1861), Worthing Voluntary Charities Report, *Nineteenth Annual Report,* Worthing and Broadwater Missionary Associations etc., 1872, WRL.
3. Kelly's *Worthing Entry* (1867), S.E. England; PO Directory 1865, Worthing, West Sussex Record Office Chichester (WWSRO); Sally White, *Worthing Through Time* (Stroud: Amberley Publishing, 2009); J.M. Bickerton, *Worthing: A Brief Account of the History of the Town from Neolithic Times to the Present Day* (Worthing Museum Publications, 1963), 29-30.
4. Davison C of E Secondary School for Girls, Worthing, *Souvenir Handbook of the*

Centenary Celebrations (May 1854–1954), 6; Drake, *Infant Schools*, 187-189; Davison memorial plaque in former St Pauls' Church, Chapel Road; *Glimpse of Old Worthing* manuscript, Davison School archive, 7.

5. The Education Commission (Newcastle) into the State of Popular Education in England, A and P, vol. IXXI, Part 1: 'Education of the Independent Poor', 1861, 28, BLL.
6. H.L. Jefferson, *St Paul's Church: A Short History* (Shoreham-by-Sea: Service Publications Ltd, Easter 1969); Broadwater Charity Annual Report 1 July 1857–1 July 1858, WRL.
7. Jefferson, *St Paul's*, 8; Arthur H. Clough (1819–1861), poet and brother of Anne Clough, reputedly coined the term 'broad church'. Possibly aligned with Mr Read's scientific interests, the term derived from the radical *Essays and Reviews* (1860) by seven academics critically exploring evidences for Christianity, e.g. Master of Balliol Benjamin Jowett's 'Interpretation of Scripture'. *Essays* outsold Darwin's *Origin of Species* (1859).
8. Mason's copy of *Hymns Ancient and Modern* (London: Novello and Co., 1861), inscribed 'CM '67, purchased in Worthing', CM2cmc24.
9. Crockford's Clerical Directories 1878 and 1882; Drake, letters to author, 8 October 1983, 5 September 1984 and 30 October 1984, author's copies.
10. *Worthing Gazette*, 27 November 1912, from Drake.
11. In a letter to the author on 25 May 1983, Drake named the mistresses: Miss Atkins and Miss Wilkins; Hetzel, *William Davison*, 28-29; the Home and Colonial Training College's recommended design in Malcolm Seaborne and Roy Lowe, *The English School: Its Architecture and Organization*, vol. 1 (London: Routledge and Kegan Paul, 1977).
12. *Souvenir Handbook*, 6; Hetzel, *William Davison*, 27-30; Drake, *Infant Schools*, 192-194.
13. Jefferson, *St Paul's*, 14-15.
14. Revd J. Brooke Pattrick, The Chapel of Ease curate, *Memorial Sermon* (Worthing: Walter Paine, printer, 21 July 1877), PNEU2Cpneu46.
15. Louisa Hubbard, letter to *The Echo*, 12 January 1871, in Hubbard's scrapbook, Bishop Otter Memorial College (BO), MS A003, Chichester University.
16. Mason, letter to Groveham, April 1861, Groveham's transcript, PNEU2Bpneu31.
17. Mason, letter to Groveham, c. May 1861, Groveham's transcript, PNEU2Bpneu31.
18. Souvenir Handbook, 'Memories', Davison School Archive, 12-13.
19. Dunning, letter to Mason, 22 October 1861, PNEU2Apneu10.
20. Groveham, letter to Kitching, 14 June 1923, PNEU2Bpneu31.
21. Mason, letter to Groveham, 'Sunday', Groveham's transcript, n.d., PNEU2Bpneu31.
22. Ibidem.
23. Mason, letter to Groveham, 'Scraps', Groveham's transcript, n.d., PNEU2Bpneu17.
24. Mason, letter to Groveham, 8 December 1861, Groveham's transcript, PNEU2Bpneu17.
25. *Christmas Exams and Class Lists*, Newsam Archives.
26. Groveham, letter to Kitching, 31 January 1924; Groveham's transcript headed 'Dates', n.d. PNEU2Bpneu31.
27. Kitching, Groveham notes, PNEU2Bpneu13; Mason, letter to Groveham (own hand), 21 January 1877, PNEU2Bpneu17.
28. C of C Report 1858–1859, minutes 26 July 1858, A and P, vol. XVI, Articles 128 and 129, BLL.

29. General Examination, Training Schools, Article 119, *Christmas Exams and Class Lists*, Christmas 1862, 58-71, Newsam Archives.
30. Mason, *Home Education*, 75.
31. *Christmas Exams and Class Lists* (1862–1863), Newsam Archives, 126–127; Rich, *Training of Teachers*, 190.
32. Salary figures from Drake to author, from Financial Section of Broadwater Charity Annual Reports, 1863–1864, WRL; Dent, *Training of Teachers*, 20, 25.
33. Augmentation Broad Sheet, at the back of the Pupil Teacher Broadsheet, *Christmas Exams etc.*, 1861–1862, Newsam Archives; C of C minutes, A and P, vol. XI, Articles 67, 122, 128, 129, 131, BLL.
34. Davison School log book with summarised HMI Reports 1863–1873, Davison C of E High School, Selbourne Road, Worthing, archives; C of C Report on *The Revised Code*, A and P, vol. XI, 1861–1862, p. xxvii, BLL.
35. Herbert Bell, 'Recollections', manuscript, CM44cmc293.
36. Fly leaf (William Read, February 1866), PNEU2Apneu7.
37. The Newcastle Commission's *Report into the State of Popular Education in England*, A and P, vol. XVII, 1861, BLL; *The Educational Blue Book and the Revised Code* in the *Home and Colonial School Society Occasional Paper*, 9 May 1869, University of London Library; Curtis, *History of Education* , 230-271
38. Ibidem; 'Worthing Education' (1815), *Worthing History Online*, ongoing publication online from Victoria County History, London (1980), recorded the school's average attendance, including the winter evening school run by Mason; *A History of the County of Sussex Volume 6*, Part 1; Davison log book.
39. Mason, letter to Groveham (own hand), c. 1863, PNEU2Bpneu17; Cholmondeley, *Story*, 7 – the letter in the middle section was quoted accurately. No originals found for the first and third excerpts on p. 7.
40. Curtis, *History of Education*, 275-9; Hetzel, *William Davison*, 57-60.
41. Davison log book.
42. Drake, letter to author, 25 May 1983, author's copy; *Worthing Education* online.
43. Davison log book.
44. Copy school registers 1864–1874, Davison School archives.
45. Davison log book.
46. Newspaper cutting in the red exercise book of Muriel Thomas, former headmistress, Davison School, kept with the school log in Davison archives; the standards attained were recorded in school registers.
47. Census, Central Bradford, 1871, Groveham family; Cholmondeley, *Story*, 6.
48. Curtis, *History of Education*, 546 on the Schools Inquiry (Taunton) Commission, vol. 1, 166; H.C. Barnard, *A History of English Education from 1860* (London University Press, 7th impression, 1971), 162.
49. Groveham, letter to Kitching, 14 June 1923, PNEU2bpneu31; Cholmondeley's biography perpetuated this misconception – see pp. 6, 8; former Davison headteacher K.S. Sandell noted, 'There was also a Middle School for girls only, the fee of which was 6d.- 8d. Per week' (*Centenary Edition*, 8).
50. Kitching, Groveham notes, PNEU2Bpneu31; letter purported to be from Mason to Groveham (Kitching's hand, dated 1863), PNEU2Bpneu17; Cholmondeley, *Story*, 8 – only the last five lines of this letter dated January 1864 are genuine (PNEU2Bpneu17).
51. Mason, letter to Groveham (own hand), n.d., PNEU2Bpneu17.
52. Huston's letter to Mason from 55 Victoria Road, Kentish Town, 4 September 1865, PNEU2Bcmc23.

53. C.M. Mason, *An Essay Towards a Philosophy of Education: A Liberal Education for All* (London: J.M. Dent and Sons Ltd, 1925; 3rd edn 1954), 10; Williams, 'Reminiscences', 57.
54. In 1927/8, the school was reclassified as The Davison Voluntary Aided C of E Girls' Secondary, under Worthing Education Committee, *five years* after Mason died; *A Brief History of the Davison School* (Worthing: Davison School, n.d.); *Inspire, Serve, Achieve,* Davison School prospectus, Bi-Centenary Celebration, 2012–2013.
55. Cholmondeley, *Story*, 8, 9; Kitching, Groveham notes, 1923, PNEU2Bpneu31.
56. Davison log book.
57. Drake, *Salary Figures*; fly leaves: Milton's *Paradise Lost* (1 January 1866), John Gill's *School Education* (1865), E. Pick's *On Memory* (1866), PNEU2Apneu7.
58. Census, Worthing, Ecclesiastical District, Broadwater, 1871; Davison log book.
59. Russell, *Morris and Birchall Genealogy* emailed to author, 21 October 2010; census, Bradford, 1861 and 1871; M.A. Coombs, 'Puzzling over Charlotte Mason's Date of Birth', *L'Umile Pianta.*
60. Pigot's Sussex Directory (1839); Burke's Landed Gentry, Brandreth, 96; Brandreth, census records, Broadwater district of Worthing, 1841 and 1851; 'Thomas Brandreth', *Dictionary of National Biography.*
61. Drake, letter to author, 30 March 1983, author's copy, for Brandreth's donation and notes on the Misses Byrom; Davison log book for Emily Brandreth's visits; PO Directory, Worthing, on Mr Lewis.
62. R.F. Drake, 'Charlotte Mason at Bishop Otter Memorial College, Part 1', *West Sussex History*, no. 41, August 1988, 13-14; Cholmondeley's *Story* is also incorrect, following Mrs Groveham's mistake (see p. 9); Emily Brandreth's will confirmed Ashton, not Arthur, was the children's father; Kitching, 'The Beginning of Things'.
63. Mason, *An Essay*, 11-12.
64. Charlotte M. Yonge (1823–1901) of Otterbourne, Hampshire, a follower of Keble and the Oxford Movement, wrote 160 books. Charlotte's favourite was *The Heir of Redclyffe* (1853).
65. Mason, *An Essay*, 9-10.
66. E. Coghlan, 'A Report of the Present Superintendent of the Mixed School of the Advantages of Early Education' (1 April 1869), *Ho and Co School Society Occasional Paper*, May 1869, 35, London University Library.
67. C.M. Mason, *First Grammar Lessons* (London: J.M. Dent and Sons Ltd, 1928), Armitt Library.
68. Mason, *Parents and Children*, 11.
69. Mason, three incomplete letters to Groveham (own hand), n.d., PNEU2Bpneu17.
70. Davison log book.
71. Mason, three letters to 'Dear Sir' (own hand), Thursday n.d., found in her blotter after death and probably not sent, PNEU2Bpneu23.
72. The Schools Inquiry (Taunton) Commission 1864–1868 led to the Endowed Schools Act of 1869, promoting middle-class secondary education; see Barnard, *English Education*, 159-166 for Taunton and 115-119 and 168 for the Education Act (1870).
73. Drake, letter to author, 2 July 1982, author's copy; Mason, letter to Groveham (own hand), n.d., PNEU2Bpneu17.
74. Mason, incomplete letter to Groveham (own hand), describing Gainsborough's *Blue Boy*, PNEU2Bpneu17.
75. Davison log book; J. Stuart Maclure, *Educational Documents in England and Wales 1816-1963* (London: Chapman and Hall Ltd, 1965) chapter 11: 'Effects of the Revised Code', 81.

10. Senior Governess at the Gentlewomen's College in Chichester, 1874–1878 (pp. 119-134)

1. G.P. McGregor, *Bishop Otter College and Policy for Teacher Training 1839-1980* (London: Pembridge Press, 1981), chapter 3, 79-124; *Bishop Otter College Magazine* (1976), BO SU 001/023; General Committee Meetings (BO MS A2003), BOC Archives, University of Chichester.
2. McGregor, *Bishop Otter*, 12-78; Janet Carter, Sue Tressler and Andrew Worsfold, *Bishop Otter Campus Tree Walk with Brief History* [leaflet] (2009), sponsored by the University of Chichester Estates Deparment with the Archives Department; University of Chichester Ordnance Survey map, 1867; Kelly's PO Directory 1867, West Sussex Record Office (WSRO).
3. Hughes, *Victorian Governess*, 40 and chapter 8, 177-203; Anon, 'The Strong-minded Woman', *St James' Magazine* (London: Houlston and Wright), vol. 15, December-March 1866; Anstruther, *Patmore's Angel*, 63-73; Curtis, *History of Education*, chapter 7; Frances Widdowson, *Next Class*, 15-18, 33-35.
4. Tropp in Widdowson, *Next Class*, 18.
5. McGregor, *Bishop Otter*, 79-92
6. Ibidem, 92.
7. Ibidem, 93.
8. Ibidem, 92, 94.
9. Widdowson, *Next Class*, 35-36.
10. Mason, letter to Groveham (own hand), summer holidays 1877, PNEU2Bpneu17.
11. Drake, 'Charlotte Mason at Bishop Otter Memorial College', 14-15.
12. Ibidem, 15; Davison log book.
13. Annual Report 1874, BO MS AOO3, BOC archives.
14. Huston, letter to Mason from 2 Herbert St, London NW, 23 October 1876, PNEU2Bpneu 23; John Thorley, 'Charlotte Mason; the Development of a Philosophy of Education 1860-1890', Part 3, 61 in Smith (ed.), *Essays on Charlotte Mason*, 61.
15. McGregor, *Bishop Otter*, 96-97 and 103.
16. Miss Trevor quoted in ibidem, 114.
17. C.M. Mason, *The Forty Shires: Their History, Scenery, Arts and Legends* (London: Hatchards and Co., 1880; 2nd edn 1881), 379-380.
18. Mason's description of Chichester owes much to Kelly's PO Directory of 1867, WSRO; *Bishop Otter Memorial College Magazine*, BO SU 001/023.
19. Ian Ker, *John Henry Newman: A Biography* (Oxford University Press, 2009); Elisabeth Jay, *Faith and Doubt in Victorian Britain* (Hampshire and London: Macmillan Education Ltd, 1986), 24-27; Keble family memoirs in Edith Olivier, *Four Victorian Ladies of Wiltshire* (Dorset: Semley Publishing, 1945/6), 24-29; Bishop Otter Practising School log book, Chichester ref. E35C/12/1, 1874–1913, WSRO; Burgon's quotation and details of Durnford's life were taken from Wikipedia to sketch in a feasible background to Mason's church life in Chichester, although there is no direct evidence.
20. E.M. Goulburn DD, *Thoughts on Personal Religion being a Treatise on the Christian Life in its two chief Elements*, Part 1, 8-23 (London: Rivingtons, 3rd edn 1863); flyleaf of Dean Goulburn's book, February 1866, from W. Read to Mason, PNEU2Apneu7.
21. McGregor, *Bishop Otter*, 94-95, 105.
22. Widdowson, *Next Class*, 10-11, 21-22, 36-37.
23. Ibidem, 35; McGregor, *Bishop Otter*, 95-96.
24. R.F. Drake, 'Charlotte Mason at Bishop Otter Memorial College, Part 2', *West Sussex History*, January 1989, 7.

25. Drake, 'Bishop Otter, Part 1', 15; McGregor, *Bishop Otter*, 98.
26. Miss Trevor's evidence to *The Royal Commission to Enquire into the Working of the Elementary Education Acts* (Cross Commission 1886–1888) in McGregor, *Bishop Otter*, 110-117.
27. Drake, 'Bishop Otter, Part 1', 10; F.C.A. Williams, 'Reminiscences', 57-58; Cholmondeley, *Story*, 12; census records, Otterton, 1871 and census, Southampton County, 1891. Fanny had a twin brother, Richard.
28. C.M. Mason, *Geographical Readers for Elementary Schools*, vol. 1 (London: Edward Stanford 1881), frontispiece.
29. Cholmondeley, *Story*, 12.
30. McGregor, *Bishop Otter*, 106.
31. General Committee Minutes 1876, BO MS AOO3; Annual Reports 1875 and 1876, BOC Archives.
32. Minutes of the Finance Committee 1877, BO MS A010.
33. McGregor, *Bishop Otter*, 98; Drake, 'Bishop Otter, Part 2', 8-9.
34. Ibidem; McGregor, *Bishop Otter*, 95-96; Bishop Otter College practising school log 1876, WSRO.
35. Deaconess Rosa Westmorland, letter to Kitching, 26 February 1924, CM51cmc454.
36. *West Sussex Journal*, Tuesday 16 January 1877 and *West Sussex Gazette*, Thursday 18 January 1877, sent by Drake to author, 15 August 1989.
37. Mason, letter to Groveham (own hand), 17 January 1877, PNEU2B pneu17; M.A. Coombs, 'Miss Read, an Important Influence on Charlotte Mason', *L'Umile Pianta*, Spring 2012.
38. Emily Brandreth, letter to Mason from Lucerne, 30 May 1877, PNEU2Cpneu46.
39. Kitching, 'The Beginning of Things'.
40. Mason, letter to Groveham from Otterbourne, Hants, autumn 1877, PNEU2Bpneu17.
41. McGregor, *Bishop Otter*, 102-105; McGregor did not find the 1877 BOC Annual report (see pp. 97 and 100), while Drake apparently read it (see 'Bishop Otter, Part 2', 9); BO MS A010 Finance Committee minutes 1877 and 12 March 1878; Telford Petrie, 'A Note on the Teaching of School Science', *Parents' Review*, vol. 39, no. 1, January 1928, 55-58.
42. Widdowson, *Next Class*, 35; McGregor, *Bishop Otter*, citing Miss Trevor's illuminating evidence, 109-114.
43. Ibidem, 115-116.
44. Drake, 'Bishop Otter, Part 2', 9: Drake found that the staff-student ratio was 1 to 13 when thirty-nine students were in residence in 1877; the Sub-Committee recorded Mason's resignation in March 1778; BOC MS AO29 account/cash book, 15 April 1878; McGregor, *Bishop Otter*, 101.
45. BOC school log book; Drake, 'Bishop Otter, Part 1', 10-11.
46. Frances Washington Epps, 'Our Daughters III: Work for Gentlewomen as Elementary School Teachers', *Parents' Review*, vol. 1, 1890 and PNEU2Cpneu46.

11. The Breakthrough in Bradford, 1879–1888 (pp. 135-155)

1. John Benson CRO, email to author, 27 March 2012. The high school was probably Queen's School for Girls (founded in 1877/8); Miriam David, *The State, the Family and Education* (London: Routledge and Kegan Paul, 1980), 119.
2. T.G. Rooper, 'The Modern Training of Girls', *School and Home Life: Essays and Lectures on Current Educational Topics* (London: A. Brown and Sons Ltd, n.d.), 303-304.

3. Mason, letter to Groveham (own hand), 20 March 1877, PNEU2Bpneu17; Thorley, 'Charlotte Mason' Part 3 in Smith (ed.), *Essays on Charlotte Mason*, 71-73.
4. Dr Foster's medical note, c. January 1878, PNEU2Bpneu17.
5. Joan Burstyn, *Victorian Education and the Ideal of Womanhood*, 74.
6. Mason, letter to Groveham from 15 Steyne (own hand), 20 March 1878, PNEU2Bpneu17; Drake, 'Bishop Otter, Part 2', 9-10.
7. Johanna Spyri, *Heidi: A Story for Children*, trans. Louise Brooks (London: Thomas Nelson, n.d.); Mason, letter to Groveham from Lucerne (own hand), 2 May 1878, PNEU2Bpneu17; Brandreth's itinerary for Mason, headed 'C.M.S.M.', 30 May 1877, PNEU2Cpneu46, shows Mason had added 'Shaw' to her name by 1877. Was she seeking a family connection, as Thomas Brandreth's middle name was Shaw?
8. Mason, letter to Groveham from Auteuil (own hand), n.d. summer 1878, PNEU2Bpneu17.
9. Groveham, letter to Kitching, 'Dates', n.d. 1923, PNEU2Bpneu31; Thorley, 'Charlotte Mason' Part 3, 73-76.
10. Mrs Winifred Smart, letter to Kitching, 3 November 1941, PNEU2Cpneu46.
11. Mason's notebook, CM1cmc9.
12. Bostridge, *Florence Nightingale*, on Lord Lawrence, 345-346, 401-404, 420, 484-485, 491, 513.
13. F. Nightingale, letter to Arthur Brandreth, 30 July 1879, PNEU2Apneu7.
14. Census, Clewer, Windsor, 1881 showed Brandreth and Maria, aka D'Arcy, probably misspelt as D'Obry; the 1891 census showed Brandreth with her brother Henry's family at Duckleburgh Rectory, Norfolk.
15. Census, central Bradford, 1871, recorded the Grovehams living at 17 Drewton Street.
16. Bradford Girls' Middle School (founded 1866), brochure (1), West Yorkshire Archive Service (WYAS), Bradford, ref. DB16/CA/7; see Kitching, Groveham notes, PNEU2Bpneu31.
17. Kelly's Directory (1881); West Riding of Yorkshire, PO Directory.
18. Census, Bradford, 1881, showed the Grovehams were now living at 2 Apsley Crescent, Manningham; brochure for Ladies' Collegiate School (2), WYAS, Bradford, ref. DB16/C4/7; Bradford PO Directory 1883.
19. Brochure for Ladies' Collegiate School (3) from WYAS stated that the school 'will be commenced on Wednesday September 10th 1879 from Mornington House, 2 Apsley Crescent'; the Boys' Collegiate School was in Lower Horton Lane; see Mason, *Home Education*, 8, for a critique of kindergarten methods.
20. Kitching, Groveham notes, PNEU2Bpneu31.
21. *Bradford Observer*, 3 March 1885; no other reports seen.
22. Groveham's letter to Kitching, 'Dates', n.d., PNEU2Bpneu31.
23. White's District Directory Part 1, Bradford, 1881; Bradford PO Directory 1891; 2 Apsley Crescent was then divided into flats; census, Yorkshire, Grassington, 1901; census, Woodbridge, 1911.
24. Russell, *Mason Genealogy*; Hannah Birchall's death certificate, 30 March 1876, Olney; Huldah J. Doyle's death certificate, 27 July 1902, Lewisham; *Entomologists' Monthly Magazine*, vol. XX1, 1884–1885, sent to author by Russell.
25. PNEU (ed.), 'Miss F.C.A. Williams'.
26. Williams, 'Reminiscences', *In Memoriam*, 58; White's Directory listed Williams appointment, 1881; Birchenough, *Elementary Education*, 146-160, 225-227.
27. Lucy Williams (Fanny's mother), letter to 'Dear Maria' (Mason), Xmas 1881, PNEU2Bpneu28.

28. Death certificate for John Groveham, 5 October 1882, Bradford Register Office.
29. PNEU (ed.), 'Miss F.C.A. Williams'; Drake, 'Bishop Otter, Part 1', 11; History of Watford Trade Directory 1884 in letter from Drake, c. January 1989; census, Fyfield, Southampton, 1891, confirmed that Williams was a training college superintendent; Mason, letters to Mrs A. Brooke in Dublin, 7 July 1890 and 17 July 1890, PNEU2Cpneu43; Brooke, letter to Mason, 17 July 1890, confirmed Williams was in Dublin, PNEU2Cpneu43.
30. Mr Joy, Hatchards Managing Director, to author by telephone, 26 January 1983; Hatchards, letters to Mason, 28 February 1880 and 19 March 1880, PNEU2Apneu5; Thorley, 'Charlotte Mason: The Development of a Philosophy of Education 1879–1890: The Bradford Years', Part 4 in Smith (ed.), 'Essays on Charlotte Mason', 82-112.
31. Mason, *The Forty Shires*, 42, 222, 224; the book was well reviewed in the *Morning Post* (6 January 1880), *Athenaeum* (26 March 1881) and several other papers at CM51cmc448.
32. Revd William Read, letter to Mason, 8 December 1880, PNEU2Apneu5.
33. A. Buckley, letter to Edward Stanford, 9 December 1880, PNEU2Apneu5.
34. Hatchards, letters to Mason, 28 and 29 June 1883, PNEU2Apneu5.
35. Memorandum between Stanford and Mason, 1 October 1880, PNEU2Apneu5.
36. Anonymous reader, letter to Stanford, n.d. c. mid-1880s, PNEUVIIpneu64; Helen Bentwich, letter to Mrs Franklin (with quotes), 2 April 1937; Lady Helen Cassel, letter to a horrified Franklin, 23 April 1937; Franklin, letter to Cassel, 28 April 1937, PNEU21pneu74; E. Bateson, *Charlotte Mason and the House of Education: A Perspective on the Role of Women as Educators in the Late 19th and Early 20th Centuries*, cited in Thorley, 'Charlotte Mason' Part 4, 97-108, listing Mason's modest royalties.
37. Mason, 'In Memoriam: T.G. Rooper', *Parents' Review*, 1903, PNEU2Apneu6; Mason, *Some Studies,* Appendix, 433-444.
38. Rooper, letter to Mason, 25 October 1884; see PNEU7pneu66 for his letters; articles at PNEU2Apneu6; he referred to Lord Macaulay's poem, 'How Horatius kept the Bridge, Lays of Ancient Rome'; no reviews of Mason's *Geographical Readers* found; Stanford, letter to Mason, 29 February 1901, when he reported £37 5s 5d loss on readers; Stanford, letter to Mason, 28 February 1903, reported the annual royalties for readers as only £2 2s since 1898 and offered the rights to cover his £60 loss, CM44cmc295.
39. Bradford Directories 1881; E.M. Willnott, Bradford Local Studies, conversation with author, 6 August 1982, described St Mark's and showed the Sunday school on an 1890 map; Bateson found Mason's pew receipt for 5s for one sitting (see *Women as Educators*, 70).
40. Groveham, letter to Kitching, 'Scraps', PNEU2Bpneu31; Mason's notes on the 'Reading Coterie' in Bradford, Kitching's hand, PNEU2Bpneu24; Cholmondeley, *Story*, 15.
41. E. Wynne, letter to Mason, 4 July 1881, PNEU2Bpneu28.
42. H. Ausubel, *In Hard Times: Reformers among the Late Victorians* (New York: Columbia Press, 1960), 64.
43. *Bradford Observer*, 28 September 1885 and 22 October 1885; Edith probably played but Mary Groveham became a piano teacher.
44. Mason visited the British Museum on 28 August 1885.
45. Kitching, 'The Beginning of Things'.
46. Young, *Portrait of an Age*, 2, 132-138; Mrs Sumner, *To the Mothers of the Higher Classes* (Winchester: Warren and Sons, 1891).

47. E. Wynne, letter to Mason, 31 March 1886, PNEU2Bpneu28.
48. Mason, *Home Education*, proof copy, annotated by C. Kegan Paul, CM51cmc416.
49. *Reading Mercury*, 1 January 1887, CM51pneu421.
50. Mary Wollstonecraft (1759–1797), *The Vindication of the Rights of Women* (1792) and *Thoughts on the Education of Daughters* (1787); the Swiss intellectual, Madame Necker de Saussure (1756–1841), wrote *L'Education Progressive* or *Étude du Course de la Vie* (1828) on educating children up to fourteen and intellectual and domestic education for women; Harriet Martineau (1802–1876) wrote *Household Education* (London: E. Moxon, 1848), to prepare men for work and women to be educated alongside domestic duties to become better wives and mothers; Sarah Stickney Ellis (1799–1872), a former Quaker, wrote extensively (e.g. *The Mothers of England; their Influence and Responsibility*, 1843), advising mothers on children's moral training; Emily Shirreff (1814–1897), *Intellectual Education and its Influence on Character and the Happiness of Women* (London: John Parker, 1858), giving a Froebelian perspective.
51. Mason, *Home Education,* viii, quoting G.H. Lewes (1817–1878), *The Physical Basis of Mind* (1877), in the second series, *The Problems of Life and Mind* (London, 1877); T.H. Huxley, 'Instruction in Physiology' (1877) in *Science and Education Essays, vol. III: Collected Essays* (London: Macmillan and Co., 1910).
52. Mason, *Home Education*, 3; M.V.C. Jeffreys, *John Locke: Prophet of Common Sense* (London: Methuen, 1967), 77-97, 100; John Locke, 'Some Thoughts Concerning Education' in Axtell (ed.), *The Educational Writings of John Locke*; Herbert Spencer, *Essays on Education Etc.* (London: J.M. Dent and Sons Ltd, 1861, 1949), 20-26; Dr W.B. Carpenter, *Principles of Mental Physiology* (Cambridge University Press, 2009); Rousseau, *Émile*; Pestalozzi, *Gertrude*; Paley, *Natural Theology,* 22, 32-34; R.H. Quick, *Essays on Educational Reformers* (London: Longmans Green, 1868; 1907), 447.
53. Mason, *Home Education*, 32, with 'Fragments', 368-369.
54. Carpenter, *Mental Physiology*, 345, 346-356; Locke, 'Education', 135, 140.
55. Mason, *Home Education*, 93, 84-105, 74-136.
56. Proverbs 2:6 (AV); Mason, *Home Education*, v, 7, 81-93.
57. Carpenter, *Mental Physiology*, 319-336; Mason, *Home Education*, 92 for T.H. Huxley's views on *artificial* reflex actions; Sigmund Freud (1856–1939), founder of psychoanalysis; J.S. Mill, *Autobiography* (London: Longmans Green, 1873).
58. Carpenter, *Mental Physiology*, 377; Mason, *Home Education,* 193-194 for attribution of Carpenter's paradigm to St Augustine; Essex Cholmondeley, 'I AM, I CAN, I OUGHT, I WILL', *L'Umile Pianta*, April 1957.
59. Mason, *Home Education,* 203-214.
60. Matthew Arnold, *Culture and Anarchy*, ed. J. Dover Wilson (1869; Cambridge University Press, 1984), 43-71; Ruskin, *Sesame and Lilies*, 148-160.
61. Mason, *Home Education,* 287-288.
62. Ibidem, 298-299; Coombs, *Some Obstacles,* chapter 5; M.A. Coombs, 'The Little Manual Called Home Education', WES/PNEU Journal, vol. 20, no. 3, October 1985.
63. White's Bradford Directory 1881, on Steinthal relatives, noted that Walmer Place used to abut Walmer Villas; Mrs Peggy Lane-Roberts (CMT 1935) (Lienie's granddaughter), letter to author, 22 April 1986; Francis Steinthal's obituary, *Ilkley Gazette*, 6 April 1934; Emeline Steinthal's obituary, *Wharfedale and Airedale Observer*, 12 August 1921; Dorothea Steinthal (Lienie's daughter) compiled a manuscript family record called *Dates from Old Diaries* (1883–1888), copied for author by Mrs Lane Roberts.

64. Dorothea Steinthal, *Dates from Old Diaries*; Petrie (Steinthal) family tree, *London Gazette*, Issue 29262, 13 August 1915, cited in David Faulders's family history research at www.faulder.org.uk.
65. C.M. Mason, 'In Memoriam: Mrs Steinthal', *Parents' Review*, vol. 32, September 1921.
66. Mason, letter to Steinthal (own hand), 23 August 1916, CM44cmc291.
67. L. Steinthal, letter to Mason from Beethoven Strasse, n.d. c. 1888, PNEU2Cpneu47.
68. D. Steinthal, letter to Kitching, 16 January 1950; Bostridge, *Florence Nightingale*, 164-166.
69. Lydia Hering, née Joss (CMT 1934), sent Kitching Alice Burn's (née Gates) memories of Mason's visit to Mrs Fleming's school by letter, n.d., PNEU2Bpneu19.
70. D. Steinthal, letter to Kitching, 25 September 1924 and 9 January 1950, CM51cmc419; P.H.J.H. Gosden, *How They Were Taught: An Anthology of Contemporary Learning and Teaching in England 1800-1950* (Oxford: Blackwell, 1969), 99-103.
71. Mason, 'In Memoriam: T.G. Rooper'; Mary Arnold, Matthew's niece and Miss Clough's former pupil at Eller How, was Mrs Humphry Ward, author of *Robert Elsmere* (London and New York: Macmillan and Co., 1888).
72. *Bradford Observer*, 6 September 1887; Mrs Munro, letter to Kitching, c. 1938, PNEU Archive.
73. Anon (Mason), 'A New Educational Departure', *Parents' Review*, vol. 1, no. 1, 1890 describes the Bradford meetings in full; Kitching, 'The History and Aims of the PNEU', *Parents' Review*, vol. 10, 1899, 411-29.
74. L. Steinthal, letter to Mason, c. 1888, PNEU2Cpneu47.
75. Sir Thomas Acland (father of Mrs Hart-Davis and Mrs Anson), letters to Mason, 1896 and 1897, PNEU2Apneu8.
76. Mary L. Hart-Davis, letter to Mason, 6 November 1887, PNEU2Apneu8.
77. Lord and Lady Aberdeen, *'We Twa': Reminiscences of Lord and Lady Aberdeen*, vol. 1 (London: W. Collins and Son, 1925), 97; Marjorie Pentland, *A Bonnie Fechter: The Life of Ishbel Marjoribanks, Marchioness of Aberdeen and Temair GBD LLD JP 1857–1939* (London: Batsford, 1952), 72.
78. Lady Aberdeen, letter to Mason, 12 December 1887 (not 1886), PNEU2Bpneu15.
79. The Rt Revd W. Boyd Carpenter, *Some Pages of My Life* (London: Williams and Norgate, 1911), 292.
80. D. Steinthal, *Dates from Old Diaries*, 1889.

12. 'Education is an Atmosphere, a Discipline, a Life', 1888–1893 (pp. 156-175)

1. Lady Aberdeen, letter to Mason, 18 May 1888 and 5 October 1888, PNEU2Bpneu15; C.M. Mason, 'Character in Children', *Murray's Magazine*, vol. 4, July-December 1888; *Macmillan's Magazine*, November 1889–April 1890.
2. Mason, letter to Archbishop Benson, 29 April and 23 May 1889, and Benson, letter to Mason, 20 May 1889, Archbishop Benson Archive, Lambeth Palace Library, London.
3. Elsie Kitching, Secretary at the House of Education, 'The History and Aims of the P.N.E.U.', *Parents' Review*, vol. 10, 1899, 8-12; Kitching, 'The Beginning of Things', 127-133.
4. Editor (Mason), 'Recollections of Miss Clough and her Connexion with the P.N.E.U.', *Parents' Review*, vol. 8, no. 1, 1897; Anna Laetitia Barbauld (1743–1825) wrote the influential *Lessons for Children*, 4 vols, n.d., and *Evenings at Home* (1793), 6 vols, encapsulating education in stories and fables via curiosity, observation and reasoning.

5. Mason, 'Miss Clough'; Mason, letter to Oscar Browning (O.B.), November 1889, OB/1/1069/A, King's College Library, Cambridge (KCLC): 'I should like much to come to tea with you, Sunday Nov 10 and Chapel would be an added pleasure.'
6. Clough, letter to O.B., November 1876, OB/1/1069/A, KCLC; Pam Hirsch and Mark Macbeth, *Teacher Training at Cambridge; the Initiatives of Oscar Browning and Elizabeth Hughes* (Portland: Woburn Press, 2004), 608.
7. *Oscar Browning: A Biography* (London: John Murray, 1983) by Ian Anstruther discusses Browning's homosexuality.
8. Mason, letter to O.B., 17 December 1889, asked O.B. to join the Cambridge PNEU committee, OB/1/1069/A, KCLC.
9. Cholmondeley, *Story*, 21, with 'Draft Proof' amendments, 23-25; Dr Benjamin E. Bernier-Rodriguez found the phrase 'Education is an Atmosphere, A Discipline, A Life' in Anon, *Oxford Democratic and Popular* (February 1890); Benjamin E. Bernier, *Education for the Kingdom: An Exploration of the Religious Foundation of Charlotte Mason's Educational Philosophy* (PhD thesis, Lancaster University, 2009), 61, published by Lulu Press USA in 2011 with the same title.
10. Mason, letter to O.B. (dictated), 5 December 1889, OB/1/1069/A, KCLC.
11. McGregor, *Bishop Otter*, 115.
12. First provisional Executive Committee Meeting (ECM), 18 January 1890, Minute Book (1890–1899), CM34cmc233 or cmc235; Kitching, 'History', 13.
13. Mason, 'Miss Clough'; Cholmondeley, *Story*, 26; Quick, *Educational Reformers*; F. Storr (ed.), *The Life and Remains of the Revd. R.H. Quick* (Cambridge University Press, 1899).
14. Mason, 'Miss Clough'.
15. 'The Parents' National Educational Union', *Parents' Review*, vol. 1, no. 3, April 1890, 40, printed as an announcement.
16. Kitching, 'History and Aims', 13-14.
17. Ibidem; Mason, letter to O.B., headed 'The Parents' Review', n.d. c. 1890: 'Financial matters have been worrying.'; Mason, letter to O.B., 25 March 1891, OB/1/1O69/A, KCLC.
18. Charlotte Mason, *How God Answers Prayers, illustrated by the Story and Origins and Development of the House of Rest* (London: Morgan Scott, 1909); E. Lawrence, *Friedrich Froebel and English Education* (London University Press, 1952); *Parents' Review* (vols 1-77) became the PNEU Journal in 1978, and then the WES/PNEU Journal from vol. 14 in 1979 to vol. 21 in 1986.
19. PNEU First Annual Report (1892), CM13cmc95, listing donations worth £150 19s 6d for *Parents' Review*; PNEU Annual Report 1900, CM43cmc273; 'Our Work', *Parents' Review*, vol. 11, 1900.
20. Mason, letter to O.B., n.d. c. 1890, OB/1/1O69/A, KCLC; Clough, letter to Mason, 4 March 1890 and 8 October 1890, CM44cmc293.
21. Mason, 'In Memoriam: T.G Rooper', *Parents' Review*, vol. 14, 1903, 481-489; Kitching, 'History', 13.
22. M. Shaw, 'Ivàn Ivànovitch: In Memoriam' (after *Dramatic Idylls* by Robert Browning (1812–1889)), *Parents' Review*, vol. 3, 1890; L. Steinthal, letter to Mason), n.d. c. June 1890, PNEU2Bpneu47.
23. Pentland, *Bonnie Fechter*, 84; Lady Aberdeen, letter to Mason, 7 February 1891, PNEU2Bpneu15.
24. 'The Parents' National Educational Union', *Parents' Review*.
25. ECM minutes, 14 February 1890, 4 June 1890, 9 July 1890 and 23 April 1891, CM34cmc233.

26. Wynne, letter to Mason from Forest Gate Vicarage, 4 July 1891, PNEU Archive.
27. Mason, letter to O.B., 7 July 1891, OB/1/1O69/A, KCLC.
28. ECM minutes, 9 July 1891; Editor (Mason), 'Obituary of Edward Wynne', *Parents' Review*, vol. 3, no. 8, 1892/3; PNEU Annual Report 1892, CM43cmc272.
29. Kitching, 'History', 20.
30. PNEU Annual Report 1892, 12-13; Helen Webb, 'A Few Recollections', *In Memoriam*, 40; Helen Webb, *Children and the Stress of Life* (London: PNEU, 1929).
31. PNEU Annual Report 1892, 13; Dr A.T. Schofield, *Physiology for Schools and Handbook of Physiology* (London: Cassell and Co., n.d.).
32. Dr A.T. Schofield, 'A New Education', *The Girls' Own Paper*, 1882; Dr A.T. Schofield, *The Mind of a Woman* (London: Methuen, 1919), 16, 44, 51, 93.
33. Mason in PNEU Annual Report 1892, 13.
34. Mason, *The Forty Shires*, 26.
35. Carnie, *Lakeland's Heart,* chapter 14.
36. Census, Ambleside, 1891; Bell, 'Recollections'; Frederick Middleton, 'Printer's Account' in Elizabeth L. Molyneux (ed.), *PUS Diamond Jubilee 1891–1951* [pamphlet] (1951), CM17cmc13.
37. 'The House of Education', *Parents' Review*, vol. 2, no. 4, 1891–1892.
38. Ruskin, *Sesame and Lilies,* 135-137; Editor (Mason), 'Tante in the Home', *Parent's Review,* vol. 2 no. 7, 1891–1892; Cholmondeley, *Story,* 32-38.
39. Editor (Mason), 'The Parents' Review School', *Parents' Review*, vol. 2, no. 4, 1891–1892; 'Our Work', *Parents' Review*, vol. 2, no. 5, 1891–1892.
40. Dorothy Richardson, *Pilgrimage*, vol. 1 (London: Virago, 1915; 1979), 241; Hughes, *Victorian Governess*, 198; by 1898, there were sixty high schools.
41. 'Notes and Queries', *Parents' Review,* vol. 1, no. 4, 1890–1891, 317; J.A. Banks, *Parenthood: A Study of Family Planning among the Victorian Middle Classes* (London: Routledge and Kegan Paul, 1954), 190-196: in 1870 there were around 12 preparatory schools and 400 by 1900.
42. PRS brochure version 1, PNEU2Bpneu41 – almost identical to 'Entry Form for Home Schoolrooms' in *A Liberal Education for All: The Practical Working Particulars of the PNEU, the PUS and The House of Education* [pamphlet], 14, PNEU23pneu161.
43. 'Our Work', *Parents' Review*, vol. 1, nos 2 and 9, 1891–1892; Mrs Spencer Curwen, 'What is Tonic Sol Fa?', *Parents' Review*, vol. 2, no. 7, 1891–1892; Mrs Franklin's report on PRS, First PNEU Annual Conference, *Parents' Review*, vol. 8, no. 8, 1897; *Aesop's Fables,* c. fifth century BC; Plutarch, *Lives of Noble Grecians and Romans* (first century AD), trans. Sir Thomas North (1579), from Amyot's French.
44. PRS fees notebook, PUS file 1891–1892, CM23cmc155; correct numbers of those in PRS/PUS remain unclear; Lane-Roberts, conversation with author, 21 November 1983.
45. Kitching, 'The Day's Work', 71.
46. Mason, *Parents and Children,* dedicated to PNEU members 'as an expression of the affection and reverence with which their efforts inspire her' (see frontispiece).
47. Quoted in Mrs Franklin's PRS report.
48. Mrs Clement Parsons, *The Principles and Objectives of the Parents, National Educational Union: An Address* [talk and pamphlet], delivered to the International Congress of Women, published by the PNEU (London: Women's Printing Society, 3rd rev. edn 1899), 15-16; CM48cmc35.
49. Jonathan Gathorne-Hardy, *The Rise and Fall of the British Nanny* (London: Hodder and Stoughton, 1972), 178; Theresa McBride, 'As the Twig is Bent: the Victorian Nanny' in A.S. Wohl (ed.), *The Victorian Family* (London: Croom Helm, 1978).

50. PNEU Annual Report 1892, 24, CM13cmc95.
51. Cholmondeley, *Story*, 37-8, cites Violet Parker's unreferenced memories.
52. Ibidem, 38; Bell, 'Recollections'; Carnie, *Lakeland's Heart*, 272; first House of Education syllabus, advance proof, CM13cmc95; some, if not all, the lecturers were initially unpaid.
53. PNEU Annual Report 1892, 24-28, CM13cmc95; François Gouin's method began with listening, then speaking, then writing.
54. Lilian Gray (CMT 1896), 'Early Days of Scale How', *L'Umile Pianta*, April 1968.
55. T.G. Rooper, *Report of Her Majesty's Inspector of Schools on the House of Education at Ambleside*, 20 November 1892; 'Our Work', *Parents' Review*, vol. 3, nos 11 and 12, 1892–1893, 949, and PNEU General Annual Report 1893, 24-28, CM43cmc272.
56. O.O., 'Notes and Queries', *Parents' Review*, vol. 1, no. 3, 1890–1891; M.L.H.D. (Mrs Hart-Davis) in 'By the Way', *Parents' Review*, vol. 1, no. 3, 1890–1891.
57. Mothers' Education Course (MEC), Programmes and Syllabus, PNEU Annual Report 1907, CM43cmc275; Mason, article on the MEC, *Parents' Review*, vol. 2, 1892.
58. Agnes B. Kinnear, letters to 'Madam' (probably Mrs Anson), 17 November 1898 and 21 November 1898, PNEU2Bpneu29.
59. Question papers, MEC examinations (1891–1914), CM22cmc143 and CM51cmc444.
60. Beatrice Wolrych-Whitmore, letter to Mrs Anson, 5 May 1897 and 17 May 1897, PNEU2Bpneu29.
61. C.S. Bremner, *The Education of Women and Girls in Great Britain* (London: Swann Sonnenschein, 1897).
62. MEC registers 1896–1907 and 1910–1914, CM22cmc143.
63. Mrs Anson, 'The Mothers' Educational Course', *Parents' Review*, vol. 8, no. 8, 1897; mothers' letters, PNEU2Bpneu29; Christina de Bellaigue, 'Charlotte Mason, Home Education and the Parents' National Educational Union in the late nineteenth century', *Oxford Review of Education*, August 2015, 13-17 on the MEC (read in draft with permission).
64. PNEU Annual Report 1893, 7-10, CM43cmc272.
65. Recorded in ECM minutes, 1893, CM34cmc233.
66. Drake, 'Bishop Otter, Part 2', 10; Miss Schofield needed a 'rest' but returned to Bishop Otter as senior governess in 1895.
67. Essex Cholmondeley, *Elsie Kitching 1870–1955: Recollections*, 4-5; Cholmondeley, *Story*, 46-48.
68. The Revd Dr Harold Costley-White, *Elsie Kitching*, 6.
69. Irene Stephens, *Elsie Kitching*, 9.
70. Mary Yates, *Elsie Kitching*, 18.

13. The 1894 Challenge and the Mason-Franklin Alliance, 1894–1897 (pp. 176-197)

1. Mason called her student governesses 'bairns', Scottish for 'child'. Drake, 'Bishop Otter, Part 2', 10; Cholmondeley, *Story*, 48; PNEU ECM minutes, 18 December 1893, CM34cmc233 (1890–1899).
2. PNEU AGM Report, 17 June 1892, CM43cmc272; ECM minutes, 7 June 1892, CMC34cmc233.
3. Helen Webb, 'A Few Recollections', *In Memoriam*, 40.

4. Michael Franklin, 'In Memoriam: Helen Webb', *Parents' Review*, vol. 37, no. 5, 1926; Mason, letter to Franklin, 23 November 1898, 16 January 1901 and 21 May 1901, CM50cmc393 (all CM50cmc393 letters are typed copies from Franklin); Gibbon, *Netta*, 50-52, 137.
5. Cholmondeley, *Story*, 48-54; Mason, *Parents and Children*, chapter 25, 268-279; John Ruskin, *Mornings in Florence* (1875–1877); *Summa Theologica* by Thomas Aquinas (1225–1274) was his compendium of Catholic teaching on the existence of God, creation, man's purpose, Christ and the sacraments.
6. 'David Margesson, 1st Viscount Margesson', *Wikipedia*, 11 June 2015, https://en.wikipedia.org/wiki/David_Margesson,_1st_Viscount_Margesson, for information on his mother Lady Isabel's ancestry; E. Shirreff, 'What is Women's Work in the World?', reprinted from the *Journal of Education* (n.d.) in 'By the Way', *Parents' Review*, vol. 1, no. 4, 1890–1891; E. Shirreff, *The Kindergarten at Home* (London: Allen, 1876).
7. Editorial note appended to Lady Isabel Margesson, 'Training Lessons to Mothers', *Parents' Review*, vol. 4, no. 1, 1893–1894.
8. Editor (Mason), 'P.N.E.U. Philosophy', *Parents' Review*, vol. 3, no. 5, 1892–1893.
9. ECM minutes, 19 December 1893, CM34cmc233, 1890–1899.
10. Lady Isabel Margesson, *What is the P.N.E.U?* (1892), quoted in Mason, *Ambleside July 9th 1894* [pamphlet], PNEU2bpneu3.
11. Mason, *Home Education* (1899), 76; compare with *Home Education* (15th edn, 1942), 99.
12. ECM minutes, 21 April 1893, CM34cmc233; the five guineas for the former students' two-year PNEU membership was later altered to life. PNEU parents paid 10s per annum.
13. PNEU AGM Report 1893, CM43cmc272 (1892–1896).
14. ECM minutes, 18 December 1893, 19 January 1894, 1 February 1894, 24 February 1894, 7 March 1894, 18 April 1894, 2 May 1894 and 8 June 1894, CM34cmc233 (1890–1899): Mortimer Margesson attended and supported his wife; Joyce Coombs, *George and Mary Sumner: Their Life and Times* (London: Sumner Press, 1965), 105-106, 108-124; the Mothers' Union shared the PNEU's aim of raising standards of Christian child training; J. Coombs noted there were 4,927 MU branches, with 234,714 worldwide members and associates by 1904 (see p. 137).
15. Mason, letter to Alfred Schofield, 16 May 1894, missing from CM51cmc439 and cmc440 PNEU Archive; William L. Mason, letters to C.M. Mason regarding the lease of Scale How, 6 August 1895, PNEU2Bpneu18. He was *not* Charlotte's half-brother William Leckey Mason; the 1901 Ambleside census showed he was born at Ulverston in 1865.
16. Blanche Whitaker-Thompson, 'Memories', *In Memoriam*, 38-40.
17. Gibbon, *Netta*, 36-7; a *chela* is a guru's pupil or disciple in Hindi.
18. Ibidem, 43.
19. Ibidem, 42 and 44. *Schwärmerei* is not a polite term in German!; Lillian Faderman, *Surpassing the Love of Men: Romantic Friendship and Love between Women of the Renaissance to the Present Day* (London: Junction Books, 1981), 170-174, 184-189: Faderman claimed that twentieth-century biographers failed to understand the subtleties of Victorian romantic friendships; Cholmondeley, *Story*, 52-54.
20. Matthew Arnold, *Culture and Anarchy*, ed. J. Dover Wilson (Cambridge University Press, 1869), 68-71.
21. Ibidem, 129, 137.

22. ECM minutes, 6 June 1894, CM34cmc233; quoted in 1893 AGM Report, *Parents' Review*, vol. 4, 1893, 373, and at CM43cmc272; Oscar Browning, *An Introduction to the History of Educational Theories*.
23. AGM Report 1894, *Parents' Review*, vol. 5, no. 5, 1894–1895, 32, and at CM43cmc272.
24. Mason, *Parents and Children*, 225; Matthew Arnold, *A French Eton or Middle Class Education and the State* (London: Macmillan and Co, 1864).
25. Editor (Mason), 'P.N.E.U. Principles' (read at the 1894 AGM), *Parents' Review*, vol. 5, no. 6, 1894–1895; Mason, *Parents and Children*, chapter 21, 225-232.
26. Mortimer Margesson offered the amendment (ECM minutes, 3 July 1894, CM34cmc233).
27. Lady Isabel quoted in Mason's pamphlet, *Ambleside 9th July 1894*, PNEU2cpneu36; 'the little manual' was *Home Education*.
28. ECM minutes, 18 July 1894, CM34cmc233.
29. Borrer, letter to Mason, 23 January 1895, PNEU2Bpneu18.
30. Lady Isabel, letter to Mason, 8 August 1894, PNEU2Cpneu36.
31. Lady Isabel's granddaughter, Gay, Lady Charteris, letter to author, 18 February 1987, author's copy.
32. Mason, *Parents and Children*, 232.
33. ECM minutes, 27 June 1894 and 18 July 1894, attended by Mason and Franklin, CM34cmc233.
34. Webb, 'Recollections', *In Memoriam*, 41.
35. Helen Webb's manuscript diary of her Ambleside visit, September 1894, CM2cmc29; Barbara Crossley, *The Armitts: Sophia and her Sisters* (Ambleside: Armitt Trust, 2012), 21-25.
36. R.A.P. (Pennethorne), 'Miss Mason of the House of Education', *In Memoriam*, 74.
37. Mrs Dallas Yorke, 'The House of Education', *Parents' Review*, vol. 8, no. 8, 1897–1898.
38. Kitching quoted in Cholmondeley, *Story*, 56-57; Mason's rooms were warm and comfortable!
39. Josephine Kamm, *How Different from Us* (London: Bodley Head, 1958), 192; Lilian Gray (CMT 1896), 'Early Days of Scale How', *L'Umile Pianta*, April 1968; D.C. Bernau (CMT 1923), 'An Easter Egg Remembers', *L'Umile Pianta*, Winter 1978, 1 ('Easter eggs' were students, accepted at Easter, who sat finals a term short); Doreen Russo (CMT 1937), *Charlotte Mason: A Pioneer of Sane Education: the Origins of the PNEU, the PUS and the Charlotte Mason Teachers* (Ambleside: Armitt Trust, n.d. 1990s); Doreen Russo's 'Pianta Memories' for author; Charlotte Mason College – PUS Diamond Jubilee Report (1891–1951), CM17cmc113.
40. P.M. Bowser (CMT 1914), 'My First Crit', *L'Umile Pianta*, Summer 1973, 6.
41. M. Gladding (CMT 1913), 'Charlotte Mason in 1923', *L'Umile Pianta*, Spring 1973, 7.
42. Eirene Manders (CMT 1922), letter to Nicholas Tucker with personal memories, n.d. c. 1987, copy with author; M.C. Harvey (CMT 1911), 'Flower Monitress', *L'Umile Pianta*, Summer 1973, 4.
43. Eileen Jay, *The Armitt Story, Ambleside* (Ambleside: Loughrigg Press, Armitt Society, 1998), xiii, xiv, 1-4, 6, 7, 10-12, 15, 18-19.
44. Bernau, 'Easter Egg'.
45. Mason, letter to Franklin, July 1895, CM50cmc393.
46. Gibbon, *Netta*, 5-6, 10-12, 17-20, 28-9, 47, 100-102, 135; Michael Franklin, conversation with author, 13 December 1983; Franklin, letters to Mason, 7 February 1894 and 16 December 1894, PNEU2Apneu12.

47. Gibbon, *Netta*, 42 (her school class started in 1894, *not* 1892); Winifred Kitching (CMT 1893), 'A London and Rickmansworth P.N.E.U. School', *L'Umile Pianta*, April 1957; 'Miss Winifred Kitching', *L'Umile Pianta*, April 1968.
48. Mason, letter to Franklin, 30 April 1896, CM50cmc393.
49. Mason, *Home Education*, Lecture III: 'Habit is Ten Natures', 74-106; Mason, *Some Studies*, 3-109.
50. Mason, letters to Franklin, 20 February 1897 and 3, 8, 14, 25, 27 and 28 March 1897, CM50cmc393.
51. Mason, letter to Franklin, 19 April 1897, CM50cmc393; Gibbon, *Netta*, 157; Mason, 'Docility and Authority', *Parents' Review*, vol. 8, no. 5, 1897, reprinted in C.M. Mason, *School Education* (London: Kegan Paul, Trench, Trübner and Co. Ltd, 1904; 3rd edn 1917), 20-22.
52. Mason, letter to Franklin, 21 May 1897, CM50cmc393.
53. Russell emailed this passage to the author from *The Times Digital Archive* (1785–1985), 27 May 1897, 14; C.M. Mason, 'P.N.E.U. Teaching in the Branches', Part I 'Moral and Religious', Part 2, 'Mental and Physical', *Parents' Review*, vol. 8, no. 8, 1897.
54. T.G. Rooper, 'The P.N.E.U. and the Poorer Classes', *Parents' Review*, vol. 8, no. 8, 1897; T.G. Rooper, 'The Tree of Knowledge and the Tree of Life', *Parents' Review*, vol. 9, no. 8, 1898.
55. Anon, 'Some Reflections on the P.N.E.U. Conference', *Parents' Review*, vol. 8 no. 7, 1897.
56. Franklin, letter to Mason, 30 May 1897, PNEU2Apneu12.
57. Mason, letter to Franklin, 31 May 1897, CM50cmc393; Dante's 'humble rush' symbolised the humility expected of the bairns – in one of *Aesop's Fables*, the rush, unlike the oak, survived by bending before the wind; in *Charlotte Mason: A Pioneer of Sane Education*, Doreen Russo explains the derivation from Dante's 'Purgatorio', Canto I, 11-13.
58. Lane-Roberts, letter to author, 21 November 1987, author's copy.
59. Mason, letter to Franklin, 8 August 1897, CM50cmc393.
60. Mason, letter to Franklin, 8 March 1898, CM50cmc393.

14. The PNEU Educational Philosopher, 1898–1905 (pp. 198-220)

1. M.H., ex-student and PUS pupil, *In Memoriam* (no. IV), 92.
2. Mason, letter to Franklin, 18 April 1897; on 23 April 1898, CM50cmc393, in which she wrote, 'Fanny is a joy to the Principal.' All Mason's letters to Franklin at CM50cmc393 are typed copies.
3. Census, St Mary's, Ambleside, 1901; Violet Curry in *Elsie Kitching 1870–1955: Recollections*, 19.
4. Cholmondeley, *Story*, 59.
5. Gibbon, *Netta*, 37.
6. J. Van Straubenzee, 'In Praise of Flitters', *L'Umile Pianta*, Spring 1973, 14; T.H. Barrow, 'Miss Mason's Love of the Country Drives', *In Memoriam*, 79-81.
7. Margery Gladding (CMT 1913), *Elsie Kitching: Recollections*, 8.
8. W.P. Primrose, 'Charlotte Mason Remembered', *L'Umile Pianta*, Spring 1973.
9. Bernau, 'Easter Egg', 15; Barrow, 'Country Drives', 80; Kitching, letter to Mrs Annie Harris (née Armitt), 1 January 1921, PNEU2Cpneu44.
10. Cholmondeley, *Story*, 59.
11. Mason, letter to Franklin, 23 April 1898, CM50cmc393.

12. Anon (Madge Franklin), Part III (no. VI): 'Childhood Memories of Miss Mason', *In Memoriam*, 94-5.
13. Mason, letter to Franklin, 20 August 1905, CM50cmc393.
14. Mason, letter to Franklin, 20 September 1905, CM50cmc393.
15. Mason, letter to Franklin, 23 April 1898, CM50cmc393.
16. Dorothy Cooke (CMT 1913), conversation with author, 11 October 1985; F.E. Garrard (CMT 1922), 'A 1921 Junior Recollects', *L'Umile Pianta*, April 1972, 7, a parody of Rudyard Kipling's 'A Smuggler's Song': 'Them that asks no questions isn't told a lie! Watch the wall my darling while the Gentlemen go by.'
17. Sheila Mary (CMT 1922), conversation with author; Beryl French (CMT 1922), conversation with author in Bristol, 19 September 1985.
18. Cooke (CMT 1913), conversation with author, 11 October 1985, and Sheila Mary, conversation with author.
19. Charlotte M. Mason, *The Saviour of the World* (London: Kegan Paul, Trench, Trübner and Co. Ltd, 1914), vol. 6, no. XVIII, 40; Cholmondeley, *Story*, chapter 10, 179-195, 'Meditations' cites poems.
20. Mineral baths cards (CM2cmc21) indicate Mason started them in 1896; prescriptions from Bad Nauheim and Ambleside, in Cook's international travelling tickets folder, CM2cmc22; Dr H.C.M. Walton, letters to author, 10 April 1982, 24 September 1982, 16 May 1983 and 3 June 1983 with notes, author's copies; Charlotte Mason's death certificate, CM1cmc3; Mrs Geraldine Walton confirmed the traditional belief in Mason's heart trouble on 10 April 1984.
21. Dr Walton, conversation with author, 10 April 1984; Mason, letter to Franklin from Villa Langsdorf, 12 August 1900, CM50cmc393, suggests that Dr Schott and colleagues believed Mason had chronic heart disease; Walton papers to be deposited in PNEU Archive, Armitt Library.
22. Violet Curry (CMT 1912), 'Charlotte Mason in 1923', *L'Umile Pianta*, Spring 1973, 7.
23. Mason, letter to Franklin, 20 May 1901, CM50cmc393.
24. E.K. Manders (CMT 1922), 'Charlotte Mason in 1923', *L'Umile Pianta*, Spring 1973, 8; Psalm 111:4, Book of Common Prayer.
25. M.H., 'Childhood Memories', no. IV, and Anon (Madge Franklin), no. VI, both from *In Memoriam*, 92, 95.
26. Cholmondeley, *Story*, 86; A. Whyte, Jacob Behman, CM1cmc12; originating in Iran, the Bahai religion peacefully proclaimed the oneness of humankind and all religion; Revd K.J. Cove, letter to author regarding Revd Frank Lewis, 17 September 1983, author's copy.
27. Cooke, conversation with author; Cholmondeley on 'Meditations', *Story*, 179-195.
28. Cholmondeley, conversation with author, 5 April 1982.
29. Gibbon, *Netta*, 55-56; Lynda Powell, *Fred Yates, Notes for an Exhibition at the Armitt Museum Nov 2001–Feb 2002,* Armitt Museum; Scale How students' diary/log, October 1901; CM9cmc61; students' letters to *Diamond Jubilee Magazine* (1891–1951), CM17cmc113; Mary Yates's diary (1907), CM17cmc123.
30. Cholmondeley, *Story*, 84-86; students' log, October 1901, CM9cmc61.
31. Franklin, letter to Mrs Walton, chair, Charlotte Mason Foundation Council, c. 16 July 1958, CM45cmc316, enclosing Mason's copied letters. They ring true.
32. ICW (ed.), *Women in a Changing World* (London: Routledge and Kegan Paul, 1966), 18-21; Franklin's scrapbook on ICW, May 1913, CM15cmc106; Lady Aberdeen was president 1904 to 1920 and Mrs Franklin from 1925 to 1927.
33. Mason, letter to Franklin, c. December 1898, CM50cmc393; Mason finally capitulated and approved PNEU affiliation with the NUWW in 1922. See Deani

A. Neven Van Pelt and Meghan Van Pelt, 'L'Umile Pianta: Charlotte Mason Educators and the "Humble Plant" from 1896-1923' in Smith (ed.), *Essays on Charlotte Mason,* 270.

34. Mary Ward founded the Women's National Anti-Suffrage League in 1908.
35. Parsons, *The Principles and Objectives of the Parents' National Educational Union*, ii, 4-24.
36. Mason, letter to Franklin, 16 August 1899, CM50cmc393.
37. Editor (Mason), 'School Books and How they Make for Education', *Parents' Review,* vol. 11, no. 7, 1900; *The Republic of Plato*, trans. F.M. Cornford (Oxford: Clarendon Press, 1941), Part II, 'Stories of Heroes'.
38. Richardson, *Pilgrimage,* vol. 3, 371.
39. Mrs M.E. Boole, 'The Preparation of the Unconscious Mind for Science', *Parents' Review*, vol. 10, no. 7, 1899, with discussion; A.T. Schofield, *The Unconscious Mind* (London: Swan Sonnenschein, 1898); Mason, *School Education* (3rd edn 1917), 113-115, her counterblast; Boole, 'Natural Priesthood', *Parents' Review*, vol. 10, 1899, said education's aim was 'to secure the closest possible harmony between conscious and unconscious cerebration'.
40. Dudley Barker, *G.K. Chesterton: A Biography* (London: Constable, 1973), 80.
41. Franklin, handwritten letter to Mason, 7 March 1900, PNEU2Apneu12.
42. Mason to Franklin, 9 March 1900, CM50cmc393; Franklin's diaries (lent by the late Joe Franklin, grandson), 17 February 1900 and 29 March 1900.
43. PNEU Annual Report 1900, 14, CM43cmc273; Joyce Coombs, *George and Mary Sumner*, 105-110 and 196.
44. ECM minutes, 7 November 1900 and 11 December 1900, CM34cmc235; Steinthal resigned as honorary organising secretary of the PNEU on 8 June 1903.
45. Franklin, handwritten letter to Mason, 7 December 1900, PNEU2Apneu12.
46. L. Steinthal, letter to Mason, 13 November 1901, and L. Steinthal, letter to Mason, 31 January 1902, PNEU2Apneu47.
47. Mason, letter to Franklin, 16 January 1901, CM50cmc393; Arnold, *Culture*, 48: culture is 'an inward condition of mind and spirit'.
48. The Hon. Mrs E.L. Franklin, 'The Home Training of Children', *Parents' Review*, vol. 19, no. 12, 1908, and *Parents' Review*, vol. 20, no. 1, 1909; Gibbon, *Netta*, 10: in childhood, Franklin had narrated the rabbi's sermon to him the following week.
49. Mason, letter to Franklin, 20 May 1901, CM50cmc393.
50. Franklin, handwritten letter to Mason, 6 June 1902, PNEU2Apneu12; Mason, letter to Franklin, June 1902, CM50cmc393; Mrs Ennis Richmond, 'Our Relations with Children', *Parents' Review*, vol. 13, 1902.
51. Editor (Mason), 'Education, the Science of Relations', *Parents' Review*, vol. 13, 1902.
52. Mason, letter to Franklin, 1 June 1903, CM50cmc393; H.F.'s diaries, 15 February, 11 April and 8 June 1903.
53. Editor (Mason), 'Studies serve for Delight, for Ornament & for Ability: A P.N.E.U. Manifesto', *Parents' Review*, vol. 14, no. 10, 1903; Francis Bacon, *Essays* (London: J.M. Dent and Sons, 1597; 1962), 150-151; Mason, *School Education,* 214, 271-300.
54. Mason, letter to Franklin, 17 June 1903, CM50cmc393.
55. 'Lady A', Netta's nickname, was teasingly linked to Sir Augustus Harris (1852–1896), a British actor, impresario and playwright; Mason, letter to Franklin, 23 September 1903, CM50cmc393.
56. Curtis and Boultwood, *English Education*, 123-126, 221-226.

57. 'Discussion on P.N.E.U. Manifesto', *Parents' Review*, vol. 14, no. 12, 1903.
58. Franklin, handwritten letter to Mason, 17 December 1903, PNEU2Apneu12.
59. Franklin, handwritten letter to Mason, 21 December 1903, PNEU2Apneu12.
60. Franklin's diary, 20 January 1894; ECM minutes, 28 January 1904, CM34cmc235.
61. Mason, letters to Franklin and Executive Committee members, 15 January 1904, CM50cmc393.
62. Mason, letter to Executive Committee, 8 February 1904, CM50cmc393.
63. Franklin's diary, 8 February 1904; Franklin, letter to Mason, 7 February 1904, PNEU2Apneu12.
64. Mason, letter to Executive Committee, 12 February 1904, CM50cmc393.
65. Mason, letter to Franklin, 12 February 1904, CM50cmc393.
66. ECM minutes, 17 February 1904, CM34cmc235; the *Synopsis* was praised and all fourteen members recommended PNEU reading courses; Franklin, letter to Mason, 17 February 1904, quoting Mrs Parsons comments on 20 March 1904, PNEU2Apneu12.
67. Mason, letter to Franklin, 21 March 1904, CM50cmc393.
68. Franklin, handwritten letter to Mason, 17 February 1904, PNEU2Apneu12; Mason, letter to Franklin, 10 February 1904, CM50cmc393; ECM minutes, 17 February 1904, CM34cmc235.
69. Mason, letter to Franklin, 7 April 1904, CM50cmc393.
70. The *Synopsis* was added to the Preface of each book in the Home Education Series in 1905.
71. E. Nesbit, *The Wonderful Garden* (London: Ernest Benn, 1911) and *The Would-be-Goods* (London, Ernest Benn, 1901; 1941).
72. Mason, letter to Franklin, 10 June 1904, CM50cmc393.
73. Mason, letter to Franklin, 22 March 1904, CM50cmc393.
74. Mason, letter to Franklin, 18 December 1903, CM50cmc393
75. Mason, *Home Education* (15th edn 1942), ix-xvii.
76. Mason, *Parents and Children*, xix-xx, chapter 21: 225-228, and chapter 25: 268-280.
77. Mason, *School Education,* front page; regarding Herbart, see 58-100, 185.
78. Ibidem, 65.
79. Ibidem, 271-299 and oral lesson plans, 329-359.
80. Mason, letter to Franklin from Romers Hotel, Grund am Hertz, 23 August 1900, CM50cmc393; Mason dictated *Ourselves* to Kitching in Germany – the manuscript is written in Kit Kit's hand, CM43cmc275.
81. Mason, *Ourselves* (2nd revised edn 1921), xix-xxii; John Bunyan, *Grace Abounding to the Chief of Sinners* (1666), *Pilgrim's Progress* (1678; Halifax: W. Milner, 1845) and *The Holy War Made by Shadai on Diabolus* (London: Religious Tract Society, 1862).
82. Mason, *Ourselves*, Book 2 includes likely past recollections: on darning, 21; 'visiting a parish', 58; and 'problems of belief', 197.
83. Bishop Tucker of Uganda, letter to Mason, 25 September 1905, PNEU2Cpneu38.
84. C.M. Mason, *Some Studies*, 158-76; Mason, letter to Kegan Paul, 23 November 1903, CM44cmc295, offering a sixth book for the series, *Max Pauli*: *A Prelude*, which was refused.
85. Mason, letter to Franklin, 10 June 1904, CM50cmc393.
86. Mason, letter to Franklin, 12 February 1904, CM50cmc393; PNEU reading courses, CM48cmc371, cmc372 and cmc163; PNEU Annual Report 1910, CM43cmc275.
87. Mason, letter to Franklin, 31 July 1905, CM50cmc393.

15. A Liberal Education for All, 1905–1922 (pp. 221-246)

1. PNEU Sixteenth Annual Report (1907), 14 for quotation, CM43cmc275.
2. Sheila Mary's memories.
3. PNEU ECM minutes, 24 May 1905, Minute Book (1903–1908), CM34cmc235; Cholmondeley incorrectly claimed Schofield opposed the *Synopsis* (ECM minutes, 17 February 1904 and Cholmondeley, *Story,* 109); ECM minutes, 14 December 1905, CM34cmc235; Lord Lytton, *Early Manhood: Its Difficulties and Responsibilities* [pamphlet] (PNEU, 1907), 3d.
4. Mason, letter to Franklin, 6 April 1905, CM50cmc393.
5. PNEU Annual Report 1905, 17, 22-23, CM43cmc272, showed eight girls', six boys' and three mixed junior schools; Mason, letter to *Morning Post,* 22 August 1905, CM44cmc300.
6. Curtis and Boultwood, *British Education,* 164-179 on the Revised Code; Curtis, *History of Education,* 327-328 on *Handbook for Teachers*; by 1900, sixteen training colleges were attached to universities.
7. Franklin, letter to Mason, 30 May 1905, PNEU2Apneu12.
8. Mason, letter to Morant, 11 July 1905, PNEU4pneu54; Birchenough, *Elementary Education,* 162-171, 358-364; Franklin's diaries, 10 July 1905 and 17 July 1905.
9. Mason, second letter to Morant, 8 November 1905, PNEU4pneu54; 'Educational Conference at Ambleside', *Westmorland Gazette,* 23 December 1905, CM44cmc313; conference with Wynn Williams, 9 December 1905, CM34cmc235; Wynn Williams, letters to Mason, 19 November 1905 and 5 December 1905, CM44cmc313.
10. Mason, letter to Franklin, 31 August 1905, CM50cmc393; Sir Robert Morant, 'The Foundress of the House of Education, Ambleside', a toast given at the PNEU Lyceum Club dinner, Piccadilly, 8 May 1911, *Parents' Review,* vol. 20, no. 6, 1911.
11. W.B. Gordon, letter to Mason, 9 May1906, CM12cmc84.
12. Tropp, *School Teachers,* note to 117-118; David, *State Education,*122-134; Article 68 of the Education Code (1890) allowed unqualified women over eighteen to teach in elementary schools with the HMI's recommendation and a vaccination certificate.
13. Inman, *Charlotte Mason,* 57-74; PNEU Annual Report 1905, 15, CM43cmc274.
14. Mrs A.M. Harris, 'A Personal Tribute', *In Memoriam,* 82.
15. W.B. Gordon, letters to Mason, 25 May 1911, 2 November 1911 and 28 December 1911 regarding the incorporation proposal, CM12cmc84; W.L. Mason's Scale How correspondence, January-March 1911, PNEU2Cpneu42; Franklin, letters to Mason, 28 January 1911 and 10 July 1911, PNEU2Apneu12.
16. Conference (1–5 June 1906), *Parents' Review,* vol. 17, no. 7, 1906; the Agenda, Discussion and Resolution are in PNEU Annual Report 1906, 17-18, CM43cmc274.
17. Mason, letter to Franklin, 17 November 1906, CM50cmc393; 'The Parents' Union School Curriculum', *Parents' Review,* vol. 17, no. 8, 1907.
18. 'What is the best way to bring up a child?', *Daily Mail,* April 1907, PNEU archive.
19. *The Tribune,* 15 July 1907; *Oxford Times,* 20 July 1907.
20. Student registers, CM10cmc62, 1891–1958; Helen Wix (CMT 1903), 'In Memoriam: Ellen Alice Parish', *Parents' Review,* June 1947; Mason, letter to Franklin, 27 April 1901, CM50cmc393.
21. Miss E.A. Parish's notebook (1907–1908), 11 October 1907, PNEU Archive.
22. Ibidem, 19, 24 October 1907; 13, 22 November 1907; 10, December 1907; 17 July; 5 October 1908.
23. Ibidem, 25 June 1908.

24. Gibbon, *Netta*, 138.
25. Ibidem, 11-12, 59-65, 99.
26. PNEU Annual Report 1914 with Branch Reports 16-32, CM43cmc276.
27. Jane Lewis, *The Politics of Motherhood: Child and Maternal Welfare in England 1900–1939* (London: Croom Helm, 1980), 61-113; Carol Dyhouse, 'Working-Class Mothers and Infant Mortality in England 1895-1914', *Journal of Social History*, Winter 1978, 248-266 and 308-318.
28. Coombs, *Some Obstacles*, 295-299, 335-346; Elizabeth Macadam, 'How the Parents' Union can help the Mothers of the Working Classes', *Parents' Review*, vol. 28, no. 1, 1917.
29. Gibbon, *Netta*, 89-92; Mrs Frances Bailey (CMT 1924), conversation with author.
30. Mason, letter to Franklin from Germany, August 1909; as noted, B.P. was a nickname for Dr Webb, CM48cmc309.
31. Franklin, letter to Mason, 10 July 1911, PNEU2Apneu12.
32. Mason, letter to Franklin, 12 July 1911, CM50cmc393.
33. Mason, letter to Bishop of Liverpool, 31 March 1908, CM44cmc294.
34. Editor (at Kegan Paul), letter to Mason, 17 April 1907, PNEU Archive; Mason, letter to Editor, 22 August 1909, CM44cmc295; *Guardian*, *Glasgow Herald* and *Tablet* reviews, CM51cmc418.
35. *The Saviour*: *The Academy*'s review, CM51cmc421; Franklin, letter to Mrs Foster, 5 July 1927, PNEU Archive.
36. Cholmondeley, *Story*, 179-195 reverently explores Miss Mason's spiritual writings; Art Middlekauff, 'Introducing the Saviour of the World' (2014) in Smith (ed.), *Essays on Charlotte Mason*, 187-211; Middlekauff's website, *Charlotte Mason's Poetry*, offers the six volumes online at http://charlottemasonpoetry.org.
37. Two extracts from the Minority Report, The Royal Commission on Divorce and Matrimonial Causes (1848–1913), HMSO, London, cited in J. Coombs, *George and Mary Sumner*, 196-198.
38. C.M. Mason, 'Two Educational Ideals', reprinted, *Parents' Review*, vol. 39, no. 1, 1928; C.M. Mason, *The Basis of National Strength* [pamphlet] (London: PNEU, 1913), reprinted from *The Times*, 7, 40, 20-21; letters regarding *National Strength*, CM44cmc306; Arnold, *Culture and Anarchy*, 202-212.
39. Mason, 'Miss Mason and the Montessori System', one of two letters to *The Times*, 3 November 1912, 8 March 1917, rebutting Montessori's own letters to *The Times Educational Supplement*, 2 and 6 November 1912, CM51cmc453; Nicholas Tucker, *The Child and the Book: A Psychological and Literary Exploration* (Cambridge University Press, 1981), 67-96 delightfully discusses the meaning of fairy tales for children.
40. J.S. Hurt, *Elementary Schooling and the Working-Classes 1860–1918* (London: Routledge and Kegan Paul, 1979), 188-189 and 210-239; Revd E. Lyttelton, letter to Mason, 15 January 1906, regarding public school classical education and the value of 'knowledge', PNEU2Bpneu19.
41. The Newbolt Report, *The Teaching of English in England being the Report of the Departmental Committee appointed by the President of the Board of Education to Inquire into the Position of English in the Educational System of England*, Board of Education, London, HMSO, 1921, Appendix III; Birchenough, *Elementary Education*, 396 and chapter 14.
42. Russell, *Mason Genealogy*.
43. 'The Children's Gathering at Winchester', *Parents' Review*, vol. 23, nos 4 and 7, 1912; 'Our Work', *Parents' Review*, vol. 23, no. 1, 1912.

44. D. Steinthal's Diary, July 1900; Florence M. Parsons, 'Courage in Education: An Elementary School Experiment', *The Nineteenth Century*, April 1917; Hurt, *Elementary Schooling*, 103-127 on the need for school meals.
45. R.A. Ambler, 'A Liberal Education in a Council School', PNEU Annual Conference, July 1916, *Parents' Review*, vol. 27, no. 7, 1916; R.A. Ambler, 'Some Experiences of a Pioneer School (Drighlington)', *Parents' Review*, vol. 27, no. 11, 1916.
46. Mrs Steinthal quoted in 'Author's Preface' in Mason, *Essay*, xxv-xxvi; see Cholmondeley, *Story*, 123-145 for a graphic first-hand account.
47. D. Steinthal's diary; some family members took Mrs Steinthal's maiden name, Petrie.
48. Mason, letter to Mrs Steinthal, 2 May 1914 and 6 May 1914, CM44cmc292.
49. Mason, letter to Mrs Steinthal, 12 May 1914, CM44cmc292.
50. Mason, letter to Mrs Steinthal, 29 May 1914, CM44cmc292.
51. Editor (Mason), 'What does the War mean to us?', December 1914, CM6cmc42; Mason, letter to Franklin, 20 August 1917, CM50cmc393; Mason, *Essay*, 1-2.
52. Mason, letter to Mrs Steinthal, 23 November 1914, CM44cmc292.
53. Mason, letter to Miss Ambler, 21 January 1915, PNEU Archive.
54. Mrs E.P. Steinthal, 'Two Visits to a P.N.E.U. Council School', *Parents' Review*, vol. 27, no. 3, 1916.
55. Florence Parsons (Mrs Clement Parsons), 'Courage in Education', *Parents' Review*, vol. 29, no. 2, 1918.
56. C.M. Mason and A. C. Drury, 'A Liberal Education in Elementary Schools: Theory and Practice', reprinted in Mason, *Essay*, Book II, Theory Applied, chapters 1 and 2; PNEU Annual Report 1916, CM43cmc276.
57. Sallie E. Bargh, letter to Miss Rush, 1 November 1917, typed copy, CM47cmc340.
58. Mason, letter to Mrs Steinthal, 28 January 1915, CM44cmc292; Willingham F. Rawnsley, 'Public Elementary Schools', *In Memoriam*, 33-38.
59. Mason, letter to Franklin, c. October 1916, typed copy, CM44cmc309.
60. Mason, 'The Scope of Continuation Schools', *Essay*, Book II, chapter III, 298; see 262-263 and 294-295 for long lists of names; H.A.L. Fisher, 'no. IX', *In Memoriam*, 27.
61. D. Gillard, 'Education in England: A Brief History', *Education in England*, 2011, www.educationengland.org.uk/history.
62. Humphrey Household (Horace's son), letter to author, 3 July 1986.
63. Horace Household, letter to Mason, 22 December 1916, CM4212cmc268.
64. Horace Household, letter to Parish, 13 December 1916, PNEU Archive.
65. H.W. Household, *Our Liberal Education for All Movement,* Gloucestershire CC Report, 1917–1918, 1-4; Household, 'Our Liberal Education for All Movement', *Parents' Review*, vol. 29, no. 8, 1918; H.W. Household, *The Teaching Methods of Miss Charlotte Mason* [pamphlet], PNEU, n.d., PNEU Archive; Geoffrey Household, letter to author, 12 May 1986.
66. Mason, letter to Franklin, 20 August 1917, CM50cmc393.
67. Charlotte Mason's will, 10 April 1919, CM1cmc8.
68. Household, 'Our Leader Still', *In Memoriam*, 42-44.
69. Mason, letter to Franklin, n.d. summer 1919, CM50cmc393; H.W. Household, *PNEU Methods of Teaching with special reference to the teaching of English*, n.d., CM16cmc10711; H.W. Household, 'The Need for a Liberal Education and how it may be given', *Parents' Review*, vol. 33, no. 10, 1922.
70. W.A. Brockington, *A Short Review of Education in Leicestershire 1925-28,* Education Committee Report; Brian Simon (ed.), *Education in Leicestershire 1540-1940* (Leicestershire University Press, 1968), 219; students' log, 22 May 1929, CM9cmc61.

71. Cholmondeley, *Story*, 167-72; D. Golding, 'Whitby Teachers' Conference', *Parents' Review*, vol. 31, no. 8, 1920; E. Hughes-Jones, 'A Tribute from an Ex-Student', *In Memoriam*, 78.
72. Franklin's diaries, 14 September 1920.
73. Mason, letters to Franklin, 24 September 1920 and 20 October 1920, PNEU2Cpneu48.
74. Student registers (1891–1948), CM10cmc62.
75. Mason, letter to Franklin, 12 January 1921 (listed as 1920), PNEU2Cpneu48.
76. The Newbolt Report (1921), Section 88: 'The Use and Enjoyment of Books in English in Elementary Schools', 36-40, 82-87, 348, 362, HMSO, London.
77. H.W Household, *The Group System in P.N.E.U. Methods: Notes for the Gloucester Conference*, 18 July 1925, PNEU, London, 1927.
78. Poem, 'The Children's Paradise', *Punch,* 18 May 1927, unattributed; Marshall Jackman, six articles in *The Schoolmasters' and Women Teachers' Chronicle*, June-July 1927, CM48cmc373, with Kitching's critical rebuttal, PNEU21pneu144; *The Schoolmistress*, 29 April 1936, cited in Stephanie Spencer, 'Knowledge as the Necessary Food of the Mind: Charlotte Mason's Educational Philosophy', in Jean Spence, S.J. Aiston and M. Meikle (eds), *Women, Education and Agency 1600–2000* (Abingdon and New York: Routledge, Taylor and Francis, 2010), 123-124.
79. PNEU membership in 1921 was 8,510, with 28 UK branches and 4 in Australia, Ceylon, India, and Jerusalem; and 160 elementary schools, 90 secondary schools and 800 children in home schoolrooms in the UK and abroad (PNEU Annual Reports 1920–1928, CM43cmc277); Cholmondeley, 'Recollections', *L'Umile Pianta*, Spring 1973. Mason did not explain to Cholmondeley her need for recognised professional qualifications or that sending her governesses into private posts ensured essential PUS income.
80. PNEU Annual Report 1921, CM43cmc277; Articles of Association, 11 August 1921, CM13cmc95.
81. Ibidem; Coombs, *Some Obstacles*, 330-359.
82. Mason, letters to Franklin, 4 August 1921 and 29 August 1921, own hand, PNEU2Bpneu22.
83. Mason, letter to D. Steinthal, 10 August 1921; Mason, letter to Francis Steinthal, 18 August 1921; F. Steinthal, letter to Mason, 19 August 1921, lent by family; D. Steinthal, letter to Kitching, 25 September 1924, CM51cmc419.
84. Kitching, letter to Mrs Annie Harris, 19 August 1921, PNEU2Cpneu44.
85. F. Steinthal, letter to Mason, 31 October 1921, PNEU2Cpneu47.
86. Mrs Steinthal's obituary, *Rochdale Observer*, 10 August 1921; Mason, letter to Franklin, 28 October 1921, PNEU2Bpneu22; Mason, letter to D. Steinthal, 21 December 1921, 18 February 1922, lent by family; Franklin's obituary, *The Times*, 8 January 1964.
87. Mason, 'Author's Preface', *Essay*, xxv.
88. Mason, letter to Franklin, own hand, 10 September 1921, PNEU2Bpneu22
89. Mason, *Essay,* Introduction, 9-10.
90. Mason, *Essay,* Introduction, 9-10
91. Mason, *Essay,* xxv-xxxxi, 5-11, 16; on curriculum, 18-20; on self-education, 23-32; on knowledge, 99-100; on reason's limitations, 139-153; on habit, 141-148; on knowledge of God, 158-169.
92. H.M. Richards, Chief Inspector, Board of Education, *In Memoriam*, 153.
93. Mason, letter to Franklin, own hand 15 October 1921, PNEU2Bpneu22.
94. Mason, letter to Franklin, own hand, 5 November 1921, PNEU2Bpneu22.

95. Mason, letter to Franklin, own hand, 11 November 1921, PNEU2Bpneu22.
96. Mason, letter to Franklin, own hand, May 1922; C.M. Mason, 'Some P.N.E.U. Principles'; *In Memoriam*, 3-6; Lady Baden-Powell and General Sir Robert Baden-Powell, 'A Field Marshall's Governess', 21-22, 22-23.
97. E.W. Hamlyn, Captain College Cadet Corps and Practising School Guide Company, 'Lady Baden-Powell at Scale How', *L'Umile Pianta*, Spring 1973; PNEU Annual Report 1922–23, CM43cmc277; C.M. Mason, 'P.N.E.U.: A Service to the State', *In Memoriam*, 1-15.

16. The Unseen Presence, 1923 (pp. 247-263)

1. Mason, *Parents and Children*, 268-274; surely Miss Mason delighted in the similarity between the Greek word for breath or spirit 'pneuma' and the beloved initials, PNEU.
2. 'An Old Pupil', 'Children's Tribute (i)', *In Memoriam*, 86.
3. W.P. Primrose (CMT 1923), *L'Umile Pianta*, Spring 1973, 4.
4. Michael Franklin, 'Children's Tribute (vii)', *In Memoriam*, 96-98.
5. Professor W.G. de Burgh, 'Some Impressions of the House of Education', *In Memoriam*, 66, 102-103.
6. Kitching, 'Day's Work', *In Memoriam*, 67.
7. Bernau, 'Easter Egg', 8.
8. Groveham, last letter to Mason, 29 December 1922, PNEU2Bpneu31; Groveham's dates (16 December 1841–21 October 1930); census, 1911, and death certificate, Woodbridge Register Office, Suffolk.
9. Mason, *last* letter to Household (Kitching's hand), 4 January 1923, CM44cmc310.
10. 'An Old Pupil', 'The Children's Tribute (i), *In Memoriam*, 86.
11. Franklin's diaries, 16 January 1923.
12. Students' log quoted in Inman, *Charlotte Mason College*, 16; Dr Jack E. Beckman, *Lesson to Learn: Charlotte Mason's House of Education and Resistance to Taxonomic Drift 1892-1960* (unpublished doctoral thesis, Cambridge University, 2004), 179: Beckman offers fascinating analysis of the resistance to change; Jack Beckman, 'The Problematic Way Forward: Miss Essex Cholmondeley (1934–1937)', *The Charlotte Mason Educational Review*, Winter 2007–2008, vol. 2, Issue 2.
13. Hough, Charlotte Mason's obituary, *Westmorland Gazette*, 20 January 1923, PNEU21pneu145.
14. Students' log in Inman, *Charlotte Mason College*, 16.
15. Elizabeth Raikes, *Dorothea Beale of Cheltenham* (London: Constable and Co., 1908), 365.
16. Frances Bailey (CMT 1924) told the author this story on 5 December 1981; she refused to view Miss Mason's corpse; Beryl French (CMT 1923), 'Memories of Miss Mason's Funeral', *L'Umile Pianta*, Winter 1992.
17. Mason's last will and testament, CM1cmc8; Ambleside Council meeting (established under the will) papers, 29 March 1923–2 July 1930, and Accounts, 31 December 1924, CM36cmc244.
18. Inman, *Charlotte Mason College*, 17; Students' Log, January 1923, CM9cmc61.
19. Ibidem; Dr Thomas and Matthew Arnold were interred at All Saints, Laleham, Middlesex.
20. Old Students, 'Agnes Drury (CMT 1902) (1874–1958)', *L'Umile Pianta*, August 1958, 5.
21. Household, letter to Franklin, c. 20 January 1923, PNEU Box XVIII ms 808, also in 'Extracts from Letters', *Parents' Review*, vol. 34, no. 3, March 1923; Anne Moreton, former CMC vice principal, conversation with author, 1983.

22. Ethel Peacey and D.S. Golding, 'Impressions' I and II, *In Memoriam*, 224-226, especially 225 for the memorial service; PNEU26pneu171; 'The 32nd Annual Report', *Parents' Review*, vol. 34, 1923: total PNEU membership was 8,680: 249 foreign, 211 elementary and 113 secondary schools, 33 classes using PUS programmes and '1,000s of children in home schoolrooms abroad and in England'.
23. Revd C.H. Chase, 'Letters to Scale How', *Parents' Review*, vol. 34, no. 3, March 1923.
24. Olive Marchington, 'The Children's Tribute', *In Memoriam*, 89.
25. E. Bicknell (CMT 1922), 'Charlotte Mason in 1923', *L'Umile Pianta*, Spring 1973.
26. 32nd PNEU Annual Report (1923), CM43cmc277; in 1979, *Parents' Review* became *The Journal of the World Wide Education Service of the P.N.E.U.*, organising the PUS and thirty remaining PNEU schools until 1989; all PNEU-named schools finally closed or were renamed by 2012.
27. Ex-Students, 'Letters to Scale How' III, *Parents' Review*, vol. 34, no. 3, March 1923.
28. Charlotte Mason, *The Times*, 17 January 1923, PNEU21pneu14, reprinted with excisions mentioned in Chapter 1; '*The Times* Obituary' VII, *In Memoriam*, 25; Sadler, 'Official Tributes', *In Memoriam*, 17-19.
29. *The East Anglian Daily Times*, 18 January 1923; *The School Guardian*, 23 February 1923, PNEU21pneu145.
30. Mason, letter to Franklin (own hand), 26 January 1922, PNEU2Bpneu22.
31. Franklin, letter to Kitching, 12 September 1923; Michael Sadler, letter to Kitching, 24 July 1923, PNEU Box 4; Lyttelton, letter to Kitching, 10 November 1923 and 3 December 1923, PNEU Box 4; Kitching, letter to Franklin, 16 January 1924; Franklin, letter to Kitching, 6 February 1924 and 31 March 1924, PNEU Box 4, pneu57 and pneu58; Lyttelton, 'Foreword' to *Essay*, first edn (Kegan Paul and Co., 1925) and third edn (London: H.M. Dent and Sons, 1954).
32. PNEU, *A Liberal Education for All: The Practical Working Particulars of the PNEU, the PUS and the House of Education*, 1928, PNEU23pneu161.
33. Franklin, letter to Kitching, 31 March 1935, typed copy, PNEUBox4.
34. *London Mercury*, July 1925; *Manchester Guardian*, 28 January 1925, CM42cmc268.
35. 'Miss Mason's Book', *Church Times*, obituary, 6 February 1925 and 20 February 1925; Mrs E.F. Duncan, letter to *Church Times*, 2 February 1925; Pennethorne, letter to *The Times*, n.d. 1925; Kitching, letter to *Catholic Herald*, 31 January 1941, CM42cmc268; Mason, *Essay*, 164.
36. 32nd PNEU Annual Report (1923), CM43cmc277; Inman, *Charlotte Mason College*, 19, and throughout for useful ensuing college history; ECM minutes, 28 March and 5 July 1923; Thorley, 'Eleven Years at Charlotte Mason College', *L'Umile Pianta*, Spring 2012.
37. Household, letter to Parish, 1 June 1923, PNEU Archive.
38. Bailey's and Sheila Mary's memories.
39. Household, letter to H.M. Richards, Board of Education, January 1927, CM42cmc268.
40. Franklin, letter to Household, 25 January 1927; Household, letter to Franklin, 30 May 1927, CM42cmc268; in 1938, Amy Pennethorne recorded 300 PNEU schools in 1934 and 138 in 1938, CM42cmc261 and cmc262.
41. Gibbon, *Netta*, 37; HRH Queen Elizabeth refused an Ambleside governess for the little princesses (PNEU22pneu155).
42. Kitching, 'Day's Work', *In Memoriam*, 70; Kitching, *Wait Half a Century*, Parts I and II, 1903–1953 [PNEU pamphlets] (Ambleside: F. Middleton, Stock Ghyll Press, 1953), PNEU Archive.

43. Robin Tanner, *Double Harness: An Autobiography* (London: Impact Books, 1987), 104-106; L.C. Taylor, *Resources for Learning* (Harmondsworth: Penguin, 2nd edn 1972), 123; L.C. Taylor, 'Charlotte Mason's Relevance to Current Educational Change', PNEU AGM 1971, Oxford, PNEU Archive.
44. Susan Schaeffer Macaulay, *For the Children's Sake: Foundations of Education for Home and School* (Westchester, IL: Crossway Books, 1984).
45. Karen Andreola (ed.), The Original Home Schooling Series (Wheaton, IL: Tyndale Press, 1989); Jennifer C. Spencer, 'Getting Personal: The Theory of Personal Integration' in Smith (ed.), *Essays on Charlotte Mason*, 211-239; The Charlotte Mason Institute, *Supporting an International Conversation towards and Authentic Charlotte Mason Education: Awakening to delightful Living*, developed from Child Light USA. Annual conferences and meetings are organised.
46. Gladys Schaefer, 'This I Know', Child Light USA blog, now Charlotte Mason Institute, 21 October 2012, www.gladysschaefer.com. See also www.charlottemasoninstitute.org/category/blog/.
47. Parish, letter to Mason, 4 August 1916, PNEU Archive.

Selected Bibliography

Guidance Note on the Charlotte Mason and PNEU Archive (© The Armitt Trust, Armitt Library and Museum, Rydal Road, Ambleside, Cumbria LA 22 9BL, www.armitt.com/Armitt_website, in collaboration with Cumbria University and Redeemer University College, Ancaster, Ontario, Canada): The Charlotte Mason Digital Collection, managed by Redeemer University College Library, is accessible at http://www.redeemer.ca/charlotte-mason. The CM and PNEU numbers refer to the Armitt archive box locations; catalogues are available on the website. The call numbers provided are accurate as of 2015. Not all records cited below are digitised or catalogued. The Help section on the Redeemer Library website is accessible at http://libguides.redeemer.ca/CMDC.

Abbreviations: AGM: Annual General Meeting; BOC: Bishop Otter College; BLL: Bodleian Law Library; CMCA: Charlotte Mason College Association; CMT (with year qualified) for all who trained at the HOE: House of Education; FHLD: Friends' Historical Library Dublin; FLL: Friends' Library London; GPDST: Girls' Public Day School Trust; HMI: Her Majesty's Inspector; KG: Kindergarten; LEA: Local Education Authority; MEC: Mothers' Education Course; MU: Mothers' Union; Pianta: *L'Umile Pianta*; PNEU: Parents' National Educational Union; PR: *Parents' Review*; PRS: *Parents' Review* School; PUS: Parents' Union School; WES/PNEU: World-wide Education Service of the PNEU.

Primary Sources

Charlotte Mason's Published Books

Mason, Charlotte, *The Forty Shires: Their History, Scenery, Arts and Legends*, London, Hatchards and Co., 1880, 2nd edn, 1881.

——, *Geographical Readers for Elementary Schools,* 5 vols, London, Edward Stanford, 1880–1884 (re-issued as the *Ambleside Geography Books* c. 1892):

vol. 1, *Elementary Geography*, 1881.

vol. 2, *The British Empire and the Divisions of the Globe*, 1882.

vol. 3, *The Counties of England* (shortened version of *The Forty Shires*), 1883.

vol. 4, *The Countries of Europe, Their Sceneries and People with Some Account of the Motions of the Earth*, 1883.
vol. 5, *The Old and the New World: Asia, Africa, America and Australia: The Causes which Affect Climate and the Interchange of Production with Maps*, 1884.

——, *Home Education: A Course of Lectures to Ladies*, London, Kegan Paul, Trench, Trübner and Co. Ltd, 1886, 3rd edn 1899. Revised and republished for the Home Education Series, 1905, 15th edn 1942.

——, *Parents and Children*, London, Kegan Paul, Trench, Trübner and Co. Ltd, 1896, 3rd edn 1904.

——, *School Education*, London, Kegan Paul, Trench, Trübner and Co. Ltd, 1904, 3rd edn 1917. Posthumously republished as *Home and School Education.*

——, *Ourselves, Our Souls and Bodies,* London, Kegan Paul, Trench, Trübner and Co. Ltd, 1905, 2nd edn 1921.

——, *Some Studies in the Formation of Character*, London, Kegan Paul, Trench, Trübner and Co. Ltd, 1906, 2nd edn 1914.

——, *The Saviour of the World*, 6 vols, London, Kegan Paul, Trench, Trübner and Co. Ltd, 1908–1914:

vol. 1, *The Holy Infancy*
vol. 2, *His Dominion*
vol. 3, *The Kingdom of Heaven*
vol. 4, *The Bread of Life*
vol. 5, *The Great Controversy*
vol. 6, *The Training of the Disciples*

Available online at *Charlotte Mason Poetry*, http://charlottemasonpoetry.org.

——, *An Essay Towards a Philosophy of Education: A Liberal Education for All*, published posthumously, London, J.M. Dent and Sons Ltd, 1925, 3rd edn 1954.

——, *First Grammar Lessons,* published posthumously, London, J.M. Dent and Sons Ltd, 1928, Armitt Library at CM3cmc32.

——, *Scale How Meditations, Dominus Illuminato Meo,* ed. Benjamin E. Bernier PhD, Lulu Press, 2011; Mason's proofs, 1906, PNEU2Apneu9.

Parents' Review Articles by Charlotte Mason (Editor)

Mason, Charlotte (Editor), 'A New Educational Departure', PR, vol. 1, no. 1, 1890.

——, 'The *Parents' Review* School', PR, vol. 2, no. 4, 1891–1892.

——, 'Tante in the Home', PR, vol. 2, no. 7, 1891–1892.

——, 'The Home School', PR, vol. 3, no. 1, 1892–1893.

——, 'P.N.E.U. Philosophy', PR, vol. 3, no. 5, 1892–1893.

——, 'Obituary of Edward Wynne', PR, vol. 3, no. 8, 1892–1893.

——, 'P.N.E.U. Principles', PR, vol. 5, no. 6, 1894–1895.

——, 'Recollections of Miss Clough and her Connexion with the P.N.E.U.', PR, vol. 8, no. 1, 1897.

——, 'P.N.E.U. Teaching in the Branches', Part 1 'Moral and Religious', Part 2 'Mental and Physical', PR, vol. 8, no. 8, 1897.

——, 'Psychology in Relation to Current Thought', PR, vol. 9, no. 7.

——, 'School Books and How They Make for Education', PR, vol. 11, no. 7, 1900.

——, 'Education, the Science of Relations', PR, vol. 13, no. 5, 1902.
——, 'Studies Serve for Delight, for Ornament and for Ability: A P.N.E.U. Manifesto', PR, vol. 14, no. 10, 1903.
——, 'Discussion on the P.N.E.U. Manifesto', PR, vol. 14, no. 12, 1903.
——, 'In Memoriam: Thomas Godolphin Rooper', PR, vol. 14, no. 7, 1904, 481.
——, 'What Does the War Mean to Us?', PR, vol. 25, no. 12, 1914, CM6cmc42.
——, 'In Memoriam: Mrs Steinthal', PR, vol. 32, no. 9, 1921.
——, 'Some P.N.E.U. Principles' and 'P.N.E.U.: A Service to the State', published posthumously, *In Memoriam: Charlotte M. Mason*, London, PNEU, 1923.
——, 'Two Educational Ideals', PR, vol. 39, no. 1, reprinted 1928.

Charlotte Mason's Other Articles and Letters to the Press

Mason, C.M., 'Character in Children', *Murray's Magazine*, vol. 4, July-December 1888.
——, Ambleside, 9 July 1894, PNEU2Cpneu36.
——, 'What is the best way to bring up a child?' *Daily Mail*, with cartoons, 2 April 1907, PNEU4pneu49.
——, *The Times Educational Supplement*, 2 November 1912, 6 November 1912 and 30 January 1913, PNEU4pneu49.
——, 'Miss Mason on the Montessori System', *The Times*, 3 December 1912, reprinted 1913, CM51cmc453 and CM54cmc499.
——, *The Daily Citizen*, 25 January 1913, PNEU Archive.
——, letters to *The Times* about Maria Montessori, 25 January 1913, CM51cmc453.
——, *The Basis of National Strength*, six letters reprinted from *The Times*, London, 1913, PNEU, CM54cmc499.
——, 'This Week's Message', *The Teacher's World*, 4 March 1914, CM51cmc436.
——, 'The War and the Teacher: Miss Mason's Advice', *Times Educational Supplement*, 2 February 1915, CM6cmc42.
——, 'Training the Future Citizen: Books and the Man', *The Mothers' Magazine*, n.d. c. 1916, PNEU Archive.
—— and Drury, A.C., A Liberal Education in Elementary in Elementary Schools: Theory and Practice', 1916, reprinted in Mason, *An Essay*, Book II.
——, 'Children as Persons', London, PNEU, n.d., proofs at CMC51cmc446.

Charlotte Mason's Personal Papers

Brandreth, Emily, Mason's itinerary, headed 'C.M.S.M.', Lucerne, 30 May 1877, PNEU2Cpneu46.
Death certificate for Charlotte Mason, CM54cmc495.
Death certificate for Joshua Mason, 1859, Liverpool Register Office; Hunter Street Quaker Burial Note, 289 QUA, Liverpool Record Office.
Death certificate for Margaret Mason, 1858, Birkenhead Register Office; funeral note, St Werburgh, Birkenhead Collection, ERC 30/6535/8, Chester Record Office.
Fly leaves of treasured books, PNEU2Apneu17.
Foster, Dr Balthazar, medical note, January 1878, PNEU2Bpneu17.

Last will, 10 April 1919, CM1cmc8.
Lesson observation ('Crits') notebooks, 1894–1897, CM1cmc7.
Mason to 'Dear Sir' (amongst the letters found in an old blotter after Mason's death) from 4 Sussex Place, Thursday, probably never sent, PNEU2Bpneu23.
Mineral baths records (1896–1919), Bad Nauheim, Germany, Builth Wells and Llangammarch Wells, Wales, and prescriptions, CM2cmc21 and CM2cmc22
Nightingale, Florence, letter to Arthur Brandreth, 30 July 1879, PNEU2Apneu7.
Notebook, 'Walks in Hampshire etc.' 1 and 2, CM1cmc9.
Pattrick, Revd J. Brooke, Curate at the Chapel of Ease, 'Sermon Miss Read', published as a pamphlet, 1877, PNEU2Cpneu46.
Sketch book, 'Northern Capitals Tour with Miss S. Armitt', 1897, CM1cmc11.
Walton, Lt Col Dr H.C.M., health analysis with Mrs Geraldine Walton (CMT 1928) for author, 10 April 1982, 24 September 1982, 16 May 1983 and June 1983, with notes, PNEU Archive

Key Correspondence

The Hon. Mrs Henrietta (Netta) Franklin CBE

Franklin donated 115 transcripts of Charlotte Mason's letters (annotated in chapter references) to Mrs Walton, Chair, Charlotte Mason Foundation, on 16 July 1958, dated from 25 February 1897 (not 1891) to 12 December 1912 and October 1916, CM50cmc303 and CM44cmc309.
Franklin to Mason, twenty handwritten letters referenced in the notes from 7 February 1894 to 10 July 1911, PNEU2Apneu12.
Mason to Franklin, handwritten letters, 9 April 1919, 12 May 1919, 20 August 1917, 12 January 1920, 16 February 1920, 18 February 1920, 20 October 1920, PNEU2Cpneu48; 29 August 1921, 15 October 1921, 5 November 1921, 11 November 1921, 28 January 1921, 26 January 1922, May 19 1922, 22 June 1922 and 6 July 1922, PNEU2Bpneu22.
Obituary, *The Times*, 8 January 1964.

Mrs Elizabeth Groveham

Groveham to Kitching, twelve handwritten letters, 28 May 1923, 31 May 1923, c. 1923 scrap of paper, 10 June 1923, 14 June 1923 and 16 July 1923; Kitching's notes from meeting Groveham at Woodbridge, 1923; 31 January 1924, 7 May 1924; two postcards, 1:30pm and 4:15pm, 23 June 1924; unauthenticated *typed* letter, 18 May 1924; final letter, 9 July 1927, PNEU2BEnv31pneu31.
Groveham's sole surviving letter to Mason, 29 December 1922, PNEU2Bpneu31
Mason's five Worthing letters transcribed by Groveham, c. March 1861, c. April 1861, c. May 1861, 'Sunday' and 8 December 1861 cited in 'Scraps', transcripted letter, Kitching's hand, dated 1863, not thought genuine, PNEU2BEnv31pneu31.
Mason to Groveham, twelve handwritten letters, incomplete letters c. 1863 regarding 'night school', 'middle-class school'; regarding teaching English; proposing a 'grand change'; regarding Mr Brandreth's death; regarding

Gainsborough's *Blue Boy*; regarding Miss Read's death, January 1877; 'Summer Holidays', 1877; autumn 1877, from Otterbourne, Hants; regarding illness and Miss Brandreth, 20 March 1878; from Lucerne, 2 May 1878; from Auteuil, Paris, c. summer 1878.

Steinthal Records

Condolence letters: Mason to Dorothea Steinthal, 10 August 1921, and to Francis Steinthal, 18 August 1921, PNEU Archive.
Mason to Emeline (Lienie) Steinthal, Kitching's hand, 6 May 1914, 12 May 1914; own hand, 29 May 1914, 2 June 1914, 23 November 1914, 28 January 1915, 6 September 1918 and 23 August 1916, CM44cmc292.
Steinthal, Dorothea, to Kitching, 25 September 1924; 9 January 1950 and 16 January 1950 regarding founding the PEU, CM51cmc419.
Steinthal, Mrs Emeline, obituary, *Wharfedale and Airedale Observer*, 12 August 1921; *Ilkley Gazette and Free Press*, 12 August 1921; *The Rochdale Observer*, 10 August 1921.
Steinthal, Francis to Mason, 19 August 1921, 31 October 1921, PNEU2Cpneu47.
Steinthal, F., obituary, *Ilkley Gazette*, 6 April 1934.
Steinthal, L. to Mason from Beethoven Strasse, c. 1887–1888, c. June 1890, 13 November 1901, 31 January 1902, 30 May 1902, last letter to Mason 26 July 1921, PNEU2Cpneu47.
Steinthal, Mrs L., Contribution to the Minority Report, *The Royal Commission on Divorce and Matrimonial Causes,* London, HMSO, 1848–1913, in Coombs, Joyce, *George and Mary Sumner: Their Life and Times*, London, Sumner Press, 1965, 196-8.

Other Correspondence

Aberdeen, Countess (later Marchioness) Ishbel to Mason, 12 December 1887 (not 1886), 18 May 1888 and 7 February 1891, PNEU2Bpneu15.
Acland, Sir Thomas (father of Mrs Hart-Davis and Mrs Anson) to Mason, 9 March 1897, 20 March 1897 and 5 May 1897, PNEU2Apneu8.
Anon to Gertrude Bell, PNEU2Bpneu18.
Bargh, Sallie E. to Miss Rushton, 1 November 1917, typed copy, CM47cmc340.
Baylee, Revd Joseph to Revd William Harrison, 2 September 1845, Lambeth Palace Library.
Bentwich, Mrs Helen to Mrs Franklin, 2 April 1937: *Geographical Readers* correspondence, PNEU21pneu74.
Borrer, Mrs to Mason regarding Lady Isabel, 23 January 1895, PNEU2Bpneu18.
Buckley, Arabella to Edward Stanford, 1880, PNEU2Apneu5.
Clough, A.J. to Mason, 8 October 1890, 4 March 1890, CM44cmc293.
—— to Oscar Browning, November 1876, OB/1/1069/A, King's College Library, Cambridge.
Dunning, Robert to Mason, Friday afternoon 1861 and 22 October 1861, PNEU2Apneu10.
Editor at Kegan Paul to Mason; Mason to Editor, 17 April 1907 and 22 August 1909, CM44cmc295.

Franklin, Netta to Edward Lyttelton regarding publication of *An Essay*, 1 April 1924, PNEU4pneu57.
—— to H.W. Household, 20 January 1927 and 25 January 1927, CM47cmc339.
—— to Ellen Parish, *L'Affaire Marovsky* (1926–1927), 10 June 1927, CM12cmc81.
Gordon, W.B. (solicitor) to Mason regarding Scale How purchase, 25 May 1911, 2 November 1911 and 28 December 1911, CM12cmc84.
Hart-Davis, Mrs Mary L. to Mason, 6 November 1887 and 21 November 1887, PNEU2Apneu8.
Hatchards and Co. to Mason regarding *The Forty Shires*, 28 February 1880, 19 March 1880, 28 June 1883 and 29 June 1883, PNEUApneu05.
Hering (née Joss), Lydia (CMT 1934) to Kitching with Alice Burn's (née Gates) memories, n.d. 1887, PNEU2Bpneu19.
Household to Parish, 13 December 1916, PNEU Box 4.
—— to Mason, 22 December 1916 and 12 January 1920, PNEU2Cpneu35.
—— to Franklin, 22 January 1923, PNEU Box 18 ms 808; 7 January 1927, 2 May 1927 and 30 May 1927, CM42cmc268.
—— to H.M. Richards, Board of Education, January 1927, CM42cmc268.
Huston, William, three letters to Mason, 4 September 1865, 5 April 1866 and 23 October 1876, PNEU2Bpneu23.
Kegan Paul, Revd Charles, publisher, to Mason, CM51cmc416 and CM44cmc296; proof copy, *Home Education,* annotated by C. Kegan Paul, CM51cmc416.
Kitching to Mrs Harris, 1 January 1921 and 19 August 1921, PNEU Box C pneu44.
Knittel, Dr to Mason, seven letters in German including several regarding translating the Home Education Series into German on 11 and 16 November 1905 and 29 September 1906, CM44cmc305.
Lyttelton, Edward to Mason regarding the value of 'knowledge', 15 January 1906, PNEU2Bpneu19.
—— to Kitching, 10 November 1923, 29 November 1923 and 3 December 1923, PNEU Box 4 pneu57.
Margesson, Lady Isabel to Mason, 2 August 1894, PNEU2Apneu36.
Mason to Archbishop E.W. Benson, 29 April 1889 and 23 May 1889, Lambeth Palace Library.
—— to Oscar Browning, November 1889, 5 December 1889 (another's hand), from Belle Vue on 23 December 1889 and 25 December 1889, 26 December 1890, 24 January 1891, 25 March 1891, 7 July 1891, OB/1/1069/A, King's College Library, Cambridge.
—— to Mrs A. Brooke, 7 July 1890 and 17 July 1890 referring to F.C.A. Williams in Dublin, PNEU2Cpneu43.
—— to Sir Robert Morant, 11 July 1905 and 8 November 1905, PNEU4pneu54A.
—— to E. Wynn Williams, 19 November 1905 and 21 November 1905, CM44313D.
—— to Bishop of Liverpool, Pan-Anglican Conference Secretary, 31 March 1908, CM44cmc294.

—— to Parish, 16 January 1915, CM34cmcm236.
—— to H.W. Household, 4 January 1923, Kitching's hand, CM44cmc310.
Mason, W.L. to Mason C.M. regarding Scale How rent and lease, PNEU2Bpneu18; regarding purchase, 28 December 1910–20 March 1911, PNEU2Cpneu42.
Montessori, Dr Maria to *The Times Educational Supplement* on 'Imagination in Childhood', 2 February 1915.
Munro, Mrs to Kitching, c. 1938, PNEU Archive.
Parish to Mason, 4 August 1916, PNEU Archive.
Read, Revd William to Mason, 8 December 1880, PNEU2Apneu5.
Reader's review of *Geographical Readers* to Stanford, n.d., PNEU7pneu64.
Rooper, T.G. to Mason, 25 October 1884, PNEU7pneu66.
Smart, D. and Smart, Mrs W. to Kitching, two letters on early memories c. 1878–1879, 19 October 1949, PNEU2Cpneu46.
Stanford, Edward, publisher of *Geographical Readers,* 1880–1884, 23 September and October 1880, PNEU2Apneu5.
Stanford to Mason, 18 March 1897, PNEU8pneu64 and pneu66; 29 February 1901, CM44cmc295.
Tucker, Bishop of Uganda to Mason regarding *Ourselves*, 25 September 1905, PNEU2Cpneu38.
Whitaker Thompson, Mrs Blanche to Mason, 10 July 1892, PNEU2Apneu8.
Williams, Mrs Lucy to 'Maria' Mason, Xmas 1881, PNEU2Bpneu28.
Wynn Williams, E. to Mason, 19 November and 5 December 1905, CM44cmc313D.
Wynne, Revd E. to Mason, 4 July 1881, PNEU2Apneu28; 31 March 1886, PNEU2Apneu28; from Forest Gate, 1 July 1891, PNEU Archive.

Charlotte Mason's Obituaries (PNEU21pneu145)

The Daily Telegraph, 18 and 20 January 1923.
East Anglian Daily Times, 18 January 1923.
Educational Times, February c. 1923.
Journal of Education, February 1923.
The Lake District Daily Herald, 20 January 1923.
North Western Daily Mail, 18 January 1923.
The School Guardian, 23 February 1923.
Teachers' World, 24 January 1923.
The Times, 17 January 1923; *The Times*' and *Times Educational Supplement*'s obituaries were reproduced in *In Memoriam*.
Westmorland Gazette, 20 January 1923, by Dr C.H. Hough.
Yorkshire Post, 18 January 1923, PNEU21pneu145.

Reviews of Charlotte Mason's Books.

The Forty Shires: *Morning Post*, 6 December 1880; *The Athenaeum*, 26 March 1880, CM51cmc448.
***The Geographical Readers*:** no press reviews found.

Home Education: *Reading Mercury*, 1 January 1887; *Pall Mall Gazette*, 13 June 1887; *Glasgow Herald*, 18 December 1886; *Liverpool Mercury*, 25 December 1886; *Guardian*, 31 April 1887; *Spectator*, 20 August 1887; *The Lyceum*, September 1887, CM51cmc452.

Parents and Children: *Manchester Guardian*, 9 February 1897; *Sydney Daily Telegraph*, 28 March 1897; *Morning Post*, 14 April 1897, CM51cmc451.

The Saviour of the World: *The Academy*, 18 May 1912, CM51cmc421; *Guardian*, *Glasgow Herald* and *Tablet*, CM51cmc418.

An Essay Towards a Philosophy of Education: *Church Times*, 6 February 1925, 'Miss Mason's Book', 20 February 1925, 'The Late Miss Mason', 27 February 1925; *Birmingham Post*, 23 January 1925; *Manchester Guardian*, 28 January 1925; *The Nation and the Athenaeum*, 14 February 1925; *Universe and Catholic Weekly*, 17 April 1925, CM42cmc268 and CM51cmc425; *Teachers' World*, 12 August 1925, CM50cmc421.

Parents' Review Articles (1890–1966)

Ambler, Miss R.A, 'Some Experiences of a Pioneer School (Drighlington)', PR, vol. 27, no. 11, 1916.

'Ambleside Teachers' Conference, no. 2' 1-5 June, PR, vol. 17, no. 7, 1906.

Anon, 'Some Reflections on the P.N.E.U. Conference', PR, vol. 8, no. 7, 1897.

——, 'The Parents' Union Curriculum', PR, vol. 17, no. 8, 1907.

Anson, Mrs, 'The Mothers' Education Course', PR, vol. 8, no. 8, 1897.

Beale, Dorothea, 'Parents' Educational Union', PR, vol. 1, no. 2, 1890.

Blogg, Frances, 'The Use of the Central Office and the Organisation of the Branches', PR, vol. 8, no. 8, 1897.

Boole, Mrs M.E., 'The Preparation of the Unconscious Mind for Science', PR, vol. 10, no. 7, 1899.

——, 'Natural Priesthood', PR, vol. 10, no. 9, 1899.

Chase, Revd Charles, 'Letters to Scale How', PR, vol. 34, no. 4, 1923.

'Children's Gathering at Winchester', PR, vol. 23, nos. 4 and 7, 1912.

Cholmondeley, Essex et al, 'Elsie Kitching: Recollections', PR, vol. 67, no. 2, 1955.

Crichton-Browne, Sir James MD LLD FRS (1840–1938), 'An Oration on Sex Education', PR, vol. 3, 1892–1893.

Dallas Yorke, Mrs, 'The House of Education', PR, vol. 8, no. 8, 1897–1898.

Epps, Mrs Frances Washington, 'Our Daughters III Work for Gentlewomen as Elementary School Teachers', PR, vol. 1, 1890 and PNEU2Cpneu46.

Franklin, Mrs E.L. to Editor, 'PR Letter Bag', PR, vol. 5, nos. 7 and 11, 1894–95.

——, 'The Home Training of Children' report to the Board of Education, PR, vol. 19, no. 12, 1908 and PR, vol. 20, no. 1, 1909.

Franklin, Michael, 'In Memoriam: Helen Webb', PR, vol. 37, no. 3, 1926.

Golding, Miss D., 'Whitby, Teachers' Conference,' PR, vol. 31, no. 8, 1920.

Hough, Dr C.H., 'Charlotte Mason', PR, vol. 34, no. 3, March 1923.

Household, H.W., 'Our Liberal Education for All Movement', PR, vol. 29, no. 8, 1918.

——, 'The Need for a Liberal Education: How It May Be Given', PR, vol. 33, no. 10, 1922.

Kitching, Elsie, 'The History and Aims of the P.N.E.U.', PR, vol. 10, no. 7, 1899.
Lytton, The Rt. Hon. the Earl of, 'Some Duties and Responsibilities of Early Manhood', PR, vol. 18, no. 12, 1906.
Macadam, Elizabeth, 'How the Parents' Union Can Help the Mothers of the Working Classes', PR, vol. 28, no. 1, 1917.
Margesson, The Lady Isabel, 'Training Lessons to Mothers', PR, vol. 4, no. 1, 1893–1894.
Old Students of the House of Education, 'Miss F.C.A. Williams ("V.P."): Some Memories', PR, vol. 36, nos 7 and 11, 1925.
Parsons, F.M (Mrs Clement), 'Courage in Education: An Elementary School Experiment', PR, vol. 29, no. 2, 1918; also in *The Nineteenth Century*, April 1917.
Petrie, Telford (Mrs Steinthal's son), 'A Note on the Teaching of School Science', PR, vol. 39, no. 1, 1928.
Richmond, Mrs Ennis, 'Our Relations with Children', PR, vol. 13, no. 8, 1902.
Rooper, T.G, 'Report of Her Majesty's Inspector of Schools on the House of Education at Ambleside' (20 November 1892) in 'Our Work', PR, vol. 3, nos. 11 and 12, 1892–1893.
——, 'The P.N.E.U. and the Poorer Classes', PR, vol. 8, no. 8, 1897.
——, 'The Tree of Knowledge and the Tree of Life', PR, vol. 9, no. 8, 1897 and other articles at PNEU2Apneu6.
Shirreff, Emily, 'What is Women's Work in the World?', reprinted from *Journal of Education* (n.d.) in 'By the Way', PR, vol. 1, no. 4, 1890.
Steinthal, E.P., 'Two Visits to a P.N.E.U. Council School', PR, vol. 27, no. 3, 1916.
Wix, Helen E., 'In Memoriam: Ellen Alice Parish', PR, nos. 6 and 7, 1947.

L'Umile Pianta Articles

Bernau, D.C. (CMT 1923), 'An Easter Egg Remembers,' Pianta, Winter 1978.
Bicknell, Ellen (CMT 1922), 'Charlotte Mason in 1923', Pianta, 1973.
Bowser, P.M. (CMT 1914), 'My First Crit.: A Lesson on Squirrels to Form 3', Pianta, Winter 1973.
——, 'The Practising School 1908–1912', Pianta, Winter 1973.
Cholmondeley, Essex, (CMT 1919) 'I AM, I CAN, I OUGHT, I WILL', Pianta, April 1957.
French, Beryl (CMT 1923), 'Thoughts on the College and the PUS', Pianta, Winter 1986.
——, 'Memories of Miss Mason's Funeral', Pianta, Winter 1992.
Frost, E. (CMT 1907), 'Botanical Garden', Pianta, Spring 1974.
Garrard, F.E. (CMT 1922), 'A 1921 Junior Recollects', Pianta 1972.
Gladding, M. (CMT 1913), 'Crits.: A Geography Lesson', Pianta, Spring 1973.
——, 'Charlotte Mason Remembered', Pianta, Summer 1973.
Gray, Lilian (CMT 1896), 'Early Days of Scale How', Pianta, April 1968.
Hamlyn, E.W (CMT 1922), 'Lady Baden-Powell at Scale How', Pianta, Spring 1973.
Harvey, M.C. (CMT 1911), 'Flower Monitress', Pianta, Summer 1973.
Hill, Winifred (CMT 1908), 'Recollections', Pianta, Spring 1973.

Kitching, E., letter to Franklin regarding the Pianta launch, 15 July 1896, PNEU Archive.
Kitching, Winifred (CMT 1893), 'London and Rickmansworth P.N.E.U. School', Pianta, April 1957.
Lane-Roberts, Peggy (CMT 1935), 'The Origins of the PNEU', Pianta, Summer 1989.
Loveday, K. (CMT 1908), 'Miss Winifred Kitching', Pianta, April 1968.
Moffatt, Ida H.C. (CMT 1919), 'Some Memories of Essex Cholmondeley', Pianta, Winter 1985.
Old Students, 'Agnes Drury 1874–1958: In Memoriam', Pianta, August 1958.
Plumtre, E.C. (1921), 'Obituary, Katherine Loveday' (CMT 1904) who impressed Baden-Powell, Pianta, Spring 1973.
Storey, N.D.E. (CMT 1932), 'At School in Ambleside Fifty Years Ago', Pianta, Summer 1982.
Tasker, Lady J.E. (CMT 1909), 'O.B.s Fifty Years On' (Oscar Browning, HOE inspector 1909–1913), Pianta, December 1959.
Van Pelt, Dr Deani A. Neven and Van Pelt, Meghan D., 'L'Umile Pianta: Charlotte Mason Educators and the "Humble Plant" from 1896-1923' in Smith, J. Carroll (ed.), *Essays on the Life and Work of Charlotte Mason*, Pennsylvania, Riverbend Press, 2014.
Van Straubenzee, J., 'In Praise of Flitters', PUS Diamond Jubilee and Pianta, Spring, 1973.

Educational Papers and Articles

Ambleside Teachers' Conference no. 1, 9 December 1905, CM34cmc235.
Brockington, W.A., *A Short Review of Education in Leicestershire 1925–28*, Education Committee, 1928.
'The Children's Paradise', *Punch*, 18 May 1927, unattributed.
Coghlan, E, 'A Report of the Present Superintendent of the Mixed School of the Advantages of Early Education' (10 April 1869), *Home and Colonial School Society Occasional Paper*, May 1869, London University Library.
'Educational Conference at Ambleside', *Westmorland Gazette*, 9 December 1905 and 23 December 1905, CM44cmc313D.
Home and Colonial Educational Paper, April 1861, iv, Brunel University Archive, Ho and Co, ref. BFSS, File 31.
Household, H.W., *Our Liberal Education for All Movement,* Gloucester County Council Report, 1917–1918.
——, *The Group System in P.N.E.U. Methods: Notes for the Gloucester Conference*, 18 July 1927, London, PNEU, 1927.
——, *Methods of Teaching with Special Reference to the Teaching of English*, PNEU, n.d. CM16cmc10711.
——, 'The Teaching Methods of Miss Charlotte Mason', *Teachers' World*, n.d., PNEU Archive.
Jackman, Marshall, 'The P.N.E.U. Method: An Investigation', six articles, *The Schoolmaster and Woman Teacher's Chronicle,* June–July 1927, CM48cmc373.
Journal of The National Society, monthly paper, April 1960–1961, Newsam Library and Archives, University College London Institute of Education.

Molyneux, E.L. (ed.), *PUS Diamond Jubilee 1891–1951*, 1951, pamphlet, CM17cmc13.
Schofield, Dr A.T., 'A New Education', *The Girls' Own Paper*, 1882.
Wix, Helen E. (CMT 1903), *Some Thoughts on Narration*, pamphlet, CM16cmc17011.

PNEU Official Records

Executive Committee Minute Book 1890–1899, CM34cmc233; 1899–1903, CM34cmc234; 1903–1908, CM34cmc235; 1908–1916, CM34cmc236; notes on the PNEU 1890–1923, CM34cmc239.
PNEU Annual Reports 1892–1896, CM43cmc272; 1897–1901, CM43cmc273; 1902–1906, CM43cmc274; 1907–1911, CM43cmc275; 1912–1916, CM43cmc276; 1917–1919, missing; 1920–1926, CM43cmc277.

PNEU Pamphlets and Articles

Kitching, Elsie, 'The Day's Work' and 'The Beginning of Things' in PNEU (ed.) *In Memoriam: Charlotte M. Mason*, London, PNEU, 1923.
——, *Wait Half a Century: Parents and Children (1901–1951) A Meeting: Science and Religion*, Ambleside, Stock Ghyll Press, F. Middleton, 1951, PNEU Archive.
——, *A Brief Account of the Life and Work of Charlotte Mason*, Ambleside, Stock Ghyll Press, F. Middleton, 1952, PNEU Archive.
——, *Wait Half a Century: Parents and Children (1903–1953) Past and Present (Knowledge and the Mind),* Ambleside, Stock Ghyll Press, F. Middleton, 1953, PNEU Archive.
——, *Children and Home and in the Parents' Union School*, pamphlet, revised 1955, PNEU Archive.
Parsons, Mrs Clement, *The Principles and Objects of the Parents' Educational Union* [talk], International Council of Women, London, Women's Printing Society, 3rd rev. edn 1899, CM48cmc357 and PNEU Archive
Pennethorne, R. Amy (CMT1898), *What Other People Are Thinking*, London, PNEU, 26 April 1951, PNEU Archive.
PNEU (ed.), *A Liberal Education for All: The Practical Working Particulars of the PNEU, the PUS and the House of Education*, 1928, PNEU23pneu161.
——, *Elsie Kitching 1870–1955: Recollections*, London, PNEU, 1956, CM48cmc363.

Unpublished PNEU and Other Records

Bell, Herbert, *Recollections*, ms.CM44cmc293
Bishop Otter statutory school log book, West Sussex Record Office, E/35C/12/1, Chichester.
Davison statutory school log book, Davison CE High School for Girls, Selbourne Road, Worthing, http://www.davison.w-sussex.sch.uk/Contact-Us-.
Kitching, Elsie, last will, 31 July 1953, CM11cmc72.

Mothers' Education Course (1892–1915) Programme and Syllabus in PNEU Annual Report 1907, CM43cmc275; letters from participant mothers, PNEU2Bpneu29.
Parish, Ellen A., notebook for Charlotte Mason, 1907–1908, PNEU Archive.
Students' Scale How diaries/log (1895–1923), CM9cmc61.
Webb, Helen, diary of visit to Charlotte Mason at Ambleside, CM2cmc29.
Westmorland, Deaconess Rosa, 'Memories', 1923, CM51cmc454
Yates, Mary, diary, excerpts 1907, CM17cmc123.

Government Reports

Committee of Council on Education Reports and Minutes, London, HMSO, call no. 100/1858/59–1898/99, Newsam Library and Archives, University College London Institute of Education; also in Accounts and Papers, BLL, Oxford.
Cook, Revd F.C., 'Teacher Education: Report on C of E Training Colleges for Women School Mistresses' in Minutes of the Committee of Council on Education 1857–1858, Accounts and Papers (A and P), BLL.
——, HMI Reports (1858) in *The Educational Blue Book* and *The Revised Code, Ho and Co School Society Occasional Paper*, London, Groombridge and Sons, May 1869.
——, *Special Report*: *C of E Training Colleges for Women School Mistresses*, commissioned by the C of C, A and P, vol. XVII, 1861, BLL, with Pidduck, J. MD, *Medical Officer's Report,* 22 Montague Street, Bloomsbury, A and P, February 1860, BLL.
Christmas Exams and Class Lists 1859-1863 with Questions and Class Lists, General Examination of Training Schools' (for candidates for Queen's Scholarships), 3-12, Newsam Library and Archives.
HMI School Reports, *Tabulated Reports on Schools Inspected in Cheshire, Shropshire and Staffordshire*, Holy Trinity National Schools, Birkenhead, by Revd J.P. Norris and Revd S.J.G. Fraser, London, HMSO, 1859–1900, call no. 1000 (1850–1860), Newsam Library and Archives.
Pupil-Teacher Broadsheet in *Christmas Examinations 1859-61-62-63-64-65-66 Questions and Class Lists,* Newsam Library and Archives, University College London, Institute of Education.
The Pupil Teacher: A Monthly Journal of Practical Education, 54 Paternoster Row, London, G.L Stevenson, 1857–1859.
Report of the Inter-Departmental Committee to Establish the Facts of State Involvement with Magdalen Laundries, Senator Martin McAleese, Dublin, 2013, chapter 3: 'History of 41 Magdalen Asylums in Ireland from 1765'.
Report on Inter-Departmental Committee on Physical Deterioration, Sir William Almeric, London, HMSO, 1904.
Royal Commission into the State of Popular Education in England, Newcastle Report, London, HMSO, 1861.
Royal Commission on the Public Schools, Clarendon Report, London, HMSO, 1864.
Royal Commission into Scientific Instruction and the Advancement of Science, Devonshire Report, London, HMSO, 1875.

Royal Commission to Enquire into the Working of the Elementary Acts, Cross Commission Report, London, HMSO, 1888.
Royal Commission into The Teaching of English in England being the Report of the Departmental Committee appointed by the President of the Board of Education, Newbolt Report, London, HMSO, 1921.
The Schools Inquiry Commission into Middle-Class Education in England, Taunton Report, London, HMSO, 1868.

Records in England and Ireland

Bishop Otter Memorial College Archives, University of Chichester

Minute Book, 2 September 1872; AGM Reports 1873–1878; Committee Minutes, BOMS/A0030; Minutes of the Finance Committee, 1877 and March 1878, BOMS A010; Accounts 1874–1878, BOMS A029; *Bishop Otter College Magazine*, BOSU 001/023; Hubbard Papers, Bishop Otter Archives.

Cumbria

'Two Centuries of the Friends' School: an active and conspicuous part to play in the educational history of Westmorland', *Kendal Mercury and Times*, 14 July 1899, reprint in File WDFC/F/1, Cumbria Archives Central, Kendal (CACK).
Westmorland Friends' Records, Kendal Central Record Office Archive Collection, Kendal Council Offices, Cumbria LA9 4RQ, www.cumbria.gov.uk/archives; Quaker Digest of Marriages (1643–1836), Westmorland Book 1216, CACK; birth records, JAC1781KRO for Gough family.

Davison Church of England Technical High School Records, Selbourne Road, Worthing

Brief History of the Davison School, Davison School, n.d.
Inspire, Serve, Achieve, Davison School prospectus, 2012–2013.
Davison School log book, excerpts July 1863–Christmas 1873, with summarised HMI reports and lists of school staff; school registers 1865–1973, Davison School.
Thomas M., Davison School, *Glimpse of Old Worthing*, in red exercise book labelled 'Log Book 1812–1902'.

The Religious Society of Friends' and Relevant Records

England: The Library, Friends' House, Euston Road, London, NW1 2BJ, www.quaker.org.uk/library.
Ireland: Friends' Historical Library Dublin, Quaker House, Stocking Lane, Dublin 16, www.quakers-in-ireland.ie/historical-library, holds a database of all Irish Friends' births, deaths, marriage, disownment and removal records, and minutes, including Carlow Friends' Monthly Meeting minutes, 1835–1842.
Northern Ireland: Lisburn, Lurgan and Moyallan Friends' records, Prospect House, 4 Magheralave Road, Lisburn, Co. Antrim, BT 28 3BD, N. Ireland:

Lisburn Monthly Meeting (LBMM) minutes, 9 February 1777–5 July 1778; Lurgan Monthly Meeting (LGMM) Family Record Book and removals records, LGM 5/2 7953 and LBMM K3, 1778–1795; Ross Chapman (LBMM records) to Joan Johnson, 29 October 2009 and 7 August 2010.
Russell, Bob, genealogical records prepared for author: *Mason, Birchall, Doyle, Leckey, Morris and Pim Genealogies.* Copies deposited at the Armitt Library and Friends Historical Library, Dublin.
Registered Deeds (© Registry of Deeds, Henrietta Street, Dublin):
Jones, Richard, Hall's Mill Deed, 1761, 253/285/16475.
Mason, Joshua junior and Adcock, Robert, Indented Deed, 19 February 1835, vol. 3, no. 270, 1835.
Mason, Joshua senior, Memorial Deed, 11 May 1840/24 November 1840, yaur Jeffares, no. 56, 21 November 1840.
Newtown School Archives (Waterford): Minutes of Munster Provincial School Proceedings (1813–1820); Newtown School Pupils' Register (1798–1882), nos 257 and 303; Library Committee of Six minutes (1811–1817); Removals List citing apprenticeships.
Waterford City Archives: List of Freemen (1700–2008), Joshua Mason's handwritten appeal, TWC1/1/1408; Liverpool Record Office list of Waterford freemen, Mason, Joshua senior and Joshua junior's certificates, Box ACC1354.
Waterford Friends' Records: Newtown Friends' Meeting House, Newtown Road, Waterford, Co. Waterford, S.E. Ireland: Monthly Meetings minutes, births, marriages, deaths, removals, disownments and burials (1802–1835).
West Sussex Record Office Chichester: Bishop Otter's practising school log, Chichester, ref. E35C/12/1.40.
West Yorkshire Archive Service: School brochures (Scruton Collection DB/6/C4/7) for Bradford Girls' Middle School Drewton St (1865), Mornington House Ladies' School (DB16/C4/7) and Mornington House Ladies' Collegiate School (September 1879), both at 2 Apsley Crescent.

Secondary Sources

Books Referring to Charlotte Mason, the PNEU or PUS

Barker, Dudley, *G.K. Chesterton: A Biography*, London, Constable, 1973.
Bernau, G.M, *The Book of Centuries and How to Keep One*, PNEU.
Berry, Marion, *I Buy a School*, London, Avon Books, 1996.
Boulter, Hugh (last director of WES/PNEU), *The Philosophy of Charlotte Mason in the 1980s*, London, WES/PNEU, 1983, at PNEU25pneu164.
Brandon, Ruth, *Other People's Daughters: The Life and Times of the Governess*, London, Weidenfield and Nicolson, 2008.
Bremner, C.S., *The Education of Women and Girls in Great Britain*, London, Swan Sonnenschein, 1897.
Carnie, J.M., *At Lakeland's Heart: Eighteen Journeys into the Past of Ambleside and its Locality from Rydal to Clappersgate until AD 1900*, Windermere, Parrock Press, 2002.

Cholmondeley, Essex, *The Story of Charlotte Mason 1842–1923*, London, J.M. Dent and Sons Ltd, 1960; 2nd unrevised edition, Petersfield, Child Light Publications, 2000 (transferred to The Orion Publishing Group Ltd, London).

Crossley, Barbara, *The Other Ambleside*, Kendal, Tim Wilson and Son, 2000.

——, *The Armitts: Sophia and her Sisters*, Armitt Trust, Ambleside, 2012.

Denton, Pennie, *A Very Remarkable Woman: The Life and Work of Angela James (née Kay-Shuttleworth) 1872–1967*, privately published, 1994.

Dyhouse, Carol, *Girls Growing Up in Late Victorian England*, London and Boston, Routledge and Kegan Paul, 1981.

Gibbon, Monk, *Netta*, London, Routledge and Kegan Paul, 1960.

Green, Fanny L., 'The House of Education', *The Monthly Packet*, half-yearly volume, ed. Christabel R. Coleridge and Arthur Innes, New Series 9, vol. 89, Jan-Jun 1895, London, A.D. Innes and Co.

Hughes, Kathryn, *The Victorian Governess*, London, Hambledon Continuum, 2001.

Inman, Revd J.P., *Charlotte Mason College*, Winchester, Cormorant Press, 1985.

Kamm, Josephine, *How Different from Us: A Biography of Miss Buss and Miss Beale*, London, Bodley Head, 1959.

Kerr, Rose, *The Story of the Girl Guides*, London, The Girl Guides' Association, 1932.

King, Jenny, *Charlotte Mason Reviewed*, Petersfield, Child Light Ltd, 1981, republished 2000.

Lively, Penelope, *Oleander, Jacaranda: A Childhood Perceived*, New York, Harper Perennial, 1995.

Lovell, Mary S., *The Mitford Girls: The Biography of an Extraordinary Family*, London, Abacus Little Brown and Co., 2001, republished 2008.

Macaulay, Susan Schaeffer, *For the Children's Sake: Foundations of Education for Home and School*, Westchester, IL, Crossway Books (a division of Good News Publishers), 1984.

McGregor, G.P., *Bishop Otter College and Policy for Teacher Education 1839–1980*, London, Pembridge Press, 1981.

Ney, Marian Wallace and Ney, John, *Charlotte Mason: A Pioneer of Sane Education*, ed. Victoria Waters, Nottingham, Educational Heretics Press, 1999.

PNEU (ed.), *In Memoriam: Charlotte M. Mason*, Victoria Street, London, PNEU, 1923.

Russo, Doreen, *Charlotte Mason: A Pioneer of Sane Education: The Origins of the PNEU, the PUS and the Charlotte Mason Teachers (1892–1992)*, CMCA, 1987.

Smyth, Charles S. (former director of WES/PNEU), *Charlotte Mason, PNEU and WES* [pamphlet], London, WES/PNEU, 1980, PNEU Archive.

Spencer, Dr Stephanie, 'Knowledge as the Necessary Food of the Mind: Charlotte Mason's Philosophy of Education' in Jean Spence, Sarah Jane Aiston and Maureen Meikle, *Women, Education and Agency 1600–2000*, Abingdon and New York, Routledge, Taylor and Francis, 2010.

Tanner, Robin, *Double Harness: An Autobiography*, London: Impact Books, 1987.

Taylor, L.C., *Charlotte Mason's Relevance to Current Educational Change* [talk], address for the PNEU AGM, Holywell Press Oxford, PNEU Archive.

——, *Resources for Learning*, Harmondsworth, Penguin, 2nd edn 1972.

Webb, Dr Helen, *Children and the Stress of Life*, London, PNEU, 1929, Armitt Library.

North American Publications on Mason Education

Andreola, Karen, (ed.), The Original Home Schooling Series, 6 vols, Wheaton, IL, Tyndale Press, 1989.

——, *A Charlotte Mason Companion* and *Personal Reflections on the Gentle Art of Learning*, Quarryville, PA, Charlotte Mason Research and Supply Co. USA, 1998.

Bauer, Susan Wise, *Charlotte Mason and Classical Education*, W.W. Norton USA, 1999.

Beckman, Dr Jack 'The Problematic Way Forward: Miss Essex Cholmondeley (1934–1937)', *The Charlotte Mason Educational Review*, vol. 2, Issue 2, Winter 2007–2008, Charlotte Mason Institute, www.charlottemasoninstitute.org.

Behlmer, George, *Friends of the Family: The English Home and Its Guardians 1850–1950*, University of Minnesota, Stanford University Press, 1990.

Bestvater, Laurie, *The Living Page: Keeping Notebooks with Charlotte Mason*, Underpinnings Press, 2013.

Buettner, Elizabeth, *Empire Families: Britons and Late Imperial India*, Oxford University Press (mentions the PUS), 2004.

Heathorn, Stephen, *For Home, Country and Race: Constructing Gender, Class and Englishness in the Elementary School 1880–1914*, Toronto University Press, 2000.

Levison, Catherine, *A Charlotte Mason Education: A Home Education How to Manual,* Champion Press Ltd, Beverley Hills, CA, new edn 2000.

Smith, J. Carroll (ed.), *Essays on the Life and Work of Charlotte Mason*, Volume 1, a publication of the Charlotte Mason Institute (www.charlottemasoninstitute.org), Pennsylvania, Riverbend Press, 2014, including Thorley, Professor John, 'Charlotte Mason: The Development of An Educational Philosophy 1860–1890'Parts 1-4; Coombs, M.A., 'A Journey of Discovery: Charlotte Mason's Secret Past and Hidden Quaker Heritage'; Middlekauff, Art, 'Introducing the Saviour of the World'; Spencer, Dr J.C., 'Getting Personal: The Theory of Personal Integration'.

Smith, J. Carroll (ed.), *Essays on the Life and Work of Charlotte Mason,* Volume 2, a publication of the Charlotte Mason Institute, Pennsylvania, Riverbend Press, 2015, including essays by Dr Lowell Monke, Professor of Education at Wittenberg University, on the role of technology in the lives of children, and Charlotte Mason, 'Reading and a Wide Curriculum' (n.d), discovered by Smith in the PNEU archive, © Armitt Library.

Quaker and Irish Sources

Bennis, E.H, 'Reminiscences of Old Limerick', *Limerick Chronicle*, 1936; reprinted Winter 1999.

Brayshaw, Alfred Neave, *The Quakers: Their Story and Message*, York, William Sessions Book Trust, Ebor Press (closed 2010), 1982.

Butler, David M., *The Quaker Meeting Houses of Ireland*, Historical Committee of the Religious Society of Friends in Ireland, 2004.

Chapman, Arthur G., *History of the Religious Society of Friends in Lurgan*, Lurgan Friends' Meeting, 1997.
——, *Quakers in Lisburn: Four Centuries of Work and Witness*, Ulster Friends Home Mission, 2009.
Chapman, George R., *Historical Sketch of Moyallon Meeting*, Lisburn, Moyallon Friends, n.d.
Cohen, Marilyn, *Linen, Family Tullyish, County Down*, Dublin, Four Courts Press, 1997.
Collins, Peter, *The Making of Irish Linen: Historic Photographs of an Ulster Industry*, Belfast, Friar's Bush Press, 1994.
Fox, George, *A Journal or Historical Account of the Life, Travels, Sufferings, Christian Experiences and Labour of Love in the Works of the Ancient Eminent and Faithful Servant of Jesus Christ, George Fox (1624–1691)*, ed. Thomas Ellwood, 1634, FLL.
Goodbody, Olive C., *Guide to Irish Quaker Records 1654–1860*, Irish Manuscripts Commission, 1967, FLL
Gough, James, *A Practical Grammar of the English Language Tongue Containing the Most Material Rules and Observations for Understanding the English Language well and Writing it with Propriety*, ed. John Gough, Dublin, Robert Jackson, 1764, 1771, FLL.
——, *Memoirs of the Life, Religious Experience and Labours in the Gospel of James Gough, late of the City of Dublin, deceased compiled from his original memoirs by his brother John Gough*, ed. John Gough, Dublin, Robert Jackson, 1781, FLL.
Gough, John, *Treatise of Arithmetic in Theory and Practice,* 4 vols, Dublin, Robert Jackson, 1767, FLL and FHLD.
——, *Tracts on Tithes: Brief and Serious Reasons why the People Called Quakers do not Pay Tithes,* Dublin, Robert Jackson, 1786. FHLD
——, *A History of the People Called Quakers from their First Rise to the Present Time Compiled from Authoritative Records and from the Writings of the People,* 4 vols, London, Darton and Harvey, 1799, FHLD.
——, *An Epistle from the National Half-Year's Meeting held in Dublin 3.5.1778 to the Monthly and Quarterly Meeting of Friends in Ireland*, Dublin, FHLD.
Harrison, Richard S., *A Biographical Dictionary of Irish Quakers*, Dublin, Four Courts Press, 1997, 2nd edn 2008.
Hodgson, J. Spence, *History of Penketh School 1834–1907*, 1907, FLL, 044.06 PEN.
Leadbeater, Mary, *Biographical Notes of Members of the Society of Friends who were Resident in Ireland*, London, Harvey and Darton, 1821/3, FLL.
Milligan, David H., *Quaker Marriage*, Kendal, Quaker Tapestry Books, 1994.
Moriarty, Christopher, 'All bloody principles and practices we do utterly deny', *Teaching Religious Education*, Issue 3, December 2008.
Newhouse, Neville H., *A History of Friends' School, Lisburn*, N. Ireland, Lisburn Friends' School, 1974.
Nolan, William and Power, T.P. (eds.), *Waterford History and Society*, Dublin, Geographical Publications, 1992.
O'Toole, Jimmy, *The Carlow Gentry: What Will the Neighbours Say?*, Carlow, Ireland, 1993.
Ottley, Charles S., *Burrin Drainage: Report and Final Award 1847*, Dublin, Alexander Thom, Carlow Local Studies, 1847.

Rankin, Kathleen, *The Linen Houses of the Bann Valley: The Story of Their Families*, Ulster Historical Society, 2007.
Shearer, M. Muriel, *Quakers in Liverpool*, Liverpool, Preparative Meeting of the Religious Society of Friends, 1982.
Thompson, Henry, *A History of Ackworth School during its First Hundred Years* and list of scholars (1779–1879), Pontefract, Ackworth School, 1879, 1959.
Wigham, M.J., *A Short History of the Religious Society of Friends in Ireland*, Historical Committee of the Religious Society of Friends in Ireland, 1992.
——, *Newtown School, Waterford: A History (1798–1998)*, Waterford, Newtown School, 1998.

Other Books

Aberdeen, Lord and Lady, *'We Twa,': Reminiscences of Lord and Lady Aberdeen*, vol. 1, London, W. Collins and Son, 1925.
Aesop's Fables, complete original translation from Greek by George Fyler Townsend, London, Forgotten Books, n.d.
Aikin, Dr John and Barbauld, Mrs Anna L., *Evenings at Home or The Juvenile Budget*, London, 1792–1796, 18th edn 1858.
Anstruther, Ian, *Oscar Browning: A Biography*, London, John Murray, 1983.
——, *Coventry Patmore's Angel*, London, Haggerston Press, 1992.
Arnold, Matthew, *A French Eton or Middle Class Education and the State*, London, Macmillan, 1864.
——, *Culture and Anarchy*, ed. J. Dover Wilson, Cambridge University Press, 1869, 1932, 1984.
Ausubel, H., *In Hard Times: Reformers among the Late Victorians*, New York, Columbia Press, 1960.
Axtell, James (ed.), *The Educational Writings of John Locke*, Cambridge University Press, 1968.
Bacon, Francis, *Essays*, 1597; London, J.M. Dent and Sons, 1962.
Baden-Powell of Gilwell, Lord Robert, *Scouting for Boys: 40th Anniversary Edition*, London, C. Arthur Pearson Ltd, 1948.
Banks, J.A., *Parenthood: A Study of Family Planning among the Victorian Middle Classes*, London, Routledge and Kegan Paul, 1954, 1969.
——, *Victorian Values: Secularism and the Size of Families*, London and Boston, Routledge and Kegan Paul, 1981.
Barnard, H.C., *A History of English Education from 1860*, London University Press, 7th impression, 1971.
Bickerton, J.M., *Worthing: A Brief Account of the History of the Town from Neolithic Times to the Present Day*, Worthing Museum Publications, 1963.
Birchenough, Charles, *A History of Elementary Education in England and Wales from 1800 to the Present Day*, London, University Tutorial Press, 1938.
Blease, W. Lyon, *The Emancipation of English Women*, London, Constable, 1910.
Bostridge, Mark, *Florence Nightingale: The Woman and her Legend*, London, Viking, 2008.
Boumphrey, Ian, *Birkenhead: A Pictorial History*, West Sussex, Phillimore Press (History Press), 1995, with picture of Holy Trinity Church.

Brown, Bishop and Baylee J., the Revd, *The Infallibility of the Church of Rome: A Correspondence between the Right Reverend Bishop Brown of Chepstow and the Reverend Joseph Baylee*, London, Longman, 1851.
Browning, Oscar, *An Introduction to the History of Educational Theories*, London, Kegan Paul, Trench, Trübner and Co. Ltd, 1881.
Bunyan, John, *Grace Abounding to the Chief of Sinners*, Halifax, W. Milner, 1666, 1845.
——, *Pilgrim's Progress*, London, Religious Tract Society, 1678.
——, *The Holy War Made by Shadai upon Diabolus*, London, Religious Tract Society, 1682.
Burgess, Dr H.J. and Welsby, Dr Paul, *A Short History of the National Society 1811–1961*, London, 1961.
Burstyn, Joan, *Victorian Education and the Ideal of Womanhood*, London, Croom Helm, 1980.
Butters, Henry, *The Etymological Spelling Book and Expositor Being an Introduction to the Spelling, Pronunciation and Derivation of the English Language Adapted to the Use of Classical and Ladies' Schools and also for Adults and Foreigners*, London, 1830.
Caine, Barbara, *English Feminism 1780–1980*, Oxford University Press, 1997.
Carpenter, Dr William B., *Principles of Mental Physiology*, London, Henry S. King and Co., 1874; reprinted 2009, Cambridge University Press.
Cassin-Scott, Jack, *Costume and Fashion in Colour (1760–1920)*, Dorset, Blandford Press, 1971.
Cheltenham Ladies' College Magazine, The Dorothea Beale Centenary Number, 1931, privately printed for Cheltenham Ladies' College.
Cholmondeley, Mary, *Red Pottage*, London, Virago Press, 1899, 1985.
Clough, Blanche, *Memoir of Anne J. Clough by her Niece*, London, Edward Arnold, 1897.
Collingwood, W.G., *The Life of John Ruskin*, London, Methuen and Co., 1900.
Coombs, Joyce, *George and Mary Sumner: Their Life and Times*, London, Sumner Press, 1965.
Crawford, Elizabeth, *Women's Suffrage Movement: A Reference Guide 1866–1928*, London, Psychology Press, 2001.
Crow, Duncan, *The Victorian Woman*, London, Allen and Unwin, 1971.
Curtis, S.J, *History of Education in Great Britain*, London, University Tutorial Press, 1953.
—— and Boultwood, M.E.A, *An Introductory History of English Education since 1800*, London, University Tutorial Press, 2nd edn 1962.
David, Miriam, *The State, the Family and Education*, London, Routledge and Kegan Paul, 1980.
Defoe, Daniel, *Robinson Crusoe*, Illustrated Classics, London, 1719, 1947.
Delamont, S. and Duffin, L., *The Nineteenth Century Woman*, London, Croom Helm, 1978.
Dyhouse, Carol, 'Working Class Mothers and Infant Mortality in England 1895–1914', *Journal of Social History*, Winter 1978.
Edgeworth, Maria, *The Good Governess and Other Stories*, London and Glasgow, Blackie and Son Ltd, n.d.

Elliott-Binns, L.E., *English Thought 1860–1900: The Theological Aspect*, London, New York and Toronto, Longmans, 1956.

Faderman, Lilian, *Surpassing the love of Man: Romantic Friendship and Love Between Women of the Renaissance to the Present Day*, London, Junction Books, 1981.

Gathorne-Hardy, Jonathan, *The Rise and Fall of the British Nanny*, London, Hodder and Stoughton, 1972.

Gill, Stephen, *William Wordsworth: A Life*, New York, Oxford University Press, 1990.

Gillard, D., 'Education in England: A Brief History', *Education in England*, 2011, www.educationengland.org.uk.

Gosden, P.H.J.H., *How They were Taught: An Anthology of Contemporary Accounts of Learning and Teaching in England 1800–1950*, Oxford, Blackwell, 1969.

Goulbern, Edward Meyrick, *Thoughts on Personal Religion Being a Treatise on the Christian Life in its Two Chief Elements, Devotion and Practice*, London, Rivingtons, 3rd edn 1863.

Gribble, James (ed.), *Matthew Arnold*, Educational Thinkers Series, London, Collier-Macmillan Ltd, 1967.

Healey, Edna, *Lady Unknown: The Life of Angela Burdett-Coutts*, London, Sidgwick and Jackson, 1978.

Heiser, F.B., *The Story of St Aidan's College, Birkenhead 1847–1947*, Chester, Phillipson and Golder, 1947.

Hirsch, Pam and Macbeth, Mark, *Teacher Training at Cambridge: The Initiatives of Oscar Browning and Elizabeth Hughes*, Portland, Woburn Press, 2004.

Hurt, J.S., *Elementary Schooling and the Working Classes, 1860–1918*, London, Routledge and Kegan Paul, 1979.

Huxley, T.H., *Science and Education Essays*, London, Macmillan and Co. Ltd, 1893, 1910.

——, 'Instruction in Physiology' (1877) in *Science and Education Essays*, vol. III: *Collected Essays*, London, Macmillan and Co. Ltd, 1910.

Inglis, K.S., *Churches and the Working Classes in Victorian England*, London, Routledge and Kegan Paul, 1963.

James, William, *Talks to Teachers on Psychology and to Students on some of Life's Ideals*, London, Toronto and Calcutta, Longmans Green and Co., 1899, 1927.

Jay, Eileen, *The Armitt Story*, Ambleside, Loughrigg Press (Armitt Trust), 1998.

Jay, Elisabeth, *Faith and Doubt in Victorian Britain*, Hampshire and London, Macmillan Education Ltd, 1986.

Jefferson, H.L., *St. Paul's Church: A Short History*, Shoreham-by-Sea, Service Publications Ltd, Easter 1969.

Jeffreys, M.V.C., *John Locke: Prophet of Common Sense*, London, Methuen and Co., 1967.

Jones, Margaret E.M., *A Brief Account of the Home and Colonial Training Institution and of the Pestalozzian System as Taught and Practised in Its Schools*, London, Groombridge and Sons, 1860.

Kamm, Josephine, *Hope Deferred: Girls' Education in English History*, London, Bodley Head, 1965.

Kazamias, A.M. (ed.), *Herbert Spencer on Education*, New York, Teachers College Press, 1969.

Ker, Ian, *John Henry Newman: A Biography*, Oxford University Press, 2009.
Lawrence, E. (ed.), *Friedrich Froebel and English Education*, London University Press, 1952.
Lewes, G.H., *The Problems of Life and Mind*, vol. III: *The Physical Basis of Mind*, Cambridge University Press, 1877.
Lewis, Jane, *The Politics of Motherhood: Child and Maternal Welfare in England 1900–1939*, Croom Helm, London, 1980.
Livingstone, R.W. (ed.), *Plato: Selected Passages*, trans. Collins William, Oxford University Press, 1940, 1951.
Locke, John, 'Some Thoughts Concerning Education' in James L. Axtell (ed.), *The Educational Writings of John Locke*, Cambridge University Press, 1968.
——, *An Essay Concerning Human Understanding*, Glasgow, 1977.
MacArthur, Ruth Brown, *The Little Mother*, London, G. Harrap and Co., 1918.
Macaulay, Rose, *Told by an Idiot*, London, Virago Press, 1923, 1983.
Maclure, J. Stuart, *Educational Documents in England and Wales 1816–1963*, London, Chapman and Hall Ltd, 1965.
Macrae, D. (ed.), *Spencer: The Man versus the State*, Harmondsworth, Penguin, 1884, 1969.
Marsden, Gordon, *Victorian Values: Personalities and Perspectives in Nineteenth Century Society*, London and New York, Longmans, 2nd edn 1998.
Martineau, H., *Household Education*, London, E. Moxon, 1848.
Mayo, Elizabeth, *Lessons on Objects*, n.d.; *Lessons on Scripture Prints*, 1840; *On Religious Instruction*, 1840; *Model Lessons for Infant Schools*, 1848–1850, University of London Library.
Mayor, E.M., *The Third Miss Symons*, London, Virago Press, 1913, 1980.
Neff, Wanda, *Victorian Working Women*, Columbia University Press, 1929.
Nesbit, E., *The Would-be-Goods*, London, Ernest Benn, 1901, 1947.
Newman J.H., *The Idea of a University*, London, Longmans Green, 1852, 1912.
Norwood, Cyril, *The English Tradition of Education*, London, John Murray, 1929, 1931.
Oldfield, Sybil, *Spinsters of this Parish: The Life and Times of F.M. Mayor and Mary Sheepshanks*, London, Virago Press, 1984.
Olivier, Edith, *Four Victorian Ladies of Wiltshire*, Dorset, Semley Publishing, 1945/6.
Paley, William, *Natural Theology or Evidence of the Existence or Attributes of the Deity, Collected from the Appearances of Nature,* ed. M.D. Eddy and D. Knight, Oxford University Press, 1802, 2008.
Pawley, B. and M., *Rome and Canterbury Through Four Centuries: A Study of the Relations between the Church of Rome and the Anglican Churches 1530–1981*, London and Oxford, Mowbray, 1974, 2nd edn 1981.
Pentland, Marjorie, *A Bonnie Fechter: The Life of Ishbel Marjoribanks, Marchioness of Aberdeen and Temair GBD LLD JP 1857–1939*, London, Batsford, 1952.
Pestalozzi, J.H., *How Gertrude Teaches her Children: An Attempt to Help Mothers Teach Their Own Children and an Account of the Method* (1801), trans. Lucy E. Holland and Francis C. Turner, London, Swan Sonnenschein, 1894.
——, *Letters on Early Education to J.P. Greaves Esq.*, trans. C.W. Barden, London, 1898.

Plato: The Republic, trans. and ed. A.D. Lindsay, London, J.M. Dent and Sons, 1935.
Plato, *The Republic*, trans. H.D.P. Lee, London and Tonbridge, Penguin, 1955.
Plutarch, *Lives*, trans. John Dryden and ed. Arthur Hugh Clough and James Atlas, Random House Inc., 2001.
Quick, R.H., *Essays on Educational Reformers*, London, Longmans Green, 1868, 1907.
Raikes, Elizabeth, *Dorothea Beale of Cheltenham*, London, Constable and Co., 1908.
Read, T.A. and Higgs, A., *Protestantism v. Roman Catholicism: Report of the Discussion between J. Baylee and M. Bridges, at Stroud 1856*, London, F.W. Harmer, 1856.
Reeder, D.A. (ed.), *Educating our Masters*, Leicester University Press, 1980.
Renton, Alice, *Tyrant or Victim: A History of the British Governess*, London, Weidenfeld and Nicholson, 1991.
Rich, R. W., *The Training of Teachers in England and Wales during the Nineteenth Century*, Cambridge University Press, 1933.
Richardson, Dorothy, *Pilgrimage*, 4 vols, London, Virago Press, 1915, 1979.
Robinson, Jane, *Bluestockings: The Remarkable Story of the First Women to Fight for an Education*, London, Viking, 2009.
Robinson, Professor Wendy, *Pupil-Teachers and their Professional Training in Pupil-Teacher Centres in England and Wales 1870-1914*, Exeter, E. Mellen Press, 2003.
Rooper, T.G., *School and Home Life: Essays and Lectures on Current Educational Topics*, London, A. Brown and Sons Ltd, n.d.
——, *Current Educational Topics*, Hull, A. Brown and Sons Ltd, n.d. c. 1880s.
Rousseau, J.J., *Émile or On Education*, 1762, trans. Barbara Foxley, London, Dent Everyman,1974.
——, *Julia or The New Éloise*, 1761; trans. anon, London, 1803.
Rusk, Robert, *The Doctrines of the Great Educators*, London, Macmillan, 1918, 1957.
Ruskin, John, *Mornings in Florence: Simple Studies in Christian Art for English Travellers*, London, George Allen, 1875–77, 2nd edn 1881.
——, *The Crown of Wild Olive: Four Lectures on Industry and War*, London, George Allen, 5th edn 1890.
——, *A Joy for Ever: and Its Price in the Market*, London, George Allen, 1893.
——, *Sesame and Lilies*, London, George Allen, 1865, 1906 edn with new preface.
——, *The Ethics of the Dust*, London and New York, J.M. Dent and Co., 1865; 1907 edn with introduction by Grace Rhys.
Schofield, Dr A.T., *Queen Anne's Hospital: Its Senators and Sufferers*, London, Swan Sonnenschein, 1889.
——, *The Unconscious Mind*, London, Swan Sonnenschein, 1898.
——, *Physiology for Schools* and *Handbook of Physiology*, London, Cassell and Co., n.d.
——, *The Mind of a Woman*, London, Methuen, 1919.
Seaborne, Malcolm and Lowe, Roy, *The English School: Its Architecture and Organization*, vol. 1, London, Routledge and Kegan Paul, 1977.
Shirreff, Emily, *Intellectual Education and Its Influence on the Character and the Happiness of Women*, London, John Parker, 1858.

——, *The Kindergarten at Home*, London, George Allen, 1876, 1894.
Showalter, Elaine, *The Female Malady: Women, Madness and English Culture 1830–1980*, London, Virago Press, 1987.
Silber, Kate, *Pestalozzi: The Man and His Work*, London, Routledge and Kegan Paul, 1960.
Silver, Harold, *Education as History*, London, Methuen, 1983.
Simon, Brian (ed.), *Education in Leicestershire 1540–1940*, Leicester University Press, 1968.
Spencer, F.H. (pupil-teacher 1886–1891), *An Inspector's Testament*, London, English Universities Press Ltd, 1938.
Spencer, Herbert, *Essays on Education Etc.*, J.M. Dent and Sons Ltd, London, 1861, 1949.
Stickney-Ellis, Sarah, *The Mothers of England: Their Influence and Responsibility*, London, Fisher and Son and Co., 1843.
Storr, Fred, *Life and Remains of the Rev. R.H. Quick*, Cambridge University Press, 1899.
Sulley, Philip, *History of Ancient and Modern Birkenhead*, Liverpool, Wirral Archives, 1907.
Sully, Dr James, *Studies of Childhood*, London, Longman Green, 1895, 1924.
Sumner, Mrs M., *Home Training*, Winchester and London, MU, 1914.
Taylor, Isaac, *Home Education*, London, 1838, 7th edn 1867.
Taylor, Whately Cook, 'Strong-minded Women', *St James's Magazine,* vol. 15, Dec-March 1866, London, Houlston and Wright.
Thackeray, William M., *The Newcombes,* London, Gresham Publishing, n.d.
Trilling, L., *The Liberal Imagination*, London, Mercury, 1940, 1961.
Tristram, H. (ed.), *The Idea of a Liberal Education*, London, George G. Harrap, 1952.
Tropp, Asher, *The School Teachers: The Growth of the Teaching Profession in England and Wales from 1800 to the Present Day*, London, Heinemann, 1956.
Tucker, Nicholas, *The Child and the Book: A Psychological and Literary Exploration,* Cambridge University Press, 1981.
Valentine, C.W. (PNEU member), *The Normal Child and Some of His Abnormalities*, Harmondsworth, Penguin, 1956, 1966.
Vicinus, Martha, *Suffer and be Still: Women in the Victorian Age*, vol. 1, London, Methuen, 1980.
——, *A Widening Sphere: Changing Roles of Victorian Women,* vol. 2, London, Methuen, 1980.
Ward, Mrs Humphry (née Mary Arnold), *Robert Elsmere*, London, Thomas Nelson and Sons, 1888.
Wells, H.G., *Ann Veronica*, London, Virago Press, 1909, 1980.
Widdowson, Frances, *Going up into the Next Class: Women and Elementary Teacher Training 1840–1914*, London, Hutchinson, 1983.
Williams, Raymond, *Culture and Society 1780–1950*, Harmondsworth, Penguin, 1958, 1966.
Wiltshire, David, *The Society and Political Thought of Herbert Spencer*, Oxford University Press, 1978.
Wohl, A.S. (ed.), *The Victorian Family*, London, Croom Helm, 1978.
Wollstonecraft, Mary, *Thoughts on the Education of Daughters*, London, 1787.

——, *A Vindication of the Rights of Woman*, London, 1792.
Women in a Changing World: The Dynamic Story of the International Council of Women since 1888, ed. M.H. Lefaucheux with representatives of the ICW in different countries, London, Routledge and Kegan Paul, 1966.
Yonge, Charlotte M., *The Heir of Redclyffe*, London, Macmillan and Co. Ltd, 1893.
——, *The Daisy Chain or Aspirations*, London, Macmillan and Co. Ltd, 1904.
Young, G.M., *Portrait of an Age: Victorian England*, Oxford University Press, 1936, 2nd edn 1964.

British Journal Articles

de Bellaigue, Professor Christina, 'Charlotte Mason, Home Education and the Parents' National Educational Union in the Late Nineteenth Century', *Oxford Review of Education*, August 2015.
Drake, Robert F., 'Charlotte Mason at Bishop Otter College', Part 1, *West Sussex History Journal*, no. 41, August 1988.
——, 'Charlotte Mason at Bishop Otter College', Part 2, *West Sussex History Journal*, no. 42, January 1989.
——, 'The Infant Schools of Broadwater Parish', *Sussex Archaeological Collections*, 1990, 128.

Journal of the World-Wide Education Service of the PNEU Articles (held at Armitt Library)

Coombs M.A., 'A Fresh Look at the Story of Charlotte Mason', WES/PNEU Journal, vol. 20, no. 2, June 1985.
——, '"The Little Manual called Home Education"', WES/PNEU Journal, vol. 20, no. 3, October 1985.
Walton, Mrs H.C.M. (Geraldine), *A Tribute to Essex Cholmondeley, 1892–1985*, WES/PNEU Journal, vol. 20, no. 3, October 1985.

L'Umile Pianta Articles (held at Armitt Library)

Coombs, M.A., 'The Thirteenth Child of Joshua Mason', Pianta, Winter 2009.
——, 'Joshua Mason Jnr.' (Charlotte's half-brother), Pianta, Spring 2010.
——, 'Puzzling over Charlotte Mason's Date of Birth', Pianta, Winter 2010.
——, 'Following Up the Story of Charlotte Mason', Pianta, Summer 2011.
——, 'Miss Read: An Important Influence on Charlotte Mason', Pianta, Spring 2012.
Early Student Memories, Pianta, July 1938, December 1959, Spring 1973, Winter 1973, Spring 1974, Winter 1978, Summer 1984, Spring 1985.
French, Beryl (CMT1923), 'Biography and Thoughts on the College and the PUS', Pianta, Winter 1986.
Inman, John P., 'Charlotte Mason: An Assessment After 50 years', Pianta, Spring 1976.
Moffat, Ida H.C. (CMT1919), 'Memories of a War-Time Winter's Journey to Ambleside', Pianta, Winter 1986.
Thorley, Professor John, 'Eleven Years at Charlotte Mason College', Pianta, Spring 2012.

Unpublished Research

Bateson, E., *Charlotte Mason, the PNEU and the House of Education: Perspectives on Female Education in the Late Nineteenth and early Twentieth Centuries*, Master's thesis, St Martin's College Lancaster, 2004, Armitt Library.

Beckman, Dr J.E., *Lessons to Learn: Charlotte Mason's House of Education 1892–1960 and Resistance to Taxonomic Drift*, PhD thesis, University of Cambridge, 2004, Armitt Library.

Bernier-Rodriguez, Dr B.E., *Education for the Kingdom: An Exploration of the Religious Foundation of Charlotte Mason's Educational Philosophy*, PhD thesis, Lancaster University, 2009

Coombs, M.A., *Some Obstacles to the Establishment of a Universal Method of Education for Parenthood by the PNEU*, MPhil thesis, Aston University, Birmingham, 1984, Armitt Library.

Cooper, Professor Hilary, *Charlotte Mason: Constructivist Approaches*, Faculty of Education, University of Cumbria.

Dowland, David, *Development of Nineteenth Century Anglican Non-Graduate Theological Colleges with Especial Reference to Episcopal Attitudes*, DPhil thesis, University of Oxford, 1993.

Eliassen, Andrea, *Assimilation and Amalgamation: The Roots of Charlotte Mason's Philosophy and System of Education*, Master's dissertation, American Public University System, Charles Town, WV.

Hetzel, Valerie, *A History of the William Davison Church of England High School for Girls, Worthing*, undergraduate dissertation, Brighton College of Education, 1975, CM47cmc336.

Lucia, Laureanda S., *Charlotte M.S. Mason: Una Filosofia Dell'Educazione*, dissertation, Sapienza Università Di Roma, Italy, 2011.

Neiwert, Professor Rachel, *Savages or Citizens: Children, Education and the British Empire 1899-1950*, PhD dissertation, University of Minnesota, 2009.

Smith, Dr J. Carroll, *Charlotte Mason: An Introductory Analysis of her Educational Theories and Practice*, PhD dissertation, Faculty of the Virginia Polytechnic Institute and State University, 2000, Armitt Library.

Van Pelt, Dr Deani A., *Charlotte Mason's Design for Education*, Master's dissertation, Faculty of Education, Faculty of Graduate Studies, University of Western Ontario, 2002, Armitt Library.

Index

Abbreviations: BOC: Bishop Otter College; CM: Charlotte Mason; CMT: Charlotte Mason Training; EK: Elsie Kitching; FN: Florence Nightingale; HF: Henrietta Franklin; HMI: Her Majesty's Inspector; HOE: House of Education; HT: Holy Trinity; LS: Lienie Steinthal; MEC: Mothers' Education Course; MU: Mothers' Union; NUWW: National Union of Women Workers; PNEU: Parents' National Educational Union; PR: *Parents' Review*; PRS: *Parents' Review* School; PUS: Parents' Union School.

#0004 - 170717 - C0 - 234/156/20 - PB - 9780718894023